CW00968626

Heidegger and Practical Philosophy

SUNY Series in Contemporary Continental Philosophy
Dennis J. Schmidt, editor

Heidegger and Practical Philosophy

Edited by
François Raffoul
and
David Pettigrew

State University of New York Press

Published by
State University of New York Press, Albany

© 2002 State University of New York

All rights reserved

Printed in the United States of America

No part of this book may be used or reproduced in any manner whatsoever
without written permission. No part of this book may be stored in a retrieval system
or transmitted in any form or by any means including electronic, electrostatic,
magnetic tape, mechanical, photocopying, recording, or otherwise
without the prior permission in writing of the publisher.

For information, address State University of New York Press,
90 State Street, Suite 700, Albany, NY 12207

Production by Judith Block
Marketing by Anne Valentine

Library of Congress Cataloging-in-Publication Data

Heidegger and practical philosophy / edited by François Raffoul and
    David Pettigrew.
        p. cm.–(SUNY series in contemporary continental philosophy)
    Includes bibliographical references and index.
    ISBN 0-7914-5343-X (alk. paper)–ISBN 0-7914-5344-8 (pbk. : alk. paper)
    1. Heidegger, Martin, 1889–1976.   2. Ethics.   3. Political science–
Philosophy.   4. Practice (Philosophy)   I. Raffoul, François, 1960–
II. Pettigrew, David, 1951–   III. Series.

B3279.H49 H345 2002
193–dc21   2002017626
                    10   9   8   7   6   5   4   3   2   1

Contents

Part I   Heidegger and Practical Philosophy

Part II   Heidegger and Ethics

Part III   The Question of the Political

Part IV   Responsibility, Being-With, and Community

Part V   Heidegger and the Contemporary Ethos

Acknowledgments

We would like to thank Dennis J. Schmidt, the series editor, for his support and guidance of this project from its earliest stages. We also are grateful to Jane Bunker, State University of New York Acquisitions Editor, for her assistance and patience throughout this process. Special thanks as well to J. Philip Smith, Vice President for Academic Affairs, and Donna Jean Fredeen, Dean of the School of Arts and Sciences of Southern Connecticut State University, for their generous support of this project. Our profound gratitude to John Cullen, Professor Emeritus of Philosophy, and Joseph Solodow, Professor of Foreign Language, Southern Connecticut State University, for their scholarly expertise and assiduous assistance in the final preparation of this manuscript. Our appreciation to James Ryan for his general editorial assistance. Thanks also to the Philosophy Department at Southern Connecticut State University, especially Philosophy Department Secretary, Ms. Sheila Magnotti, for her kind support in the innumerable ways that are indispensable to the production of such a manuscript. We also recognize our colleagues from the Heidegger Conference and the *Collegium Phaenomenologicum* for their constant inspiration and support in this endeavor.

Jean-Luc Nancy's "Heidegger's 'Originary Ethics'" is reprinted from *Studies in Practical Philosophy* (vol 1, no. 1, 1999) with the permission of Ms. Melissa Emero. The diagram "Exactitude/Truth" in Professor William J. Richardson's chapter is reprinted from *Lacan and the Human Sciences*, edited by Alexandre Leupin, with the permission of the University of Nebraska Press (University of Nebraska Press, 1991). We greatly appreciate as well the assistance of Janelle Finch, a graphic designer in the Southern Connecticut State University Public Affairs Office, who prepared the diagram for inclusion in this book.

Finally, we are indebted to the contributors and translators who made this book possible.

Abbreviations

German Texts of Martin Heidegger
(following the *Gesamtausgabe*)

GA 2   *Sein und Zeit* (Frankfurt am Main: Vittorio Klostermann, 1976).

GA 3   *Kant und das Problem der Metaphysik* (Frankfurt am Main: Vittorio Klostermann, 1991).

GA 5   *Holzwege* (Frankfurt am Main: Vittorio Klostermann, 1977).

GA 9   *Wegmarken* (Frankfurt am Main: Vittorio Klostermann, 1976).

GA 12   *Unterwegs zur Sprache* (Frankfurt am Main: Vittorio Klostermann, 1984).

GA 13   *Aus der Erfahrung des Denken* (Frankfurt am Main: Vittorio Klostermann, 1983).

GA 16   *Reden und andere Zeugnisse* (Frankfurt am Main: Vittorio Klostermaun, 2000).

GA 19   *Platon: Sophistes* (Frankfurt am Main: Vittorio Klostermann, 1992).

GA 21   *Logik: Die Frage nach der Wahrheit* (Frankfurt am Main: Vittorio Klostermann, 1976).

GA 24   *Die Grundprobleme der Phänomenologie* (Frankfurt am Main: Vittorio Klostermann, 1975).

GA 25   *Phänomenologische Interpretation von Kant's Kritik der reinen Vernunft* (Frankfurt am Main: Vittorio Klostermann, 1977).

GA 26   *Metaphysische Anfangsgründe der Logik* (Frankfurt am Main: Vittorio Klostermann, 1978).

GA 27   *Einleitung in die Philosophie* (Frankfurt am Main: Vittorio Klostermann, 1996).

GA 28   *Der deutsche Idealismus* (*Fichte, Schelling, Hegel*) (Frankfurt am Main: Vittorio Klostermann, 1997).

GA 29/30   *Die Grundbegriffe der Metaphysik* (Frankfurt am Main: Vittorio Klostermann, 1983).

GA 31	*Vom Wesen der menschlichen Freiheit* (Frankfurt am Main: Vittorio Klostermann, 1982).
GA 39	*Hölderlins Hymnen "Germanien" und "Der Rhein"* (Frankfurt am Main: Klostermann, 1980).
GA 40	*Einführung in die Metaphysik* (Frankfurt am Main: Vittorio Klostermann, 1983).
GA 42	*Schelling: Vom Wesen der menschlichen Freiheit* (Frankfurt am Main: Vittorio Klostermann, 1988).
GA 43	*Nietzsche: Der Wille zur Macht als Kunst* (Frankfurt am Main: Vittorio Klostermann, 1985).
GA 45	*Grundfragen der Philosophie: Ausgewählte "Probleme" der "Logik"* (Frankfurt am Main: Vittorio Klostermann, 1984).
GA 47	*Nietzsches Lehre vom Willen zur Macht als Erkenntnis* (Frankfurt am Main: Vittorio Klostermann, 1989).
GA 53	*Hölderlins Hymne "Der Ister"* (Frankfurt am Main: Vittorio Klostermann, 1982).
GA 55	*Heraklit* I, II (Frankfurt am Main: Vittorio Klostermann, 1979).
GA 61	*Phänomenologische Interpretationen zu Aristoteles: Einführung in die phänomenologische Forschung* (Frankfurt am Main: Vittorio Klostermann, 1985).
GA 65	*Beiträge zur Philosophie (Vom Ereignis)* (Frankfurt am Main: Vittorio Klostermann, 1989).
GA 77	*Feldweg-Gespräche* (Frankfurt am Main: Vittorio Klostermann, 1995).

Other Texts

G	*Gelassenheit* (Pfullingen: Neske, 1985).
NI	*Nietzsche*, Vol. I., 5th ed. (Stuttgart: Verlag Günther Neske, 1989).
NII	*Nietzsche*, Vol. II., 5th ed. (Stuttgart: Verlag Günther Neske, 1989).
SZ	*Sein und Zeit*, 9th ed. (Tübingen: Max Niemeyer, 1960).
ZS	*Zur Sache des Denkens* (Tübingen: Max Niemeyer, 1969).

English Translations of Martin Heidegger's Texts

BP	*The Basic Problems of Phenomenology*, trans. Albert Hofstadter (Bloomington: Indiana University Press, 1982).
BTa	*Being and Time*, trans. John Macquarrie and Edward Robinson (New York: Harper & Row, 1962).
BTb	*Being and Time*, trans. Joan Stambaugh (Albany: State University of New York Press, 1996).

BW   *Basic Writings* (New York: Harper & Row, 1977).

C   *Contributions to Philosophy* (*From Enowning*), trans. Parvis Emad and Kenneth Maly (Bloomington: Indiana University Press, 1999).

CT   *The Concept of Time*, trans. Will McNeill (Malden, Mass.: Blackwell, 1992).

DT   *Discourse on Thinking*, trans. John M. Anderson and E. Hans Freund (New York: Harper & Row, 1966).

EGT   *Early Greek Thinking*, trans. David Krell and Frank Capuzzi (New York: Harper & Row, 1975).

EP   *The End of Philosophy* (New York: Harper & Row, 1973).

FCM   *Fundamental Concepts of Metaphysics*, trans. William McNeill and N. Walker (Bloomington: Indiana University Press, 1995).

HCT   *History of the Concept of Time*, trans. Theodore Kisiel (Bloomington: Indiana University Press, 1985).

I   *Hölderlin's Hymn "The Ister,"* trans. William McNeill and Julia Davis (Bloomington: Indiana University Press, 1996).

IM   *An Introduction to Metaphysics*, trans. James Manheim (New Haven, Conn.: Yale University Press, 1984).

KPM   *Kant and the Problem of Metaphysics* (fifth ed., enlarged), trans. Richard Taft (Bloomington: Indiana University Press, 1997).

MFL   *The Metaphysical Foundations of Logic*, trans. Michael Heim (Bloomington: Indiana University Press, 1984).

Ni   *Nietzsche*, Vol. 1, trans. and ed. David Farrell Krell (San Francisco: Harper & Row, 1991).

Nii   *Nietzsche*, Vol. 2, trans. and ed. David Farrell Krell (San Francisco: Harper & Row, 1991).

Niii   *Nietzsche*, Vol. 3, trans. Joan Stambaugh, David Farrel Krell, Frank A. Capuzzi; ed. David Farrell Krell (San Francisco: Harper & Row, 1991).

Niv   *Nietzsche*, Vol. 4, trans. Joan Stambaugh, David Farrel Krell, Frank A. Capuzzi; ed. David Farrell Krell (San Francisco: Harper & Row, 1991).

OWL   *On the Way to Language*, trans. Peter D. Hertz (New York: Harper & Row, 1971).

P   *Pathmarks*, ed. William McNeill (Cambridge: Cambridge University Press, 1998).

PLT   *Poetry, Language, Thought*, trans. Albert Hofstadter (New York: Harper & Row, 1971).

PR   *The Principle of Reason*, trans. R. Lilly (Bloomington: Indiana University Press, 1991).

QCT   *The Question Concerning Technology and Other Essays* (New York: Harper & Row, 1977).

S   *Plato's Sophist*, trans. Richard Rojcewicz and André Schuwer (Bloom-
             ington: Indiana University Press, 1997).
TB   *On Time and Being*, trans. Joan Stambaugh (New York: Harper &
             Row, 1972).
WCT   *What Is Called Thinking?*, trans. Fred Wieck and J. Glenn Gray (New
             York: Harper & Row, 1968).

Other Selected Texts

CPR   Immanuel Kant, *The Critique of Pure Reason*, trans. Norman Kemp
             Smith (New York: St. Martin's Press, 1965).

Introduction

FRANÇOIS RAFFOUL AND DAVID PETTIGREW

H eidegger often has been reproached for his alleged neglect of practical issues, specifically his "inability" to propose or articulate an ethics or a politics. The reasons offered in support of such a claim vary. They include, for
example, his supposed privileging of "the Same" as opposed to an authentic thought
of "the Other"; his "contempt" for ontic or concrete affairs due to some Platonic es-
sentialism; his "dismissal" of the intersubjective or collective dimension of human experience; and last but not least, his troubled relation to Nazism. Others have argued
that Heidegger's thought of being suffers from a certain theoreticism. Whatever the
reasons advanced, Heidegger's thought of Being, it has been concluded, cannot contribute to ethics or politics, or to practical philosophy broadly conceived as a domain
of action and collective existence.

This charge, however, might ultimately rest on a radical misunderstanding: one
seeks to find in his work a classical problematic, does not find it, and concludes from
this that Heidegger ignored the practical dimension of existence. For instance, where
Heidegger takes issue with traditional conceptions of ethics, or where he actually rejects ethics as a discipline in the metaphysical tradition, it is concluded that his
thought is an-ethical, if not unethical. In fact, however, his "rejection" of the tradition of ethics is done in the name of a rethinking of a more "originary" ethics that he
attempts to pursue. This is why, in contrast to these traditional interpretations, this
book, *Heidegger and Practical Philosophy*, will instead investigate the extent to which
Heidegger's thought can be read as an important and indeed a crucial resource for
practical philosophy and for the possible articulation of an ethos for our time. For the
issue, as Françoise Dastur reminds us, is not to enframe Heidegger's thought of the
other, for instance, in preestablished schemas, but rather to approach and question
his thought "with respect to the way in which [it] encountered and posed the question of the other."[1] The purpose of *Heidegger and Practical Philosophy* is to demonstrate that Heidegger did not neglect the practical dimension of existence but instead
radically transformed the way it is to be thought.

In fact, recent publications of his early lecture courses in the *Gesamtausgabe* have made manifest that Heidegger developed his *own* thought through an appropriative reading of practical philosophy and its fundamental categories. For instance, his 1924–1925 course on the *Sophist* offers a detailed reading of key passages from Aristotle's *Nicomachean Ethics*. Other courses from that period also testify to the influence of practical-ethical categories in the genesis of Heidegger's thought and vocabulary. The reappropriation of Kant's practical philosophy, the object of several chapters in this book, also figures prominently in this respect. Besides the crucial issue of tracing the genesis of Heidegger's ontological categories in the tradition of practical philosophy, there is also, in *Sein und Zeit* particularly, an entire rethinking of praxis: the emphasis on "concern"; the analyses of everyday being-in-the-world; the rethinking of entities in terms of the "πράγματα"; the reevaluation of the "pragmatic"; the genealogy of "theoretical comportment," and so on. All of these motifs testify not so much to a simple priority of the practical over the theoretical, as we read sometimes,[2] but rather to an attempt to rethink the very status of the practical, which no longer would be situated within the traditional theory/praxis dichotomy. In a word, they testify to an attempt at thinking praxis in its *ontological* sense, and no longer within a metaphysical structure. One also could note here other factors that demand a new focus on Heidegger and practical philosophy. Recent works, for instance, Jean-Luc Nancy's, have drawn their own rethinking of community, of "being-in-common," from an avowed radicalization of Heidegger's thought of Being and of existence. It then becomes unavoidable and necessary to revisit those texts in order to retrieve in them a sense of community that perhaps was not noticed sufficiently in previous commentaries. Another important aspect of Heidegger's relation to practical philosophy, besides his drawing from that tradition and his own rethinking of the practical, is the way in which his celebrated texts on technology, nihilism, the atomic age, and so on represent an important resource for reflecting on our times, and our contemporary ethos. All of these motifs constitute the *raison d'être* of this book, and its *foci*.

This book will endeavor to explore, then, the practical dimension of Heidegger's thought. By this we do not mean, it should be stressed from the outset, a mere "application" of Heidegger's thought to various practical concerns, as though his thought—or thought in general, for that matter—could be used as a tool, following a consequentialist or utilitarian model. The current and growing development of so-called "applied ethics" in the curriculum conceals a peculiar and paradoxical neglect of a genuine philosophical questioning concerning the meaning of ethics, at the same moment that it betrays an almost desperate need for ethics in our age. But this need arises out of the fact that ethics is left groundless. It is then ethics itself that is in need of a philosophical foundation. It is to such a foundation that this book would like to contribute. Further, its working hypothesis is that Heidegger's thought transforms the way in which the very realm of practice is to be conceived and calls for a radical rethinking of what is meant by the "ethical," the "political," or the "practical" as such. The "practical," "ethical," and "political" are to be thought from the thought of Being, because such a thought includes them eminently. As Dastur explains, "For Heidegger, 'ontology' thus understood is always 'practical,' always 'engaged,' and thus bears an intrinsically ethical dimension. This is doubtless the reason why Heidegger has not written on ethics: because he surely does not need 'to add' it on to an ontology that would then itself be conceived only as a part of philosophy."[3] It is in this sense that this book is concerned with fleshing out the practical senses of ontology, and the ontological senses of praxis. In a striking formulation, Dastur writes: "Thus, for Heidegger, ethics is ontology itself" (HPP, 87).

Various specialists from several countries explore here how Heidegger has positioned, in his own way, the question of ethics and politics, as well as the practical scope of his thought. This does not mean so much investigating how his thinking can be included within preestablished practical categories, or even how Heidegger has "ontologized" practical categories. Heidegger *did not* "ontologize" practical philosophy, even when he found his own thought through a destructive/appropriative reading of this very tradition. Instead, he has circumscribed or delimited the traditional and derivative opposition of theory and praxis (as well as the "poietical") and has begun to think anew the "practical" itself. In "Letter on Humanism," for instance, Heidegger makes the striking remark that "the deed of thinking (*das Tun des Denkens*) is neither theoretical nor practical" (BW, 263). In one sentence, he has at once stepped out of the theory/praxis opposition and reinscribed another sense of praxis ("deed of thinking") at the heart of thinking as the "adventure" into Being. "Thus thinking is a deed. But a deed that also surpasses all praxis" (BW, 262). This is why he is able to also state in that essay that "such thinking has no result. It has no effect" (BW, 259). It has no effect, not because it is solely theoretical or contemplative (in fact, it "exceeds all contemplation" [BW, 262]), but because the praxis here evoked is no longer understood as the production of effects on the basis of a theory, within the end/means operatus. The essence of action, he reminds us in the very first lines of "Letter on Humanism," is not that which causes an effect, nor that which is governed by the value of utility. What is at stake in the critique of the theory/praxis opposition, as well as the instrumental conception of action, is an attempt at freeing praxis itself as the action of being itself. What is praxis when no longer the act of mastering beings? When it is freed from the tyrannical imperative to produce effects, that is, results, from the tyrannical imperative that all beings *have a use*? When it is freed from the manic, frenetic, or frantic race to exploit all resources, including the "human" resources? What does Heidegger mean when he speaks of such a deed in terms of the "humbleness of its inconsequential accomplishment" (BW, 262)? What is thinking when no longer understood as the contemplative *theoria* on the basis of which effects can take place? In fact, thinking does not need to be put into action, as it were, for when action is defined as the "accomplishment" of man's relation to Being, then thinking becomes itself an act ("Thinking acts insofar as it thinks" [BW, 217]). It is in that sense that this book speaks of "practical philosophy": in the sense that Heidegger advances when he states that thinking is *l'engagement par l'Etre pour l'Etre* (engagement by Being for Being)" (BW, 218). It is therefore not simply a matter here of stating that Heidegger's thought has a practical and an ethical dimension, but above all, of beginning a search into the *ontological* senses of what has been called, in the tradition, "practical philosophy," "ethics," and its fundamental categories. *The ethical, the practical, take place at the ontological level*, and it is at that level that the following contributions situate themselves.

This book attempts to elucidate the full scope and significance—as well as certain limits—of Heidegger's thought for practical philosophy in five parts: Heidegger and Practical Philosophy; Heidegger and Ethics; The Question of the Political; Responsibility, Being-With, and Community; Heidegger and the Contemporary Ethos.

In Part I, the focus is placed on Heidegger's relation to the *tradition* of practical philosophy, in particular, his interpretive reading and appropriation of Aristotle and Kant. It is perhaps not emphasized enough that Heidegger has an important thought of freedom, approached in positive terms. It is true that *Vom Wesen der menschlichen Freiheit, On the Essence of Human Freedom*, volume 31 of the *Gesamtausgabe*, is not yet available in English, which is why the properly Heideggerian understanding of freedom is taken up with profit in this part in three of its four chapters. If it is the case, as John Sallis states, that "freedom is the very origin or non-origin of action, its condition of possibility, its wellspring" (HPP, 3), it then becomes crucial to an elucidation of Heidegger's practical philosophy to reflect further on the ontological senses of freedom. However, freedom is approached outside of the theory/praxis opposition, outside of the metaphysical constructs of free will, subjectivity, and causality. Let us think here of that passage, among many others, from *The Question Concerning Technology*, in which Heidegger asserts firmly that, "The essence of freedom is originally not connected with the will or even with the causality of human willing."[4] As Dennis Schmidt writes: "This sense of freedom is one not grounded in any ontology of the subject, not governed by any sense of agency or the will, indeed it does not even coincide with anything which we might call a subject" (HPP, 169). What, therefore, would a nonmetaphysical account of freedom be? What sort of action is freed when substracted from those categories? What does it mean to say, as John Sallis reminds us, that Dasein is characterized as "being free [*Freisein*] for its ownmost potentiality-for-being" (SZ, 191), or that Dasein's "being toward a potentiality-for-being is itself determined by freedom" (SZ, 193)? It appears that the issue, in the end, is to think of freedom as being originary to Dasein's Being, and in a sense to Being itself. Schmidt remarks that the essence of freedom is the essence of being itself (HPP, 169). The metaphysical ways of enframing freedom (in subjectivity, in the Will, in causality, etc.) prove inadequate to an authentic thought of freedom, of the "free-ing" in freedom, what is freeing in our being, what makes us free. This is why the encounter with Kant is so crucial. The turning point in the thought of freedom takes place in Heidegger's reading of Kant's moral philosophy. As Frank Schalow shows: "In his 1930 lectures on Kant, Heidegger summarizes his destructive-retrieval of the concept of freedom in this way. 'Freedom ceases to be a property of human being,' and instead 'man becomes a possibility of freedom'" (HPP, 33). This transformation is followed in careful analyses and demonstrations. The relationship to Kant's moral philosophy also is addressed in Jacob Rogozinski's chapter, although in a more critical light. Rogozinski argues that in the ontological reduction of the moral Law, Heidegger runs the risk of not being able to account for the "radicality of evil." The chapter then draws the limits of the Heideggerian deconstruction of metaphysics by wondering whether Heidegger has really broken with the tradition of ontodicy, whether he has not substracted Being from the possibility of Evil. He asks: "Would not this persistence of an undeconstructed configuration mark the limit of Heideggerian deconstruction—of *any* deconstruction?—the irreducible abutment of the logical reduction that it cannot break up, because it has not taken the step toward ethics?" (HPP, 59). Another central figure in this confrontation of Heidegger with the tradition of practical philosophy is of course Aristotle. In his chapter on Heidegger's interpretation of *aretê*, Jacques Taminiaux continues a work begun several years ago on this issue, developed in several essays and books. As Taminiaux puts it, in relation to the problematics of *aretê* in Heidegger's text, "the manner in which Heidegger approached this thematic in his first courses at Freiburg and then at Marburg, engages a cluster of closely related questions which are pertinent to practical philosophy" (HPP, 13). More specifically, it informs questions and debates pertaining to the development of ethical theories in contemporary continental thought. Through a close reading of the 1924–25 winter semester course on *Plato's Sophist*,[5] as well as the 1922 essay, "Phenomenological Interpretations with Respect to Aristotle: Indication of the Hermeneutical Situation,"[6] Taminiaux shows how the Heideggerian reading of Aristotle, although said to be founded on the phenomenology of Dasein, in turn is founded on a *certain reading* of Aristotle, a certain reappropriation of the *Nicomachean Ethics*.

In Part II, the difficult issue of Heidegger and ethics is taken up. For if Heidegger rejects traditional understandings of ethics, and even ethics itself as a discipline, one might argue that his thought allows us to envisage ethics in a different way. In fact, one could argue that the thought of Being itself is to be approached in ethical terms, that Being exhibits its own "ethicality." In a rich chapter, Jean-Luc Nancy attempts to understand further Heidegger's claim in "Letter on Humanism," that the thinking of Being is an "originary ethics," at the very moment Heidegger rejects ethics as a discipline. To account for this difficulty, Nancy proposes the following hypothesis: "There is no 'morality' in Heidegger if what is meant by that is a body of principles and aims for conduct, fixed by authority or by choice, whether collective or individual. But no philosophy either provides or is by itself a 'morality' in this sense. Philosophy is not charged with prescribing norms or values: instead it must think the essence or the sense of what makes *action* [*l'agir*] as such, in other words of what puts action in the position of having to choose norms or values" (HPP, 66). Nancy then unfolds what we could call the ethicality of Being, which would allow him to justify that the thought of Being has an ethical dimension. From another perspective, this is also what Françoise Dastur attempts to show through a reflection on the phenomenon of conscience. Refusing to choose between Lévinas, who asks us to contemplate "otherwise than Being," and Heidegger, who leads us to another way of thinking about Being, Dastur insists that ontology, for Heidegger, is an ontology of finitude, that is, an ontology that pays attention to "the fact that we have to welcome the at once frightening and marvelous alterity of a being at the origin of which we are not and which is also among other things—ourselves" (HPP, 89). In contrast to Levinas' interpretation, and in resonance with Paul Ricoeur, Dastur argues that the other is present in Dasein's very being, and that the relation to the other is intrinsic to Dasein's Being. Focusing on Heidegger's 1928–29 winter semester lecture course, *Einleitung in die Philosophie*, Jean Greisch proposes "to pursue the question concerning his relation to the problem of grounding a philosophical ethics" (HPP, 99). Greisch recognizes that Heidegger's contribution to ethics is miles away "from the questions of a content-based ethics." In a sense, it must be so if what is at stake is a reflection on the very *possibility* of ethics, what constitutes the ethicality of ethics. In that perspective, Greisch begins by emphasizing that being-with others belongs to the very being of human Dasein, so that the relation to the other—definition of ethics for Levinas—is constitutive of Dasein. Addressing several objections traditionally directed at Heidegger (on the issue of Dasein's "indifference," for instance, or on the value of the "with" in Being-with, contrasted to Levinas' "for," in being-*for*-the-other), Greisch argues that on the question of indifference, "the very experience of being-alone (of growing isolation in all material and psychical forms) shows just how little indifferent the other actually is for Dasein"; further, he stresses that in that 1928–29 course, unconcealment signifies "necessarily and essentially a sharing [*Sichteilen*] in truth" (GA 27, 118), so that Heidegger, as Greisch remarks, does not need to trouble himself "over the concept of a so-called 'communicative reason'" (HPP, 103)! Finally, in response to Levinas' charges that Heidegger's "philosophy" is a philosophy of power and domination, Greisch is careful to insist on Dasein's finite and factical *powerlessness*, its abandonment to the other entity, and to the other as such. "In abandonment (which obviously also includes being delivered over to the other!) the constitutive powerlessness of factical Dasein expresses itself" (HPP, 111). It is that very finitude and facticity which come to constitute the "philosophical basis" for ethics, as Heidegger approaches it. In "*Homo prudens*," Chapter 8, Miguel de Beistegui reflects on the thought of "man" in Heidegger's work and on its nonanthropological scope. De Beistegui shows that in this nonanthropological definition of the human, Heidegger reveals an "originary openness" in the human that exposes it to "a constitutive and non-human otherness" (HPP, 117). De Beistegui then attempts to understand this openness and excess in ethical terms: "This particular opening to that which always and from the very start has begun to open itself in [man] . . . is also, I would like to suggest, ethical" (HPP, 118). He develops that project through a detailed analysis of "anticipation" (*Vorlaufen*) in *Sein und Zeit*, of resoluteness (*Entschlossenheit*), and *Augenblick*. Once thought outside of the metaphysical representations of ethics (in the theory/praxis opposition, etc.), "resoluteness could come to designate the origin of proper action, and thus to delimit the sphere of ethics itself" (HPP, 126).

Part III is concerned with the philosophical implications of Heidegger's political choices and his thinking with respect to a possible politics. Theodore Kisiel enters Heidegger's "text" via the Rectoral Address as well. He develops the historical context of the address by identifying three distinct levels of the political in Heidegger's analytic of the Dasein of the German people—the phenomenological, metaphysical, and *seynsgeschichtliche*—levels that he subsequently unfolds as phases in Heidegger's thinking of the political (HPP, 137). Kisiel finds in the Rectoral Address and in Heidegger's lectures of the time a "resistance" "to the increasingly absolutist regime's campaign of total coordination" (HPP, 138). He interprets this resistance in light of Heidegger's political thought in 1923—a thought he characterizes as fundamentally Aristotelian (i.e., the phenomenological one). He then discusses what he calls a Platonic "metaphysical" concept of the political (e.g., in the 1933–34 winter semester course), where Heidegger focuses on the "relationship between a *people* and its *state*, which constitutes the essence of the political" (HPP, 145). Finally, Kisiel describes the third concept of the political, born of a "regress to German-Greek Da-sein that generates the third concept of the political, the archaic (poietic, *seynsgeschichtlicher*) concept," one "facilitated especially by Hölderlin's poetic German translations of Greek tragedy" (HPP, 152). Kisiel asserts that this return (undertaken, for example, in the 1935 summer semester course, *Introduction to Metaphysics*, and in the 1942 summer semester course, *Hölderlin's Hymn "The Ister"*) involves nothing less than "a matter of restoring the originative power of one of the most influential words in the Greek language, πόλις, the root of the political" (HPP, 153). This is a perspective on the basis of which Kisiel makes the striking comment that Heidegger "criticizes the Nazi claim of the totalitarian character of the political" (HPP, 154). By distinguishing three concepts of the political operative in Heidegger's thought, Kisiel not only complexifies an issue that can be too often caricatured, but he also sheds light on all future debates on this difficult question. In his chapter, Dennis Schmidt focuses on the Rectoral Address. "In the end," he writes, "any reflection on the topic of Heidegger and political life must begin by confronting the Rectoral Address" (HPP, 161). Significantly, Schmidt reads the Rectoral Address "Self-Assertion of the German University" in relation to Plato's 7th Letter, stating, "No greater parallel can be found in the history of philosophy to serve as a sort of model for understanding Heidegger's astonishing political naiveté than the case of Plato" (HPP, 162). Schmidt argues that Heidegger's address was principally related not to politics or community but to the place of the university amidst the politics of the time. Here Schmidt emphasizes that Heidegger's effort to renew the university through philosophy is plagued by a naiveté concerning the limits of theory in the political arena. While the Rectoral Address may have marked Heidegger's political failure, Schmidt advances the idea that it is, in contrast, Heidegger's *Beiträge* that "might prove to be the entry into Heidegger's real contribution to a possible politics" (HPP, 167). In this text, he argues, Heidegger opens our thinking to the "full force of freedom in such matters" (HPP, 169). Charles Scott attempts as well to situate Heidegger's engagement with politics in relation to the period associated with the Rectoral Address. Scott proceeds with extreme caution to situate his discourse in such a way as to wrestle "the positive and practical implications of Heidegger's thought for our lives" from the debacle of his political failure. Scott asserts early on that what especially "strikes" him as "having the most practical value in his thought is found in its movement that overturns any possible, final authority that a person might give to his specific claims" (HPP, 178). And he finds this movement "even in his Rector's Address of 1933" (HPP, 178). Scott elaborates on what we might call this "deconstructive" move in Heidegger's thought by interrogating the 1942 lectures on Hölderlin's poem *Der Ister*. Here Scott finds within Heidegger's thought the theme of an attunement to the "questionableness" of being, an attunement with deconstructive potentialities with respect to concepts of authority or violence. Scott argues that Heidegger "finds in Hölderlin's poetry a way of speaking that provides that opening," an opening to attunement and destiny. Scott suggests finally that the opening attunement has the potential to bring about, as Heidegger apparently wished, a "revolutionary transformation of German language, understanding, values, and practices" (HPP, 181). Peg Birmingham's chapter traces Hannah Arendt's debt to Martin Heidegger in several respects. Specifically, Birmingham suggests that Arendt adopts Heidegger's critique of the modern stance toward the world, namely, the *Gestell*, "a technological enframing in which everyone and everything is understood in terms of a worldless functionality" (HPP, 194). Arendt agrees with Heidegger, that the modern world of enframing takes place through a stifling technological language. Birmingham asserts that Arendt's notion of "natality" allows for the "unexpected word" that is perhaps the only possible response, in its "vulnerability and infelicity," to this very *Gestell*. Birmingham rejects, however, Arendt's opposition of her theme of "natality" to Heidegger's themes of Being-towards-death, or finitude. Birmingham shows that Heidegger's thinking of finitude implies a radical opening—a radical possibility—that already harbors any thinking of natality and launches an authentic thinking of freedom. This thought of freedom is related to nothing other than life.

In Part IV, several contributions engage the issues of community, of our being-in-common, and responsibility in Heidegger's thought. François Raffoul's chapter engages the question of responsibility in Heidegger and attempts to address it in terms of Heidegger's thought of Being, that is, outside of the traditional enframing of responsibility in a subject-based thinking (i.e., as accountability). Further, Raffoul considers that Heidegger's understanding of responsibility sheds light on many debates raging today around the question of ethics. The focus is placed on the connection between responsibility, facticity, and otherness in Heidegger. Several questions lead this reflection: How does the concept of Dasein involve responsibility? What are the ontological senses of responsibility? Does it exceed an egocentric and subjectivistic enclosure? To what extent does it manifest an essential exposure to otherness?

Raffoul begins to show that the very concept of Dasein means to be a responsibility for itself, as the term *care* clearly indicates. Dasein is a concern for Being, for its being, and for the being of other entities. Raffoul further elaborates on that sense of responsibility in terms of the finite constitution of Dasein, through analyses of Dasein's facticity, "guilt," or Being-guilty (*Schuldigsein*). The origins of responsibility: Dasein is called to appropriate the inappropriable of its own "existence," its birth, its death, its whole being. However, this inappropriability reveals the otherness at the heart of Dasein. Raffoul unfolds the presence of this otherness in an analysis of the call of conscience in *Being and Time*, echoing what Dastur also says in this book about "the most intimate alterity." Stressing the irreducible place of otherness in the being of Dasein, Raffoul concludes by arguing that "it is in such a nexus of responsibility, facticity, and otherness that the site of ethics, of an "originary ethics," is to be situated in Heidegger's work" (HPP, 218). David Wood's self-confessed "experimental" chapter attempts to "show that Heidegger's problematic can be effectively developed through a consideration of the complex temporality of human maturation and development" (HPP, 219). Beginning with a reflection on what reading, and reading responsibly, can mean, Wood stresses that Heidegger "distinguishes two kinds of interpretation: recapitulation and real explication, and emphasizes the need for the risk, violence, daring needed for the latter" (HPP, 221). In light of this distinction, Wood himself engages in that risk and raises a question that would challenge any assumption regarding the strictly "adult" status of Dasein. As Wood puts it, "Dasein, for the most part, seems to mean adult Dasein" (HPP, 225). He then proceeds to reflect on possible analogies or proximities between child development (if we understand that "the whole issue of human development is like a courtyard opening onto, and opened onto by, the most pressing concerns of our time—historical, political, educational, and environmental") and various features of historical Dasein, on the basis of the claim that "the truth about Dasein's temporality lies in its developmental incompleteness" (HPP, 227). It is our "continuing responsibility," David Wood believes, to keep "exploring these passages, opening these doors" (HPP, 232). From the outset, Walter Brogan, in his chapter, states clearly his goal: "I will argue in this chapter that *Being and Time* provides, in several essential respects, the appropriate philosophical basis for a contemporary, postmodern understanding of ethical relationships and political community" (HPP, 237). Further, Brogan insists that this understanding of "post-metaphysical" community—one "that does not erase the singularity and alterity of those who participate" (HPP, 237) in it—is further pursued by Heidegger and developed in the later *Contributions to Philosophy*. Brogan first attempts to show that death, as understood in Heidegger's analysis, is "the precondition for a philosophy of community that remains faithful to the utter singularity and finitude of each of the members of the human community" (HPP, 237). Although this claim may seem paradoxical, it only appears so if one begins with an understanding of being-with as a negation of singularities. But Brogan argues that being-towards-death is "the limit condition that prevents the co-optation and appropriation

of the being of another" (HPP, 237). He develops in several analyses the features of
what he thus calls a "mortal community." Moving to the recently published *Contributions to Philosophy*, Brogan fleshes out Heidegger's sense of community in this last
work. The central insight is that community in Heidegger's later thought is "the community of those to come, is a community of singular beings" (HPP, 244). This
demonstration is done through analyses of several passages from the *Beiträge*.
Lawrence Hatab reflects on empathy as a crucial ethical motif and how it figures in
Heidegger's thought. The following themes are considered: the ecstatic nature of Dasein's finite being-in-the-world; the ecstatic conjunction of being-in and being-with;
the primacy of *Befindlichkeit* and *Stimmung*; and Heidegger's remarks on empathy
(*Einfühlung*). Hatab insists on Heidegger's overcoming of the modern, isolated, individual subject. He writes that "in *Being and Time* Heidegger undermines the subject-
object bifurcation and the notion of an isolated, unencumbered self by showing how
human Dasein is being-in-the-world" (HPP, 250). Emphasizing the ec-static nature of
Dasein, as well as the place of moods, in this overcoming of subjectivity, Hatab proceeds by reflecting on empathy as a "moral mood." He clarifies that in Heidegger's
critique of empathy, "It is not the phenomenon of shared feeling that is rejected, but
rather the theoretical model that presumes isolated selves that somehow must venture 'out' to each other" (HPP, 255). In fact, Heidegger's critique lies in the argument
that empathy presupposes isolated subjects, which he wants to dispute by insisting on
the *originary* being-with of Dasein (therefore not needing empathy to "step in" in
order to relate to the other). As Hatab writes in a striking formulation: "No, the
shared affect just *happens*" (HPP, 256). Heidegger's critique can then help us challenge
the subjectivistic assumptions that prevail in the social sciences. Hatab illustrates this
Heideggerian contribution in the domain of child development. The author then develops several analyses that reveal both the value and the limits of empathy for ethics.

   Part V considers Heidegger's relation to a number of questions that define our
epoch. Thomas Sheehan focuses on Heidegger's reflections on nihilism, reflections that lie at the heart of his thought and inform his relation to practical philosophy throughout his career. In this vein, Sheehan writes: "The task of Heidegger's
philosophy would be to 'annihilate nihilism,' to overcome it by drastically limiting
the power and reach of technology and making room again for nature" (HPP, 276).
Accordingly, Heidegger's thought would lead us to "turn our backs on industrialization, techno-science, the exploitation of the earth" (HPP, 276). It was this philosophical motivation that led Heidegger to be aligned with National Socialism.
However, in his chapter, Sheehan takes a remarkable step in opposing Heidegger's
critique of *technē*, writing: "Entities are endlessly available to human engagement
and manipulation. The technological domination of the globe is the *gift* of the finite open. Far from having a philosophically negative valence, *die Technik* is the
positive outcome of *Ereignis*" (HPP, 295). Indeed, Sheehan's chapter suggests "that
what Heidegger has to say about the essence of nihilism—important though it might
be—cannot realistically serve as a philosophical platform for grounding political op-

tions" (HPP, 297). More telling is his assertion that "Heidegger's ideas on histori-cal-cultural nihilism—for whatever light they may shed on the question of essential nihilism—will not help one bit with changing the real powers that drive τέχνη today (HPP, 297). Pierre Jacerme, in contrast, asks in Chapter 18, "Is There an Ethics for the 'Atomic Age'"? Ethics for Aristotle, Jacerme asserts, is concerned with habit: "Its name *ethike* is one that is formed by a slight variation from the word *ethos* (habit)," and "moral virtue comes about as a result of habit."[7] But, with Hiroshima, Jacerme asks, do we not see the appearance of the *inhabitual*; the *strangest* and most *uncanny?* Jacerme reads Heidegger's work in 1949—in the Bremen lectures on technology (*The Thing, The Ge-Stell, The Danger, The Turning*)—as an at-tempt to configure an *êthos* of man that would correspond to the uncanny "danger" that "concerns" his being. Jacerme's reflections on Heidegger's engagement with the "atomic age" are interwoven with notes from Hiroshima by Kenzaburo Oe and Hersey's *Hiroshima.* Jacerme asserts that after Hiroshima the uncanny undermines any possibility of a normative ethics, thus the uncanny becomes what must be thought in a "positive" way in order to delineate an originary ethics. "Man" has ab-rogated his position as the measure of all things, and it is Being—in its very un-canny event—that emerges as the measure of an originary ethics. Andrew Mitchell engages Heidegger's thinking with respect to praxis in relation to Nietzsche. Mitchell suggests that "the thought of life, the ground of both art and knowledge for Nietzsche, is ultimately what is at stake in the Heidegger-Nietzsche confronta-tion." Life likewise provides the context for Heidegger's considerations of practice in *The Will to Power As Knowledge.* Life is that embodiment which opens out onto chaos, inseparably joined to a surrounding world of will to power (HPP, 318). For Mitchell, the "traditional view of praxis as a 'deed' or 'activity' by which goals are realized and intentions carried out" misses the necessity of praxis for life. Mitchell states that, for Heidegger, "praxis first means neither 'deed' nor 'activity,' but rather the sheer 'performance of life' (*Lebensvollzug*)" (HPP, 321). Further, Mitchell insists that with Heidegger, the performance of this life is always at the limit of fini-tude. But the limit that praxis encounters is always only to be transgressed—it must be, for life is nothing more than this transgression. Life is born of such overstep-ping that first begins from the limit. "Life begins at the limit, this is the fruit of Hei-degger's Nietzsche confrontation," writes Mitchell, and it is through the confrontation of these two thinkers that he engages Heidegger's thought of the character of a praxis for our time—in Heidegger's notion of *Gelassenheit,* or release-ment. Releasement is the practice of life at its limit, a practice that no longer over-steps that limit but rather first lets it be. This letting be, Mitchell suggests, is Heidegger's renewed conception of praxis, thus echoing what Heidegger had al-ready said of letting-be in the 1928–29 course as the "originary practice [*Urhand-lung*] of Dasein" (GA 27, 112, 183, 199). William Richardson gives thought to the relation between Heidegger and Lacan and in turn to the truth of psychoanalytic praxis. He asks what happens to the truth of psychoanalysis when the positivist ideal of classical science is rejected, as is the case with Lacan. "The truth of the subject," he writes, "comes about, then, through the speaking that constitutes the psychoanalytic process" (HPP, 345). This is a "revelatory" truth born from a "historicizing process." "Founded thus in language itself, truth has an inexhaustible resilience" (HPP, 345). Yet Richardson points out that with this inexhaustibility, there is no "truth of this truth—no final standard. There is only the momentary event of the enunciation." In order to interrogate this psychoanalytic proxis, Richardson, in his contribution to this book, draws from Heidegger's own treatment of the Greek *a-lêtheia*.

After years of sterile polemics regarding Heidegger's relation to ethics and politics, it is our hope that this book—through the contributions of its authors—will open the way to a genuine philosophical engagement with the practical dimension of Heidegger's thought.

Notes

1. Françoise Dastur, "Le Temps et l'autre chez Husserl et Heidegger," *Alter*, no. 1 (1993) (Fontenay-aux-Roses: Editions Alter), p. 386.

2. We do not follow here the otherwise illuminating analyses of Franco Volpi, who accounts for the Heideggerian critique of reflection as an *inspecto sui* by the hypothesis of a priority given to the "practical" over the "theoretical." "Being and Time: A 'Translation' of the Nicomachean Ethics?," in *Reading Heidegger from the Start* (Albany: State University of New York Press, 1994), pp. 195–211.

3. Françoise Dastur, "The Call of Conscience: The Most Intimate Alterity," *Heidegger and Practical Philosophy* eds. François Raffoul and David Pettigrew (Albany: State University of New York Press, 2002), p. 87. Hereafter cited as *HPP*, followed by page number.

4. Martin Heidegger, "The Question Concerning Technology," *BW*, p. 330.

5. Martin Heidegger, *Plato's Sophist*, trans. Richard Rojcewicz and André Schuwer (Bloomington and Indianapolis: Indiana University Press, 1997).

6. Martin Heidegger, "Phenomenological Interpretations with Respect to Aristotle (Indications of a Hermeneutical Situation)," trans. Michael Baur, *Man and World* XXV (1992): 355–393.

7. Richard McKeon, *Introduction to Aristotle* (New York: Random House, 1947), p. 331.

Part I

Heidegger and Practical Philosophy

1

Free Thinking

John Sallis

Freedom appears unconditionally practical. Surely one will grant, without further ado, without limiting qualifications: freedom is unconditionally practical. Surely one will grant, too, grant by way of explanation, that freedom is the very origin or nonorigin of action, its condition of possibility, its wellspring. There would be no reason for surprise, then, if even a theoretical discourse oriented to the *concept* of freedom were compelled to remain, in the end, a discourse entirely on the practical. A discourse, for instance, on practical reason.

And yet the appearance is anything but sure, and the prospect of surprise prematurely suspended. For the *Critique of Practical Reason* does not restrict the concept of freedom to the domain of the practical, even though it grants from the outset that the decisive attestation—the proof—of the reality of freedom occurs within this domain. Kant writes: "The concept of freedom, insofar as its reality is proved by an apodictic law of practical reason, is the *keystone* of the entire edifice of the system of pure reason and even of speculative reason."[1] Binding the entire structure together, freedom belongs to neither part exclusively; as such, it is anterior to the distinction between theoretical and practical. Not only action but also thinking would, in its proper dignity, arise from freedom.

A corresponding anteriority with respect to the distinction between theoretical and practical is found in *Being and Time*, an anteriority not only of freedom but indeed of the entire existential analysis. To be sure, Heidegger can be said to privilege what one would readily call the practical. By situating the preparatory analysis (Division One) within the horizon of everydayness, Heidegger orients that analysis to the domain of Dasein's dealings with tools and articles of everyday use. Within this domain, Dasein comports itself to these beings primarily by taking them up and using them. It is even in this practical domain that Dasein first comes upon itself: "Dasein initially finds 'itself' in *what* it does, needs, expects, has charge of—in what is ready-to-hand for its concern in the surrounding world" (SZ, 119). Likewise, it is in this world that others are first of all encountered not as objectively present beings but precisely *as* they are in this world, as they show themselves in their engagements in this world: "They are what they do" (SZ, 126). Indeed, Dasein's engagement with what is ready-to-hand for its concern is such that only in exceptional circumstances involving interruption of its concernful dealings does Dasein even momentarily cast its gaze upon these beings as merely things present. But even if that gaze were to be extended, it still would not be theoretical in the sense of a knowing detached from the concerns of the everyday surrounding world. Indeed, Heidegger questions the very possibility of simply distinguishing theoretical and practical, that is, the possibility of delimiting either domain as thoroughly detachable from the other. It is not such that "on the one hand we observe and on the other we *act*." Rather, observation is an engaged concern (*Besorgen*) "just as primordially as action has *its own* kind of seeing" (SZ, 69).

In the case of the basic existential moments that constitute the *there*, the nondifferentiation, the anteriority with respect to the distinction between theoretical and practical, is more radical. Understanding, for instance, is equally theoretical and practical; that is, it is indifferent to the distinction. When Dasein projects itself upon a possibility, it comports itself toward a potentiality and thus orients itself to something that can be realized through action.[2] At the same time, Dasein is disclosed to itself from this possibility, while also letting unfold from it a significational whole that infuses significance into Dasein's world. Much the same indifference is displayed by dispositions or moods: while attuning Dasein to its world, putting it in touch with its practical concerns and directives, they also serve to disclose the world—indeed, to disclose being-in-the-world as such—and so to hold open the horizon within which things can be thematized in their meanings, that is, cognitively.

The case of freedom is otherwise only in that *Being and Time* supplies no developed analysis of freedom comparable to those of understanding and disposition. Functioning as an operative rather than a thematic concept, this determination provides Heidegger with a powerful resource for expressing the comportment of Dasein to its own possibilities, as when Dasein is characterized as "being free [*Freisein*] *for* its ownmost potentiality-for-being" (SZ, 191). Heidegger writes even that Dasein's "being toward a potentiality-for-being is itself determined by freedom" (SZ, 193). With regard to the occurrence of anticipation (*Vorlaufen*) as authentic being-toward-death, it is said to be a matter of "becoming free for one's own death" as sheer possiblity (SZ, 264). In a way that emphasizes the bearing of freedom on Dasein's comportment to possibility, Heidegger introduces a doubling of freedom—for instance, in the discussion of anxiety: "Anxiety reveals in Dasein its *being toward* its ownmost potentiality-for-being, that is, its *being free for* the freedom of choosing and grasping itself" (SZ, 188). Though free to choose, Dasein may indeed not choose, not choose to choose, letting its choice be made instead by the they-self rather than itself, or rather, by the they-self that is the self of inauthentic Dasein. Freedom requires, therefore, its doubling: not only being free, but being free for one's freedom.

As with the basic existentials that belong to the constitution of the *there*, freedom pertains not to Dasein's comportment to this or that being but to the very clearing of a space, of a significant world, within which particular beings can come to show themselves as they are. Freedom pertains to the occurrence of disclosedness (*Erschlossenheit*) which, indifferent to the distinction, is presupposed equally by theory and practice.

In the lecture courses and essays that immediately postdate *Being and Time*, freedom as an existential assumes a more thematic role, or rather it is made to play more thematically the role already assigned to it in *Being and Time*. For instance, in the 1928 lecture course *Metaphysical Foundations of Logic*, Heidegger focuses on the relation of freedom to the for-the-sake-of (*Umwillen*). This designation, taken directly from *Being and Time*, denotes the possibility in which all of the various instrumental references (those designated by the phrase in-order-to) converge and are gathered. The for-the-sake-of is that possibility of Dasein for the sake of which the various instrumental operations within the surrounding world would be carried out. It is also the kind of possibility upon which Dasein, existing for the sake of itself, projects. It is precisely the structural moment that binds projection to delineation of a world, so that, with projection, a corresponding significance comes to be infused into the world. In *Metaphysical Foundations of Logic*, Heidegger is explicit about the connection between the for-the-sake-of and freedom: "In freedom, such a for-the-sake-of has always already emerged." It is not, however, as though the for-the-sake-of were simply present (*vorhanden*), so that freedom could then come into relation to it. On the contrary: "Freedom is itself the origin of the for-the-sake-of"—not in the sense that there would first have been freedom and only then the for-the-sake-of. Most precisely expressed: "Freedom is, rather, one with the for-the-sake-of" (GA 26, 246f).

The direction of the analysis is unmistakable: freedom is being set at the very center of understanding, that is, at the heart of projection. Thus, "Freedom gives itself to understand; it is primal understanding [*Urverstehen*], i.e., the primal projecting of that which freedom itself makes possible." Still further, Heidegger specifies that free projection not only puts into play the possibility on which Dasein projects itself but also, in that very projecting, sets up a counter to freedom, something binding (in somewhat—though not identically—the manner in which, according to *Being and Time*, Dasein is bound by the corresponding referential totality, especially as that in which Dasein finds itself already thrown). The 1928 lecture course explicitly sets freedom at the very center of Dasein's existential constitution: "As free, Dasein is world-projection. But this projecting is only projected in such a way that Dasein holds itself in it and does this so that the free hold binds Dasein. . . . Freedom itself holds this binding over against itself. The world is maintained in freedom counter to freedom itself. The world is the free *counter-hold* [*freier* Widerhalt] of Dasein's for-the-sake-of. Being-in-the-world is accordingly nothing other than freedom" (GA 26, 246f).

These developments are confirmed and consolidated in the 1929 essay "On the Essence of Ground." Again, Heidegger refers to the for-the-sake-of and identifies as freedom that which casts something like a for-the-sake-of projectively before it. Now freedom becomes fully thematic: "Surpassing in the direction of the world [or: passage beyond to the world—*Der Überstieg zur Welt*] is freedom itself. . . . *Freedom alone can let a world prevail and let it world* [Walten und welten lassen] *for Dasein*" (GA 9, 163f). Freedom is neither a characteristic nor even the wellspring of Dasein's comportment toward beings, neither of its theoretical nor its practical comportment; freedom is not something that belongs—not even as origin—either to vision or to action. Rather, freedom is the passage beyond beings—in this sense, transcendence—that lets prevail a world in which beings can come to be present.

Yet if confirmed and consolidated in the 1929 essay, these developments through which freedom becomes thematically central first take on a more radical cast in the following year. This is the year to which Heidegger refers when, much later, he marks the inception of his efforts to submit *Being and Time* to an immanent critique. He characterizes this effort as "the attempt, undertaken again and again since 1930, to shape in a more originary way the *Fragestellung* of *Being and Time*" (ZS, 61). It would have been, ever since this year, a matter of venturing to pose the question of *Being and Time* in a more originary way, of seeking to let the question posed in that work take shape more originarily.

It was in this same year that Heidegger first drafted his essay "On the Essence of Truth." First presented as a lecture in 1930, it was presented again and again and repeatedly revised before finally being published in 1943. It is preeminently in this essay that Heidegger takes over and radicalizes the thematic centering of freedom. For here he ventures to think freedom as the essence of truth.

"On the Essence of Truth" puts into question not only the essence of truth but also the very sense that *essence* has in this phrase, puts into question the truth of essence. What the initial sections of the essay thus produce is a double series of redeterminations, of essence, on the one hand, of truth, on the other hand; the redeterminations are carried out regressively, moving from the ordinary to the more originary.

The ordinary concept of truth is circumscribed as accordance, correspondence, and correctness. It is the accordance of a thing with its operative preconception or the accordance of a statement with that about which it is asserted that makes the thing or the statement true. Such accordance is what is had in common by everything that can be called true. Taking essence to have the sense of "the common" (Κοινόν), one may say that the essence of truth is accordance (correspondence, correctness).

Heidegger's strategy is to unsettle this determination, specifically to show how it is dependent for its very sense on the medieval determination of truth as *adequatio rei et intellectus* and, ultimately, on the medieval articulation of being that provides the foundational schema for this determination. Once the apparent obviousness of the ordinary concept of truth has been thus undermined, two questions arise. Now one must ask, first of all: What precisely is the character of the accordance that constitutes truth? In particular, what is the character of a statement that is accordant and thus true? What is a correct statement, a *true* statement? The most direct answer to this question is found not in the 1943 published version of the essay but in the initial draft from 1930: "It is only because the statement is also a comporting [Verhalten] that it can in its way accord with something." In other words, a statement can be accordant with the thing of which it speaks, only because it is not itself a thing (which would somehow have to be like another, very different thing, the thing spoken of) but rather a comportment to the thing spoken of, a way of intending the thing itself. Specifically, an accordant—and thus true—statement is a comportment that presents the thing *as* it is.

The second question now unavoidable concerns the possiblility of such statements: What is required in order that it be possible for a statement to occur that, intentive of a thing, presents that thing as it itself is? In other words, what do such statements presuppose? What is the condition of their possibility? Heidegger's answer: what is required is that beings show themselves within an open region in which the statement, the verbal comportment, can subordinate itself to them, take its standard from them, to say them *as* they are. The comportment must be open to beings to take its standard from them, to let the saying be measured by the things said; thus what is required is, in Heidegger's phrase, "openness of comportment." It is this openness of comportment that makes possible the truth of statements, their accordance with the things spoken of, and thus, Heidegger concludes, openness of comportment can in a more originary sense be called the essence of truth. With the redetermination of essence as condition of possibility (as making-possible, enabling: *Ermöglichung*), the essence of truth proves to be the openness of comportment.

Posing the question of ground launches a further regression: What is the ground of the possibility (the ground of the making-possible, of the enabling) of truth as correctness? That is, what is the ground of the openness of comportment? Heidegger carries out this move with utmost economy. He refers to the way in which such comportment is given its standard by the things themselves, that is, the way in which the verbal comportment is pregiven a directedness to the things of which one speaks. He asks: How can such pregiving occur? What is its ground? His answer enacts the regressive move: The pregiving can occur "only if this pregiving has already entered freely into an open region for something opened up that prevails there and that binds every presenting. To free oneself for a binding directedness is possible only by *being free* [Freisein] for what is opened up [*zum Offenbaren*—hence also, for what becomes manifest] in an open region. Such being free points to the heretofore uncomprehended essence of freedom. The openness of comportment as the inner condition of the possibility of correctness is grounded in freedom. *The essence of truth is freedom*" (GA 9, 185f).[3] With the redetermination of essence as ground of possibility, the essence of truth proves to be freedom.

Nothing could be more astonishing. Nothing could seem stranger, more alien. Nothing could appear more foreign to truth than freedom. For if one were to suppose that here it is only a matter of the one who enacts a statement having to be free (unimpeded) in order to carry out the act, one would have missed the point entirely.

Rather, it is a matter of the *essence* of truth: freedom is the very essence of truth itself. What could be more astonishing than—as seems thus inevitable—submitting truth to human caprice? One would more readily suppose that human caprice is at the root of all kinds of untruth (lies, deception, semblance). Indeed, sound common sense would not hesitate to attribute to human caprice virtually all that goes to constitute the very opposite of truth itself, the opposite of that pure essence of truth that holds sway above and beyond the sphere of the merely human, all-too-human. What, then, could seem stranger than to declare freedom the essence of truth? Stranger still would be perhaps only the declaration that this freedom that is the essence of truth is not anything that belongs to human beings, that it is not a property of the human being. But what, then, is freedom that it can be the essence of truth?

Needless to say, there is less difficulty in saying what it is not. In fact, Heidegger himself includes, in the lecture course on Schelling from this period, an extended discussion of the various traditional concepts of freedom. The discussion is designed to introduce Schelling's unique concept of freedom (as the capacity [*Vermögen*] for good and evil), which Heidegger sets apart from all traditional concepts of freedom, just as, no doubt, he would set equally apart from them the determination of freedom as the essence of truth. Heidegger distinguishes five traditional concepts of freedom. The first identifies freedom as the capability of self-beginning, that is, as the self-ability to initiate a series of events without recourse to any further ground. Freedom also is conceived, secondly, as not being bound to something, that is, as negative freedom in the form of freedom *from*. The third concept is positive freedom: being free *for* something in the sense of committing oneself to something. The fourth, inauthentic concept construes freedom as the mastery of spirit over sensibility, as the dominance of reason over drives, desires, and inclinations. In the fifth, authentic concept, freedom is thought of as the independence that consists in "self-determination in the sense that what is free gives itself the law of its own essence on the basis of this essence itself" (GA 42, 145).[4] This is freedom as it came to be thought only with Kant: self-determination as self-legislation (*Selbstgesetzgebung*).[5]

Freedom as the essence of truth is distinct from freedom in all of these senses, though not entirely lacking traces of certain traditional concepts. As being free for what comes into the open so as to be manifest and so that a directedness is pregiven, freedom is indeed a kind of freedom *for*; yet it is a freedom not *for* any particular thing or action upon things but rather *for* things as such, *for* the very openness that lets them come forth manifestly and bindingly in the open. The freedom that is the essence of truth also is in a sense self-determination, but it is a matter of determining oneself to a submission to the open manifestness of things.

Heidegger expresses this concept of freedom as letting be, as letting beings be (*das Seinlassen von Seiendem*), as letting beings be the beings they are. Heidegger declares that such letting be is not a matter of neglect and indifference. In a marginal comment written in his copy of the first edition of "On the Essence of Truth," Heidegger remarks that letting be is to be taken "not in the negative sense" but as "granting—preservation." Another such comment describes letting be as "leaving that which is present its presencing, and not importing or interposing anything else." The drift of the language of letting be, its drifting toward tautology—letting beings be the beings they are—serves notice, on the other hand, that it is not a matter of producing beings, of bringing them about in an ontically creative way. The first of the marginal notes just cited continues, "not as an ontically oriented effecting" (GA 9, 188). Neither is it a matter of constituting beings, as, in a transcendental philosophy, objects are regarded as constituted as such by the subject. Nor, on the other hand, is it just a matter of dealing with particular beings in the sense of tending, managing, or planning with regard to them. Rather, "To let be—that is, to let beings be as the beings that they are—means to engage oneself with the open region [*sich einlassen auf das Offene*] and its openness into which every being comes to stand, bringing that openness, as it were, along with itself" (GA 9, 188). The parallel with the passage that thematizes freedom in "On the Essence of Ground" is striking. In the 1929 essay, freedom is characterized as the passage beyond innerworldly beings to the world itself, as the surpassing of beings that lets a world prevail for those very beings passed over, letting them be thus innerworldly. Correspondingly, "On the Essence of Truth" characterizes freedom as a passage to the open; but now there is more evident insistence that passage beyond is not carried out in such a way as to escape beings and leave them somehow behind, that, instead, it is precisely such as to come back to them as beings within the open, as being themselves the beings they are. Freedom is letting oneself into engagement with the open, in the open, in such a way that beings can stand forth in their open manifestness, that is, be the beings they themselves are.

Still more remarkable is the move that Heidegger now ventures, a move that has the effect of differentiating this essay decisively from the 1929 texts. For once the regression to freedom has been carried out, Heidegger neither terminates the movement nor lets it simply resume as regressive. To be sure, one could, up to a point, easily mistake the move as mere iteration of the movements toward the more originary. For now the question explicitly becomes that of the *essence* of freedom. One might well suppose, even on the basis of the topography of the essay, that Heidegger's discussion of freedom as letting be is already oriented to determining the essence of freedom. One notices, however, that, in contrast to the previous stages that have produced the double series of determinations, Heidegger now forgoes specifying the operative sense of *essence*. Nonetheless—and especially if one draws on other texts of this period[6]—one would hardly be too far off the mark if one were to take *essence* here in its basic, classical sense: then *essence* would designate that which one asks about in asking the question "τί ἐστι?"—that is, in asking *what* something is. This seems to be just the direction that the questioning takes when, in the section entitled "The Essence of Freedom," freedom is characterized as letting be. At least within certain— still unmarked—limits, the essence of freedom is letting be.

Yet at just the point where letting be is characterized as engagement in the open, there is a peculiar interruption in the flow of the text, or rather, there is inscribed a trace of a remembrance of the beginning of Western thinking. Heidegger writes: "Western thinking in its beginning conceived this open region as τὰ ἀλήθεια, the unconcealed [*das Unverborgene*]. If we translate ἀλήθεια as 'unconcealment' rather than 'truth', this translation is not merely 'more literal'; but it contains the directive to rethink the ordinary concept of truth in the sense of the correctness of statements and to think it back to that still uncomprehended disclosedness [*Entborgenheit*] and disclosure [*Entbergung*] of beings" (GA 9, 188). This remembrance and this translation with its inherent directive have the effect of turning the previously regressive movement in what could be called simply—for want of a more appropriate figure—a different direction. It is not a matter of extending the regressive series to a still more originary term of the same order; it is not a matter simply of moving from the essence of truth to the essence of the essence of truth. Rather, what the remembrance and the translation put into play is the referral of the essence of truth to that which, though called now *the open*, was called ἀλήθεια by the Greeks and thereafter translated as *truth*. Were that translation to be—at least for the moment—retained, then one also could translate in the following way what Heidegger writes about freedom as the letting be that consists in engaging oneself in the open: the essence of truth—so the translation would run—consists in self-engagement in (what has been called, translated as) truth. In short, the essence of truth is engagement in truth.

But for Heidegger ἀλήθεια is to be translated back into *unconcealment*, into the disclosedness of beings. And it is back to these translations that the ordinary concept of truth is to be thought. Such thinking is precisely what Heidegger ventures in the wake of the remembrance. Freedom he now determines as exposure (*Aussetzung*) to the disclosedness of beings, as being set out into the unconcealment in which beings come to be disclosed. As such, freedom is also "ek-sistent," a standing out outside itself, out into the disclosedness of beings. Thus freedom comes to be determined *from* (in reference to) the disclosedness of beings, and what Heidegger says will become evident begins indeed to become evident: "But here it becomes evident also that freedom is the ground of the inner possibility of correctness only because it receives its own essence from the more originary essence of uniquely essential truth" (GA 9, 187). Freedom receives its essence from—is essentially determined from—the more originary essence of uniquely essential truth, that is, ἀλήθεια, the disclosedness of beings. Determined from ἀλήθεια, freedom as letting be—the essence of freedom— proves to be exposure and ek-sistence.

"On the Essence of Truth" includes a subtext on untruth. Initially—and ironically—set aside as the mere opposite of truth, which falling outside of truth can appropriately be left aside, untruth comes to be more and more insistently in question until finally, in the later sections of the essay, this subtext virtually takes over. Rather than constituting a mere external opposite, untruth proves to be an "untruth that is most proper to the essence of truth" (GA 9, 193). For instance, as the concealment that Heidegger calls the mystery, "Precisely because letting be always lets beings be in a particular comportment that relates to them and thus discloses them, it conceals beings as a whole. Letting be is intrinsically at the same time a concealing" (GA 9, 193). Or, as errancy, this "essential counteressence [*Gegenwesen*] to the originary essence of truth" (GA 9, 197) occurs as a double movement, on the one hand, concealing the mystery—that is, the concealment—that holds sway in the unconcealment of beings while, on the other hand, turning away from the mystery toward readily available beings.[7] Thus there is no pure essence of truth; rather, the essence of truth is such as to yoke together truth and untruth, unconcealment and concealment (in its various compoundings).

But then, this is to say that freedom, as exposure to the unconcealment of beings, is at least equally exposed to concealment. Freedom as letting be is exposure to the complex of unconcealment and concealment as which the essence of truth holds sway.

The course of "On the Essence of Truth" is repeatedly interrupted by references—either in remembrance or otherwise—to beginnings. In *Contributions to Philosophy*, this theme will constitute one of the major axes, the opposition between the first beginning and another beginning. In the essay, however, this axis is still less than fully in play.

One such reference occurs in the midst of Heidegger's discussion of freedom as exposure and as ek-sistence. He writes about what he will venture to call even the beginning of history: it is in any case the beginning that occurs "at that moment when the first thinker takes a questioning stand with regard to the unconcealment of beings by asking: what are beings? In this question unconcealment is experienced for the first time." This is, then, a beginning in which "beings themselves are expressly drawn up into their unconcealment and conserved in it" (GA 9, 189f).

Another such reference comes after the introduction of untruth into the essence of truth. In this context, the eruption of thinking that constitutes a beginning can no longer be limited to a renewed experience of unconcealment but must include equally—even perhaps above all—a manifold contention with concealment. Thus Heidegger declares that there can arise "resolute openness [*Ent-schlossenheit*] toward the mystery." He continues: "Then the question of the essence of truth gets asked more originally. Then the ground of the intertwining of the essence of truth with the truth of essence reveals itself." Opening to the mystery, dispelling the errant concealing of concealing, one ceases to orient the question of the essence of truth to readily available beings and the correctness pertinent to them. Instead, one redoubles one's exposure to the unconcealment of beings, exposed now as an unconcealment to which concealment belongs. And instead of being oriented to mere particular beings, one questions the essence of those beings; one asks now the question of the truth of essence. Such is the eruption of questioning: "The glimpse into the mystery out of errancy is a questioning—in the sense of that unique question of what beings as such are as a whole. This questioning thinks the question of the *being* [Sein] of beings" (GA 9, 198).

The question—another question, the question of this questioning—is whether the eruption of questioning is not precisely a redoubling of freedom. The question is whether the interruption effected when one poses the question of what beings as such are and thus comes to experience unconcealment and no longer merely to live along, as it were, in one's concealed exposure to it—the question is whether this break with errancy is not precisely a matter of becoming—unaccountably—free for one's freedom. The question is whether the beginning of philosophy—every beginning of philosophy, every enactment of philosophical beginning—is not, in precisely this sense, a matter of free thinking.

The eruption of questioning is most extreme, yet whatever is done will always be done from a distance, with distance. It is only through the originary distances that Dasein gives itself in its freedom—and, at the extremes, in its freedom redoubled— that a true nearness to things comes to arise, allowing Dasein to be true to things. And it is only by being able to listen into the distance that Dasein awakens to the response of another. In every case, then, Dasein's action—always, it seems, anterior to the distinction between theoretical and practical—is an action at a distance, and Dasein itself is, in Heidegger's phrase, *ein Wesen der Ferne* (GA 9, 175).

Notes

1. I. Kant, *Kritik der praktischen Vernunft*, in *Werke: Akademie Textausgabe*, vol. 5 (Berlin: Walter de Gruyter, 1968), p. 3.

2. In another text from the same period, Heidegger stresses the connection to action, though to action determined in a fundamental way: "Understanding as self-projecting is Dasein's fundamental mode of *happening* [*Grundart des* Geschehens]. As we can also say, it is the authentic meaning of action [*Handelns*]"(GA 24, 393).

3. In the *Gesamtausgabe* edition, the final sentence in this passage reads: "*Das Wesen der Wahrheit, als Richtigkeit der Aussage verstanden, ist die Freiheit.*" The phrase "*als Richtigkeit der Aussage verstanden*" does not appear in the first edition of *Wegmarken*, nor in any of the earlier editions of the essay.

4. This lecture course was presented during the summer semester of 1936.

5. Elsewhere Heidegger offers this account: "In subjecting myself to the law, I myself to myself reveals, discloses as such, me to myself in my *dignity*" (GA 24, 192).

6. See especially, GA 45, 60-62.

7. The operation of the subtext on untruth, and the monstrosity of truth that results, is discussed in detail in *Double Truth* (Albany: State University of New York Press, 1995), chap. 6.

2

The Interpretation of Aristotle's Notion of *Aretê* in Heidegger's First Courses

JACQUES TAMINIAUX

The specific point that I would like to address is the Heideggerian interpretation of Aristotle's notion of *aretê*, commonly translated as *Tugend* in German and *vertu* in French, translations that Heidegger chose not to use. The term *aretê* does not figure anywhere among the Greek terms used in *Sein und Zeit*, but one can note that the thematic of *aretê* plays an important role in the genesis of this book, if we follow the courses that Heidegger taught at Marburg. Moreover, the manner in which Heidegger approached this thematic in his first courses at Freiburg and then at Marburg engages a cluster of closely related questions that are pertinent to practical philosophy. In fact, one would be able to show that the first heirs of Heidegger, those who were influenced by these courses before *Sein und Zeit*—notably Hannah Arendt, Hans-Georg Gadamer, Hans Jonas, and also Leo Strauss—staked out, each in his or her own manner, their own field of research, specifically in relation to a debate, sometimes explicit, sometimes inexplicit, with Heidegger's reappropriation of the thematic of *aretê*.

I

I will recall, roughly, the context of this reappropriation of Aristotle, which was Heidegger's focus during his last years as an assistant in Freiburg. One finds a programmatic outline of this in the famed report of 1922 to Natorp and to Misch.[1] In relation to these two judges—*captatio benevolentiae*—Heidegger characterizes this context as a contribution to the *history of ontology and logic*. At first this characterization is purely formal and conventional. The real scope only appears when one pays attention to the long preamble in which Heidegger determines the style and stakes of his contribution. These are announced in the title of the report, *Phenomenological Interpretations with Respect to Aristotle*, a title indissociable from its subtitle, *Indication of the Hermeneutical Situation*. To interpret is a double activity of explication or exegesis *and* understanding, which is intrinsically situated within, or bound to, a hermeneutic situation. The characteristics of this situation denote from the outset Heidegger's insistence on a central motif of inquiry, a motif dear to Husserl, namely, *sight*. The hermeneutic situation is determined by a *point of view*, an orientation of *vision*, a *visual* horizon. Even if an interpretation assumes argumentation, debate, or a dialogue with others, it is ultimately a matter of vision. More precisely, it culminates and is accomplished in a *Durchsichtigkeit*, a transparence of the "living present" (the term is borrowed from Husserl), which marks the situation of the interpreter, and which he or she must take on resolutely. Under these conditions, the interpretation of the past of philosophy could only be a reappropriation of the present where the power of elucidation is measured by the radicality of the interpreter's philosophical interrogation. Instead of devoting oneself to historiographical research, the interpreter must engage in philosophical research. This research, Heidegger insists in 1922, thematizes human Dasein, insofar as it is questioned with respect to its Being-character (*Seincharakter*). In other words, the object of this research is factical life in its fundamental movement, that is, "In the concrete temporalizing [*Zeitigung*] of its Being it is concerned about its Being" (PIA, 359). Furthermore, far from being a distant observer of factical life, this research accompanies its proper movement and itself belongs to it, because this research deliberately confronts factical life in all of its gravity. I will recall briefly the "constitutive" characteristics of this factical life, considered in its motion. Factical life is through and through animated by a *concern* for either the environing world (*Umwelt*), the with-world (*Mitwelt*), or the world of the self (*Selbstwelt*), and it is therefore defined in relation to a world, a relation that, according to Heidegger, is the cradle of all meaning and the true "original intentionality." It is as a modality of this intentionality of care that Heidegger introduces the second characteristic that is constitutive of factical life: *fallenness*. As a concernful relation to the world, original intentionality is accompanied by a tendency that is itself intentional, namely, to identify with the world and in this way to detach itself from itself. This fallenness substitutes tasks that are easy to master for the fundamental anxiety of factical life and obliterates the radical selfhood of this life under the leveling reign of publicness and of "the They." *Proper* original intentionality is in this way the constant prey of an *improper* modality of intentionality. This persistent tension between the proper and the improper is particularly detectable in the third constitutive characteristic of factical life, that is, in the relation that this life has with its own end, *death*. The imminence and the ineluctable nature of death are constitutive of "the character of Being" of facticity and determine it intrinsically. On this point as well, the motif of vision is paramount. In its ineluctable imminence, death is the "phenomenon" that makes life visible (*sichtbar*) to itself (PIA, 365), that is, it brings "the specific temporality of human Dasein" (PIA, 366) into view (*Sicht*). But access to this view, since fallenness accompanies original intentionality as its shadow, assumes the detour of a countermovement that resists *Verfallen* and opposes the original primacy of a negativity to the positivity with which it is identified.

Such being the constitutive factors of factical life—the object of philosophical research—it is easy to define more precisely the specificity of the philosophical problematic taken up by Heidegger; from the outset, he announces to Natorp and Misch that such problematics will contribute to the history of ontology and logic. Indeed, the style of this problematic reveals that it is both ontological and logical. It is ontological, since its theme is factical life with respect to its Being-character, thus giving this problematic the status of an ontology of facticity. But Heidegger clarifies that this ontology, far from being a regional ontology, has the status of *prinzipielle Ontologie* in comparison to other regional ontologies. The ontology of facticity is the foundation and meaning of the various problematics of regional ontologies. This fundamental ontology also is a fundamental *logic*, since it belongs to the very being of factical life to articulate the intentionality that is constitutive of it, to articulate for itself the many ways in which this intentionality is temporalized. The various ways in which facticity relates to the world, and to itself as a relation to the world, the ways in which it offers itself in a *logos*, are just as many categories and categorial structures to be interpreted, keeping in mind the fundamental tension between authenticity and inauthenticity.

It is significant that in the presentation of this logical problematic of the ontology of facticity, Heidegger amalgamates the language of Kant with the language of Husserl's *Logical Investigations*. The categorical structures through which factical life articulates itself are, he says in Kant's language, "conditions of possibility," but they are not reduced to simple "logical forms" because they are susceptible, he adds, following Husserl, to being rendered visible and to offer themselves up to an *Anschauung*.

By its insistence on sight, on the necessary demarcation of authentic intentionality from all of the modalities of inauthentic intentionality, on the living present, on the distinction between regional and principal levels, on the intuition of categorical structures—the Husserlian echoes are evident throughout all of these characteristics—it goes without saying that this hermeneutic problematic proclaims itself as phenomenological through and through.

Why is Aristotle involved in this problematic? It would be much too simplistic to believe that the Aristotelian *corpus* was only a possibility among others for this problematic to find an application and a justification after the fact, as if it could have developed independently of this *corpus*. Rather, it is through a meditation on Aristotle that it developed its own approach.

That is what I would like to show and to examine with respect to a specific theme, *aretê*.

But before proceeding it is essential to emphasize that it is the phenomenological character of the problematic taken up by the young Heidegger that led him to study the Greek texts. He wrote: "The philosophy of today's situation moves inauthentically within the *Greek* conceptuality . . . [Recall the Husserlian use of words like *idea, apophantic, apodictic, category, noêsis,* etc.]. The basic concepts have lost their primordial functions of expression, functions that are particularly suited to particularly experienced regions of objects. But in all of the analogizing and formalizing that have penetrated these basic concepts, there remains a particular character of origin; these basic concepts still carry with them a part of the genuine tradition of their primordial meaning, insofar as there is still detectable in them the meaning-direction that goes back to their objective source" (PIA, 370, tr. slightly modified). The phenomenological hermeneutic must illuminate the sources that are themselves intentional, since they consist in the specific experiences of certain regions of an object of a specific type. The name for this illumination of intentional sources is *Destruktion*.

It would be naïve to think that the deconstruction of inherited concepts consists in valorizing a sort of Greek golden age of the hermeneutics of facticity. Aristotle deserves to be deconstructed no less than the moderns. In 1922, at the beginning of his interpretation of Aristotle, Heidegger did not fail to emphasize the limitations of the Aristotelian understanding of factical life. A first limit is that logic and ontology derive from physics in Aristotle, therefore, his inquiry is concerned with the movements of nature and not the intrinsic motion of human Dasein. Secondly, Aristotle's logic and ontology are determined by an anticipatory understanding of the meaning of Being that is quite narrow, since it is taken from the specific experience of a determinate objective region: the experience of *poiêsis* in the general sense of the production of artifacts or production of effects. For Aristotle, Being first means to be produced. Now production is not an activity by which factical life sights itself but rather is an activity by which it turns away from what is most proper to it by being absorbed by intraworldly objects, therefore, it is an activity that belongs to the fallenness that accompanies factical life as its shadow.

II

Having determined this interpretative context, we are now prepared to investigate the Heideggerian reappropriation of the thematic of *aretê*.

Because the 1922 text is quite elliptic and elusive on this theme, I would like to take a look at the 1924 course on Plato's *Sophist*, a course where the introduction is a long analysis of the *Nicomachean Ethics*. In this course, the pages most explicitly focusing on *aretê* are found in a paragraph (§8) where Heidegger looks at Aristotle's analysis of *phronêsis* in Chapter V of Book VI of the *Nicomachean Ethics*. Why does Heidegger comment on this analysis in a course devoted to Plato's *Sophist*?

A simple reminder of the themes that are debated in the *Sophist* will enable us to clearly sketch out the meaning of Heidegger's recourse to Aristotle in view of ensuring good phenomenological-hermeneutic conditions for his reading of Plato. These themes are enunciated as contrasts—Being and non-Being, truth and appearance, knowledge and opinion—that need to be understood phenomenologically, that is, seen and described, as well as interpreted, in relation to human beings. As soon as the series of contrasts are enunciated, it is easy to perceive that the themes that they evoke are closely linked: knowledge is associated with truth, and truth is associated with beings as beings, while opinion is associated with appearance that sometimes passes for truth. What is at stake in Plato's struggle with the Sophists is the quest for true knowledge as opposed to opinion. The detour through Aristotle is designed to establish that in such a quest a certain human way of being is involved. And since ultimately it is truth that connects knowledge to beings as beings, the detour through Aristotle attempts to establish the way in which truth, while it characterizes the being of the entities to which human beings relate, also characterizes through various modalities that remain to be determined the way of being of human beings.

Furthermore, in Greek, the word for truth is *alêtheia*. The privative character of this word, which Heidegger translates as "un-concealment, " is enough to indicate, he states from the start, that for the Greeks truth such as they understood it is not immediately accessible but must be wrested from an initial concealment. It is this very wresting, Heidegger asserts, that mobilized all of Plato's energy and animated his struggle against the Sophists and rhetoricians. As an inheritor of Plato's teachings, Aristotle not only emphasized, like him, that the true, in the sense of the unconcealed, is a character of the entity and of its Being, but also, and more clearly than his master, he put the state of unconcealment of the entity and its Being in relation to human beings. They are able to uncover (*alêtheuein*) because they are the only living beings who speak.

As we see, the recourse to Aristotle in this 1924 course consists in a reappropriation in terms of the existence of all of the themes evoked above. Far from raising these themes as distant objects of study for the history of ideas, for Heidegger, it is a matter of showing that these themes, these techniques of analysis, comparison, and genealogy, dear to specialists of this history, also are questions that concern the very existence of those who undertake the study. While he departs from the usual methods of this history—to clarify texts in relation to those that precede them, for example, to explicate Plato in relation to the pre-Socratics—he substitutes something altogether different from a retrospective method—to clarify Plato in light of Aristotle—that is, a prospective method. It is not simply a matter of substituting the latter for the former under the pretext that the students are better informed than their masters, or that the closest is easier to know than the farthest. If Heidegger had recourse to the *Nicomachean Ethics* to introduce Plato, it is because in Aristotle's treatise the very axis of his own philosophical interrogation stood out. And this is why the language in which he expresses his lecture on Aristotle is already the language that he will use in *Sein und Zeit*. In other words, what he discovers already in the *Nicomachean Ethics*, as he clearly asserted in the 1926 lecture on "The Fundamental Concepts of Ancient Philosophy," is an "ontology of Dasein." How does *aretê* enter into this context, and how is it defined here?

It is fitting to note first that Heidegger's recourse to the *Nicomachean Ethics* exclusively focuses on Books VI and X, thus neglecting the long analyses of Books I to V devoted successively to the Good and to happiness, to the relation between the mean and the extremes, as well as to the properly ethical *aretai* that are courage, self-control, generosity, magnificence, kindness, benevolence, sincerity, and justice. And if Heidegger retains only Books VI and X of Aristotle's treatise, it is, we will see shortly, because *alêtheia* and the investigation of the ways in which the living beings who speak (human beings) relate to it play a determining role here. We would be wrong to think, however, that the Heideggerian retrieval of the thematic of Aristotelian *aretê*, such as it is developed in these books, is strictly epistemological. In fact, the so-called intellectual *aretai* treated in these books are approached neither from an ethical nor an epistemological perspective, but rather from an essentially ontological one. In other words, he approaches them as modes of unconcealment of Being as such. Let us follow this interpretation.

Book VI of the Aristotelian treatise begins by recalling that the right principle (*orthos logos*) that governs each of the ethical dispositions examined in the preceding books consists in choosing the mean, at equal distance from excess and defect. It recalls also that the *aretai* of the *psychê* are divided into two groups: the ethical *aretai* and the dianoetical *aretai*. The latter, which belong to the part of the *psychê* that has *logos*, are subdivided into two groups: those where the *psychê* considers beings whose principles (*archai*) are unchangeable, and those where it considers the beings that are changeable. The first group is called intellectual, while the other is called deliberative. That being the case, the task defined by Aristotle in Book VI is to determine which is the best disposition (*beltistê hexis*) for the dianoetic aptitudes of the *psychê* of either group, which amount to determining, on the one hand, which would be the intellectual *aretê*, and, on the other hand, which would be the deliberative *aretê*. Moreover, each of the dianoetical aptitudes of the *psychê* has an aletheic function. As a consequence, in order to identify the *aretê* specific to each of the two groups, it is important to determine the aptitude in each that best exercises the aletheic operation.

It is at this point that Heidegger begins his interpretation by emphasizing that Aristotle introduces his research by a programmatic enumeration of the modes of *alêtheuein*, which are *technê, epistêmê, phronêsis, sophia,* and *nous* (Book VI, 3, 1149b 15). And Heidegger leaves no doubt about the way in which he understands these modes. While Aristotle attributes them to *psychê*, Heidegger does not hesitate to attribute them to the "human Dasein." He also does not hesitate to translate *alêtheuei hê psychê* as "Dasein is uncovering," or even by the expression that he will use in *Sein und Zeit*: "Dasein is in truth," by specifying that unconcealment is a determination of the Being of Dasein (§4). Furthermore, since Dasein is uncovering, an uncovering that determines it in its Being in relationship to beings, Heidegger does not hesitate to introduce in his translation of the Aristotelian enumeration of the diaonetic modes of *alêtheuein* the word "being," even though Aristotle never mentioned it explicitly.

One already suspects, under these conditions, that the interpretation of the Aristotelian problematic of *aretê* will consist for Heidegger in defining, with respect to Dasein, the ontological capacity to uncover, which is inherent in each of the modes enumerated by Aristotle to better determine their scope. And since Aristotle defines *aretê* in general as the best disposition, it will be a matter of discerning for each of the two fundamental modes of disclosure (intellectual and deliberative) "its most genuine possibility to uncover beings as they are and to preserve them as uncovered" (S, 21).

Now, Aristotle maintains that the best intellectual disposition is *sophia,* and he relegates *epistêmê* to an inferior rank. As for the deliberative disposition, it is *phronêsis* to which he attributes the dignity of *aretê,* from which *technê* is excluded.

The question that occupies me is therefore to ascertain if Heidegger subscribes to these two hierarchies and what meaning he attributes to them.

As I indicated above, it is only in these pages devoted to the Aristotelian analysis of *phronêsis* that Heidegger expressly uses—several times—the word *aretê.* This frequent usage itself suggests that it is *phronêsis* to which he attributes the dignity of *aretê.* This permits us to presume, given the hermeneutic context that we have roughly recalled, that the Aristotelian analysis of *phronêsis* to his mind is of paramount importance. But since manifestly *sophia* is for Aristotle also an *aretê,* and even the highest *aretê,* we can assume that it will also be a matter for Heidegger of questioning this preeminence and to situate it in relation to the *aretê* of *phronêsis.*

For anyone familiar with *Sein und Zeit,* it is easy to perceive that the capital importance that Heidegger attributes to the Aristotelian analysis of *phronêsis,* two or three years before the publication of his *opus magnum,* lies in the fact that Heidegger sees in it the central axis of his own analytic of Dasein.

There is no need to follow the detail of the text to be convinced of this. A few indications will suffice.

The Heideggerian interpretation of Aristotelian *phronêsis* in §8 of the course on the *Sophist* begins by recalling the aletheic character of the two intellectual modes and the two deliberative modes. Heidegger emphasizes that neither *epistêmê* for the first mode nor *technê* for the second is able to assume the rank of *aretê.* And it is at this point that he gives his own definition of the word: *aretê* signifies the authentic and fully developed possibility of unconcealment (S, 33).

Paragraph 8 asks, then, by what right *phronêsis* can assume the rank of *aretê,* in the sense of authentic (*eigentlich*) possibility of unconcealment, while *technê* cannot.

The reason is simple: *phronêsis* is able to assume the rank of *aretê* insofar as it unvovers Dasein itself.

It is this response that we must now consider.

Like *technê,* recounts Heidegger, *phronêsis* involves a deliberation. As is the case for *technê,* the deliberation of *phronêsis* is, as such, relative to something that is able to be otherwise. But there the resemblance between the two deliberative modes ends: they are essentially different regarding their goal and principle. The *telos* of the kind of action revealed by *technê*—an action that pertains to *poiêsis,* to production or the making of something—is some thing other than Dasein, an entity that is "over and against" Dasein, an *ergon* or a work that falls outside of Dasein. On the other hand, the action revealed by *phronêsis,* far from being an involvement with exterior entities, is *praxis,* understood as the conduct of the very life of man, that is, as the very way in which Dasein exists. And the goal that *phronêsis* takes into view is not, moreover, exterior (*para*), because it is nothing else than the accomplishment of *praxis, eu prattein*, that is, the accomplishment of the way in which Dasein exists. It is in Dasein itself, and not in the things that fall outside of it, that the *houneka* of *phronêsis* resides. The difference between *technê* and *phronêsis* is no less defined if one considers the *archê*, or principle, of each. On the one hand, the *archê* that guides *technê* in the production of a work also is by nature external to Dasein, because it is the *eidos*, the form or the model of the external product that is being produced. On the other hand, the *archê* of *phronêsis* is not exterior to Dasein, because it is nothing else than the mode in which Dasein uncovers itself.

As a mode of unconcealment, the function of *phronêsis* is, therefore, according to Heidegger, to render man "*transparent to himself*" (S, 36) and to wrest this transparency from anything capable of covering it. Because, Heidegger insists, "it is not at all a matter of course that Dasein be disclosed to itself in its proper Being" (S, 36).

What is remarkable in this Heideggerian interpretation of Aristotle, first, is the insistence with which it moves into the sphere of *Eigentlichkeit*, of the authentic Self. What is also remarkable is the insistence with which it channels the ethical into the ontological, in accordance with this stress on the self over the other. When Aristotle writes that the *phronimos* is the one who deliberates well with respect to things that contribute to a good life shared by all (*poia pros to eu zên olôs*) (1140 a 28), for example, Pericles, Heidegger does not hesitate to translate: "the one who deliberates in the right way . . . regarding 'what is conducive to the right mode of Being of Dasein as such and as a whole'" (S, 34). When Aristotle writes that *phronêsis* is an "aletheic disposition relative to action and concerning the things that are good for human beings (*ta anthrôpina agatha*)" (1140 b 5), Heidegger does not hesitate to translate as: "a disposition of human Dasein such that in it I have at my disposal my own transparency" (S, 37).

One will no doubt object that Heidegger's introduction in his interpretation of the Aristotelian *phronêsis* of the notion of *Gewissen*, commonly translated as "moral conscience," indicates all the same a sort of resistance to a radical ontologizing that defines his reading, in my view. I believe, on the contrary, that the introduction of *Gewissen* confirms this ontologizing.

We first note that it is after having pursued the comparison between *technê* and *phronêsis* that Heidegger suggests a proximity between the latter and *Gewissen*. It is remarkable, he says, that *technê* is susceptible to development and improvement as a result of its failures, while *phronêsis* obeys the law of all or nothing. It cannot be "more or less" complete. Either it is or it is not, so that one cannot say, unlike *technê*, "that it has an *aretê*"; one must rather say that it "is in itself ἀρετή" (S, 38). Furthermore, while that which *technê* has produced is able to fall into oblivion, because the know-how inherent in it can be lost, on the contrary, with respect to *phronêsis*, "there is no possibility of falling into forgetting," because it "is in each case new" (S, 39). It is at this point that Heidegger introduces *Gewissen*. He writes about 1140 b 28: "Certainly the explication which Aristotle gives here is very meager. But it is nevertheless clear from the context that we would not be going too far in our interpretation by saying that Aristotle has here come across the phenomenon of conscience" (S, 39). And he adds "φρόνησις is nothing other than conscience set into motion, making an action *transparent*. Conscience cannot be forgotten" (S, 39). In other words, the *Gewissen* that is evoked here is not understood as a sense of good in opposition to bad, of justice in relation to injustice, but as the power each time renewed that the singular Dasein has of being revealed to itself as a whole and authentically. It is indeed in these terms that *Sein und Zeit* will analyze (§54) *Gewissen* as the attestation in each Dasein in the *Augenblick* of resoluteness of an "authentic potentiality-of-being-a-Self." I do not think that there is on my part any retrospective projection here, because the analysis of *Gewissen* in *Sein und Zeit* expressly returns in a note[2] to theses enunciated by Heidegger in the celebrated lecture "The Concept of Time," pronounced at Marburg in 1924 shortly before the course on the *Sophist*.[3] *Gewissen* does not figure by name among the theses that enumerate some fundamental structures of Dasein, such as Being-in-the-world, Being-with-others, speech as self-interpretation of Dasein, *Jemeinigkeit* and *Jeweiligkeit*, the domination of "the They" in everydayness, care, and so on. But even if this lecture does not expressly name *Gewissen*, it is indeed what it announces when it insists on the *Gewissheit* with which each Dasein is able to apprehend at any moment "its most extreme possibility of Being," namely, Being-towards-death. Further, this lecture is evidently in the background of the course on the *Sophist*, since Heidegger does not fail to clarify that his interpretation of Aristotle is "founded on a phenomenology of Dasein." Such a phenomenology could not explicitly be exposed in the context of these lectures (§9c), but of course the auditors knew that Heidegger had just exposed its outlines in the lecture on "The Concept of Time." What of the *aretê* of *sophia*, and how does Heidegger situate it in relation to the *aretê* of *phronêsis*?

"What is most striking now," he says, "is that Aristotle designates σοφία as the ἀρετή of τέχνη (Nic. Eth. VI, 7, 1141 a 12). The highest mode of ἀληθεύειν, philosophical reflection, which according to Aristotle is the highest mode of human existence, is at the same time the ἀρετή of τέχνη. This must seem all the more remarkable in view of the fact that τέχνη has as its theme beings which can also be otherwise, whereas the theme of σοφία is in a preeminent sense what always is" (S, 39-40).

It is not possible for us to follow the details of the Heideggerian interpretation of *sophia* as an *aretê* of *technê* (1141 a 12). Since Aristotle also characterizes *sophia* as an *aretê* of *epistêmê*, Heidegger is committed to pinpoint the continuity between *technê* and *epistêmê*. More precisely, he wishes to show how *technê*, which is based in the everyday empirical world, is able to raise the everyday to the highest level of unconcealment; through this metamorphosis, *epistêmê* is prefigured and in turn prefigures *sophia* through an overcoming of the uncovering capacity of *technê*.

This genealogy of *sophia*, as the *aretê* not only of *epistêmê* but also of *technê*, allows one to show at the same time that *sophia*, in the Greek sense, that is, as the *bios theôrêtikos* of the philosopher, remains rooted in the everyday empirical world and in the *technê* that extends it. This is the case despite the fact that the four "essential moments" that constitute *sophia*—namely, openness to the whole, the capacity to unveil that which remains hidden to the *polloi*, the pursuit of foundations, and the resolve to see for no other purpose than seeing, beyond all care (§14)—are clearly not characteristics of the everyday world.

We will restrict ourselves to the fourth moment—sight for the sake of sight—because Heidegger focuses on it in order to interpret the specific *aretê* of *sophia*. Relying on the first book of Aristotle's *Metaphysics* (I, 2), Heidegger emphasizes that *sophia* owes the autonomy of the uncovering that it performs to its theme: that which is both the finality and principle of beings. When Aristotle says, in this regard, that *sophia* aims for the highest good, the *malista agathon*, Heidegger hastens to give him credit for having achieved "for the first time a fundamental ontological understanding of the ἀγαθόν" (S, 85). Credit, in order words, for having grasped the *agathon* as a name for Being. *Agathon*, he insists, is "nothing else than an ontological character of beings" (S, 84). For Aristotle, this character is proper to the being which always is and which as such is its own proper principle and proper finality. It is such a being that gives *sophia* its proper theme, and pure *theôria* is the only correct comportment toward such a being. The divine and therefore autonomous character of the pure contemplation that defines *sophia* (and which is its *aretê*) therefore lies in the fact that its object is the *aei*, that which always is (and as such is divine). It also lies in the fact that *sophia* itself consists, as contemplation, in being constantly present to the *aei*.

Under these conditions, *phronêsis*, whose object is human Dasein, could only accede to the rank of *sophia* if Dasein was from "all the entities in the world an entity in the most authentic sense," that is, an entity always identical and remaining so always. Such is obviously not the case. Instead of being always and forever, the "Being of man arises and passes away; it has its determinate time, its αἰών" (S, 94). The privilege that Aristotle attributes to *sophia* over *phronêsis* thus ultimately lies for Heidegger in the fact that *sophia* alone relates to those beings that "have for the Greeks ontological priority" (S, 94), the beings which for the Greeks are in the proper sense (i.e., always are).

However, Heidegger notes that the privilege that Aristotle attributes to *sophia* over *phronêsis*, therefore, the superior *aretê* of the first in relation to the second, does not only lie in the ontological preeminence of the object of *sophia* in relation to the object of *phronêsis*, it also lies in the specific structure of the *alêtheuein* exercised by *sophia*, as opposed to the one exercised by *phronêsis*. With regard to this structural comparison, Heidegger writes: "The appropriate question is whether the mode of being of the respective ἀληθεύειν is higher or lower. Even if neither of these two could accomplish anything, the question of the genuine character of their ἀρετή would still be necessary. For the ἀρετή is something like a τελείωσις; it is that which brings some being to itself in its most proper Being" (S, 116).

To Heidegger's mind, this *teleiôsis* resides in *eudaimonia*, an Aristotelian notion that one must understand, he insists, in a sense that is still "strictly ontological," because the notion constitutes the proper Being of human Dasein (S, 118).

The question is therefore of knowing with respect to *eudaimonia*, thus ontologically understood, in what sense *sophia* has priority over *phronêsis*. The answer is that the *theorein* in which *sophia* is established and settles, this pure vision that Aristotle calls *nous*, satisfies all of the structural components of *eudaimonia*: the most excellent disposition, the pure aptitude of grasping (*noein*), the uniform and uninterrupted perseverance, the pure presence to the unconcealed, the autarchy, the property of embracing the complete course of life instead of occasionally appearing. On all of these points, the vision that *phronêsis* attains at the end of its deliberation—a vision that is beyond discourse, *aneu logou*, and that consists in the moment of vision of a decision—is deficient because it remains weighed down by the action it serves, by the shifting circumstances it faces, therefore, by a renewed search, and finally by an absence of autarchy to the extent that "all possibilities of Being with regard to the πρᾶξις . . . are dependent . . . on Being with others" (S, 121).

Schematic as it is, this excursion suffices to show, we believe, that there is indeed in this Heideggerian interpretation of Aristotle a thought of *aretê*, and that this thought encompasses at the same time *phronêsis* and *sophia*.

As Heidegger himself says that his interpretation is "founded on an ontology of Dasein," that he will not explicitly expound on in his course, the question is whether or not and to what extent this phenomenology appropriates what it claims to be Aristotle's doctrine of *phronêsis* and *sophia*, as well as the preeminence of the *aretê* of the latter over the former. It seems to me beyond doubt that this phenomenology of Dasein, which is an ontology, assumes the Aristotelian doctrine of *phronêsis* and its preeminence over *technê*, insofar as *phronêsis* is understood as Dasein's view of his own-most being (i.e., as the *Gewissen* that makes transparent the most proper possibility of being a self). On the other hand, everyday *technê* only reveals beings whose mode of being is other than that of Dasein. That the phenomenological ontology of Dasein assumes what the 1924 course considers Aristotle's doctrine in the preeminence of *sophia* is less clear, since *sophia* in Aristotle refers to beings whose mode of being is that of constant presence and therefore of an infinite temporality that in no way pertains to Dasein. However, upon closer reflection, the insistence with which Heidegger stresses the excellence of the *bios theôrêtikos* and maintains throughout his course that philosophical existence is one of the most extreme possibilities of human Dasein (§1c) and the attention he lends to the structural components of the *theôria* to which philosophical existence devotes itself suffice to indicate that Aristotelian *sophia* also is able to be reappropriated by a phenomenological ontology of Dasein. Under which conditions? The 1924 course does not say, but it suggests an answer when Heidegger implies, on the one hand, that *aretê* is Dasein's own-most possibility of unconcealment and accomplishment of its Being, and that, on the other hand and paradoxically, the most eminent *aretê*, *sophia*, not only uncovers beings whose permanent mode of being in no way pertains to Dasein, but also through this very uncovering acquires an immortality that does not belong to Dasein's existence.

This suggests that the phenomenological ontology of Dasein undertakes to resolve this contradiction, although this is not explicitly stated in the course on the *Sophist*.

The solution will consist in assigning to *sophia* the task of not taking into view the eternal mode of being of Heaven primarily, but the mode of Dasein's Being. This solution is only touched upon in the 1924 course. It appears when Heidegger raises the question "as to the meaning of Being which provides the guiding line, on the basis of which Aristotle reaches the point that he can attribute to σοφία a priority over φρόνησις" (S, 113). To this question Heidegger responds further that this meaning of Being consists in "the eternal presence" of that which does not need to be produced, and he clarifies that the Greeks had "gathered this meaning of Being, Being as absolute presence, from the Being of the world" (S, 122), understood as nature against the background of the environing world of equipment; from then on they had the tendency to accommodate "the temporality of human Dasein to the eternity of the world" (S, 122). In other words, the last component of the Greek *eudaimonia* was the possibility of immortalizing oneself, of "not coming to an end" (S, 122).

The solution wrought by Heidegger for the contradiction that I just formulated and that, it goes without saying, was obvious to him, will consist for the phenomenological ontology of Dasein in accommodating the *bios theôrêtikos* to the most proper mode of Dasein's Being, that is, its finite and mortal temporality—a central theme, we insist, of the 1924 lecture on "The Concept of Time"—instead of aligning it as the Greeks had with the improper mode of Being of the infinite temporality of nature. It is not an exaggeration to say that this accommodation will consist at the same time in aligning *sophia* with *phronêsis*, if *phronêsis*, once ontologized and radicalized, is no longer understood simply as a discerning relative to human affairs and to the decisions called for in view of the good life within human plurality, but rather as *Gewissen* in the strict Heideggerian sense of the word, that is—as will be made clear in *Sein und Zeit*—as a preontological attestation in each Dasein of its own-most possibility of being a Self, its being-towards-death. It also is not an exaggeration to maintain, from the same perspective, that the way in which *Sein und Zeit* characterizes *Gewissen*, that is, a purely ontological version of *phronêsis* once it is taken out of its insertion in human affairs will be strongly dependent—hermeneutic circle *oblige*—on the features that Heidegger noted in 1924 in the structural components characteristic of the inherent *alêtheuein* of *sophia*, namely, the pure, silent vision, the solitary autarchy, and the reassembling of the complete course of life.

III

The Heideggerian reading of Aristotle is said to be founded on the phenomenology of Dasein, but it seems clear to me—hermeneutic circle *oblige*, once again—that this phenomenology, in its turn, is founded on a *certain reading* of Aristotle, a certain reappropriation—without doubt more meticulous and detailed than my brief excursion is able to indicate—of the *Nicomachean Ethics.* This alone will suffice to explain why many readers of *Sein und Zeit* cannot help at first to give an ethical connotation to the binary movement of the description undertaken by the book, that is, the contrast made between *Eigentlichkeit* and everydayness, between care and concern.

In any case, the result of this circularity is that the deliberate orientation of the phenomenology of Dasein toward Dasein's most proper mode of Being and its mortal temporality is accompanied by—except for the alignment with the eternality of nature—the assumption of what this phenomenology of Dasein recognizes in the Greek text: unconcealment as a wresting from distortion, forgetfulness, appearance; the overcoming of *technê* and *poiêsis* inherent in the everyday; Being-in-truth; language as an expression of being as such; the autarchy of the *bios theôrêtikos*; the orientation of the latter toward an ultimate vision, *aneu logou.*

There is no doubt that the first heirs of Heidegger were led to question the various aspects of this interpretation in a way similar to ours. I will mention two briefly in order to conclude.

With regard to Gadamer, who always proclaimed his debt to the first teachings of Heidegger—on the *Nicomachean Ethics* in particular— it is remarkable that although he claimed to be inspired by the master, his own hermeneutic used in reappropriating the Aristotelian notion of *phronêsis* in no way follows the speculative version that Heidegger had proposed. In treating the deliberative character of *phronêsis,* Heidegger praised Aristotle for having substituted the solitary *dianoetic* for the dialogic dear to Plato, thereby showing that language is only the provisional intermediary of a vision that in the end leaves language behind. However, the Gadamerian analysis of *phronêsis* emphasizes the irreducible dialogical character of language. Gadamer's emphasis restores to *phronêsis* its prudential, altruistic, and properly ethical connotation that Heidegger had labored to minimize. Believing he read Aristotle through the lens of Heidegger, in reality, he read Aristotle totally differently, as he himself recognized in a little preface that he wrote for the *Dilthey Jahrbuch* to the famous report of 1922. He had read and reread this text in his formative years but had lost it at the end of the war and then reread it with astonishment when it was rediscovered fifteen years ago. For proof of this confession: "What struck me today is that in the manuscript of Heidegger, it is not at all *Phronêsis* which comes to the fore but rather the *aretê* of the *bios theôrêtikos, sophia.*"[4] No less striking, he adds, is the insistence placed on *Durchsichtigmachen,* as if an irreducible opacity was not essential to the history and destiny of humans (IPA, 14). And, finally, this: "What on the whole strikes me the most is the preponderance of the ontological interest which goes as far as to include the general analysis of *phronêsis,* to such an extent that in this programmatic writing the concept of *êthos* is hardly mentioned at all."

With respect to Hannah Arendt, I will not dare to claim as I just did for Gadamer that she thought that she was working under Heidegger's authority. Heidegger's attitude in 1933, his Platonic-Nazi proclamations at the time of the Rectorate, spurred

Arendt to deliberately question the pertinence, the limits, and the blind spots of the teachings that she had received from him. This interrogation led her to perceive that the deconstruction practiced by Heidegger, far from being wholly faithful to the phenomena as he claimed, suffered from the start from a bias consisting of maintaining the priority of the *bios theôrêtikos* and pushing this priority to the point that this *bios* ends by becoming blind to many phenomena and by destroying "in it the plurality of the human condition."

To restrict myself to the thematic that I have developed, I believe that one can say, as Arendt herself suggests in a letter to Heidegger where she mentions that she will be sending her book on, *Vita Activa*, that this book has been conceived as a point-by-point rebuttal of the Heideggerian reappropriation of the Greeks, as was done in the Marburg era.

Whereas Heidegger focuses on the eminent *aretê* of the *bios theôrêtikos*, Arendt sheds light on the *aretê* that this *bios* tends to obliterate, that is, the *aretê* of the *bios politikos* celebrated by Thucydides, for whom Heidegger had nothing but contempt.

As he subscribed to the priority of the *bios theôrêtikos*, Heidegger deplored that for the Greeks this *bios*, because it is devoted to the contemplation of what is eternal in the movements of nature, overlooks the mortality of Dasein. On the contrary, Arendt does not fail to underline that for Plato's disciples the immortality of contemplation aimed first at disparaging a former claim—properly political—to immortality, understood by Pericles as a collective memory of deeds and words, a justified aim, she insists, in the sense that the most human form of the active life, *praxis* properly defined, is only taken up fully in the stories, the narratives, for which Heidegger shared Plato's disdain in the *Sophist*.

More generally, while Heidegger read the *Nicomachean Ethics* from the perspective of an ontology of solitary Dasein, Arendt emphasizes that which in this treatise continues to echo the *bios politikos*, and its condition of possibility—the sharing of acts and words within the human plurality.

While Heidegger, treating the two Aristotelian definitions of human Being—*zoon politikon* and *zôon logon echon*—does not hesitate to relegate the former to the fallen everyday *Mitsein* and to channel the latter toward an apophantic dimension, then toward a saturating but solitary *dianoetic* dimension, Arendt insists on the necessity of assigning the same rank to both and refuses to see in the former the inauthentic reign of the they and its idle talk and in the latter the precursor of an ultimate vision.

From this results a readjustment of the Heideggerian reappropriation of Aristotle. We find no trace in her work of the depreciation of the everyday and the public sphere. There is a refusal in her work to confuse, under the same rubric of *Öffentlichkeit*, the social and the political. Whereas Heidegger assigns to *poêisis* the status of an immersion within the world and an evasion of proper existence, Arendt emphasizes that the production of works makes possible the permanence of a properly human dwelling beyond the consuming cycle of *zôê* and is therefore the condition *sine qua non* of the temporal unfolding of the existence of someone who is irreplaceable.

As for *praxis*, Heidegger poses that the Aristotelian *houneka* ultimately means that Dasein is deliberately for the sake of itself, and that the *phronêsis* that clarifies praxis in the end signifies, within Dasein [*for intérieur*], the confrontation of its own being toward death beyond all communication. On the contrary, Arendt poses that the *per quam* condition of *praxis* is plurality, that the question "Who?" does not emanate from the self turned in on itself but is imposed on each by others in a common world of appearances. She also poses that *phronêsis*—indistinguishable from an interaction and an unsurpassable interlocution—far from leading to the individual's transparent possession of his or her own proper identity, consists for him or her in prudently realizing at each step the profound ambiguity of his or her action and his or her speech, which affect others as much as they are affected by them in such a way that the individual is in no way master of his or her identity.

At the time when Heidegger's ambition was to radicalize phenomenology, he emphasized that this involved three steps: reduction, construction, and deconstruction. To us who are the heirs of his heirs—I have only cited the two closest—one would of course have to cite others not as close—Levinas, Merleau-Ponty—the question that continues to call upon us is, in my opinion, that of knowing if these three steps—return to the phenomena, articulation of these in appropriate concepts, dismantling of inherited schemes, theses, principles whose deeply buried phenomenal sources may be other than claimed—then, as he understood them, correspond to the demand that justifies them when they assume that the *bios theôrêtikos* enjoys the intangible privilege of an ultimate vision.

Notes

This chapter was translated by Jennifer Hansen.

1. Martin Heidegger, "Phenomenological Interpretations with Respect to Aristotle: Indication of the Hermeneutical Situation," *Man and World*, translated by Michael Baur (1992), pp. 25 (3-4), 355-93. Hereafter cited as PIA, followed by the page number.

2. SZ, 268/BTa, 312.

3. Martin Heidegger, *The Concept of Time*, translated by Will McNeill (Malden, Mass.: Blackwell, 1992).

4. *Interprétations Phénoménologiques d'Aristote* (Toulouse: TER, 1992) p. 12. Hereafter cited as IPA.

Freedom, Finitude, and the Practical Self
The Other Side of Heidegger's Appropriation of Kant

Frank Schalow

From 1926 to 1929, Heidegger turned to Kant's *Critique of Pure Reason* in order to provide a historical context to amplify the key motifs of his *magnum opus*, *Being and Time*, including temporality, finitude, and transcendence.[1] Soon thereafter, in a lecture course from 1930 entitled *Vom Wesen der menschlichen Freiheit*,[2] he shifted his attention to the task of appropriating Kant's moral philosophy as outlined in his *Critique of Practical Reason*. Unlike Kant's first *Critique*, however, the second *Critique* lacks a temporal orientation. Initially the atemporal focus of Kant's second *Critique* would seem to be more of a drawback than a benefit to Heidegger's attempt to reask the question of being. Yet the rational remnants of Kantian metaphysics also provide a further occasion for Heidegger to wield the sword of his quest to deconstruct the philosophical tradition. By showing that the key elements of Kant's ethics (e.g., freedom) can be recast in terms of human finitude, and conversely, that the explication of praxis is crucial for mapping the topography of the question of being, Heidegger charts a new path for hermeneutics. Given this observation, we arrive at the controversial thesis that Heidegger further radicalizes his hermeneutical project by retrieving the concrete dimension of human praxis.

Though Heidegger does not embrace the theory-praxis distinction, it becomes important insofar as the elevation of the former over the latter constitutes a permutation of the metaphysics of presence. That is, the presumption of favoring knowledge over action leads to a parallel substantialization of the self in terms of the Cartesian *cogito*, of pure reflective awareness. By inverting this priority and allowing what has been subordinated under the heading of "praxis" to come to the foreground, Heidegger can elicit the constellations of issues—freedom, transcendence, historicality—which shape the landscape of the question of being. In particular, a treatment of freedom holds the promise of returning philosophy to its origin in Dasein's worldly comportment.

In echoing Kant, who says that philosophy is primarily "practical" in nature,[3] and Schelling, who maintains that freedom is the "beginning and end" of philosophy,[4] Heidegger remarks: "*The question concerning the essence of human freedom is the most basic question of philosophy in which even the question of being is rooted*" (GA 31, 300). Given that the Cartesian *cogito* is essentially "worldless," Heidegger's 1930 lectures on freedom plot the coordinates by which to locate the "practical self" along the arc of finite transcendence. And insofar as the appropriation of Kant's problematic of temporality constitutes the first stage in "destroying" the history of ontology,[5] his exposition of the practical self contributes to the dismantlement of the Cartesian *cogito*, the projected second stage of the phenomenological destruction.[6] Thus it is not surprising that the third stage of the destruction would target Aristotle's thought, to whom Heidegger turned early on in order to glean a sense of the "ethos" as the source of Dasein's situated dwelling.[7]

I

With few exceptions, Heidegger concentrates his dialogue with Kant on appropriating the motifs of temporality and finitude as outlined in the first *Critique*. In a lecture course from 1928 entitled *Phänomenologische Interpretation von Kants Kritik der reinen Vernunft*, which bears the name of Kant's major work, and in its sequel in 1929, *Kant and the Problem of Metaphysics*, Heidegger argues that Kant was on the threshold of recognizing that a prior orientation to temporality governs any attempt to understand being. In his earlier lecture course *Logik* (1926), Heidegger also appeals to Kant's examination of our knowing capacity, to the schematism of categories and their root in the transcendental imagination, in order to address the possibility of understanding of being.[8] Yet an almost deafening silence emanates from these works about the import of practical reason and its key elements, including freedom and responsibility.

While also accenting the Kantian problematic of temporality in the *Basic Problems of Phenomenology*, Heidegger briefly examines Kant's portrait of moral respect. In a section devoted to addressing Kant's rendition of the self in its practical as well as its theoretical dimension, Heidegger remarks: "Respect reveals the dignity before which and for which the self knows itself to be responsible. Only in responsibility does the self first reveal itself—the self not in a general sense as knowledge of an ego in general but as in each case mine, the ego as in each case the individual factical ego" (GA 24, 193-94;BP, 137). In the process, Heidegger acknowledges that "Kant's interpretation of the phenomenon of respect is probably the most brilliant phenomenological analysis of the phenomenon of morality that we have from him" (GA 24, 188-89;BP, 133). This remark in turn prefaces Heidegger's succinct attempt in the Kant book (covering only four pages) to show that human finitude shapes our moral self-consciousness,[9] and hence that both theoretical and practical reason have their origin in the time-forming power of the transcendental imagination.

Given Heidegger's overarching strategy to destroy the philosophical tradition, the paucity of treatment of Kant's moral philosophy in the major works that comprise Heidegger's dialogue with his predecessor throughout the 1920s may not be surprising. For Kant's emphasis on the atemporal origin of practical freedom would seem to exclude the motif of human finitude, which Heidegger identifies as the crux of his critical appropriation of Kant's transcendental philosophy. While moral respect exhibits an experiential side that is open to phenomenological description, Kant relegates freedom as the "presupposition" of morality to a higher plane apparently divorced from any such treatment (GA 3, 168-70;KPM, 118-19). And just as this presupposition appears inaccessible on phenomenological grounds, so the importance that an examination of freedom would have for bringing Kant's thought as a whole within the scope of Heidegger's "destructive" task can hardly be denied. The attempt to chart the crossover between the issues of finitude, facticity, and temporality and the apparently incongruent corollaries of moral governance, freedom, and praxis would contribute to Heidegger's effort to map the topography of the question of being in greater detail. Hence, we must welcome Heidegger's effort in 1930 to extend his dialogue with Kant in order to include the basic thrust of his moral philosophy. Not only do these 1930 lectures rectify an omission in Heidegger's treatment of Kant's thought, but they also exemplify the manner of debate between the two as a mode of *Auseinandersetzung* or "setting apart" and "placing in opposition" thinkers joined in their common concern for the matter itself [*die Sache des Denkens*].

Two reasons stand out as to why Heidegger brings the topic of freedom into the foreground in his 1930 lectures on Kant. First, in 1929, Heidegger had already begun to address freedom as the pivot of all philosophical inquiry. As became evident in his essay "On the Essence of Truth" (1930), he linked the phenomenal dimension of unconcealment (truth) with Dasein's capacity to let be (freedom) (GA 9, 187-91;P, 143-47). Second, Heidegger's radical appropriation of transcendental philosophy in the Kant book was as controversial as it was successful. This controversy came to a head in Ernst Cassirer's review of the Kant book in 1930 and in his celebrated conversation with Heidegger at Davos in 1929. As Cassirer remarks in the "Davos Disputation," "The extraordinary significance of the schematism cannot be overestimated. The greatest misunderstandings in the interpretation of Kant creep in at this point. In the ethical [*Ethischen*], however, he forbids the schematism. There he says: our concept of freedom, etc. are insights (not bits of knowledge) which no longer permit schematizing" (GA 3, 267;KPM, 195). In prefiguring his claim from the 1930 lecture course on Kant, that freedom holds the key to philosophy, Heidegger defends his more radical portrayal of human praxis against Cassirer's interpretation: "I spoke of a freeing in the sense that the freeing of the inner transcendence of Dasein is the fundamental character of philosophizing itself. The authentic sense of this freeing. . . . is to be found in becoming free for the finitude of Dasein" (GA 3, 289;KPM, 203).

For Heidegger, freedom and finitude are essentially interdependent, even though Kant suggests otherwise in relegating practical freedom to the infinite realm of things in themselves. But since Kant's analysis of freedom revolves around ethical action, and his practical philosophy provides the entryway for Heidegger's discussion of freedom, the latter must reopen the question of ethics as well. Insofar as the possibility of ethics hinges on freedom, and freedom unfolds as a finite dimension of human existence, ethical inquiry also must proceed from a finite orientation. As Heidegger remarks to Cassirer:

> This concept of the [Categorical] Imperative as such shows the inner relation to the finite creature. . . . This inner relation, which lies within the Imperative itself, and the finitude of ethics, emerges from a passage in which Kant speaks of reason as self-supporting, i.e, of a reason which stands purely on its own and cannot escape into something eternal or absolute, but which also cannot escape into the world of things. [The] essence of practical reason . . . [lies in] being open to others. (GA 3, 279–81;KPM, 196–97)

As becomes evident in his disputation with Cassirer, Heidegger addresses the issue of freedom according to a double gesture that retrieves the crux of Kant's analysis while deconstructing its metaphysical underpinnings. In light of a strategy of "repetition" practiced in *Being and Time*, Heidegger upholds Kant's claim that ethics depends on a prior insight into the nature of freedom. And yet at the same time Heidegger maintains that it is necessary to address not only how ethics depends upon prior metaphysical assumptions concerning freedom, but that it is equally important to question the roots of that metaphysics. This doubling of the question would offset two levels of forgetting that occlude Kant's insights into the possibility of ethics: (1) the privileging of one dimension of time in order to understand being, namely, the present, so that its idealized form or eternity marks the origin of freedom (i.e, an unconditioned will) and (2) the truncation of time as a series of nows in contrast to eternity, in such a way that the realm delimited by the former or nature stands in stark opposition to the domain circumscribed by the latter or freedom.

Rather than to make the concern for freedom an afterthought of the metaphysics of presence, as Kant does, Heidegger addresses freedom as housing a set of issues that brings into question the temporal determination of being. Freedom must now be defined in its alliance with finitude rather than in opposition to it, in kinship with the ecstatic trajectory of temporality (transcendence) versus the stasis of time as eternity. Thus Heidegger dismantles the remnants of Kant's archaic cosmology; this cosmology pits the eternal realm of freedom against the transient realm of nature, while assuming a schism between the former as the haven of values and the latter as the haven of fact. Freedom then reemerges as a power or force in which we participate, insofar as we belong to the dynamic process whereby nature embodies the tension of unconcealment-concealment. Correlatively, Heidegger dismantles the elements of Kant's obsolete rational psychology; rational psychology construes the self as a privileged agent separated from the flux of experience and defines its "power" indeterminately as the abeyance of any external influence by natural events, as an uncaused cause or as pure spontaneity. Instead, the self is a participant in the larger process of unconcealment. Hence, the agency proper to the self or freedom reemerges as a power with which Dasein is endowed, rather than a capability it possesses.

In his 1930 lectures on Kant, Heidegger summarizes his destructive retrieval of the concept of freedom in this way. "Freedom ceases to be a property of human being," and instead "man becomes a possibility of freedom" (GA 31, 134). Put in other terms, Dasein becomes the "manager" of freedom, the vehicle for the distribution of its power, rather than its possessor (GA 31, 134-35). This radical change in the proprietorship of freedom becomes fundamental for Heidegger. The solitary self ceases to be the sole benefactor/possessor of freedom, but Dasein receives freedom as belonging to a relationship (i.e., through its partnership with being). Because freedom arises in conjunction with being, the discharge of the power to be free occurs through the nexus of relationships, including Dasein's being with others, which comprises its worldly existence. Dasein receives the power of freedom through its readiness to reciprocate for this gift of being—the openness I already am—through the self's willingness to safeguard freedom for the benefit of others.

Through his destructive retrieval of Kant's practical philosophy, Heidegger undertakes a displacement of the subject as the agency of moral choice. But we should not then conclude, as others have, that he leaves no room for moral decision making and the practical self embodying this freedom. On the contrary, Heidegger reopens the question of how the self can engage in praxis, can exercise choice, and can display responsibility. And this questioning, which "overturns" ontology in favor of a new set of issues that stems from Dasein's situatedness among beings, accompanies Heidegger's attempt to address the possibility of ethics. As he remarks in his 1928 lectures on the foundations of logic:

> As a result, we need a special problematic which has for its proper theme beings as a whole [*das Seiende im Ganzen*]. This new investigation resides in the essence of ontology itself and is the result of its overturning [*Umschlag*]. . . . I designate this set of questions *metontology*. And here also, in the domain of metontological-existentiell questioning, is the domain of the metaphysics of existence (here the question of an ethics may properly be raised for the first time). (GA 26, 199;MFL, 157)

In the subsequent sections of this chapter, let us then consider the impact that Heidegger's novel treatment of freedom has on (1) redefining the practical self and (2) spelling out the nature of responsibility that lies at the heart of the Kantian ethics.

In this way, we will reenact the "repetition" that Heidegger undertakes in radicalizing Kant's ethics, the decentering of an ethics of normative guidelines in favor of its origin in the openness of finite freedom.

II

We have spoken of repetition to describe the strategy by which Heidegger appropriates Kant's philosophy in terms of new possibilities of thinking, yet that strategy has its factical root in the historical withdrawing, preserving, and granting of being's truth to human beings and hence in the way that their historicality allows for the reemergence of the past in the future in order to make way for the arrival of the present. Insofar as Heidegger undertakes an *Auseinandersetzung* with Kant on the issue of freedom, and the transmission of insight on this topic occurs historically, Heidegger's thinking must already be infused with the freedom he brings into question. The self-referential character of Heideggerian discourse has an important repercussion, namely, that the direction of his inquiry into freedom exhibits the chief element(s) constitutive of it, the component of facticity, the dimension of "alreadiness" whereby human beings acquire the power to be free by receiving it and reap its benefits by safeguarding it. Put in terms that are most conversant with Kant's thinking, the experience of freedom is always finite, that is, the allocation of limits accompanies the dispensation of that "power," an empowerment that springs from our relation to being.

We might employ the term *economy* to describe the dynamics involved in the distribution of the power of freedom. Heidegger brings this economy into question in order to address in a positive way that dimension of freedom which for Kant remains indeterminate due to his metaphysics of presence, namely, the manner of freedom's transmission. For Kant, freedom can have the privileged character of a spontaneous cause only when relegated to an eternal domain divorced from the nexus of cause/effect relations of nature. But the enigma then arises how the individual agent can embody this pristine freedom and yet become the instigator of actions bearing absolute moral worth in a world preoccupied with relative or "instrumental" ends. Indeed, the specter of paradox overhangs Kant's attempt to describe the constitution of the moral agent or the nature of the practical self. How can there be a supersensuous/sensuous practical reason, an unconditioned/finite freedom?

On the one hand, this paradox appears alien to Heidegger, because he does not first subscribe to a dichotomy between freedom and nature. On the other hand, its resolution becomes instructive, because Kant must indirectly invoke the vestige of human facticity in order to explain how we can identify the "reality" of freedom. Since it remains unknowable as an idea of reason, freedom becomes evident only when it is attested to by an action having moral worth. The action indicates an agent's conformity to an unconditioned ethical standard (i.e, the moral law), and only because a being with commensurate freedom can absolutely comply to such a standard, an action having moral worth testifies to this freedom. As Heidegger summarizes the matter: "The factuality [*Tätsachlickheit*], which corresponds to the reality of freedom, is praxis" (GA 31, 271). Though Kant speaks of it as an idea, freedom nevertheless can be experienced only through its enactment in concrete praxis. In other words, freedom is to be found in its exemplification in the (maxim of) a given action. And the way in which the example testifies to (the idea) of freedom—so that its instantiation is evidence of its reality—means that human freedom resides in facticity, thus Heidegger alludes to the "facticity of freedom" [*Faktizität der Freiheit*] (GA 31, 273). Praxis then defines the mode of concretion in which finite beings encounter the possibility of freedom.

If freedom does not entail the stasis of eternity but instead springs from the influx of temporality, as Heidegger contends, then how can the power of freedom preserve itself in its finitude? If human freedom is dynamic rather than static, then must it not exhibit a kind of kinesis or motion by which the self becomes "engaged" in whatever action it does? Such motion cannot be, as it was for Kant, a linear process which, because it includes a determinate beginning and end, must eventually dissipate. On the contrary, in order to sustain an agent who upholds "absolute ends," the dictates of the moral law, such freedom must display a completely different dynamism. And since Heidegger does not accept an atemporal locus of freedom, its dynamism must exhibit the interplay of the temporal ecstases in such a way that any direction forward is simultaneously a returning to (oneself). The power that pervades human choice unfolds its possibilities only insofar as the act of choosing proceeds from Dasein's openness, from the open expanse of being. In making choices Dasein rediscovers who it already is, in such a way that its own-most possibilities are precisely those that hold forth a path of self-return. The temporalizing, elliptical movement of Dasein's return to itself channels the power of freedom, which is steeped in finitude and facticity. In a contrary way to the dissipation of linear motion, this movement of "self-choosing," or "resolve," recovers the abundance of its origin, the hallmark of "repetition."

But what does the ecstatic movement of repetition, which Heidegger first describes in *Being and Time* as resoluteness, have to do with morality in Kant's sense? Not only does Heidegger refrain from endorsing any ethic—Kantian or otherwise—he also suggests that his discussion of authenticity is primarily an ontological account without ethical import. And yet through his account, Heidegger outlines the historical situation of human existence, which defines the ethos from which any awareness of ethical concerns arises. Given that the Kantian sense of freedom can only be "formally indicated" in concrete praxis, and the self who engages in praxis finds himself or herself oriented by the fabric of beliefs, customs, and mandates comprising an ethos, moral self-consciousness (respect for the law and self-respect) exhibits facets of authentic existence. The self-choosing of resolve is endemic to the formal determination of freedom by which a moral agent applies the law to itself. Kant calls the self-legislation of the moral law "autonomy."[10]

When recast in factical terms, the mode of freedom that Kant identifies can most simply be described as the renewal of a commitment. That is, morality is a way of keeping before oneself those very concerns that define the essence of the person and enable the individual to lend himself or herself to those demands whose fulfillment best exemplifies his or her nature. As Heidegger states in the Kant book, "The submitting, self-projecting onto the entire basis possibility of what authentically exists, which the law gives, is the essence of the acting Being-itself, i.e., of practical reason" (GA 3, 159;KPM, 111). In his 1930 lectures on Kant, Heidegger underscores this point by maintaining that responsibility defines the essential nature of the self, "the basic modality of being that determines all human comportment" (GA 31, 262).[11] While Kant describes freedom in abstract terms as the spontaneity of self-determination, it turns out, quite paradoxically, that the fulfillment of obligations is a way in which the practical self "lets itself be" defined by those concerns most indicative of its constitution as care [Sorge]. And this way of abiding in a commitment by letting be is the essence of self-respect. Thus moral responsiveness lies at the heart of the self-legislation of the law or "autonomy." Insofar as this responsiveness entails a responsibility for one's existence, and this responsibility defines the facticity of freedom, the legislation of the moral law in Kant's sense equals self-responsibility. Thus in one of the most pivotal passages from his 1930 lectures on Kant, Heidegger states: "Practical Freedom as autonomy is self-responsibility [Selbstverantwortlichkeit], the personhood of the person, the authentic essence, the humanity of the human being" (GA 31, 296).

By shifting from a sense of freedom as the spontaneous determination of the will to the openness of letting be, Heidegger displaces the locus of the moral agent from subjectivity to the open expanse of being. In Being and Time, he prefigures this development by describing conscience as a "call" that elicits from the individual a readiness for commitment, a summons to take action in compliance with the demands of the situation. A receptivity to be governed unfolds insofar as the self reciprocates for its admission into the open expanse of being. Given this new locus for human praxis, the initiative of choice as spontaneity hinges on an accompanying receptivity, whose inducement of openness relocates practical freedom in Dasein's finitude.

In the Kant book, Heidegger first argues that a receptive spontaneity and a spontaneous receptivity mark a more radical origin for both theoretical and practical reason in the transcendental imagination (temporality). In his 1930 lectures on Kant, Heidegger shows that the Kantian precept of moral autonomy exhibits the same binary dimension of human finitude. We can no longer define human freedom through the clash between activity and passivity. Rather, freedom arises through another mode of configuration—that of "middle-voice"—which balances activity and passivity, spontaneity and receptivity, and thereby charts a new landscape for ethical action.

On the one hand, Heidegger displaces the subjectivity of the moral agent; on the other hand, he reiterates the importance of the self as undertaking moral praxis, as exercising responsibility. Does Heidegger then retain a vestige of the metaphysics of subjectivity that would inhibit his attempt to reopen the question of ethics? Does he inadvertently swing the pendulum in the direction of the self's response to its own conscience in a way that turns a concern for the other's welfare, of the other as other, into something of an afterthought, as Levinas suggests?[12] Does Heidegger's repetition of Kant's ethics—with its emphasis on a "metaphysics of morals"—implicitly reaffirm the priority of ontology over ethics in a way that Levinas rebukes? If we are to appreciate fully Heidegger's appropriation of Kant's practical philosophy, we must be able to address these questions.

III

Ethics primarily considers the welfare of the other (person), as emphasized by Levinas, who perhaps was inspired by a desire to resolve the dispute between Heidegger and Cassirer that he witnessed while attending the Davos seminar.[13] While Levinas was not the first thinker to arrive at this insight, his criticism of Heidegger for his apparent omission of this concern most poignantly defends the interests of the other.[14] Yet the obvious is not only an occasion for forgetfulness, it also is the sheltering of the truth in which remembrance can occur. Because of the advantage of historical hindsight, we can accentuate Heidegger's apparently incidental allusion to practical philosophy and thereby prepare for such remembrance. If only in a discrete way, the "other" appears as the indelible "face" of finite freedom. For the other recalls the fact that freedom resides in its nonpresence. That is, freedom is a "power" that the self acquires only by first preparing to distribute its benefit to the other. And this interplay of deferral/acquisition means that the "owned" dimension of freedom takes a "relational" rather than a "solitary" form. As a power that can only be transmitted through an appropriative act, freedom catapults Dasein beyond itself through its affiliation with the other. The economy of freedom allows for a plurality of participants within the open expanse of being, in such a way that "I" can experience myself as free only through a "reciprocal rejoinder" [*Erwiderung*] linking me with the other.[15] By heeding the other's welfare, for example, as a unique voice in a dialogue, the self is first "cleared" in its freedom to let the other be in the pursuit of his or her own possibilities.

In *Being and Time*, Heidegger describes this way of responding to the welfare of the other, which acknowledges the singularity of his or her own way of being-free, authentic or emancipatory solicitude. Through solicitude, Dasein encourages the other to participate in the freedom that is essential to fostering the "owned" dimension of individuality. This owned dimension, however, is not a property of the self but, on the contrary, it pervades the nexus of relationships by which the individual experiences his or her companionship with the other, the fabric of community. Insofar as the owned dimension of freedom always unfolds through an ever-widening circle of participants, Dasein comes to itself in the process of honoring its obligation to others. In this way, Heidegger brings to fruition his insight drawn early on from Kant's idea of a "kingdom of ends" and Schleiermacher's notion of "free sociality" that life within a community—friendship, family, church, and state—provides the setting for the self to enact its freedom.[16]

Through this emancipatory solicitude, Dasein champions the welfare of others in such a way that its interests, its administration of care, can extend to all corners of the world. Within an Enlightenment context, Kant had first characterized the autonomous will as a kind of "hero" who rises above petty desires in order to act in behalf of all human beings, that is, become a "citizen of the world" [Weltbürgers].[17] In his 1930 lectures on Kant, Heidegger develops this motif in the guise of the essentially worldly human being [Weltwesen Mensch] (GA 31, 264). The Weltwesen Mensch embodies the emancipatory solicitude that invites each individual to participate in freedom and share its benefits with others. Through his emphasis on the essentially worldly human being, Heidegger suggests that the commitment of resolute self-choosing and the responsiveness of conscience help shape the êthos of Dasein's interaction with others. While Heidegger maintains that the call of conscience provides the first clue to Dasein's participation in the disclosive power of language, scholars often overlook the dialogic power of this silent voice.[18] For in saying "nothing,"[19] the call of conscience illustrates that hearing precedes saying, and hence it is only by first "listening" that human beings acquire the power to speak (GA 12, 28–30;PLT, 209). Insofar as Dasein is both thrown into language and resides there, hearing distinguishes the primary way in which the self can respond to the concerns of the other.

To appreciate Heidegger's understanding of the practical self, we must spell out an etymology around which a cluster of meanings gravitates: responsibility as responding, responding as answering, answering as hearing. Through conscience Dasein not only heeds its appeal to be itself but, because this plea is always the voice [Stimme] of care, each of us also experiences the attunement [Stimmung] that echoes the claim [Anspruch] of the other. While Levinas criticizes Heidegger for neglecting the "face" of the other, the latter's reply to this omission lies in maintaining the priority of the other's voice. In this regard, the voice of alterity reverberates in Dasein's responsibility as a mode of responsiveness. The concluding passage from On the Essence of Ground (1928) illustrates this intimate link between the aural dimension of language and the disposition to act in behalf of the other:

> And so the human being, existing as a transcendence that exceeds in the direction of possibilities, is a creature of distance. Only through originary distances that he forms for himself in his transcendence with respect to all beings does a true nearness to things being to arises in him. And only being able to listen into the distance awakens Dasein as a self to the response of the other Dasein in whose company [Mitsein] it can surrender its I-ness so as to attain itself as an authentic self. (GA 9, 174;P, 13)

Heidegger's insight from his 1928 essay provides the impetus for his retrieval of Kant's practical philosophy in 1930. Very seldom do we find in Heidegger's thought such an explicit reference to the ethical problematic as we do in his 1930 lectures on human freedom. And yet the paucity of remarks on human praxis, as exemplified in the Kant book, may not so much indicate neglect or a tendency to subordinate ethics to ontology; on the contrary, his reluctance to formulate directly an ethic instead bears witness to a deeper inquiry that would reintroduce the practical self as a focal point in executing his destructive retrieval of the tradition. In this regard, we cannot ignore the element of facticity in his thinking, namely, that the concern for ethics withdraws with the question of being, so that the incubation of the latter prefigures the rediscovery of the latter. Thus the displacement of the metaphysical subject and the recovery of the practical self are two sides of a movement that subverts the metaphysical presumption of presence.

The destructive retrieval of the practical self contributes to the *Auseinandersetzung*, which Heidegger undertakes with his predecessors, from Kant to Kierkegaard, from Aristotle to Nietzsche.[20] The more we participate in this *Auseinandersetzung*, the more we can benefit from Heidegger's insights into the economy of freedom and its relevance for reshaping the landscape of ethical inquiry.[21] In the end, Heidegger's retrieval of the practical self provides another avenue to overcome the metaphysics of presence and to evoke a more radical disclosure of being from the ruptures and dislocations of human praxis.

Notes

1. Martin Heidegger, *Logik: Die Frage nach der Wahrheit*, pp. 354ff. Also see *Phenomenological Interpretation of Kant's Critique of Pure Reason, Kant and the Problem of Metaphysics*.

2. GA 31, 262ff.

3. Immanuel Kant, *Critique of Practical Reason*, translated by Lewis White Beck (Indianapolis: Bobbs-Merrill, 1957), p. 126. Kant states: "Nor could we reverse the order and expect practical reason to submit to speculative reason, because every interest is ultimately practical, even that of speculative reason being only conditional and reaching perfection only in practical use."

4. F. W. J. Schelling, *The Unconditional in Human Knowledge*, translated by Fritz Marti (Lewisburg, Penn.: Bucknell University Press, 1980), p. 82.

5. GA 2, 63;BTb, 35.

6. See Frank Schalow, "The Topography of Heidegger's Concept of Conscience," in *Heidegger*, edited by John D. Caputo, *American Catholic Philosophical Quarterly*, vol. LXIX/2 (spring 1995): 256.

7. Franco Volpi, "Being and Time: A 'Translation' of Nichomachean Ethics," translated by John Protevi in *Reading Heidegger from the Start: Essays in his Earliest Thought*, edited by Theodore Kisiel and John van Buren (Albany: State University of New York Press, 1994), pp. 195–211.

8. See Frank Schalow, *The Renewal of the Heidegger-Kant Dialogue: Action, Thought, Responsibility* (Albany: State University of New York Press, 1992), pp. 7–25. Also see Reiner Schürmann, *Heidegger on Being and Acting*, translated by Christine-Marie Gros (Bloomington: Indiana University Press, 1987), p. 7. See Schürmann's discussion of the "practical a priori."

9. GA 3, 155-60;KPM, 109–12. See Kant, *Critique of Practical Reason*, p. 90.

10. Immanuel Kant, *Foundations of the Metaphysics of Morals*, translated by Lewis White Beck (Indianapolis: Bobbs-Merrill, 1959), p. 59.

11. I am grateful to Professor François Raffoul for providing me with this reference.

12. Emmanuel Levinas, *Collected Philosophical Papers*, translated by Alphonso Lingis (The Hague: Martinus Nijhoff, 1987), pp. 54–56.

13. I am grateful to Professor Wayne Froman for pointing this out to me.

14. In a critical way, Levinas remarks: "Heideggerian philosophy precisely marks the apogee of thought in which the finite does not refer to the infinite (prolonging certain tendencies of Kantian philosophy: the separation between the understanding and diverse themes of transcendental dialectics), in which every deficiency is but weakness and every fault committed against oneself—the outcome of a long tradition of pride, heroism, domination, and cruelty" (*Collected Philosophical Papers*, p. 53).

15. Stephen Watson, *Tradition(s)* (Bloomington: Indiana University Press, 1997), p. 3.

16. See John van Buren, *The Young Heidegger: Rumor of the Hidden King* (Bloomington: Indiana University Press), p. 346.

17. Martin Heidegger, *Vom Wesen des Grundes*, in GA 9, 153;P 119). See also GA 3, 206;KPM, 145. And see Kant, *Critique of Practical Reason*, p. 90. As Kant remarks: "This idea of personality awakens respect; it places before our eyes the sublimity of our own nature (in its [higher] vocation."

18. For a compelling critique of Heidegger on this point, see John McCumber, "Authenticity and Interaction: The Account of Communication in *Being and Time*," in *The Thought of Martin Heidegger*, edited by Michael E. Zimmerman, *Tulane Studies in Philosophy* 33 (1984): 45-51.

19. GA 2, 363;BTb, 252.

20. GA 28, 6, 231;GA 3, 249;KPM, 175. Also see Frank Schalow, *Language and Deed: Rediscovering Politics through Heidegger's Encounter with German Idealism*, (Amsterdam & Atlanta: Editions Rodopi, 1998), pp. xvii, 39.

21. Charles E. Scott, *The Question of Ethics* (Bloomington: Indiana University Press, 1990), pp. 7-15.

4

Hier ist kein warum
Heidegger and Kant's Practical Philosophy

JACOB ROGOZINSKI

The rose is without why: it blooms because it blooms.

—Angelus Silesius

And it was in fact so. Driven by thirst, I eyed a fine icicle outside the window, within hand's reach. I opened the window and broke off the icicle but at once a large heavy guard prowling outside brutally snatched it away from me. "*Warum?*" I asked him in my poor German. "*Hier ist kein warum*" ("Here there is no why"), he replied, pushing me inside with a shove.

—Primo Levi, *If This Is a Man*

What is the relationship between Heidegger's and Kant's practical philosophy? Are we to take his meditation on Kant's work as one of the main "sources" of his thought? By engaging Kant, and specifically his practical philosophy, is it not the case that Heidegger exposes his own thought to danger? What would be the consequences of this exposure for a radical reflection on praxis and ethics? In order to attempt to answer these questions, I will begin with the well-known 1943 text "On the Essence of Truth."

"Man wanders." He "always finds himself already wandering," forgetful of the truth of being, and this straying plunges him into distress. Such is also the position of philosophy when, from the depths of this wandering, it opens itself to the call of the question of Being. Oscillating between the welcome of the enigma and the threat of wandering, torn between its desire to go beyond beings and its refusal to submit itself to an injunction from Outside, it suffers the distress of thought. "Kant had already anticipated" this distress, writes Heidegger, but he was not able to think it, much less to indicate a way out: "Kant, whose work introduces the final turning of Western metaphysics, envisions a domain which to be sure he could understand only on the basis of his fundamental metaphysical position, founded on subjectivity, and

43

which he had to understand as the keeping of its laws (. . .) However, whether philosophy as 'keeper of its laws' fulfills its primordially decisive essence, or whether it is not itself first of all kept and appointed to its task as keeper by the truth of that to which its laws pertain—this depends on the primordiality with which the original essence of truth becomes essential for thoughtful questioning."[1]

Reading this 1943 text, the situation seems clear: in Heidegger's eyes, or at least in those of a certain Heidegger, Kant's adherence to the metaphysics of subjectivity is not in any doubt. The Kantian demand that thought be the "guardian of its laws" is interpreted here, at the cost of some distortions, as the guardianship by subjectivity of its "own laws," as autonomy. Establishing the "supremacy of the Law" would then consist in instituting the domination of the Subject prescribing its own Law to itself. Kantian philosophy could then be challenged in the name of a more "initial" decision, closer to the *Anfang*, to the "originary essence of truth," in which thought finds itself called to the guardianship of its laws by "what makes its laws be laws," by the discovery of the truth of being. As no law is sufficiently primordial to make law by itself, any determination of the "law"—theological or ethical, juridical or scientific—appears to be derived, inessential, indeed metaphysical, insofar as it misrecognizes its own origin, that which is Beyond the Law and which gives it the force of law.

Would what goes for practical philosophy in 1943 also go for the *Critique of Pure Reason*? Would Kant's work be "metaphysical" through and through? To that question one cannot give too simple an answer. The Heideggerian interpretation of Kant, and especially of the first *Critique*, in fact undergoes very remarkable variations. In the early period, from 1927 to 1929, Heidegger accords to the *Critique of Pure Reason*, cleansed of its neo-Kantian misinterpretations, a notable privilege: it inflicted on "the traditional metaphysical edifice" its "first and deepest shaking." In initiating a refoundation of ontology that places at the forefront the "finitude" of knowledge (i.e., its rootedness in originary temporality), Kant was "the first and only thinker" of Western history to have tried to think Being within the horizon of time (SZ, 23;BTa, 45). This attempt, however, remains precarious and inconsistent, suffering an evident retreat after the second edition of the *Critique*, making all the more urgent the task of a "repetition" of the Kantian foundation within the framework of fundamental ontology. An ambiguous attitude, at once of filiation and of rupture, in which the recognition of a proximity, of an essential debt to Kant, is allied with the demand to surpass his limits in fidelity to his project—we find here what we could refer to in Hegel and Nietzsche as parricidal gesture. The difference is that Hegel situates the decisive contribution, Kant's legacy, in the second *Critique*, with the discovery of the principle of autonomy, whereas Heidegger looks to the first *Critique* and the discovery of original finitude. In both cases, however, it is a matter of playing off Kant against himself, extracting from the "formalist" or "metaphysical" matrix of his system its core of truth, the sign heralding a more authentic thought. In contrast to Hegel, Kant's ontological privilege will not be maintained by Heidegger. Nevertheless, if it initially seems to be displaced, transferred in a 1930 seminar to the second

Critique, and later in a 1936 course to the third *Critique*, it will soon be abandoned, as the dialogues with Nietzsche, and above all with Hölderlin, deepen and as Heidegger's thought reaches its "turning point," its *Kehre*. Finally, the whole of Kant's work, including the first *Critique*, will be relegated to the metaphysics of subjectivity.[2] Yet through these variations something remains constant: the setting aside of practical philosophy. With the brief and singular exception of the 1930 seminar, Heidegger seems always to have regarded it as a blind spot of Kantian thought. Not only in its implications (i.e., the practical reestablishment of speculative ideas) but already in its initial orientation would Kantian ethics demand to be deconstructed. How does this deconstruction of the Law work, and where does it lead us? Will it succeed in finishing its task of reducing or destroying *without remainder* the Law of ethics?

According to Gadamer, it is "after his meeting with Cassirer in Davos" that "Heidegger relegated Kantian philosophy to the history of the forgetting of being, as his later works on Kant show."[3] This is perhaps an overstated assessment, but it is true that this 1929 debate with the heir of Marburg neo-Kantianism brings to light the fundamental stakes and the limits of the Heideggerian interpretation of Kant. The quarrel bears on the problem of "finitude" above all, and more precisely on that of practical " finitude": on the question of whether Kant's practical philosophy is to be understood as an ethics of "finitude." Cassirer is not hostile to a Heideggerian reading of the first *Critique* and accepts without difficulty the thesis of the impassable "finitude" of human *knowledge*, which rests on the reduction of theoretical reason and on the understanding of the transcendental imagination as originary temporality. He nevertheless refuses to extend this reduction to practical reason. His interpretation of Kant is indeed based on a "determined and radical dualism" between the theoretical and practical, the sensible world and the intelligible world, on the opposition between the *temporality* of phenomena and noumenal *freedom*. Kant's ethics would be "decisively metaphysical," entailing a "breakthrough" toward the intelligible world in which the freedom of the moral subject breaks the circle of temporality and rises to the supersensible.[4] If the temporal schematism of the imagination imprisons us in finitude, we nonetheless participate in the infinite, in the Absolute, through the irreducibility of our practical reason to the schemata of the imagination and through our free submission to the demands of a universal Law (KPM, 172–73). He asserts moreover that "anxiety throws the earthly from you" (KPM, 180). To this Heidegger objects that the categorical imperative is addressed only to reasonable and finite beings, that the notion of duty itself, of practical obligation, with the implication of its essential incompletion (i.e., that it remains unachieved), reveals the finite character of Being-obliged, that the sense of the Law as a constitutive element of Dasein testifies to the "finitude of ethics"(KPM, 174–75, and § 38). It is impossible, therefore, to remove the Law from time: when Cassirer invokes the atemporal dimension of the noumenon, Heidegger can easily answer that this eternal permanence still presupposes an inauthentic ontological determination of time as persistence in the presence of the eternally present. Moreover, Cohen's and Cassirer's neo-Kantian problematic constantly presupposes the very practical temporality that it challenges: that is, in conceiving freedom as something ordained—a practical finality—or in conceiving autonomy as autotelic and the Law as "final goal," it reintroduces time into the heart of ethics in the form of the temporal horizon of the future, as the aim of infinite progress toward an end that is always still to come. And, were it necessary, this would confirm the criticism leveled at them by Heidegger.

The ethical breakthrough to which Cassirer lays claim was merely a regression, a lapse into the most classical prejudices of metaphysics. But if there is retreat, it is first of all Kant's retreat. Cassirer's analysis indeed embraces the dominant orientation of Kantian philosophy; it gives a faithful account of the theme of the "third step," the passage to the supersensible, and thus to the atemporal. It is indeed Kant who, in his practical philosophy, hardens the demarcation between the sensible and the intelligible, lays stress on the immutable permanence of the intelligible character, and claims that freedom is impossible in time. The neo-Kantian interpretation is no less univocal: it ignores the fact that in another aspect of his thought Kant reaffirms the temporal character of the Law, of the ethical decision, of the Sovereign Good and radical evil, thus sketching out another thought of Passage, which would no longer involve the super-sensible but which would step toward originary sensibility, the affective site of the Law. To bring these subterranean fracture lines, where the work of thinking detaches itself from the metaphysical frame that holds it, will be one of the aims of our reading. Failing that, Kant's ethics appears entirely a prisoner of an inherited ontology, metaphysical through and through. Such is precisely Heidegger's position: Heidegger considers Kant's ethics the main reason for his "falling back," for the disastrous *volte-face* that occurred between the first and the second editions of the *Critique of Pure Reason*. In reducing reason and understanding to transcendental imagination, in determining pure reason as finite, "i.e., sensible" reason, the 1781 edition seemed to subject rationality to sensibility, to hurl it into the "abyss," threatening the total dissolution of the rational in the sensible, contrary to the Kantian plan of founding an ethics, of establishing a priori principles of pure practical reason. To fight practical empiricism—the ethical nihilism that reduces the good to sensible happiness—to save the Law of practical reason, it was necessary for him to push aside the temporalizing imagination in favor of the understanding and reason, to restore the ancient primacy of the *ratio* and the *logos*: in thus canceling out the ontological advance of the *Critique*, the 1787 edition clears the ground for the *Critique of Practical Reason* (KPM, 146).The ethical project is the evil genius that diverts Kantian thought from its own truth. Therefore, the fundamental ontological repetition of the Kantian foundation will have to eliminate this obstacle, to reduce ethics, in the sense of a phenomenological reduction-destruction. Having shown that theoretical reason derives from transcendental imagination, Heidegger will extend this reduction to practical reason: his analysis will uncover, in the feeling of respect for the Law, the fundamental structure of auto-affection, namely, transcendental imagination as temporality and ipseity, already at work in theoretical reason and understanding. At the same time, it will eliminate the distinction between theoretical reason and practical reason, making impossible the affirmation, fundamental for Kant, of the primacy of practical reason. This dissolution is no accident but rather satisfies a constant demand of phenomenology: "Reason, Husserl declared, is not to be divided into theoretical, practical or aesthetic, etc.," and if the phenomenological reduction requires a "universal ethical *epoche*," a putting-out-of-play of any determination of value,[5] it is the same for the ontological reduction planned by Heidegger. Here again, the distinction between theory and practice and moreover every ethical determination find themselves pushed aside, submitted to the veiling/unveiling of the truth of Being.[6]

"Soon after *Being and Time* appeared a young friend asked me, "When are you going to write an ethics?" (BW, 231). At a time of disarray, of a darkening of the world, the wish for an ethics that would help us overcome our anguish becomes even more pressing. This request is nevertheless naive: the "young friend" had not noticed that the Heideggerian "ethics" had already appeared, that the thought of Being "is in itself the original ethics" (BW, 235). More efficacious than any praxis, more open to the clearing of truth than any theoria, "such thinking is neither theoretical nor practical. It comes to pass before this distinction" (BW, 236, 240).[7] For it thinks, more authentically than any ethics, man's ethos, the dwelling or site where he is asked to stand—an archi-ethics that no longer has anything to do with "ethics." It implements an ontological reduction of the Law that leads it back through a series of conditions, to the originary domain from which the beinglaw of all law is addressed. From ontic laws—juridical or moral—it is a matter of going back to their condition of possibility, to the injunction (*Fugung*) that confers on them their imperative vocation, that is, to the commands (*Weisungen*) that dominate each epoch, determining its preunderstanding of the law—as law of God or of practical Reason, of Nature or of History. Then we have to reassign these "historical" injunctions to their ultimate ontological condition, their sending from the unveiling of the truth of Being, which offers itself while withdrawing itself—as *phusis, logos, idea,* and finally as subject and will—and gives its " imprint" (*Prägung*) to each of these eras. So it is only "from Being itself (that) the assignment of those directions [can come] that must become law and rule for man" (BW, 238). More originary than any law is the sending of Being, whose call claims man and grants him his dwelling. This gift is a "grace" (*Huld*), the "giving of maintenance" (*Halt*) which gives to man his basis. It is nevertheless a summons that snatches man from his everyday fallenness, from the values and norms of the "They," to involve him in the "ek-static" opening of truth. This call presents itself as the violence of anxiety, the unbearable, *to deinon, das Ungeheuer,* in which "the singularity of the event bursts forth," "bursting what so far appeared normal." The originary dimension of ethics then reveals itself as essentially distinct from any common "value" and any "morality": as the paradoxical site of an *unheimliche ëthos* in which the call to dwell in the Open throws the existent far from its *Heim,* leaving it "solitary, anxious, trapped in the middle of Being"[8]: exposed, uncovered in face of the clearing.

The Heideggerian deconstruction of every "ontic" ethics, however, involves some presuppositions that we must question. Its reduction-destruction of the Law is founded on the priority of the ontological claim, that of the truth of Being, over any ontic prescription. That the ultimate requirement, the call or the sending from which every assignation proceeds, should be identified as that of Being remains for Heidegger too obvious to question. It also is self-evident that the concept of law only ever applies to an ontic regional determination, that all law is law in beings. What would happen if the Kantian thought of the law could not be reduced to this kind of determination, could not be assigned to a region of being; if it revealed itself in the feeling of the sublime as the binding form of the world, in the feeling of respect as the injunction that gives the subject its basis and gives existence its orientation? Should one not acknowledge in its imperative a dignity at least equal to that of Being? Would not the ethics of the Law give access to an *êthos* as originary as the dwelling under the truth of Being? These questions are underpinned by a primordial question: that of the ontological status of the Law, of the connection between the question of the Law and the question of Being: "beneath this proximity, this metonymy perhaps [the law, another name for Being, Being, another name for the law; in both cases "transcendent" as Heidegger says of Being], the abyss of a difference is perhaps hidden and maintained."[9] Admitting that the Law as conceived by Kant is not one ontic norm among others and certainly not a moral rule—but rather that it designates the pure form of the *Gesetzmässigkeit*, the meta-prescription from which any prescription receives its force as law, thus recognizing that the law is nothing in beings, still leaves indeterminate its ontological status, its essential *situation* relative to Being itself.

Two divergent perspectives then present themselves. It could be, as Heidegger maintains, that *nomos*, the originary sense of the Law, names "the assignation hidden in Being's decree," that the Law is one of the possible names of Being. As one of Heidegger's students suggested as early as 1931, it would be in the second *Critique* that one would from now on have to situate the decisive ontological breakthrough.[10] The Heideggerian interpretation of Kant should be partially amended, but without undermining its main lines of thought or the history of Being. Or is it necessary to take the step, to risk a more audacious hypothesis that would dig up again between Being and the Law "the abyss of a difference," to attempt to situate the gift of the Law *epekeina tes ousias*, beyond the essentiality of Being, to think, following Levinas, of ethics as a tearing away from Being?

Heidegger will hear nothing of this question. For him, the ontological reduction of the Law participates in a wider gesture, in the destruction of ethics, in the deconstruction of duty and good, as well as of any other authority that would presume to oppose itself to Being and impose its law on it. *The Introduction to Metaphysics* analyzes at length the system of four limitations of Being, four cleavages that cut across the history of Western philosophy.[11] These four scissions, in which Being finds itself each time restricted by a limiting determination, are supported by the same metaphysical determination of Being as constant presence, as eternally identical permanence, and so they contribute to the forgetting of the truth of Being. It is with the fourth, with the ethical domination of Being by the ought-to-be, that the eclipse becomes total. It can be seen first in Plato: when it is determined as idea, the morning light of the truth of Being has already receded. Seized in the evidence of theoretical vision, "Being no longer provides the measure," it has lost its initial potentiality, the power to make appear what is. This power of the May-be has been transferred to the ideality of the idea, to the highest Idea that Plato names the Good—which must not be understood as the moral good, which is aptitude, the valor of the possible, what "lends to Being the power to be (*wesen*) as idea, as model" and thus situates itself beyond it. This violent deposition of Being by the Good is only possible because Being has already degraded itself. Yet the hidden truth of Being still reigns in the Good that supplants it, as it alone can confer to the Good its power to make law. The Good, the Law, and the *Sollen* are mere derivative determinations, usurping the place of their originary condition. They are nothing but simulacra, shows of Being. Initiated by Plato, this degradation "is completed in Kant," in the "philosophy of values," "and in particular (in) what is laid on the market today" in 1935—"as philosophy of national-socialism."[12] In short, a single filiation leads from Plato to Kant, and from Kant to the Hitlerian ideologists. In Nazism, as the realm of moral values, the fulfillment of goodness, the ancient victory of the Good over Being, unfolds its most extreme consequences.

This rather surprising assertion only develops in all of their implications the presuppositions of Heideggerian ontology and most of all those of this essential presupposition: that Being alone is what "provides the measure," that it is the irreducible condition of any reduction, the originary One that precedes all scission, that which prevails and suffers no restriction—in such a way that the ethical opposition between Being and what ought to be, in dividing Being from itself and in limiting it in order to submit it to an ontic law, does it violence. But if the Good and the Law can confront Being and belittle it, it means that they compete with it on the same ground. In asserting without justification that the originary and authentic meaning of the *agathon* and the *nomos* has nothing to do with ethics, that they have meaning only in the horizon of Being, Heidegger helps himself in advance to what he was supposed to prove: he prejudges their ontic character, thus inevitably subordinating them to the injunction of Being.

In this context, in which the Law is but a degenerate avatar of the Platonic Good, the Kantian project of freeing the Law from its ordination to the Good would represent only an unimportant detour in the history of a long decline. It is inconceivable to Heidegger that this "Copernican" gesture, in emancipating the Law from the tutelage of the Good, of God, even of the Subject, could shield it from all ontic foundation, expose it to the abyss, to the enigma of its gift.

For Heidegger, Kant's ethics would belong unreservedly to metaphysics—not only in its conditions and implications, but in its aim itself, that of a "practical philosophy," of a "morality" underpinned by the disastrous scission of *Sein* and *Sollen*. In all of this, Kant would be simply persevering in an old blindness, yet bringing to it a special inflection, the mark of an epoch or rather of a turn from one epoch to another. The history of metaphysics is the reign of nihilism: in the ontological sense, insofar as the supreme Principles of beings usurp Being, while Being itself is considered as nothing; but also in the ordinary ontic sense, as the dissolution (*Verwesung*) of the super-sensible, the collapse of supreme ideals, as the Principles arising from the nothingness of Being return to their nothingness, where "the Ideas of Reason, God, *the moral imperative*, Progress, Universal Happiness, Culture and Civilization successively lose their constructive power, finally to fall into nullity.[13] Modernity is defined by the predominance of a unique Principle, the Subject, of which the Cogito, Pure Reason, Absolute Spirit, and Will to Power are merely modes. That epoch is called modern in which "man becomes subject," in which the human subject rises to the place occupied long ago by the Idea of Good, and later by the God of onto-theology,"[14] a problematic that permits the characterization of the "*historical*" *situation* of Kantian philosophy, as a phase of transition between the Cartesian inauguration of the metaphysics of the Subject and its culmination in Hegel and Nietzsche. In conceiving the *I think* as the fundamental condition of all knowledge, Kant "safeguards the metaphysical aspect of modern metaphysics"[15] he confirms and consolidates the modern *handing over* of the Principles (i.e., from God to the Subject). Since the *Kehre*, Heidegger's judgment of Kant has indeed been modified: the *First Critique* loses its ontological privilege, and the whole Kantian project is relegated to the history of wandering. What never varies, however, is the unremittingly negative judgment upon the practical philosophy, which remains the accursed share of the system, the heart of its blindness. Nevertheless, it no longer will be dismissed for having restored the primacy of Reason, but rather for having initiated the terminal phase of the metaphysical decline, the "absolute nihilism of the "will to will" (*Wille zum Wille*). It is with Kantian practical reason that the insurrection of the will breaks out, that the I think at last steps forth as an I will that already possesses the essential characteristic of the nihilistic will to will, its lack of aim (*Ziel-losigkeit*) (EP, §21). The will of the autonomous subject is not considered "nihilist," because it wills nothingness, the empty abstraction of the Law, instead of willing itself, but on the contrary because it does not will anything else but itself, and so "can only will the nullity of nothingness" (EP, §3). This is a will of No Other, an unbridled will, endless, lawless, as it does not know any other end or law but itself. One will note that the Heideggerian analysis depends upon, without ever calling into question, the dominant interpretation since Hegel of Kantian autonomy as "will which wills will," as the power of the Subject to prescribe to itself its own law that frees it from all external law. Heidegger contents himself with reversing its meaning, seeing the most forlorn wandering, the deepest forgetfulness, just where Hegel celebrated the advent of the Absolute. "Kant's thesis on the Law," or rather Heidegger's thesis on Kant's Law, would be that the *Gesetz* is (*selbst*) *Setzung*, the self-positing of the subject, that *the Law is the Law of the Subject*. To suppose that this thesis does not hold, that the Kantian thought of the Law cannot be reduced to it, no doubt would be to call into question the Heideggerian interpretation of Kant in its entirety, and with it his conception of modern metaphysics and the very plan of the history of Being. Here we can pose once again the capital question whether Law is "another name for Being," or whether it refers to an otherwise-than-Being—and approach it in a more specifically delimited and more practicable manner. In putting into question its determination as law of the metaphysical Subject, perhaps we will discover in the ethics of Law a breakaway, an *irreducible* excess, which could not be *reduced to Being*—to the *forgetfulness of Being*, which would mark the limit of the ontohistorical reduction of ethics.

It is advisable, considering the importance of the stakes, to take a closer look at Heidegger's thesis on Law: to search for what led him to identify it with the will to will of the Subject. For the early Heidegger, the main trait of the Kantian conception of the Subject is its *ontological indetermination*, a direct consequence of its Cartesian filiation (SZ, 24;BTa, 46). It is the marvel of the first *Critique* that despite this "fatal indetermination" it progresses so far as to touch the "unknown root," the knot of the subject, of the imagination and of temporality, a miracle that bears no fruit, for the originary identity of transcendental apperception and of time glimpsed there is constantly missed. Because of his "vulgar" conception of time, which he assimilates to the intratemporality of *Vorhanden*, to a continuous succession of nows, Kant can understand the temporal self-identification of the self only within the horizon of the present, as the constant presence of a subsisting being,[16] thus distorting his conception of freedom, understood within this framework of substantial permanence as a mode of the "objective" causality of being presentat-hand (GA 31, 173, 299–300). Heidegger says nothing of what could have been for Kant, if he had thought beyond himself, an authentic reappropriation of the finite transcendence of the Self in the originary temporalization of its freedom. We, however, know that in the problematics of *Being and Time*, Dasein "originally temporalizes itself from its future," through the anguished anticipation of its own death. What a 1925 course said of the cogito sum also would go for the "Cartesian" Kant: that it deals merely with the "appearance" of Dasein whose "authentic statement and fundamental certainty" should be *sum moribundus*: I am mortal, I am "having to die." For "it is only in dying (*im Sterben*) that I can in any way absolutely say "I am.""[17] In the anguish of my *being-toward-death* and the resolute decision that it makes possible, the Dasein that I am regains authentically in its singularity, which is always mine, in its "finitude," its freedom. And it is no longer, as with Kant, the permanence of a *Vorhanden* but instead the maintenance of this free resolution that "gathers and unifies the existence of Dasein throughout its history.[18]

If this orientation is not found in Kant, is it only through neglect, owing to his "Cartesian" incapacity to understand existence? If he escapes this logic of ontothanatology, is it not in accordance with an *other* thought of freedom: of a freedom that would no longer or not only?—reveal itself under the horizon of death but in the *factum* of Law? Would it be possible to understand ethical "finitude" from the horizon of Law and no longer in terms of *being-toward-death*, and yet without abstracting it from temporality? Perhaps Heidegger is mistaken about Kant when he accuses him of reducing the temporality of the subject to that of a subsisting being-at-hand, as if the Kantian ethical subject did not temporalize itself in its progress toward the final end that Law prescribes to it, and as if its temporal persistence did not require a free decision, a "choice of the intelligible character," and a constant resolution to maintain itself in this decision. If it is true that practical temporality exceeds the horizon of *being-toward-death*, if death is not the absolute Master, the meaning of "finitude," of transcendence, of freedom, the status of the ethical self in its rapport with itself and the other would all be upset.

Death is "always essentially mine"—it is "the own-most possibility of Dasein"—it "interpellates (it) in its singularity." In tearing it away from its everyday fallenness, from the anonymity of "one dies," the anguished anticipation of its death permits Dasein to grasp itself in its authenticity—a recovery that demands a preliminary "attestation" of its being-able-to-be-itself, which it undergoes in the "voice of conscience" (*Gewissen*), as a "call" (*Ruf*) which calls it back to its "debt" (*Schuld*).[19] The "moral" connotations of these motifs should not lead us astray; as ever, the existential analytic presupposes a reduction-destruction of values and moral meanings, of the misinterpretation of the call as an imperative of a "universal moral-conscience," of the misunderstanding of being-in-debt as "ethical fault" and as responsibility toward others. The notion of debt must be "freed from any rapport with duty and law," from any relation to a "moral wrong,"[20] an onto-existential reduction whose main target is "Kantian ethics," above all in its neo-Kantian versions—notably that of Cohen and Cassirer, who understand the Kantian subject as an intersubjective "universal conscience." And perhaps, in rescuing it from its traditional interpretations, this reduction will be able to bring out the core of Kantian ethics: the singular imperative of the Law, beyond the semblance of an objective, universal rule, beyond the negative determination of wrong as privation and defect, the assertion of a "positive evil," of an originary debt, which is "the most personal of all," a radical fault that sinks into existence.

In the call of *Gewissen*, ethics and the access to *êthos* are at stake: in this anethical archiethics, the existent reaches its own dwelling only by exposing itself to dispossession. To this deprivation—this disappropriation that Heidegger calls *Unheimlichkeit*, disquiet, uncanniness—"I am called," "in an unfamiliar voice," an injunction addressed "from the distance and into the distance," which "tracks down and threatens (my) loss which is forgetful of itself." What does the silent voice say? "In all rigor—nothing," no fault committed, no duty to respect, nothing but the indeterminate pure form of the call, its summons. A Voice from Outside, which is nevertheless not the voice of Another, of "a foreign power which would penetrate Dasein," which is the call of No Other, that is, of Self: "in *Gewissen*, Dasein calls itself." It calls itself away from its inauthentic and fallen Self to its possible authenticity—it calls on itself to come back to itself from its alienation, its foreignness.[21] Everything happens as if, having detected the original phenomenon of the call in its pure, indeterminate form, Heidegger rushed to submit it to a certain determination, to impose on it the structure of a recall to oneself, to either reappropriate it for or repatriate it to the Self. And this is because he understands the phenomenon of the call from within the horizon of being-toward-death, the "existential solipsism" where Dasein, isolating itself in its "ownness," projects itself toward its own-most possibility. Inflected in this direction, the phenomenological description of the call will simply echo a problematic already previously established. In its self-directedness, the call to itself testifies to the essential property of Dasein: that it only exists for the sake of itself (*umwillen seiner*) a property that we could designate as its *adseity*. Thus oriented, does description remain phenomenologically faithful to the thing itself? Does it sufficiently respect what was revealed in the phenomenon of the call, namely, its uncanny and faraway character? Is this to say that the call that calls me back to myself could come from an "other," and if so, from which other, and in what way? Is it possible only under the horizon of freedom-for-death? Would another thought of death and freedom be required, which would take into account this rapport with the other? Unless the task is to free the thought from death, to understand differently, in another ontological dimension, according to other affects and another temporality, the finitude of existence and its singularity that is always mine. In viewing its alteration as originary and pre-solipsistic, perhaps we already transgress the framework of the ontological analytic of Dasein, of this being for whom in its Being its own Being is at stake, this being which "relates to its Being as to its ownmost possibility."

So many questions that for Heidegger do not even arise, from the moment he encloses the call in the circle of the recall to self. Following a gesture influenced by Kant, or at least by his own reading of Kant, in which the relation to the Law that Kant also designates as a "voice" of *Gewissen* that reminds us of our "debt" (*Schuld*) is reduced to an auto-affection of Self. Having shown that theoretical reason, in its receptive spontaneity, is founded in the spontaneous receptivity of the transcendental imagination, the *Kantbuch* attempts to find the same structure in the "constitutive feeling" of practical reason. Respect for the Law, as free submission to a Law that the Self prescribes to itself, would reveal the same synthesis of spontaneity (freedom) and of receptivity (submission), the same structure of auto-affection, namely, the transcendental imagination identifying itself with originary temporality, with the "ipseity" of the finite self. Auto-affection is the ecstatic transcendence of the Self, its "exit from self," which opposes to itself a resistance, a blockage, in order to return to itself,[22] which is to assimilate the *autonomy* of practical reason to the *auto-affection* of Self, to the "adseity" of Dasein, to consider Law as a temporal and "imaginary" self-determination of the finite "ipseity," as the law of the subject. This is the basis of Heidegger's thesis on the Law. It is difficult, when reading the *Kantbuch*, not to let oneself be seduced by the violent radicality of the interpretation and its apparently flawless rigor; it is even more difficult when no philosophical "tribunal" exists, no "law" that would assign to interpretative violence its reasonable limit. A work can resist a certain type of reading, however, if its prejudices contradict and disfigure its essential aims, and whose apparent radicality reveals itself as the surety for an arbitrary violence. Heidegger's initiative, as has just been seen, is backed by a notion of respect as the "constitutive feeling" of practical reason, where "respect for the Law is respect for the Self acting before itself," the authentic relation of the self to itself when it "refuses to dispel the hero from its soul."[23] Once again, one will notice that Heidegger presupposes what he had to prove—that respect for the Law is respect for oneself, autoaffection. He thus ignores Kant's text, which on the contrary defines it as respect for *others*, for "the man whom I see before me," who presents the Law to me as in an "intuition" (*anschaulich*) in which my self-sufficiency is dashed.[24] That a law of pure reason may thus give itself in a quasi-intuition, that a feeling that nevertheless presents itself only through the other—these are major difficulties for Kantian ethics. This should, however, forbid us to identify the "affect" of respect with auto-affection. Should we conclude that the Law of autonomy is not reducible to the self-determination of the Subject? Should we conclude that practical reason does not conform to the same structure as theoretical reason, does not refer itself back to the imagination, that it appeals to a destination that "totally exceeds the domain of imagination" (GA 31, 261–97)? Un-imaginable, should we also think its Law as infinite, atemporal, properly metaphysical? Or would it devolve back to another dimension of finitude, of temporality, of transcendence? For what could a temporality and an "egoity" prior to the imagination consist in? What would be, in this other mode of temporality, the limit assigning the existent to its finitude?

So many problems evaded by Heidegger. Although he managed to guard himself from the main neo-Kantian misinterpretations, he never called into question the most massive prejudice of the traditional interpretations, the presuppositions shared by Jacobi, Hegel, and Nietzsche, that the autonomous Kantian will is "will of self," will that wills will. It is in the 1930 course on *The Essence of Human Freedom* that the structure of auto-affection and "adseity" of the ethical Self will be reinterpreted in that sense. Having examined Kant's "first path" toward freedom, the transcendental freedom of the first *Critique*, where that transcendental freedom, reduced to causality, is not thought authentically from out of existence, Heidegger turns to the "second path," the path of "ethical praxis": only there, and for the first time in Western history, would Kant approach the realm proper to freedom (GA 31, 134–35, 300). Contrary to earlier writings, this course confers on Kantian practical philosophy a notable privilege: that of opening the "fundamental question of philosophy," the essence of freedom as "the foundation of the possibility of Dasein," "root of being and time" (GA 31, 277–78). If freedom "stands behind being and time," if the question of being is rooted in the question—perhaps rendering it a more radical question— of the essence of freedom revealing itself in "ethical praxis," does that mean that the archi-ethics of freedom would be more originary than the thought of Being? That, irreducible to any ontology, it would expose itself to an otherwise than Being, to a dwelling more primordial than the truth of Being? These are questions that find no place in Heidegger's work. This freedom that is more originary than man will be immediately identified as will, as an "autonomous" will willing itself as will: "A good will is absolutely good (. . .) insofar as it only wills the will, and so only wills"—"pure will signifies: willing the proper essence of will." There is no other "good," no other "duty" than this will to will oneself. Hence, the practical law is a "formal law," the pure form of oneself. The law *of* the will is the will itself, the Law *as* will: "the law only exists because and insofar as it wills." Not for one moment does Heidegger consider that the Law may not will at all, may not belong to the will; precisely because it is the will's condition and assigns to it its limit. In any case, what the law "wills" must for Heidegger remain indeterminate: "What it demands is that I should really will, i.e., that I should be decided, that I should will decisively." "But will what? This is again a vain and misleading question" (GA 31, 279, 289). As the call of *Gewissen*, the Law states nothing, does not stipulate any duty or any end, does *anything else* but itself, its pure will of decision, its pure decision to Will.

Will of the will, willing itself without end: in 1930, such would be for Heidegger the most secret root of Being. The very one that he stigmatizes a few years later as the worst anguish, the darkest forgetfulness. For, in the meantime, the *Kehre*, the turning point of his thought, had taken place, interrupting the path it had set upon since *Being and Time*: "This interruption is motivated by the fact that (. . .) (this endeavor) runs the risk of becoming, against its will, a consolidation of subjectivity."[25] The task of the deconstruction of metaphysics must consequently be understood, at least in part, as a self-deconstruction that radicalizes the ontology of Dasein by extricating it from a schema that retained the imprint of a metaphysical Subject. Thus will be abandoned the problematics, central to *Being and Time*, concerning the access to "authenticity" through resolute decision; the ontological privilege of Dasein likewise will be abandoned.

After the turning point, it is no longer Dasein that opens the horizon of the understanding of Being, but Being itself that summons man, asks him to comply with the unveiling of its truth, with these sendings that punctuate the epochs of its history. From then on, "man," to whom the sending is addressed, could not be a singular individual but is instead the "historical Dasein," the type of man characteristic of each era. With the exception of rare thinkers or poets reached by the remote echo of the call, the singular existent *has no choice* but to answer, cannot choose either to submit to the wandering of its time or to escape from it.[26] In his effort to overcome the voluntarism of "resoluteness," Heidegger comes to dispossess the existent of all responsibility, of all power to determine the sense of its existence, of the demand to be answerable for its free decision. With the abandonment of "existential solipsism," the foundational possibility of its freedom also has been lost; it is the very question of the singularity of existence, of its truth "which is always mine," which is evacuated as residue of the metaphysics of subjectivity. That my life's mineness does not necessarily come down to a solipsist auto-affection, that finite ipseity or "egoity" is not necessarily identical to subjectivity—that the pure Ego is not a Subject—Heidegger pays no attention to these considerations. It is not only the "subjectivization" of Dasein that is thereby interrupted, but with it the Kantian "second path," an ethical praxis rooted in the finite transcendence of human freedom, while the privilege previously accorded to Kant is withdrawn.

What never varies throughout the reversal of the problematic is Heidegger's thesis on the Law, constantly determined as law of the subject, of the will that wills itself as will: the "turn" consists here only in reversing the sense of this determination, in henceforth denouncing the worst nihilism where he previously believed he discovered the root of Being. That Kantian autonomy amounts to an auto-affection, to an indeterminate self-determination of the will of the self, will never be questioned. Is this not a disfiguring misinterpretation? In denouncing what he formerly celebrated, has not Heidegger burdened Kant—a pseudo-Kant—with the responsibility for his own nihilism of 1930? At any rate, before and after the *Kehre*, the same project persists: to deconstruct ethics, to reduce the Law, to assign it to a subordinate place, sometimes as the authentic determination of the will of Dasein and sometimes as a "historical command" of the metaphysical Subject. In the end, this reduction is equivalent to a total destruction in the aimlessness of the will to will, in which the Kantian concept of autonomous will "reaches perfection," only to sink straightaway "into the nullity of nothingness"—*Selbstaufhebung der Moral* as the apotheosis of nihilism: of the Law, nothing remains. Yet in the text in which its liquidation is announced, something of Law recurs, in a brief moment, as a call to what could resist disaster, assign a limit—as a resistance to the surging will to will. And it is precisely what a Will without an end cannot tolerate, namely, an end, irreducible to the commands of the epoch, to the "programs" of *Gestell*, unconditioned, absolutely valid in itself—an end in itself. "The will to will denies any end in itself, can only tolerate an end if it is a means to win itself in play deliberately, and to organize a space for this play" (EP, §23), an incongruous and belated resurgence of a Kantian ethical motif, presented in opposition to the will to will, as a line of resistance—perhaps impossible to endure—to the nihilistic culmination of the autonomous will. Kant against Kant: only the respect for the end in itself, the second formula of the categorical imperative, could counter the ultimate consequences of the autonomy of willing, the third formula of this imperative, as if the fracture of a dispute, a "differend," crossed the practical philosophy, setting two representations of imperative, two modes of giving the Law, in conflict with one another. For it is still the Law—this same Law abrogated in the absolute will to will—whose imperative is to treat every reasonable being "always at the same time as end and never simply as a means." The forgetfulness of Being entails the negation of every end in itself, its reduction to the rank of means, a simple unit of stock, a cog in the machinery. Is this not to acknowledge that the vocation of this Law that stipulates the respect for this end is to resist nihilism, perhaps to deliver us from it? That the call of the Law could save us from the forgetfulness of Being, even save Being itself from its forgetfulness? This furtive avowal, in an isolated passage without consequences, is indeed confirmed in another text in a new resort to Kant. As to what this end in itself, this pole of resistance to the hold of *Gestell*, could consist in, Heidegger gives us no clue. For Kant, this term designated the personhood of the reasonable being as an object of respect—an apparently "humanist" conception brushed aside by the thought of Being, which denounces as metaphysics every "humanist interpretation of man as rational animal, as person, as spiritual being endowed with a soul and a body" (BW, 210). Not that such a thought "pleads for the inhuman," but on the contrary, because "even the highest humanist determinations of the essence of man do not reveal the proper dignity of man (*die eigentliche Wurde des Menschen*)."[27]

It is in the name of man, of this concept, central in Kant, of human dignity, that his humanist determinations, including the Kantian "person," are challenged as unworthy of man. Kant *versus* Kant, once again. It is well known, however, that the "personhood" of the reasonable being is not reducible, for Kant, to *human* personality, which makes it more difficult to assimilate his ethics to a "metaphysical humanism." It could be that his attempt to free a nonmetaphysical and nonhumanist concept of man and of his dignity takes Heidegger closer to Kant than he would like to admit. In the *Groundwork of the Metaphysics of Morals*, the distinction between the dignity (*Wurde*) of the person "which does not admit of any equivalent," and "value" (*Wert*), which is always relative, coincides with that between the end in itself, which "cannot be replaced by another end," and merely "subjective," conditioned ends.[28] Is it legitimate to dissociate, as does Heidegger, the dignity of man from personhood as an end in itself, as an irreducible singularity whose Law commands respect? Why should the "dignity" of which the "Letter on Humanism" speaks not coincide with the "end in itself" threatened by the will to will, evoked by *The Overcoming of Metaphysics*, that is, coincide *also* with the individual's singularity or the always-being-mine of Dasein, itself endangered by the mass leveling of *Gestell*? One could not then avoid establishing a connection between the Heideggerian concept of the "dignity of man," on the one hand, as an "ek-sisting" opening onto the clearing of Being, and the Kantian concept of "disposition for personhood," on the other hand, as an ethical exposition welcoming the Law. This would once more raise the question of the relationship between the ethics of the Law and the thought of Being. Finally, in conferring on "man" such an eminent "dignity," is one not led to introduce a *Sollen*, an unconditional demand to respect, to defend this threatened dignity? Such is, as a radical "young Hegelian" wrote, "*the categorical imperative to overturn all relations* which make of man a humiliated, enslaved, abandoned (*verlassenes*), contemptible being."[29]

Heidegger would not take this step in the direction of ethics. It would have been necessary for him to revise the plan of the history of Being, to entirely reconsider his ontological reduction of the Good, of the Law, of *Sollen*, perhaps also of the *Subject* and the *Ego*. Without a doubt, it was impossible for him to make use of the Kantian concepts of end in itself and of *Endzweck*. For him, the notion of "end" is always understood as the telos of a *technê*, from the point of view of fabrication: as early as Aristotle, the understanding of praxis has been distorted by the primacy of *poiêsis*, by the domination of the categories of production.[30] A more essential thought of action would have to emancipate itself from the reign of ends, from the obsession with the why. Like the rose, existence has no why; it is without reason and without aim. To finally let existence bloom without a why is the Turning point and Salvation (*Rettung*), the still-distant coming of *Ereignis*.[31]

Paradoxically, in fact, this absence of end, this "freedom from any aim," is also what characterizes the "play with itself" of the will to will; hence, the recourse, briefly attempted by Heidegger, to the Kantian end in itself, which recourse must be in vain if the notion of end is already subordinated to the very thing it was supposed to counter. But is this really so? To what extent are the practical concept of the end in itself and the aesthetic concept of finality without end still subjected to a techno-metaphysical teleocracy? Is it impossible to conceive of an end removed from the telos of production? In failing to explore this possibility, the Heideggerian deconstruction of finality is caught in a very remarkable aporia. If every end is "technical" (i.e., metaphysical), our salvation can only be found in a play without why and without aim. But the essence of technology is itself a play without end, and this play hurls us into the darkest distress. One cannot answer that it is not the same play, the same mode of being-without-an-end, for Heidegger's thought gives us no criterion, no law that would permit us to distinguish them, to differentiate the two faces of Janus' head. For want of Law, *Ereignis* and *Gestell* become indiscernible: the thought of Being would fall into an abyss, would reach its point of collapse. Here again, the existent has no choice, no power to decide whether to heed the call or wander in forgetfulness. There would not even be any difference between the opposing poles of being, between the wonder of the without-why sung by Angelus Silesius and the horror of the *kein Warum* evoked by Primo Levi.

The ontological reduction of ethics thus stumbles over an irreducible residue, over the demand for an end in itself, of a *Sollen*, of a Law, to which it cannot accede, except by giving up its own premises, and to which it has nevertheless to yield, for fear of collapsing into the undecidable. This is the logic of a failed parricide: the revocation of Kantian ethics cannot do without the Law it revokes. From the Kantian critique of skepticism to Hegel and Nietzsche, and then to Heidegger, we discover the same orientation—so many ever-more radical attempts to overcome nihilism, each criticizing its predecessors for their lack of radicalism, their insufficient delimitation of *nihil*, the persistence of an illusion they had not overcome, causing each of them to fall back into nihilism, into a "bad skepticism," an "incomplete" or "inauthentic" nihilism. In determining nihilism ontologically—in the sense that Being is nothing for it—and in positing that the essence of nihilism is Being itself in the nothingness of its withdrawal, Heidegger gave us its most radical delimitation, a promise of its *Verwindung* to come. It might be that such a radical deconstruction leaves in its turn a residue, an undeconstructed remainder, the indication of another mode of nihilism, unnoticed by the thought of Being and all the more threatening for that: like the enduring path of the "practical empiricism" spotted by Kant, the path of ethical nihilism—namely that *the Law* is nothing, that there is no Law, no basis to distinguish between good and evil, so that evil is *nothing*, nothing existing—a simple privation—and nothing more than the good. If the demarcation of good and evil dissolves into the dialectical *Aufhebung* of the Law, is it not the same with the ontological reduction of good and the Law? What has happened to evil in the thought of Being?

We had noted that, in *Being and Time*, the existential analysis of *Schuld* at once brushed aside any "vulgar" interpretation of debt as moral misdeed and wrong toward others. For the ontic notion of misdeed or evil, conceived here classically as *privatio boni*, "the lack of something which ought to be," is not the path to the thought of the ontological *Nichtigkeit* of Dasein at the foundation of its debt. It is indeed the difference between good and evil itself that is challenged as "inauthentic," *indifferent* to thought. Admittedly this purely negative conception of evil will be abandoned soon enough and, after the *Kehre*, Heidegger will endeavor to thematize the effective reality of evil as a fundamental ontological stake. One may wonder, however, whether he will really succeed in doing so, whether the thought of Being does not fail to think the "radicality" of evil: if, positing a "co-presence of evil in good and good in evil," in bringing then to an originary unity that "makes possible their scission," and finally to the "absolute indifference" of the abyss and Nothingness, one does not risk sublating or effacing their difference, of justifying evil by good, of leading thought into its indifference to evil.[32] In asserting that the harm of evil does not reside in human agency, that "Being itself is the battlefield" between "fury and salvation (*Heile*),"[33] do we not still deprive the existent of any power of decision, of any responsibility, of any duty other than that of waiting? Is it not also to reduce evil to nothing, if only to the Nothingness of Being, to justify in advance the disaster (*Unheil*), the devastation of "Fury," as a fatal consequence of its withdrawal, the inevitable reversal of its selfgiving, in such a way that nothing or nobody has any longer to answer for it? *Theos anaitios*: what is highest in beings is not implicated, is free from any mistake or debt. Or again: the Absolute absolves itself. From Plato to Hegel, Western philosophy has always made efforts to reject the wrong, to absolve the supreme Principle of its beings. Has Heidegger really broken with this tradition of ontodicy?[34] Has he not repeated that same gesture of absolution at a greater depth, by extending it to Being itself? Would not this persistence of an undeconstructed configuration mark the limit of Heideggerian deconstruction—of *any* deconstruction?—the irreducible abutment of the logical reduction that it cannot break up, because it has not taken the step toward ethics?

Notes

1. Martin Heidegger, "On the Essence of Truth," in BW, p. 139. See the commentary on this passage by H. Birault in *Heidegger et l'expérience de la pensée* (Paris: Gallimard, 1978), pp. 86–90.

2. "Kant's Thesis about Being," translated by T. E. Klein and W. E. Pohl, in *The Southwestern Journal of Philosophy* 4 (1973): 733.

3. H .G. Gadamer, "Heidegger et l'histoire de la philosophie," *Cahiers de l'Herne—Heidegger* (Éditions de l'Herne, 1983), p. 174.

4. "Davos Disputation between Ernst Cassirer and Martin Heidegger," in KPM, p. 173.

5. Cf., for instance, E. Husserl, *Erste Philosophie* (1923–1924), *Zweiter Teil: Theorie der phänomenologischen Reduktion* (The Hague: M. Nijhoff, 1959), p. 110.

6. Apparently, this is the case for all "ethical" motifs that Heidegger evokes, which are one by one ontologically deconstructed and reconstructed: *Schuld, Gewissen* and *Verfallenheit* in *Being and Time,* and later such Platonic concepts as *agathon* or *dikê,* and so on.

7. On the metaphysical determination of the opposition between "theory" and "practice," cf. Ni, 238.

8. Martin Heidegger, *An Introduction to Metaphysics,* translated by R. Manheim (New Haven, Conn.: Yale University Press, 1959), p. 152. On this notion of *unheimlich êthos* as the "proper ethos of the nonproper," see J. L. Nancy *L'impératif catégorique* (Paris: Flammarion, 1978), pp. 124–25.

9. Jacques Derrida, "*Prejugés—devant la loi,*" in *La faculté de juger* (Paris: Minuit, 1985), p. 124.

10. G. Kruger, *Critique et morale chez Kant* (Paris: Beauchesne, 1997).

11. IM, pp. 93–206. On the fourth limitation, see pp. 196–99.

12. Ibid., p. 199. One can find here the (in)famous declaration on the "greatness and internal truth" of the Nazi movement.

13. On Nietzsche's phrase, see "The Word of Nietzsche: "God is Dead,"" in QCT, pp. 53–112.

14. "The Age of the World Picture," in ibid., pp. 115–54.

15. "Overcoming Metaphysics," in EP, pp. 103–09, §5. See also §§17–18.

16. GA 25, 112, 342, 395.

17. HCT, 316. See BTa, §64.

18. See §§54–60 of BTa.

19. BT, §58.

20. SZ, 283;BTa, 328. For all of these items, see my study "Dispelling the Hero from Our Soul," in *Research in Phenomenology,* vol. XXI (1991).

21. GA 25;390–91;KPM, §34.

22. BP, 131–37;KPM, §30. For a critique of the Heideggerian reduction of respect and of reason to the transcendental imagination, see H. Declève, *Heidegger et Kant* pp. 163–66.

23. Immanuel Kant, *Critique of Practical Reason*, translated by L. W. Beck (Indianapolis: Bobbs-Merrill, 1956), p. 80.

24. Immanuel Kant, *Critique of Judgment*, translated by James Meredith Creed (Oxford: Clarendon Press, 1952), §29. As we will see, this will constitute the main concern of the Analytic of the Sublime.

25. Niv, 141. It is not insignificant that this declaration is inscribed in an analysis of European nihilism.

26. M. Haar, *Heidegger et l'essence de l'homme* (Grenoble: J. Millon, 1990), pp. 195-97.

27. BW, 210. See the analysis given by Derrida in "The Ends of Man," *Margins of Philosophy* (Chicago: University of Chicago Press, 1982), pp. 123-31.

28. Immanuel Kant, *Groundwork of the Metaphysic of Morals*, translated by H. J. Paton (New York: Harper & Row, 1964).

29. Karl Marx, *Critique of Hegel's "Philosophy of Right,"* translated by Annette Jolin and Joseph O'Malley (Cambridge: Cambridge University Press, 1972).

30. On the supremacy of the "attitude of the producer" as a fundamental idea of the ontological heritage, see BP. On the link established by Aristotle between *technê, eidos*, and *telos*, see "On the Being and Conception of *Physis* in Aristotle's *Physics* B, 1," translated by T. Sheehan, *Man and World* 9 (1976): 231.

31. Cf. the verse by Angelus Silesius cited in PR, 35-38. See also the beautiful book by R. Schürmann, *Le principe d'anarchie* (Paris: Seuil, 1982), pp. 97-98, 121-25.

32. See Heidegger's *Schelling's Treatise on the Essence of Human Freedom*, translated by J. Stambaugh (Athens: Ohio University Press, 1985), p. 157.

33. "Letter on Humanism," BW, 237.

34. See the analysis provided by J. L. Nancy in *L'expérience de la liberté* (Paris: Galilée, 1988), pp. 169-74, which finds in Heidegger "a silent justification of Being" (an "ontodicy") persisting until the end.

Part II

Heidegger and Ethics

5

Heidegger's "Originary Ethics"

Jean-Luc Nancy

Presenting Heidegger's thinking of ethics involves a threefold difficulty, the terms of which inevitably need setting out, at least in brief. First of all, Heidegger's Nazi engagement, then his almost complete silence on the camps, marked his memory (even aside from any proper political judgment) with a moral taint that many have seen as invalidating any ethical proposition on his part, if not the whole of his thinking. It is not our purpose to analyze these particulars (and moreover the case has already been well investigated by some important works; for the record: Bourdieu, Habermas, Faye, Pöggeler, Lacoue-Labarthe, Derrida, Granel, Parfait, Janicaud, Wolin, Sluga, etc.).[1] We will confine ourselves to positing the following: it is right to infer from the moral error a certain style or a certain professional intellectual conduct (across the entire works), but it is wrong to draw such an inference when what is at issue is the logic by which a thinking sought to analyze what constitutes man as the one through whom "Being" has as its original "sense" (or *êthos*) the choice and conduct of existence. That this thinking was not equal to the dignity (*Würde*) that it thus took as its theme must give rise to further thinking. But that is possible only if one takes Heidegger's thinking as one's point of departure (not forgetting to ask oneself what the precise ethical expectation was to which the political engagement sought to respond).

Aside from the previous consideration, some have thought it possible to deny that there is any ethical dimension to Heidegger's thinking, basing their claim on his own objection to ethics as a "discipline," on the corresponding absence of a "moral philosophy" in his work, and on his refusal of any moral interpretation of the analytic of *Dasein*. On this score, for this chapter to have the least relevance, one would need to begin by demonstrating the falsity of this argument and by reconstructing the possibility of a properly ethical approach to Heidegger. Not only is there no space here for this task, but it can be considered quite unnecessary. Only those who have read Heidegger blindly, or not at all, have been able to think of him as a stranger to ethical preoccupations. Moreover, there are already enough works in existence to refute this prejudice. It will suffice, then, to spell out the following (which the rest will complement): there is no "morality" in Heidegger if what is meant by that is a body of principles and aims for conduct, fixed by authority or by choice, whether collective or individual. But no philosophy either provides or is by itself a "morality" in this sense. Philosophy is not charged with prescribing norms or values: instead, it must think the essence or the sense of what makes *action* [*l'agir*] as such, in other words, of what puts action in the position of having to choose norms or values. Perhaps, incidentally, this understanding of philosophy is itself already Heideggerian in origin, or at least for us, today, it is necessarily Heideggerian in modality. That would not prevent one from showing how appropriate it is to Spinoza, Kant, Hegel, or Husserl, or from showing how, doubtless for specific historical reasons, it chimes in with those contemporaries of Heidegger (each quite different from the others), Bergson, Wittgenstein, or Levinas, which amounts to saying that, in general terms, there would be a case for showing how, with Heidegger and with Heidegger's period, philosophy understood itself (once again) as "ethics," let us say, for the sake of speed, rather than as "knowledge," presupposing, in particular, a distinction between "ethics" and "morality," which our whole present age has inherited (even if at times confusedly). But that is not our purpose here: we have simply to sketch out an internal explication of Heidegger himself, striving to be as strictly faithful as possible, while avoiding piety.

The third difficulty conflicts with the above. If ethics constitutes, paradoxically, at once a discreet, unobtrusive theme in Heidegger's work and a constant preoccupation, an orientation of his thinking, then one would need to undertake a general examination of this thinking. In fact, we will have to show the extent to which the "thinking of Being"—which is, after all, the principal, even exclusive title of this thinking—is nothing other than a thinking of what Heidegger called "original ethics," and that it is this throughout, in all of its developments. In particular, it would not be difficult to show that the celebrated "turning" (the *Kehre*), characterized most succinctly as a "passage from onto*logy* to *onto*logy" (in the terms of the *Beiträge*), basically corresponds to an accentuation, a reinforcement or a "folding" of the ethical motif. And this, one can suppose, was not wholly unrelated to a reflection silently tensed and perturbed by the National Socialist aberration. It is, therefore, just as much ruled out *de jure* to isolate a Heideggerian "moral philosophy" as it is *de facto*, owing to the economy of a dictionary, to cover the whole of Heidegger's work. So we will confine ourselves to explicating the basic intention of the text in which the motif of "original ethics" is brought to light, that is, the "Letter on Humanism." Linked to this will be some essential reminders of what paved the way to this motif in *Being and Time* and *Kant and the Problem of Metaphysics*. As for the rest, suggestions will have to suffice ("the rest" would be above all: (1) the thinking of freedom as an "ungrounded foundation"; (2) the thinking of language and poetry as a true *êthos*; (3) the thinking of "technics" as a retreat from moral foundations and the delivery of a different ethical demand).

To sum up the situation, two overwhelming objections could be raised: "Heidegger has a bad morality," and "Heidegger has no morality." These are not so much ruled out here as reserved for a different scheme of analysis. The only kind that is appropriate here needs instead to take as its theme Heidegger's thinking conceived of itself, throughout, as a fundamental ethics.

The "Letter on Humanism" announces itself forcefully and distinctly, in its very first sentence, as a reflection on *action*. It is very clear that the question of humanism is, for Heidegger, the question of what man is (of his *humanitas*) insofar as he has to act or to "conduct himself" (*conduct*, or action, insofar as it is its own end, action that is not "causing an effect" (BW, 217), seems to us an appropriate term for rendering the German *Handeln* as well as the Greek *praxis*, especially in the present context).

But what man is insofar as he has to act is not a specific aspect of his Being: it is his very Being itself. If Dasein—according to the opening formulations of *Being and Time*—is the being for which "in its very Being, that Being is *at issue* for it" (SZ, 12), it is because this "is at issue" [*"Il s'agit de"*] (*es geht um,*" it is about") does not bring into play an interest that is merely theoretical or speculative. Rather, it destroys the supposed autonomy of such an interest. If, in Dasein, Being is at issue [*il s'agit de l'être*] (and if, without playing on words more than language itself does, Being is an action [*l'être est de l'agir*]), that is because Being, as the Being of Dasein, *is* what is at stake [*l'enjeu*] in its conduct, and its conduct is the bringing into play [*la mise en jeu*] of Being.

This point of departure—and more than that, this axiom or this transcendental absolute of all thinking of Being—could also be expressed as follows: because the difference between Being and beings is not a difference of Being (it is not the difference between two kinds of Being of beings), it is not a difference between two realities, but the reality of Dasein insofar as it is in itself, of itself, open and called to an essential and an "active" relation with the proper[2] fact of Being.

This relation is that of *sense*. In Dasein, it is a case of giving sense to the fact of Being—or, more exactly, in Dasein the fact of Being is making sense [*le fait d'être est: faire sens*]. This "making sense" is not theoretical, nor is it practical in a sense opposed to the theoretical (but on the whole, it would be more in accordance with Heidegger's thinking to call it "in the first instance" practical). For knowledge, or the understanding of Being as sense, is identical to the action of sense, or action as sense. To be is to make sense. (In a direct line from Kant, pure reason is practical insofar as it is theoretical.)

But this "making" is not a "producing." It is, precisely, acting, or conducting oneself. Conduct is the accomplishment (*Vollbringen)* (BW, 217) of Being. As sense's conduct, or the conduct of sense, it is essentially "thinking." The essential action is thinking, but that does not close action back up on a "(merely) theoretical practice." If the *Letter*, along with many other texts, seems to restrict action—and with it original ethics—to an activity that one would be inclined to call abstract, speculative, and "active" through metaphor (the metaphor of the "thinkers" and the "poets"), then this is the effect of an inadequate reading. In reality, "thinking" is the name for action, because sense is at issue in action. Thinking (and/or poetry) is not an exceptional form of action, it is not the "intellectual conduct" to be preferred to others, but it is what, in all action, brings into play the sense (of Being) without which there would be no action.

This, indeed, is why action as thinking—the bringing into play of sense—is "desired" by Being. This desire is love (BW, 220) as ability (*Mögen*) (BW, 220), in other words, having a taste, an affection, or an inclination for, and the ability to do something. Being desires thinking (one might say here, in a direct line from Hegel, "the Absolute wants to be close to us"). It desires it in that thinking can accomplish the sense that it is. What thinking names is this: that sense desires itself as its own action. (It would be necessary to develop elsewhere how the concept of such a "desire" is *not* that of object-desire.)

This means that Being as the fact of Being—the fact that there is something in general—constitutes by itself the desire that this fact be accomplished (unfolded, acted) as sense. But this proposition must really be understood in all of its radicality and in its originariness. There is not first a brute fact (the Being of beings, the "there is"), then a desire for sense (for this Being). For if this were the case, sense, action, and ethics would have to come after and from somewhere other than the fact of Being. Now, on the one hand Being is not a "fact" in this sense—it is not something given, but that there is a gift—and sense cannot be conferred on it as a signification brought to it from elsewhere. (Moreover, such a problematic is not truly encountered in any great philosophy. It shows through only where it has been possible to posit Being as a brute fact of existence "in itself" in the face of which a subjectivity has to assume a giving of sense "for itself." This is an aspect of Sartre's thinking—explicitly targeted in the "Letter"—or of philosophies of the absurd. The specificity of Heidegger consists, however, in thinking Being as the fact of sense, and sense as the gift of Being.) On the other hand, sense conceived as signification conferred or found in addition to Being itself could not properly be the sense *of* Being, still less Being itself as sense. Now it is established in *Being and Time* that "[t]he sense of Being can never be contrasted with beings, or with Being as the supporting 'ground' of beings, for a 'ground' becomes accessible only as sense, even if it is itself the abyss of senselessness" (SZ, 152).

The fact of Being—as Dasein—is *eo ipso* the desire, ability, and love (ability-love) of sense. But the given [*donnée*], or the "deal"[*"donne"*] is precisely the "gift of essence" (BW, 220) in which Being gives itself essentially as the action of sense. Thus the "given" is the making sense of Being, and what is thus given or desired, given as desired (even if, once again, the sense of these words would need reevaluating elsewhere), is to "say the truth of Being" (BW, 218) or to "bring [it] to language" (BW, 217).

Making sense is not a production of sense. Let us say, to clarify things, that it is not an activity that can be compared to that by which, according to Lévi-Strauss, an existential given, itself reducible to a senseless materiality, is turned into an operative sense. (Moreover, one can add, still by clarification, that in a world not related to the otherworld of a principle, a gift or an origin, a creator or a world-subject in general, there is, strictly speaking, no other "fundamental" possibility than the alternative represented in these ways by Heidegger and Lévi-Strauss, unless there is still a means of going beyond both formulations of the alternative, which is another story—perhaps ours.)

If action is an "accomplishing," it is because Being itself accomplishes itself in it as the sense which it is. But Being is itself nothing other than the gift of the desire of/for sense. So making sense is not of sense's making; it is making Being be, or *letting* it be (BW, 220), according to the ambivalence of the German *lassen: bauen lassen*, to have something constructed = to let, to give to the constructing activity as such; *sein lassen*, to let be, to give, to entrust to the activity of Being as such.

Letting be is not a passivity: it is precisely action itself. It is the essence of action insofar as action is the essence of Being. It is a case of allowing Being to be/to act the sense that it is/desires. In Dasein, Being as such—the fact that there are beings in general—is no more "present" than anywhere else (the Being of beings in general is no more present or absent in one place or another), but it is the "that there is" of Being as sense. This sense is not a property *of* the "that there is," it properly *is* (or *makes*) the "that there is" as such. It engages it and engages itself in it: "that there is" is what is at stake in sense. That Being, absolutely and rigorously considered as such (which also means, to allude to other developments in Heidegger, considering it according to its unnominalized value as a verb—the "that Being" rather than "Being"—and moreover understanding it as transitive—Being *is* or *exists* beings, it "makes" them be, in other words, it makes them make sense), is essentially its own "engagement" (BW, 218) as the action of sense: that is the decisive axiom of this thinking. Thus ontology is from the outset, within or beyond itself, Being's *conduct of sense*, or the conduct of the sense of Being, according to the strongest value of the expression (in other words, according to its most ethical and least directional value).

Sense's conduct—or the conduct of sense—makes Being as Being acted by and as Dasein. Dasein is Being insofar as it is at stake as that being which man is. The conduct of sense is thus indissociable from a "liberation of man for the dignity of his *humanitas*" (BW, 225). Dignity (*Würde*) is that which is to be found beyond any assignable value, that which measures up to an action that is not regulated by any given. *Humanitas* needs to be measured against this measurelessness of action, or rather, against action itself as absolute measure. Humanism is inadequate, because it rests on an interpretation of beings that is already given (BW, 225f), in other words, on an interpretation that has already fixed sense (e.g., according to a definition that is Christian, or Marxist, etc.—cf. BW, 225). By fixing sense—the signification of sense—humanism conceals or loses sight of the import of Kant's fourth question, *What is man?*, as a question that is concerned not with a determinable essence of man but with what is more originally in man than man, namely, Dasein as finitude (KPM, §§38–41).

The finitude of Dasein is the finitude of Being as the desiring action of sense. "Finitude," then, does not mean a limitation that would relate man—negatively, positively, or dialectically—to another authority from which he would derive his sense, or his lack of sense. Instead, "finitude" means precisely the non-fixing of such a signification: not, however, as the powerlessness to fix it, but as the power to leave it open.

"Finitude" thus means unaccomplishment as the condition of the accomplishment of action (or that action *is*) as sense. This does not mean "loss of sense," or "sense produced through the mediation of its loss." It means sense itself as "the relation of Being to the essence of man" (BW, 226), that is, that Being is at issue in man, or that man consists in (has his *humanitas* in) the making be of sense, and the making sense of Being, which could therefore never be reduced to a fixing of the sense of Being. For such fixings (significations) to be brought about (to be determined, chosen, and to regulate conducts), Being must still be exposed to—and as—the action-of-sense as such, or as the gift of the desire of/for this action, in other words the *non-given of sense*, which is the very fact of Being as sense—and thus finitude.

This is why "[t]here is and must be something like Being where finitude has come to exist" (KPM, §41). But existence is not the factual given. One could say there precisely is no "factual given" before there is the gift of the "there is" itself. There is no "fact" before the gift of Being, which itself constitutes the gift [*le don*], or the abandonment [*l'abandon*], to sense. Nor is existence *actualitas*, or the entelechy of an essence (BW, 229f). It is "ek-sistence," the way or conduct of Being as Being "outside" of itself, in other words as Being-to-sense, or again as making sense or action. (One could try saying ek-sistence is the entelechy of what is neither essence nor power, but the sense of Being.)

Yet, for all that, one must not think of ek-sistence as an ontological category alien to concrete existence. Just as this word is but a different way of writing "existence," so the structure it designates only takes place right up against concrete existence. What *Being and Time* calls the "facticity" of Dasein (SZ, 56, 135) is doubtless not the "factum brutum" of any "within-the-world" being, nor is it detached from the simple factuality of a concrete existence. The "fact" *that* Dasein *is* in that it is desired as the action of Being takes place *right up against* the fact *that* such and such a concrete man, in each case, exists, and that his "ontical" existence *as such* has the ontological structure of Dasein. In general, that which people have gotten into the bad habit of translating as "authentic" but which is in fact the "proper"(*eigen*, *Eigentlichkeit*) takes place nowhere other than right up against the "improper," right up against everyday existence—and what is more, in the very mode of the improper's "turning-away" in relation to the proper (SZ, 44, 136, etc.;cf. BW, 236). Putting it another way, factual existence is "proximally and for the most part" (SZ, 136) constituted in ignorance of the facticity of sense, which is the ontological fact of existence itself. "The pure 'that it is' shows itself, but the 'whence' and the 'whither' remain in darkness" (SZ, 134). But it is precisely this darkness, in other words this

Being-not-given of sense, that first of all gives access to the proper dimension of sense as what is, in Being and of Being, desired and to be accomplished (acted). In the ordinary impropriety of simple existing, Being's propriety of sense—which consists precisely in a having-to-make-sense, and not in the disposition of a given *proper sense*—both dissimulates *and* reveals itself.

It follows:

1. that ontical existence has, as such, the structure of ontological ek-sisting;

2. and that, correlatively, the fact of Being (of Dasein) has, as such, the structure of making sense or of action.

In its principle, the ethics that thus announces itself refers to nothing other than existence. No "value," no "ideal" floating above anyone's concrete, everyday existence provides it in advance with a norm and a signification. But it is this anyone's everyday existence that finds itself requested to make sense (cf. the celebrated apologue on Heraclitus, BW, 256–57). This request, in turn, emanates neither from a heaven nor from an authority of sense: it is, in existence, the proper request of its Being. Only on the basis of this original request will it be possible for the existent, in its action, to give itself ideas or values—and what is more, this will have *sense* only according to the original action that is at issue in the request.

Hence, this thinking strives to take most rigorously into account the impossibility, which has arisen with and as modernity, of presenting an already given sense, with the evaluations that would be deduced from it. (Although this is not the place, one ought to ask oneself whether this problematic is not in fact that of the whole of philosophy, already present with Plato's *agathon* and first radicalized with Kant's imperative.)

To clarify things, one could say that the ethics that engages itself in this way engages itself on the basis of nihilism—as the general dissolution of sense—but on the exact reverse of nihilism—as the bringing to light of the making sense as action requested in the essence of Being (BW, 248–49). So it also engages itself according to the theme of a total and joint responsibility toward sense and toward existence. (One can only signal in passing the importance of the motif of responsibility. Discreetly explicit, like that of ethics itself, this motif tends toward nothing less than "Being's Being-responsible towards itself, proper Being-its-self" (KPM, §30). The latter, in principle, has nothing solipsistic or egoistic about it but on the contrary contains the possibility and the necessity of Being-responsible towards others.)

So ek-sistence is the way of Being of Being as Dasein (BW, 228). This way of Being is immediately a conduct: the conduct of Being open to making sense, a Being open that is itself opened by (or rather, whose opening consists in) the desire/ability of sense. In that it is thus opened, this conduct is a setting-outside-itself, or ex-position as the very position of the ek-sistent. This Being-outside-itself, or this "ecstatic essence" (BW, 229), does not occur to an already given "self." It is, on the contrary, through it that something like a "self" (a subject, and a responsible subject) can come about. "Ecstasis," as it is to be understood here, is not exaltation beyond the bounds of the ordinary. (Besides, ecstasis as exaltation is not at all, as such, the mark of an accession to authenticity (SZ, 134). This is indeed why the word "ecstasis" also undergoes a modification into "standing-out" (BW, 230).

Being in ek-sistence consists in "Being the there" (BW, 229). *Dasein* must be understood not adverbially and locally (Being there), but verbally, actively, and transitively: Being the there. Hence, *Dasein* is definitely not the name of a substance, but the sentence of an action. "Being there" in fact presupposes the dual prior given of a being and a place. But "Being the there" implies that Being properly ek-sists as its "clearing" (BW, 229). By this "clearing" one must understand not in the first instance an illumination or a revelation that comes and brings Being to light—but Being itself as an opening, a spacing out *for* possibilities of bringing to light (SZ, 170). Being ek-sists (is) in that, as such, it opens Being. The *there* is the open in that, right up against an existence *hic et nunc*, making sense is at issue. The *there* is the place in that, on the basis of it, of its opening, something can take place: a conduct of sense.

The *ek* of ek-sistence is the conduct proper to Being the there in full measure (and it is measure itself, to the extent that there is no ethics without measure), in which by Being the there—by Being *that there is there* an existence—Being is sense. Sense, indeed, is "the structure of the opening" (SZ, 123). But such a structure is not the disposition of a distance (like the given opening of a source, for example, from which sense could spring): it is the activity of opening, or of opening oneself, as making sense. (Let us note in passing that action as opening essentially implies "Being-with-one-another" as its "foundation." The opening of making sense is utterly impossible in a solipsistic mode (cf. SZ, 124). Nevertheless one cannot derive from this the prescription of an "altruistic" morality. What is established is rather that, whatever the moral choice, the other is essential to opening, which is essential to sense, which is what is essential in the action that makes the essence of Being.)

Being is thus essentially a making sense (-of-itself), and one can specify the scope of this expression by considering all of the definitions that have now been acquired. But the fundamental definition is undoubtedly this: the sense that it is a case of "making" is no more a sense that can be assigned according to something other than Being than Being can make sense through the simple positing of a Being there. There is, in principle, neither a simple transcendence nor a simple immanence. If it is legitimate to say, without any verbal acrobatics, that the sense of Being is the Being of sense, this will mean that sense (the sense of human existence, but along with it, of the world) is in principle nothing other than action, or conduct. Conduct is thus the proper transcendence of the immanence that is.

Let us stop here at the objection that will doubtless arise: this sense is thus identical and coextensive with all action, whatever its signification and whatever its value. This supposed "ethics" thus leads to an indifferentism (a subjectivism or a moral relativism), even if that indifferentism is a kind of "morality of action." To this, consider two responses:

1. In fact, the determination of Being as the desire/ability of making sense is ontologically and logically prior to any evaluation of a determinate sense. This is indeed necessary if what is at stake in the first instance is an absolute *dignity* as the character of Dasein. Transposed into different terms, only a subject that is entirely responsible for sense, and for its own existence as making sense, without prior subjection to any fixed sense, can be a fully fledged ethical subject. Nothing else was at stake, already, in Kantian dignity, for which (setting aside the model of a "law of nature"—which precisely is *only* an analogical model) the "universality of the maxim" meant the totality of responsibility, while the condition of "respect" meant engagement by and before oneself as "*acting* self" (KPM, §30). There is no subjectivism in Heidegger any more than there is in Kant. For subjectivism, in fact, evaluative, moral decision making is represented as a good in itself (the "freedom to choose"), the only real "good," already appropriated by every subject as such: fundamentally, subjectivity itself as good. In contrast, the dignity of Dasein consists in needing, in each choice, to engage what can be called, for want of a better term, the objectivity of Being (and, consequently, humanity and the world). It is most remarkable that what is undoubtedly one of the most significant of contemporary ethical investigations in the Anglo-Saxon context, Charles Taylor's investigation into the "ideal of authenticity," is left as though hanging halfway between these two directions. To the extent that it challenges subjectivism but without invoking a transcendent authority, it actually indicates—unconsciously—the necessity of an ontology of making sense. In general, it is instructive to note the extent to which the contemporary Anglo-Saxon debate on the (non-) foundation of morality (between Aristotelian-Thomist proponents of a determinable "good" and liberal proponents of a "justice" between individuals with differing subjective "goods") has at its back, as though unwittingly, the same ontological demand. What is at issue is nothing other than the end of a metaphysico-theological foundation to morality *to arrive at ethics as the ground of Being*. So Heidegger will at least have marked out the particulars of the problem.

2. If no norm or value is yet determined on the fundamental level where what is at issue is the valueless value, the unevaluable dignity of a making-oneself-the-subject (or agent) of possible evaluations, in contrast, one can consider that this immediately indicates a prior

attestation to what can, if one dare say, quasi-orientate action as such: nothing other than the truth of ek-sistence. But one must not fail to recall that this truth takes place right up against existence, or that it is its very event (event and appropriation, *Ereignis*—a theme that cannot be developed here). One might be tempted to say that respect for existence, such is the imperative. But this imperative precisely does not provide sense or value. What it enjoins is to have to make the sense of existence *as* existence. It cannot be reduced, for example, to a "respect for life," as though the sense of life or life as sense were given. On the contrary, talk of a respect for life immediately exposes one to all of the problems of determining what is "life," "human life," how it does or does not differ from "animal life" (or "plant life"), its conditions of recognition, of dignity, and so on. From this one can grasp how all of the problems raised today by "bioethics" as well as by "human rights" bring to light the necessity of heading back toward an ontology of action, not so that they can be resolved once and for all, but so that one can apprehend the absolute making sense of the action that puts itself in the position of having, for example, to decide what *is* a "human life"—without ever having the ability to fix this *Being* as a given that has been acquired once and for all. (We know very well that these considerations are entirely extrapolated from Heidegger, but it is necessary at least to indicate that such an extrapolation, of which Heidegger will doubtless have been unaware, is not only possible but necessary.)

The "proper dignity" (BW, 233) of man, that which does not depend on any subjective evaluation (BW, 251), thus derives from Being's entrusting itself to him by exposing itself as the opening of making sense. Man who is no longer either the "son of God" or the "purpose of nature" or the "subject of history"—in other words, man who no longer is or has sense—is the existent in which Being exposes itself as making sense. One could risk an expression such as man is no longer the signified of sense (which would be man according to humanism), he is its signifier, not in that he designates its concept, but in that he indicates and opens its task, as a task that exceeds all assigned senses of man. "Dasein" means the making sense of Being which exceeds in man all significations of man.

Exposed in this way, Being *is* properly the entrusting to Dasein of the "guarding" of its truth. It is in this sense that man is called "the shepherd of Being" (BW, 234). We must stop here for a moment, since this "pastoralism" has so often raised a laugh or a smile. To be sure, words such as "shepherd," "guarding," and "protective heed" are not free from evangelistic, backward-looking connotations. They evoke a preserving, a conserving of what ought only to be opening and risk. A reactive tone becomes discernible here, in which Heidegger was far from alone in sharing, and which often befalls moral discourses ("preserving values," etc.), as though inaugural dignity, brought to light without any acquired protection, without the reassurance of any given sense, itself needed to be protected, safeguarded. Now what has to be "guarded" is the open—which the "guarding" itself risks closing up again. The dignity of the open might then be substituted by an emblematic value of its guardians, these latter coming to be identified, moreover, in the determinate figures of the "thinker" and the "poet." All of this must pose a problem, and we will need to indicate it. It remains the case that, quite logically, the "guarding" of the "open" can ultimately only be its very opening, without protection or guarantee, and that the pastoral tone must not conceal the indication of an absolute responsibility. Here one doubtless finds the crux of a radical thinking of ethics: in the possibility of confusing original making sense with an assignable origin of sense, or opening with a gift (or again, what is lodged here is the whole ambiguity of the "gift," to which we will return). Thinking the origin as *êthos*, or conduct, is not the same as representing an originary *êthos*, but it is easy to slide imperceptibly from one to the other (the difficulty is not specific to Heidegger and could no doubt, equally be found in Levinas or Spinoza).

However that may be, let us remember for the moment that these same words—guarding, protective heed, the solicitousness of the shepherd—indicate the order of a *conduct*. It is less a case of leading [*conduire*] a flock than of conducting oneself in such a way that "beings might appear in the light of Being" (BW, 234).

But this "appearing" is not the effect of a production. Man does not produce beings, nor does he produce himself: his dignity is not that of a mastery (which, in general, is not susceptible of dignity but of prestige or impressiveness). In fact, "[m]an does not decide whether and how beings appear"; this is a matter for the "destiny of Being" (BW, 234). *That* there is something, and that there are *such* things—*this* world—is not for us to decide. This, then, is given. But what is properly given with this gift, or what is properly the destination of this "destiny" (and without which there would be neither "gift" nor "destiny" but *factum brutum*) is what *is* not, in other words, the Being of beings as the desire/ability of sense. What is properly given—that which Being gives and that which Being gives itself—is the having-to-make-sense of beings and in beings as a whole (their "appearing in the light of Being"). It is in this sense that man is responsible for Being, or that in man, Dasein is the Being-responsible of/for Being itself.

"*Es gibt,*" *das Sein* (BW, 238) is the expression that needs to replace "Being is": "the essence of Being" is an "essence [. . .] that is giving, granting its truth" (BW, 238). What Being gives is Being itself. Being gives of Being. (The) Being (of beings) is thus not a "gift" that it "gives." This is the whole ambiguity of the theme of the "gift," and it is the reason, as we see again, one may prefer "letting" to "giving": Being lets beings be. Being does not "give" anything: Being is the letting be through which something is. Hence their very Being, or their essence, "gives" itself, "lets" itself, or "transfixes "beings as "truth," in other words, as that which opens to sense—and precisely not as a sense or as an appropriable horizon of signification. The "gift" as "gift" is inappropriable, and this is exactly what it "gives"—or "lets" (hence, what we receive as a present does not become our property as something we have acquired; the gift becomes "mine" without alienating its inappropriable essence as gift; for these essential reasons, what is called "gift" here, on account of the idiomatic expression *es gibt*,—"it gives"—cannot designate "a gift"). The gift becomes "mine" without alienating its inappropriable essence as gift. Conversely, and correlatively, what is "let" becomes "mine" without retaining anything of a giver, which otherwise would not *let* be—or let *make*—its own letting be.

This is why it is a case of corresponding to this "gift," or this "letting be/make" as such. It is a case of responding to it and Being responsible for it, of Being engaged by it. It is a case of finding the fitting gesture, the right conduct ("*das Schickliche[. . .], das diesem Geschick entspricht*") (BW, 234) toward the giving or the letting be/make as such. In other words, toward Being: for Being is not, one must insist on this, the giver of the gift (*es* gibt—from whichever angle, there is no owner of the gift as long as, following Heidegger, we retain the motif of the gift, the analyses of it that Derrida has given need to be referred to here). Being is the gift itself, or rather, Being *is* to let be, just as it *is* "the clearing" (BW, 235), which is to say that it ek-sists the existent, so it does not "give" it existence, it *is*, transitively, ek-sisting.

The fitting gesture is the one that "touches" (BW, 235) upon Being. (It would be necessary to develop here the difference between touch as simply a sense, in German *Tast, tasten*, and the *rühren* used by Heidegger, which means more dynamically to stir, affect, move.) If it is a case of "touching" upon Being or of touching it, this is because it is "the nearest" (BW, 235), and it is so insofar as it is the transitivity of ek-sisting. If, in Dasein, Being "is at issue," it is by this intimate nearness—existence touches itself, in other words, it also "moves" itself, sets itself moving outside of itself and affects itself with its own *ek-*. Action, this action of "touching," is thus what is at stake in the Being "which is at issue." (One could also say that the theme of originary self-affection is renewed here, outside the sphere of consciousness and affect, as the theme of an originary *êthos*.)

"Nearness" and "touching" evoke what would need to be called the intimate distance according to which "Being" is related to "the essence of man," in other words, according to which "Being itself is the relation" (BW, 235). Being = the relation of existence to itself as the action of sense. Being, for the existent, is precisely not purely and simply Being there but opening to an accomplishment of sense.

The relation of existence to itself as the opening of sense and to sense is nothing other than the relation of the "improper" to the "proper" (BW, 236). The improper of ordinary existence reveals itself as "improper" in that it has an essential relation with the "proper"—even if it is in the mode of fleeing or avoiding, which means it has a relation with its own "proper" [*son propre "propre"*], with what is most proper and nearest to it, the call to make sense. One could transcribe this as nothing is more ordinary than the call, most often an undeceived one, to the "sense of existence," and nothing is rarer than responding to this call in a fitting ("responsible") way, in other words, without being deceived by a "sense" supposedly given to existence, as if from within or beyond it, instead of confining oneself to the making sense of ek-sisting.

But the rarity of this does not mean, in an oppressive way, that it is a privilege that is reserved for a few or very difficult to obtain: it means that it is of the essence of the sense of Being not to give itself as a laid-down sense (and thus, to repeat once again, not properly to be *given*), and that the dignity of man comes from his Being exposed to this essence of sense as that which touches him most closely of all, that which touches him—or that which he touches upon—but which does not let itself be incorporated, appropriated, and fixed as an acquisition. If sense had been acquired, or what amounts to the same thing, if it were to need acquiring, there would be no ethical possibility. If, however, the action of sense is the exercising of the relation (of the "touching") with what is nearest but cannot be appropriated as a being, then not only is there an ethics, but ethics is the ontology of ontology itself (as for appropriation, it is the event of Being, the *Ereignis*).

"The nearness occurs essentially as language itself" (BW, 236). This essential role of language does not contradict the primacy of action. It is not a case of saying that the exercising of language is the only real action, relegating "practical" actions to second place. Later on we will doubtless have to indicate a certain reservation toward the role that Heidegger entrusts to language, although the potential for countering this reservation lies with none other than Heidegger himself. But first we must situate the place of language as accurately as possible.

Language is not a superior kind of conduct. It is the element in which conduct confirms itself as conduct-of-sense. On the one hand, language experiences sense as what is to be asked or questioned. It is "a questioning that experiences" (BW, 246). On the other hand, what it experiences—the sense of Being, in other words, Being as sense (BW, 240)—it experiences or undergoes as "the *transcendent* pure and simple" (BW, 240). Language responds to Being as the "*transcendens*," but it does not respond to it by assigning the *transcendens*; it responds by co-responding to the transcendence of the *transcendens*, and it thus responds to transcendence by taking responsibility for it. This is how it is itself "the house of Being, which is propriated (*ereignet*) by Being and pervaded by Being" (BW, 236f), in other words, it is, as structure of language, much less a "lodging" for a designated sense than the very *Ereignis* of sense, event-appropriation (desire/ability) of sense (on *Ereignis*, many more developments would be necessary). It is so in that it is properly the element of sense. But it is not the element of sense as a production of significations. It is so in that significations can only ever be signified on the ground of making sense, which is not itself a signification (and which refers perhaps rather to "due silence" (BW, 246).

In truth, "language" designates here much less the order of the verbal (cf. BW, 236) than that on the basis of which this order can take place, and which is, precisely, the experience of transcendence (or more exactly, experience as transcendence, and as its responsibility). Nevertheless, transcendence must be understood very precisely, not as that which might transcend existence toward a pure "beyond" (and which, by

the same token, would no longer pertain to language but to a different experience, a—
let us say mystical—experience of the *transcendens* as such, rather than of transcendence), but as that which structures existence itself into a "beyond," into ek-sistence
(cf. BW, 252, "'world' is in a certain sense precisely 'the beyond' within existence and
for it"). The transcendence (of the sense) of Being is a transcendence of immanence
and for immanence: it is nothing other than the desire/ability of making sense and
this desire/ability *as* making sense.

On this basis, the transcendence of Being can and must be explicitly expressed
as "the original ethics" (BW, 258). Sense, in fact, does not relate the existent to a transcendent signification that sublimates it outside of itself. Sense appears instead as
"the demand [. . .] for an obligating intimation and for rules that say how man, experienced from ek-sistence towards Being, ought to live in a manner befitting his destiny" (BW, 255). Such an intimation is not necessary, because there would need to be
an obligation to enforce a law, about which, moreover, one would still know nothing.
It is, on the contrary, the manifestation of sense as such, as the sense of action. (If
one wants to put it thus, one can say: sense is the law.) Heidegger writes, with regard
to Kant (KPM, §30), "the respect before the law [. . .] is in itself a making-manifest of
myself as acting self," whereas "[r]eason, as free, gives to itself that for which the respect is respect, the moral law." (Let us take the opportunity here to emphasize once
again the importance of the Kantian source. It is as though Heidegger's concern was
to regain the point where Kantian subjectivity frees itself, by itself, from its subjective
foundation (from representation, from signification) and confirms itself as acting, in
other words as exposed to a sense that is not given.)

What *ethics* is here is not the effect of a distribution of disciplines that would distinguish the order of moral significations (values) from the order of cognitive or natural significations ("logics" or "physics") (BW, 255f). "Disciplines" can only find their
place, in fact, as regimes of signification, "after" making sense as such. This latter is
prior to such partitions, and it is so as an "intimation," just as the conduct of existence is prior to any determination of significations. (From which one ought logically
to deduce that all of the discipline orders are "originarily ethical"—the cognitive, the
logical, the physical, and the aesthetic just as much as the moral.)

Êthos needs to be thought of as "abode" (according to Heraclitus's saying *êthos
anthropoi daimon*) (BW, 256). The abode is the "there" in that it is open. The abode
is thus much more a conduct than a residence (or rather, "residing" is above all a
conduct, the conduct of Being-the-there). The thinking of this conduct is thus the
"original ethics," because it thinks of *êthos* as the conduct of/according to the truth
of Being. This thinking is thus more fundamental than an ontology: it does not think
"beings in their Being," but "the truth of Being." It was already in this sense that the
thinking of *Being and Time* "designated itself as fundamental ontology" (BW, 258), so
it becomes clear not only that the thinking of Being involves an ethics but, much
more radically, that it involves itself as an ethics. *"Original ethics" is the more appropriate name for "fundamental ontology." Ethics properly is what is fundamental in funda-*

mental ontology. Nevertheless, one cannot substitute the first designation for the second without risking losing sight of the following, which is essential: *ethôs* is nothing external to or superimposed on Being; it is not added to it and does not occur to it, nor does it give it any rules that come from elsewhere. But Being *is*—because it is in no way a being—what ek-sists the existent, what exposes it to making sense. Being is the ek-sistent conduct of Dasein. This is also why, in preference to any term that might evoke a "moral philosophy" deduced from a "first philosophy," Heidegger retains the expression "thinking of Being," stating that it is "neither ethics nor ontology," "neither theoretical nor practical" (BW, 259).

This thinking "has no result" (BW, 259, 262): it does not give either norms or values. This thinking does not guide conduct; it itself conducts (BW, 260) toward the thinking of conduct in general—not as that which is to be *normed* or finalized, but as that which constitutes dignity itself: having, in one's Being, to make sense of Being. (Besides, if thinking as original ethics were to provide "maxims which could be reckoned up unequivocally," it "would deny to existence nothing less than the very *possibility of acting*" (SZ, 294).

That which is deliberately provocative in the expression "this thinking has no result" requires precise consideration. This expression also amounts to saying that such a thinking is its own result, or "effect" (BW, 259), not because it goes round in circles in the purity of its speculation, but because it is only possible as a thinking (in the manner of all true thinking) insofar as it is itself a conduct, an existential action. It posits and posits itself actively, which is also to say that it obligates itself, to encounter human dignity insofar as this latter is incommensurable with a fixing of signification and a filling out of sense: in other words, ultimately, incommensurable with all "thinking" in the standard sense of the word (idea, concept, discourse). Neither a sense projected indefinitely beyond ("philosophy of values") nor a sense captured and fixed as pure autonomy (subjectivism of free choice) can ensure such a dignity. (Both, moreover, bring about disappointments that are bitter in a different way from that which seems at first sight to emerge from Heidegger's "without result," and this is indeed what is attested to by the contemporary moral confusion, for what it fails to find is both values and free will. But it shows by this that it has no sense of ethics.)

Dignity is possible only if it measures up to finitude, and finitude, as will now have been understood, means the condition of Being of which sense makes the ground and the truth *as making sense.* (Infinitude would be the condition of a Being of which sense would be the result, produced, acquired and related back to itself.) To abbreviate: ek-sistence *is* sense, it *has* no sense.

Existence, for its part, has numerous senses (and non-senses); it can and it must have them, receive, choose, and invent them. Their number and their scope remain incommensurable with the single sense of dignity. *Touching* upon this sense—in other words not absorbing it as a signification, but exposing oneself to it—this is the conduct toward which thinking strives. What marks it as a conduct is that it knows it is conducting itself to the "shattering" that consists in "shattering against the hardness of its matter" (BW, 246). But this is neither a conduct of shattering nor a way "to 'philosophize' about shattering" (BW, 246). It is the conduct that conducts itself to take the measure of the incommensurable interval between every "thinking" (idea, representation, etc.) and the fundamental action that makes it itself think. It takes the measure of the absolute interval, which sense is.

There is nothing mystical about this: what is mystical is the thinking that immediately projects its insufficiency into the sufficiency of a signified effusion beyond itself. But here thinking merely experiences the relation of the improper to the proper as that which is properly to be thought, when it is precisely not an "object of thinking," when it is the gesture of conduct, and more than the gesture, the event of Being that ek-sists as the conduct of sense. What is called "thinking" is thus not a discursive and representational elaboration "on the subject" of this conduct: it is Being engaged in it.

Let us recall briefly how this event of Being is indicated in *Being and Time* as a "call of conscience" (SZ, §§56–57). This call "creates" a "Being in debt" (SZ, 280). The "debt" is neither an indebtedness nor a guilt. It is "a predicate for the 'I am'" (SZ, 281). In this, it is the responsibility (SZ, 282, cf. 127), which is incumbent upon me in that I am "the ground of a negativity" (SZ, 283), in other words, the "ground" of ek-sisting as such. (One might see this as an articulation of Kant in Hegel: the moment of negativity as imperative, and vice versa, which amounts to converting the propriety of the negative of *poiêsis* into *praxis*.) In the terms of the *Letter on Humanism*, one is responsible for the gift as such. *The call or the gift is already by itself an "acting on itself"* (SZ, 288). At the same time, responsibility is not played out between an impersonal "Being" and an isolated "self": there is no "impersonal Being"; Being is rather, if one wants to put it this way, the person-Being of Dasein, or again, in a formulation that would beat the same time provocative and humorous, the personal Being of Dasein (cf. the complex relation to the word "person" (SZ, §10). Consequently, responsibility only ever takes place as responsibility with and toward others (SZ, 288).

Thinking, in its sense of "original ethics," is the experience of this absolute responsibility for sense. Nevertheless, this "experiencing" is not a "feeling" (the word, moreover, is not in the text and is used here only as a provisional recourse). This ethics is no more anaesthetics than it is a mysticism. It is not a case of feeling the sublime sentiment of incommensurable dignity, and the action of thinking does not consist in savoring its mixture of pleasure and pain. It is a case of exposing oneself to the absence of concept and affect (once should think, once again, of Kantian respect—but also, if one rereads the texts closely, of the sublime as *apatheia*), which very exactly makes the articulation of Being as ek-sistence, or as making sense. The intimation of sense, and/or its desire, is without concept and without affect. Or rather, the original *êthos* is the ek-sistent a priori synthesis of concept and affect in general, and it is only in this way that it is not the object but the business of thinking.

Opening oneself to making sense as such, as what is at stake in Being, means at the same time opening oneself to the possibility of evil. For "Being nihilates—as Being" (BW, 261). In other words, strictly speaking, the gift as the possibility/intimation of making sense also gives itself as the possibility of not receiving the gift as gift (without which it would be neither "gift" nor "desire" nor "intimation"—nor what is more properly the synthetic a priori of these three categories). It is not a case of a human "badness" to be denounced (BW, 260), as against the generosity of Being. This generosity itself offers the possibility of the "nothing" in the essence of Being. That does not mean there is no difference between the two antagonistic possibilities, for in that case they could not be called "evil" and "good." It means that evil is possible as the "rage" (BW, 260) that precipitates Being into this nothing that it also is. How can the ek-sisting precipitated in this way into its nothingness be distinguished from ek-sisting exposed to its most proper possibility of sense? Fundamentally, how can one nothingness be distinguished from the other? Heidegger wants at least to make it understood that no distinguishing ("normative") proposition has any real sense if thinking is not firmly upheld in the face of the possibility that making sense might "nihilate," destroy itself as such. No doubt, the tension, which one can detect on reading the text, in the refusal to attempt the slightest determination of evil can have something disquieting about it, to which one would need to return elsewhere. But the following has to be conceded: any determination of evil would leave us in retreat from the necessity of thinking the possibility of evil as a possibility of ek-sistence. It would leave us in retreat from the possibility of Being as ek-sistence.

This is, moreover, what is indicated by the passage in which Heidegger sketches out a recent history of negativity "in the essence of Being" (BW, 261) (revealing "nihilation" to be indissociable from "the history of Being"—or Being as history—which brings it to light in its essential character). He notes that negativity appears in Being with speculative dialectics, but only so as immediately to observe that "there Being is thought as will that wills itself as the will to knowledge and to love": in other words, dialectics sublates evil in this knowledge and this love. In this most recent form of theodicy, "nihilation" remains "veiled in the essence," or again: "Being as will to power is still concealed." So it is as will to power that nihilation has manifested itself without dialectical resorption. One can gloss this indication by thinking of the date of the text, 1946. If Heidegger is not more explicit, it is surely because he refuses to separate the question of Nazism from that of an essential "*Weltnot*" (BW, 170, 265), a distress or deficiency in the modern world, linked to the unleashing of "technics" (which it is insufficient to oppose with a moral protest), which means at least that the modern world—or Being in its most recent "sending"—brings to light, to a harsh light, an unreserved "engagement" of ek-sisting in the complete responsibility for sense (which may mean, moreover, that the demand to which the Nazi engagement was intended to respond was ethical, *and* that Nazism itself revealed itself to be this demand turning over into "rage"). In this, "original ethics" is not only the fundamental structure, or fundamental conduct, of thinking, it also is what is delivered at the end, and as the accomplishment, of the history of "the West" or of "metaphysics." We can no longer refer to available senses; we must take absolute responsibility for the making sense of the world. One cannot ease the "distress" by filling up the horizon with those same "values" whose inconsistency it was—once their metaphysical foundation had collapsed—that precisely let the "will to power" unfold. But this means that the "ground" needs to be considered differently: as ek-sistence.

This is how original ethical conduct encounters its law, its proper *nomos*: the *nomos* of the "abode," in other words, of "upholding" according to ek-sistence (BW, 260). It is a case of upholding oneself and "bearing oneself" in a way befitting the injunction of Being—which is an injunction to be ek-sistent. Conduct, dignity, is a matter of bearing. One must bear oneself: bear up before the responsibility for making sense, which has unfolded unreservedly. Man must understand himself according to this responsibility.

This bearing is above all that of language. "Thinking" action consists in "bringing to language." That which is to be brought to language is not of the order of maxims. These latter, as such, do not need to be properly "brought to language": they are available significations, at least to a certain extent. (To take up that example again, one can express a "respect for life," but that says nothing about what does or does not make sense through "life" and "respect" for it.) The bearing of and in language is nothing other than respect or care for making sense, the refusal, consequently, to reduce it to facile moralizations or aestheticizing seductions (hence, for example, *Being and Time* was able to dismiss interpretations of "responding to the call" as "wanting to have a 'good conscience'" (or as) "cultivat[ing] the call voluntarily" (SZ, 288), which does not rule out the fact that the *Rectoral Address* fell into these traps).

Hence, it is with regard to the bearing of language that the "Letter on Humanism" expresses what are, properly speaking, its only maxims, the maxims of "bearing" itself: "rigor of meditation, carefulness in saying, frugality with words" (BW, 265). This triple maxim does not propose any values, nor is it possible to use it simply for measuring the "ethicity" of a given discourse. The careful—even fastidious—restraint which they evoke, and which for its own part has a whole Kantian (sublime prose) and Hölderlinian tradition, can always just as easily turn into puritanical affectation. The ethics of "bringing to language" cannot be confused with a morality, still less a policing of styles. The triple maxim is merely the maxim of the measure of language in its relation with the unmeasurable of making sense.

This is why Heidegger can take as an example of the "inconspicuous deed of thinking" (BW, 263) the use of the expression "bring to language" itself (which he has just said is to be taken "quite literally" (BW, 262). If we think it, he says, "we have brought something of the essential unfolding of Being itself to language." This means that "bringing to language" does not consist in expressing through words a sense laid down in the thing which is Being (Being is precisely not a thing). It means literally (one ought to say "physically," if one had the time here to explain oneself on this point) *bringing* Being itself, as ek-sisting, to the advent or the event that it is: to the action of making sense. Language makes Being be, it does not signify it. But "making Being be" means opening it to the conduct of sense that it is. Language is the exercising of the principle of responsibility. Hence, saying "man," or the *humanitas* of man—provided one has "bearing"—cannot amount to expressing an acquired value. It will always mean—so to speak—letting oneself be conducted by the experience of a question—What is man?—which already experiences itself as beyond any question to which a signification could give a response. Language is action in that it obligates itself indefinitely to action. "Bringing to language" does not mean entrusting oneself to words: on the contrary, it means entrusting the acts of language, like all acts, to the conduct of sense, in other words to the finitude of Being, the ek-sistence in which "man infinitely exceeds man."

If it is not going too far, we will allow ourselves in conclusion three brief remarks that extend beyond the scope of this chapter. It is not pertinent to develop them here, but it is undoubtedly pertinent to mention them, since it would be lacking integrity not to indicate the perspectives from which it will have been possible to present, here, Heideggerian ethics (perspectives in line, it must be pointed out, with a whole post–Heideggerian elaboration, above all, in France, Italy, and the United States).

1. Unquestionably, Heideggerian ethics is far from stressing "Being-the-there-with-others," which is nevertheless essentially co-implicated in ek-sistence according to *Being and Time*. That sense is or makes sense only in the sharing that finitude also *is* essentially, this is what is, at least, not emphasized, which is no doubt also the reason it will have been possible to treat a "people," without further ado, as an individual. To be rigorous the analysis would need to proceed as far as plural singularity as a condition of ek-sistence. This singularity is not that of the "individual" but that of each event of Being in "the same" individual and "the same" group. Moreover, the singularity of the event of Being also needs to be considered insofar as it affects the totality of beings. It also will be necessary to "bring to language" the Being or the ethical sense of non-human beings. At any rate, "bringing to language" is indissociable from a "communicating" that Heidegger does not linger over. This is not the communication of a message (of signification) but of making sense in common, which is different from making a common sense. It is finitude as sharing.

2. At the same time, the attention given to language—particularly in the form of poetry—is always (above all, in the Heidegger of the writings on language) on the point of privileging as the unique and final (no longer the "original") action a silent enunciation that might prove to have the structure, nature, and appearance of a pure utterance of sense (and not of the "conduct of sense"). Poetry—and/or thinking—

would give sense, even if silently, instead of opening to it. So it is at this precise point, at the apex of the action that "brings to language," that one would need to think how it is the "bringing," bringing Being itself, which is properly action, more than language as such, or how existing exposes itself outside language through language itself, which would take place, in particular, within making sense in common, in other words, through a language that is in the first instance an *address*. (One could say ethics would be "phatic" rather than "semantic." We propose also to say it in these terms: making sense *exscribes* itself rather than inscribing itself in maxims or works.)

The first two remarks amount to saying that "original ethics" still does not think sufficiently the responsibility for its own ex-position (to others, to the world), which nevertheless constitutes its true logic.

3. By claiming the title "original ethics," and by identifying it with a "fundamental ontology" prior to all of the ontological and ethical partitions of philosophy, Heidegger cannot but have kept deliberately quiet about the only major work of philosophy, *Ethics*, which is an "ontology" as well as a "logic" and an "ethics." His silence on Spinoza is well known: it is no doubt here that it is at its most "deafening." There would be a great deal to say about this, but the shortest of observations will suffice: stating that *êthos* is the ek-sisting of existence itself might be another way of saying that "[b]lessedness is not the reward of virtue, but virtue itself" (*Ethics*, V, prop. 42).

Notes

This chapter was translated by Duncan Large.

1. Translator's note: cf. especially Pierre Bourdieu, *The Political Ontology of Martin Heidegger*, translated by Peter Collier (Stanford, Calif.: Stanford University Press, 1996; Cambridge: Polity, 1991); Jürgen Habermas, "Work and 'Weltanschauung,'" in *Heidegger: A Critical Reader*, edited by Hubert L.Dreyfus and Harrison Hall (Oxford: Blackwell, 1992); Jean-Pierre Faye, *Le piège: la philosophie heideggerienne et le nationa lsocialisme* (Paris: Balland, 1994); Otto Pöggeler, *Philosophie und Nationalsozialismus. Am Beispiel Heideggers* (Opladen: Westdeutscher Verlag, 1990); Philippe Lacoue-Labarthe, *Heidegger, Art, and Politics: The Fiction of the Political*, translated by Chris Turner (Oxford: Blackwell, 1990); Jacques Derrida, *Of Spirit: Heidegger and the Question*, translated by Geoffrey Bennington and Rachel Bowlby (Chicago: University of Chicago Press, 1989); Gérard Granel, *Écrits logiques et politiques* (Paris: Galilée, 1990); Nicole Blondel-Parfait, *Théorie et pratique chez Heidegger: histoire d'une erreur*

(Lille: ANRT, 1987); Dominique Janicaud, *L'ombre de cette pensée: Heidegger et la question politique* (Grenoble: Millon, 1990); Richard Wolin, *The Politics of Being: The Political Thought of Martin Heidegger* (New York and Oxford: Columbia University Press, 1990); Richard Wolin, ed., *The Heidegger Controversy: A Critical Reader* (Cambridge, Mass., and London: MIT Press, 1993); Hans D. Sluga, *Heidegger's Crisis: Philosophy and Politics in Nazi Germany* (Cambridge, Mass., and London: Harvard University Press, 1993).

2. Translator's note: Except for two instances of "authenticity," Nancy uses "*propre*" (proper, own, authentic) and its derivations in all cases, where Heidegger uses terms based on the root "*eigen*" (especially "*eigentlich*" and "*Eigentlichkeit*"). The special case of "*Ereignis*" is addressed in the text.

6

The Call of Conscience
The Most Intimate Alterity

Françoise Dastur

Should we consider, as Lévinas does, that there is an unquestioned primacy of ontology in the Western tradition that does not allow us to take account of the other's alterity?[1] We know Lévinas' argument: the other is not a "being" or an "entity," susceptible of being conceptually grasped and understood on the basis of the ontological dimension: such an act would objectify and do violence to the other. What Lévinas names the face is the other insofar as it does not come from me and who calls forth my responsibility. It is this ethical call of the other that fundamentally questions the privilege of Being and authorizes Lévinas in *Totality and Infinity* to attribute the role of first philosophy to ethics and no longer to the science of Being. Indeed, at the end of his book, he declares solemnly that "morality is not a branch of philosophy but first philosophy."[2]

But is there really an incompatibility between ontology and ethics, and must the other be irreconcilably opposed to Being? Does not ontology itself already have a practical and an ethical dimension, which determines it in a fundamental way? Heidegger tells us in his "Letter on Humanism" that the thought of Being is itself "a primordial ethics" (BW, 258), because in accordance with the fundamental sense of the word *ethos*, which signifies abode, a place of habitation, it understands Being as the primordial element of human existence. Thus, for Heidegger, ethics is ontology itself.

But what kind of ontology is this? Of course, this is not the Greek or classical ontology, which posits Being outside or "before" man—what for Heidegger is an ontology of substance, of presence-at-hand, of *Vorhandenheit*, because such an ontology in principle excludes the properly human dimension—but what Heidegger calls "fundamental ontology" in *Being and Time*. Such a fundamental ontology grounds all claims about "Being" on the relation of man to Being and understands man as this particular entity who is not indifferent to Being, who questions—first in a practical way, prior to theory *in a philosophical context*—his own Being as well as other beings. He does this precisely because he is not "given" to himself, indeed, because he has to be his own Being, to "become what he is"—in a word, because he exists and can only exist as his own project. It is clear here that ontology for Heidegger is not without a practical dimension: it does not give priority to pure seeing, to pure *theoria*, but on the contrary to the "practical" freedom of existence. Such an existence unfolds historically as a relation to self and to the other, and such a relation constitutes humanity.

For Heidegger, "ontology" thus understood is always "practical," always "engaged," and thus bears an intrinsically ethical dimension. This is doubtless the reason Heidegger has not written on ethics: because he surely does not need "to add" it on to an ontology that would then itself be conceived only as a part of philosophy. Here it is implicit that he thinks Being in a way that is different from the tradition—which identifies Being with substance. Heidegger, like Lévinas, is critical of the Western tradition. His thought unfolds "beyond" or at the "end" of philosophy, as he clearly lets it be known after the "turn."

Do we really have to choose between Lévinas, who asks us to contemplate "otherwise than Being," and Heidegger, who leads us to another way of thinking about Being? Moreover, is it possible to think without opposing Being and the other? It seems to me that Ricoeur takes up this question in the last pages of *Oneself As Another*, pages in which I see the culmination of the dialectic of otherness and selfhood that constitutes the most fundamental level of his hermeneutics of the self, a hermeneutics that wants "to hold itself at an equal distance from the Cogito exalted by Descartes and from the Cogito that Nietzsche proclaimed forfeit."[3]

This dialectic of otherness and selfhood—whose "the main virtue" is to keep "the self from occupying the place of foundation" (OA, 318)—cannot be raised to the properly speculative level of the meta-categories of the Same and Other without keeping the hermeneutic dimension of truth (*alêtheia*). This dimension can only be conceived of in terms of the implication—and not in terms of the exteriority—between the interpreter and the interpreted. This dialectic is without doubt what profoundly prevents considering the tenth chapter of *Oneself As Another* as constituting a truly superior degree of interpretation, that would have thus attained a level of independence relative to his preceding nine analyses. But such an independent speculative ontology would in principle fail to account for an alterity that can only be given according to the dimension of attestation and that is by definition disparate and broken. In this respect, the ironic tone of the last page of *Oneself As Another* (356) in no way appears to be a simple evasion. Ricoeur effectively invokes Socratic irony and plagiarizes Plato's *Parmenides* in alleging that only the kind of discourse that leaves the various modalities of alterity in a state of dispersion belongs to the very idea of alterity itself, "under penalty of otherness suppressing itself in becoming the same as itself." The refusal to make alterity an inclusive meta-category—that is, a genre—does not depend on Ricoeur's decision to leave the three modalities of alterity (which invoke the three great experiences of passivity: one's own body, the Other, and conscience)[4] in a state of dispersion, nor is it to pose a question mark after ontology as he does in his tenth chapter, precisely titled, "What Ontology in View?" (OA, 297). On the contrary, this refusal is implied by the very type of ontology that is here proposed—and "engagement" is its essential dimension. This engagement places the finitude of the interpretative look at the heart of a project that can only be defined as an ontological *approach* and never as a systematic construction. At the onset, we understand why Ricoeur opposes the shortcut of the Heideggerian analytic of *Dasein* and calls forth a longer way of interpreting existence, one that passes through the detour of the epistemological question. This is why, from this perspective, Ricoeur already emphasized in *The Conflict of Interpretation* that ontology remains "a promised land," only glimpsed: "In this way, ontology is indeed the promised land for philosophy that begins with language and with reflection; but like Moses, the speaking and reflecting subject can only glimpse this land before dying."[5]

Here is where the reference to another hermeneutic of the self seems to arise, the Heideggerian hermeneutics of care. Perhaps it is necessary to briefly recall that if for Heidegger ontology is something else than a promised land, this is not because finitude is overcome, but on the contrary because ontology is, as he clearly says in the Davos lecture, the "index of our finitude."[6] For "ontology requires only a finite creature" (GA 3, 252;KPM, 175), and what within us properly testifies to the necessity of interpretation, of the projection of a horizon of understanding, is the fact that we have to welcome the at once frightening and marvelous alterity of a being at the origin of which we are not and which is also among other things—ourselves.

According to Heidegger, his whole project focuses on a task that Kant had already taken up: the elaboration of an analytic of *Gemüt*, that is, the determination of the self as a "receptive structure" (OA, 354) for the other than oneself, and it is in this perspective that he rejoins with the Aristotle of the *Nicomachean Ethics* just as much as with the Aristotle of the *De Anima*, who says that the soul is in some ways all things, a phrase that Heidegger cites at the beginning of *Being and Time* to testify to the ontic-ontological privilege of *Dasein*, and which makes the latter the condition of possibility for all regional ontologies (BTa, 19).

A careful rereading of *Kant and the Problem of Metaphysics* would show that it is the Kantian theory of pure sensibility, that is, a sensibility that pre-forms what it is prepared to receive, which leads to seeing in time (as self-affection) the very structure of the *selfhood* of a finite subject (GA 3, 183;KPM, 120). This selfhood can no longer be understood according to the substantial model of the self but must essentially be defined as care. Above all, care is alone this capacity of self-solicitation or self-address, the *Sich selbst-angehen* that allows the assignation to receptivity: "*angewiesen auf Hinnahme*," says the German text of the *Kantbuch* (GA 3, 129–30;KPM, 183). It is the implication of *Sich-selbst-angehen* with *Angewiesenheit*, of self-concern with assignation, that thus defines what Heidegger terms *Existenz*: "Existence means dependency upon the being as such in the submittance to the being as such which is dependent in this way" (GA 3, 156;KPM, 222).

One clearly sees here that if care is always self-concern, "care for oneself"—Heidegger explicitly says that "care for oneself . . . would be a tautology" (BTa, 237)—this

could not be understood as a closing in of the self: "'Care' cannot stand for some special attitude towards the Self; for the Self has already been characterized ontologically
by 'Being-ahead-of-itself,' a characteristic in which the other two items in the structure of care—Being-already-in . . . and Being alongside . . . —have been *posited as well*"
(ibid.).

Only by misunderstanding the existential sense of care, which implies reference
to the other, would one want to replace self-affection with the "hyperbole" (Ricoeur's
term) of a hetero-affection, which would have as its presupposition the "exteriority"
of the other of which Lévinas speaks. Ricoeur clearly states that, "By hyperbole, it
must be strongly underscored, we are not to understand a figure of style, a literary
trope, but the systematic practice of excess in philosophical argumentation" (OA,
337). And, after having analyzed how for Lévinas, both in continuity and in rupture
with Kantian ethics, the other absolves itself of all relation and absolutizes itself, he
concludes: "In truth, what the hyperbole of separation renders unthinkable is the distinction between self and I, and the formation of a concept of selfhood defined by its
openness and its unveiling function" (OA, 339). A pure hetero-affection is in effect
as unthinkable as a pure self-affection. One can indeed chastise Heidegger for having
too unilaterally placed the stress on self-affection up until 1929, and of thus only
defining Being as the self-projection of *Dasein*. But the meaning of the "turn" (which
unfortunately Lévinas does not make much of) is to think more profoundly still
about finitude and to open thinking to "the event" of the co-appropriation of Being
and man, that is, a thinking of the encounter as simultaneity of the call and response.

To come back to the period preceding the turn, it should be said that if finitude
(i.e., receptiveness) has come to exist, as Heidegger declares in *Kant and the Problem
of Metaphysics*,[7] self-affection only occurs in view of this eminent capacity of hetero-
affection that characterizes man and distinguishes him from animals. Animals are
not open to being as such, because they are not open to themselves as non-substi-
tutable singularities. Animals cannot say "I," but if man says it, if existence is in each
case mine—in the distributive sense of *Jemeinigkeit*—this is because this being which is
man is not "indifferent" to his Being (BTa, 68), and that non-indifference is a concern
for what is most proper to *Dasein*, namely, its death, which cannot be relieved by anyone. The "self" in oneself only arises through death, which explains why Heidegger
was able to write *sum moribundus*, the I is always in the process of dying, is dying. As
he says in his course of the summer semester of 1925: "If such pointed formulations
mean anything at all, then the appropriate statement pertaining to Dasein in its being
would be *sum moribundus* ["I am in dying"], *moribundus* not as someone gravely ill or
wounded, but insofar as I am, I am *moribundus*. *The* MORIBUNDUS *first gives the* SUM *its
sense* (HCT, 31).

But it must be added that this hermeneutics of care, insofar as it is a hermeneutics of finitude and mortality, is a hermeneutics of attestation. This is effectively a
hermeneutics of the self understood, not as a representational self, as Kant would
have it—that is, according to the dimension of an exclusively theoretical reason—but

as an essentially active and responsible self. And in this regard there is no doubt that the concept of care (*Sorge*), which itself has a noble tradition,[8] should be brought together with the Aristotelian *praxis*, as Ricoeur emphasizes, in stressing the works of Franco Volpi and Jacques Taminiaux (OA, 311). This is because the essentially temporal structure of self-affection necessarily carries a teleological sense: all behavior presupposes a "towards which," an *Umwillen*, which always concerns the Being of *Dasein* (BTa, 115) and which refers just as well to the Aristotelian *eu zên* as the Kantian *Endzweck*.

But by the same token, this implies that responsibility be understood as a constitutive structure of a being that understands itself only by responding for itself, assuming responsibility for itself, since its facticity, far from being assimilable to the *factum brutum* of a natural being, must on the contrary be understood as that which constrains Dasein to assume responsibility for its own Being. It is a question of a *Faktizität der Überantwortung* (BTa, 174), the facticity of Dasein being delivered over to itself, as Heidegger clearly stipulates. In his reading of Heidegger, Patocka often stressed this ontologization of responsibility that will later allow Heidegger, in his "Letter on Humanism," to see primordial ethics in ontology itself. But Patocka does not see an "ethical elision" here (this is the expression Ricoeur uses to characterize Heidegger in a 1988 interview);[9] on the contrary, he sees the abolition of the modern distinction between the representing subject and the acting subject, "the fatal distinction which is in part responsible for the false moralism of modern times and which motivated Nietzsche's attacks against morality."[10] In any case, it is clear that this ontologization of responsibility demands that fundamental ontology pass by way of *Bezeugung*, by way of attestation.

One cannot be content to remain at the *ontological-existential* level, this secondary level of philosophic speculation (*meta*-level, Ricoeur would say), without raising—in relation to it—the suspicion of a purely artificial construction. It is therefore necessary to go back to the level previously bracketed, the *existentiell-ontic* level. To get back to the existentiell-ontic level is not, however, to appeal to facts and experience insofar as these would be considered facts of nature to be described, in terms of what Heidegger calls *Vorhandenheit*. But one could invoke another kind of fact here, what Kant in the second *Critique* calls "fact of reason" (*faktum der Vernunft*),[11] and for him this would be nothing other than the conscience of the moral law that imposes itself upon us. This "fact of reason," insofar as it is a metaphysical fact, resists any description, because it includes within itself the dimension of the constitutive attestation of *Gewissen*, of moral conscience.

In the same manner, Heidegger seeks the attestation of a potentiality of being oneself in a "*Faktum*," a fact recognized by common conscience, since it derives from the everyday self-explication of *Dasein*: the voice of conscience, *die Stimme des Gewissens*. But this fact is not a natural *Tatsache*, a fact of nature, since its reality is rightly subject to controversy—it is essentially suspect, Ricoeur would say. And like him, Heidegger sees in the "ambiguity" of this fact the proof that this is an original phenomenon of Dasein, because only that which needs to be attested and not pre-sented as a fact of nature can also be contested following this strict logic according to which the dimension of belief and faith is inseparable from doubt. Ricoeur force-fully emphasizes that this vulnerability of attestation follows upon its practical and nontheoretical essence, with the fact that the discourse of attestation is not a foun-dational discourse (OA, 22), and that it consequently calls for continually renewed "practical" confirmations.

It should be stressed[12] that for me what makes for the paradigmatic character of moral conscience, insofar as it is an experience of alterity and passivity, is that the di-mension of attestation primordially constitutes it directly, that it is inscribed in it. What in fact is moral conscience? In French, the word *conscience, cum scientia*, to which it is not always necessary to add the adjective "moral" to distinguish it from psychological consciousness—[*conscience*]—is perhaps in a sense more precise than the word in German, *Gewissen*, which rather refers to the notion of certainty, because it recalls the Greek *syneidêsis*, and especially because it preserves the trace of the *cum*, of the *syn*, of the "with" that implies a relationship to alterity. In Greek, *synoida* has the sense of "knowing with another," "being complicitous with," and also "being a witness of," just as much as knowing oneself, knowing oneself from within. This in-terior knowledge thus supposes in some way that one makes oneself witness to one-self, perhaps in what should be called in German *Mitwissen* rather than *Gewissen*. But this witnessing of oneself demands that this Being-with-oneself be experienced in a rigorous dissymmetry, and this is brought forth by the call of the voice of conscience. To quote Ricoeur:

> In this intimate conversation, the self appears to be called upon and, in this sense, to be *affected* in a unique way. Unlike the dialogue of the soul with itself, of which Plato speaks, this affection by another voice presents a remarkable dis-symmetry, one that can be called vertical, between the agency that calls and the self called upon. It is the vertical nature of the call, equal to its interiority, that creates the enigma of the phenomenon of conscience. (OA, 342)

And a little earlier it was a question of "this unprecedented passivity" for which "the metaphor of the voice, at once inside me and higher than me, serves as the symptom or the clue" (OA, 342).

What is here essential for the verticality of the call (which constitutes the self as self)—that is, within the self-affection through which selfhood occurs, in the imma-nence of the self—is a breach of transcendence (i.e., the dimension of hetero-affec-tion). But this union of incompatibles, of self-affection and hetero-affection, comes forth as the voice, as the call: "Here is found the feature that distinguishes the phe-nomenon of conscience, namely, the sort of call (*Ruf*), of appeal (*Anruf*), that is indi-cated by the metaphor of the voice" (OA, 342). And Ricoeur quickly points out the necessity of thinking about the unveiling capacity of metaphoricity in referring back to the analysis of the seventh chapter of *La métaphore vive*, which ends with the idea of "metaphorical truth."

A little further, after passing the test of suspicion, called for by the metaphorical character of conscience itself—which designates conscience as "bad conscience," in Hegel and Nietzsche—Ricoeur returns to Heidegger and emphasizes that the latter has the merit of separating off conscience from the false alternative of a good and a bad conscience, in not referring it to some capacity for distinguishing good and evil "in themselves" that the voice of conscience would allow us to know. He says, "We are all the more attentive to Heidegger's analysis as we owe to him the starting point of this entire discussion of the metaphor of the voice" (OA, 348). Thus, for Heidegger, there is a truth to the "metaphor" of the voice that is related to the fact that the voice "says" nothing and thus, against neo-Kantian value theory and Scheler's material ethics, conscience is placed, in a perfectly Kantian fashion, "beyond good and evil." Because even for Kant, and this is what explains the formal character of the imperative, good and evil cannot be determined prior to the moral law. Kant declares this in the second *Critique*: "The concept of good and evil must not be determined before the moral law (of which it seems as if it must be the foundation), but only after it and by means of it." [13] This "paradox," in Kant's own terms, is at the foundation of the notion of autonomy, since heteronomy is characterized precisely by the fact of separating the good from the will and of making it the object of the will and not the form of the will. Consequently, it seems to me that Heidegger's position, which consists in depriving all content from the silent call of conscience, remains within the strict line of Kantian thought.

For Heidegger, then, the phenomenon of conscience points back to the idea of autonomy: "In conscience Dasein calls itself" (BTa, 320). Here we find the very identity of the caller and the called, of the agent and the patient, which had already characterized the phenomenon of anxiety. In the structure of the call, we find the threefold temporal structure of care: the one who is called is the fallen *Dasein*, captivated by the world in the present; the one who calls is *Dasein* in its pure facticity, Dasein as being-thrown, who is in the past; and that to which it is called is the authentic *Dasein*, which projects itself insofar as it is authentically being-toward-death in the future. It is thus because it does not call for this or that, but uniquely to *be, according to another mode, or to will otherwise,* that the call has a formal character, just like the Kantian imperative.

Nonetheless, we have to conjugate the identity of self-affection as autonomy with the foreignness of the call, and this will effectively enable us to go beyond the simple dialogue with oneself: "The call comes *from* me and yet *from beyond me and over me*" (BTa, 320). This foreignness is precisely that of a self who is not primordially "at home" but who is always already thrown in the world. It comes, as Ricoeur emphasizes, from the radical passivity of a being who is not his own origin and who is thus, with regard to himself, in the position of receptivity. *It follows that facticity itself gives rise to the superiority of the call (which inscribes alterity in the very heart of the*

self), and which thus makes every autonomy at the same time a heteronomy. It should be
noted in this respect that it was Heidegger who reminded Cassirer (who seemed to
forget this) at Davos that the Kantian imperative only makes sense for a finite being,
and that it is intrinsically inscribed in its very constitution. To Cassirer, who sees
Kantian ethics as the overcoming of finitude, Heidegger remarks, "I believe that we
proceed mistakenly in the interpretation of Kantian ethics if we first orient ourselves
to that to which the ethical action conforms, and if we see too little of the inner
function of the law itself for Dasein "(GA 3, 175;KPM, 251). In his interpretation of
the *Critique of Pure Reason*, Heidegger specifically wants to show that for Kant, the
infinity of the ontological understanding of being remains principally tied to ontic
experience.

Now this strange union of the ontic and the ontological, of infinity and finitude,
and of immanence and transcendence, occurs within the voice and as voice. It is this
latter trait that I would like to emphasize. Heidegger insists on the fact that one must
take everyday discourse literally: "Characterizing conscience as a call is not just giving
a 'picture,' like the Kantian representation of conscience as a court of justice" (BTa,
316). Here there is no metaphor for Heidegger but, on the contrary, a genuine experience of what voice is. This is because it is not essential that discourse be phoneti-
cally articulated to be language (*Sprache*), and because voice (*Stimme*) does not in
German have the purely vocal sense of the Greek *phônê*, but rather a juridical sense,
that of giving one's judgment by a vote. This is why Heidegger emphasizes that "the
'voice' is taken rather as a giving-to-understand" (BTa, 316). Thus there can be a
silent voice, which does not speak, as a pure phenomenon of comprehension, a pure
phenomenon of meaning, just in the same way there can be an understanding, which
is not reduced to simple acoustic perception.

One can ask if what one understands by meaning does not always presuppose
this dissymmetry or temporal noncoincidence with oneself, which is experienced in
the call, or if meaning should not be essentially placed in relation with temporality.
This also is what Merleau-Ponty says in *The Prose of the World*; "in any language at all
there is nothing but understandings," and that "the very ideas of a complete expression and of a signifier that would exactly cover the signified are both inconsistent,"
since "the meaning is beyond the letter, the meaning is always ironic."[14] Voice here
does not signify immediate self-presence: on the contrary, it reveals that the self is not
intimate with itself, or at best, only exists in the noncoincidence between two voices,
everydayness and conscience—and that it only knows itself as a "proximity in the distance" with itself or as a partial coincidence.[15] The silence of the call, its formal and
nonphonetic character, is thus to be inscribed within the dimension of a selfhood
that exists always according to the mode of a promise of oneself, that is, according to
the mode of a constancy of oneself, of a *Selbt-ständigkeit*, which has nothing to do with
the substantiality of an ego.

Could we speak as Ricoeur does of the "de-moralization of conscience" (OA,
351, tr. modified) with regard to Heidegger? It seems to me—at least this is what I

have tried to show in making the parallel between Kant and Heidegger—that this could only be done from a Hegelian point of view—which is certainly a legitimate one—that is, through a critique of the *moralische Weltanschauung*, the "moral world-view." Hegel also insists on the fact that the abstract Kantian morality is the very principle of immorality, that is, that any immoral or unjust conduct could be justified on the basis of the definition of duty as a simple, formal agreement with oneself.[16] In this regard, the critique of resoluteness, as a "resolve to nothing," addressed to Heidegger, curiously recalls the critique of the beautiful soul, the Kantian *schöne Seele*, which is characterized by Peguy's often cited and strikingly brief phrase, "Kant has clean hands, but he does not have any hands."

Nevertheless, this critique should be taken seriously, since it shows that for Heidegger, like Kant, moral realization is problematic—and doubtless more so for Heidegger than for Kant, precisely because for him practice is no longer distinguished from theory, and additionally, thinking seems to constitute the whole of morality. Does not Heidegger effectively claim at the beginning of the "Letter on Humanism" that "thinking acts insofar as it thinks," and that "such action is presumably the simplest and at the same time the highest, because it concerns the relation of Being to man"? (BW, 217). What finally allows us to distinguish Kant's interpretation of conscience from Heidegger's is the status of the "you must," of the second person imperative, which is not delineated *as such* for Heidegger. This is why Ricoeur's asking that the phenomenon of attestation be closely tied to that of the call (OA, 351) constitutes the transition to a real ontology of action. Thus the passivity of the being called is decisively related to another alterity, the alterity of the Other (the alterity of *aliud*), which appears within the constitutive alterity of the self (the alterity of *alter*), which is for Heidegger essentially temporal.[17]

That the alterity of the Other appears within the alterity of conscience does not mean that they are identical. And it is precisely on this point that Ricoeur distances himself from Lévinas by questioning his reductive move (OA, 354). Ricoeur sees in Lévinas a reduction of the alterity of conscience to the exteriority of the Other, and for Ricoeur, this parallels the Heideggerian reduction of being-guilty to the uncanniness of the facticity of Being in the World. Ricoeur proposes an alternative between Heidegger's uncanniness and Lévinas' exteriority. He proposes a third solution, one that anticipates the very structure of selfhood within the Being-called. This is why he severely criticizes the Lévinasian "phenomenology of separation," in which he sees rather a "phenomenology of egotism," marked by the hyperbolic stamp that leads Lévinas to make statements of such a kind: "In separation, the ego ignores the other" (TI, 34). Ricoeur also emphasizes that the hyperbole of the absolute exteriority of the other takes a paroxystic turn when, in order to affirm an unconditioned assignation of responsibility, Lévinas goes all the way to say in *Otherwise Than Being or Beyond Essence* that "selfhood in its anarchic passivity of identity is hostage."[18] What the hyperbole of an absolute heteronomy renders unthinkable—carving out an abyss between identity and alterity—is precisely what Ricoeur wants to bring forth, namely, selfhood as a welcoming structure of the other, an other who is no longer "scandalously" identified as an offender or as a persecutor.

The double response that Ricoeur gives to Lévinas, on the one hand, that the call is primordially attestation, and to Heidegger, on the other hand, that attestation is primordially a call, seems to me to constitute a strict fidelity to a hermeneutics of the self, which is authentically a hermeneutics of finitude. This is because such a hermeneutic refuses the speculative ease with which we always tend to generalize—that is, to generalize and thereby erect alterity into a homogenous genre. For Ricoeur, it is a question of "the need to maintain a certain equivocalness of the status of the Other on the strictly philosophical plane." This is why *Oneself As Another* ends with the phrase: "With this aporia of the Other, philosophical discourse comes to an end." That there is an aporia of the other (OA, 355) is perhaps ultimately what the philosopher has to contemplate, because his discourse comes to an end: he is mortal, he is incapable of totalization, that is, he neither knows absolutely what there is about the Other, nor does he absolutely understand himself with the help of the meta-categories that serve as the traditional philosophical themes of speculation.

To resonate with Ricoeur's final remarks, but also with the primordial ethics of Heidegger, I conclude by saying that the philosopher also should be capable of remaining silent on the subject of ethics, for such a silence is perhaps exactly what makes possible an opening to a *practical* ethics.

Notes

This chapter was translated by David Allison and Emily Lee.

1. This is a revised and an updated version of a text published in French in *Paul Ricoeur, L'herméneutique à l'école de la phénoménologie* (Paris: Beauchesne, 1995), and in German in *Der Anspruch des Anderen*, edited by B. Waldenfels and I. Därmann (Münich: Fink, 1998).

2. E. Lévinas, *Totality and Infinity*, translated by Alphonso Lingis (Pittsburgh: Duquesne University Press, 1969), p. 304. Hereafter cited as TI.

3. Paul Ricoeur, *Oneself As Another*, translated by Kathleen Blamey (Chicago: University of Chicago Press, 1992), p. 23. Hereafter cited as OA.

4. OA, 355.

5. Paul. Ricoeur, *The Conflict of Interpretations*, translated by Kathleen McLaughlin (Evanston, Ill.: Northwestern University Press, 1974), p. 24.

6. "[. . .] for ontology is an index of finitude. God does not have it. And the fact that the human being has the *exhibito*, is the strongest argument for its finitude, for ontology requires only a finite creature." See GA 3, 252;KPM, 175. One finds in

this fourth edition the *Davoser Vorträge* and the *Davoser Disputation*, in which Heidegger and Cassirer debated in April 1929, just prior to the publication of the *Kantbuch*.

7. GA 3, 222;KPM, 156: "*Dergleichen wie Sein gibt es nur und muss nur geben, wo Endlichkeit existent geworden ist*" ["There is and must be something like Being where finitude has come to exist"].

8. It would doubtless be necessary to trace its geneology beyond Seneca and the Stoics all the way back to the preoccupation with death (*meletê thanatou*) which is philosophy itself for Plato in the *Phaedo* (81a), in *The Collected Dialogues of Plato*, edited by Edith Hamilton and Huntington Cairns and translated by Hugh Tredennick (Princeton, NJ: Princeton University Press, 1985).

9. See interview with P. Ricoeur in "A quoi pensent les philosophes?" in *Autrement* 102 (November 1988): 175.

10. See Jan Patocka, "Heidegger penseur de l'humanité," in *Epokhè* 2 (1991): 389ff.

11. I. Kant, *The Critique of Practical Reason*, translated by Lewis White Beck (New York: Bobbs-Merril, 1956), p. 31.

12. This is the reason for the superlative in my title: *the most* intimate alterity is, in accordance with one of Ricoeur's own phrases, an awareness of "*the most* deeply hidden passivity" in contrast with other passivities—for example, the experience of one's own body and of one's relations with others (OA, 318).

13. Kant, *The Critique of Practical Reason*, Book I, Chapter 2 (p. 154).

14. M. Merleau-Ponty, *The Prose of the World*, edited by Claude Lefort and translated by John O'Neill (Evanston, Ill.: Northwestern University Press, 1973), pp. 29–30.

15. To say this in terms borrowed from Merleau-Ponty, referring to the experience of another passivity and alterity, the flesh.

16. Cf. G. W. Hegel, "The Moral Vision of the World" in *Phenomenology of Spirit*, translated by A.V. Miller (Oxford: Clarendon Press, 1977). See also G. W. Hegel *Philosophy of Right*, translated by T. M. Knox (Oxford: Clarendon Press, 1967), § 135.

17. Let me refer to my article in "Le temps et l'autre chez Husserl et Heidegger," in *Alter*, Revue de Phénoménonologie, ENS, no. 1 (1993).

18. E. Lévinas, *Otherwise Than Being or Beyond Essence*, translated by Alphonso Lingis (Dordrecht: Kluwer Academic Publishers, 1991), p. 180.

The "Play of Transcendence" and the Question of Ethics

Jean Greisch

The considerations in this chapter are tied to ideas I developed in the second part of my essay, "The Great Game of Life and the Overwhelming."[1] The textual basis has remained the same: Heidegger's winter semester 1928/29 Freiburg lecture course *Einleitung in die Philosophie*. The frame of inquiry, however, has changed. It is not my concern here to discuss the thematizing of the question of God in Heidegger's concept of a "metaphysics of Dasein," but rather to pursue the question concerning his relation to the problem of grounding a philosophical ethics.

Many skeptics would object that this is a hopeless undertaking. Is not every attempt to make Heidegger's fundamental ontology fruitful for a meditation upon the foundation of ethics comparable to a trek through the desert? To this objection I would like to oppose the title of a Walt Disney film: *The Living Desert!* Or less colloquially, How is one to understand Heidegger's thesis in the last Marburg lecture course that the "metaphysical isolation of the human" in no way issues out into a solipsism, but that precisely the "existential solipsism," which §40 of *Being and Time* speaks of, itself makes possible an existential understanding of being-with-others? Naturally, I am well aware that fundamental questions of this type are miles away from the questions of a content-based ethics. Nevertheless, a concern for such preparatory questions is worth the trouble.

In order to lend further precision to the "hermeneutical situation" here staked out, I mention two authors who openly or silently have influenced my reading of Heidegger's lecture course. On the one hand, behind my interpretation stands a concern with Paul Ricoeur's projected "hermeneutic of the self" in *The Self As an Other*. In this respect, my question is, briefly put, the following: Can the dialectic of sameness [*Selbigkeit*] and selfhood [*Selbstheit*] developed by Ricoeur—and along with this the dialectic of selfhood and otherness, especially decisive for Ricoeur's determination of the task of ethics—be grounded in Heidegger's analytic of Dasein and fundamental ontology?

On the other hand, and perhaps still more decisive, in any case more demanding, in the background of my questioning stands the Levinasian concept of a fundamental ethics that claims to occupy the place of "first philosophy." Is the "entanglement of alterity" set up by Levinas as ethical ground structure, that is, the structure of "being-for-the-other" ("*l'un-pour-l'autre*"), wholly and entirely incompatible with Heidegger's understanding of Dasein and of Being, or not?

The following meditation upon a few central themes of Heidegger's lecture course seeks to follow the contour of these two main questions.

Prelude [Vorspiel]:
Being-with-Others As Essential Structure of Dasein

By introduction, the general frame of inquiry in the lecture course is briefly to be recalled. The concern in this "Introduction" is to lay open an existential access to philosophizing and then to advance to an essential conception of philosophy by a double meditation on the difference between philosophy and science [*Wissenschaft*], on the one hand, and philosophy and worldview [*Weltanschauung*], on the other hand. The following thesis forms from the outset the basis for all of these considerations: "We do not philosophize then and when, but constantly and necessarily, insofar as we exist as humans [*Menschen*]. . . . To be a human [*Menschsein*] means already to philosophize. Already and according to its essence, not opportunely or inopportunely, the human Dasein as such stands in philosophy" (GA 27, 3). That philosophy so understood is no mere "knowledge of wisdom" (GA 27, 25) has to do with the "innermost essence of philosophy, for the longest time not grasped in its central function": its finitude. "This is not thereby conceived such that one in apparent modesty and with a certain emotion finally admits that our knowledge would be a patchwork. Philosophy is not for this reason finite [*endlich*], since it never comes to an end [*zu Ende kommt*]. The finitude does not lie in the end, rather at the beginning of philosophy; this means that finitude in its essence must be taken up into the concept of philosophy" (GA 27, 24). The metaphysic of Dasein is accordingly a philosophy of finitude in a marked sense.

The unfolding of the first question, that is, the quest after an existential understanding of science, leads Heidegger just as quickly to the question of an original essence of truth, and thereby to a meditation on the position of Dasein in relation to truth. The task of the philosopher consists in bringing simple insights to expression, such as the insight into the fact that the conception of truth as judgment is in no way false, but nevertheless fails to grasp the original essence of truth as unconcealment. Once the insufficiency of propositional truth is recognized, then the task of an adequate description of the phenomenon of truth presents itself. This presupposes that behind the much-touted subject-object-relation the more original phenomenon of "being with," in the sense of "residing with" [*Aufenthaltes bei*], comes into view.

At the same time, it is necessary not only to differentiate distinct types of beings, that is, to order them along a hierarchical stepladder, but to differentiate distinct ways of Being. With this a new light falls on the unique privilege of the human way of being: "Dasein exists, and only it. Only the human [*Mensch*] has existence" (GA 27, 71). For our question, what is important is that Heidegger's discussion of the ontological difference of the distinct ways of being proceeds from two extreme poles: on the one hand, the being-present-at-hand-together of the multiple things of the world (illustrated by two boulders) and, on the other hand, the social [*mitmenschliche*] being-with-another (illustrated by two hikers who observe the two boulders). In this context, Heidegger comes to speak for the first time on the relation to others, wherein he makes the following fundamental clarification: "Now as for beings which have our type of Being—since we are just as much not ourselves as rather each is the other, another Dasein—the Dasein of another is not simply present-at-hand next to us with perhaps still other things in-between. Rather, another Dasein is there with us, Dasein-with; we ourselves are determined through a Being-with the other. Dasein and Dasein are a with-one-another" (GA 27, 84–85).

Only a phenomenological attitude is able to hold fast to the essential difference between the two ways of Being, for language here plays a similar trick upon us of leveling the difference, as in the realm of the copula. The same particle "next" [*neben*], in regard to its linguistic application, can be applied just as well to two houses as to two humans. One house stands "next" to another; one can speak just so of a human and his or her neighbor ["*Neben*"-*Mensch*]. Only the sharpened essential insight of the phenomenologist recognizes that the neighboring-human [*Nebenmensch*] in the first place is a fellow-human [*Mitmensch*], and that the prefix "with-" is only applicable to the relation of two beings whose mode of Being is existence. Correspondingly, Heidegger stresses: "Only what is itself Dasein is able to be there with us [*mit-dasein*]" (GA 27, 85). Otherwise said: only one who understands what Dasein means can understand what constitutes the existential sense of "with." Consistent with this, Heidegger states: "Dasein-with [*Mit-dasein*] means not only: being also at the same time, even simply qua Dasein, but rather the mode of Being of Dasein first brings authentic sense to the 'with.' 'With' is to be grasped as participation [*Teilnahme*], whereby foreignness as participationlessness is only an alteration of participation. The 'with' therefore has an entirely determined sense and does not mean simply 'together,' nor the being-together of such that have the same mode of Being. 'With' is a proper [*eigene*] way of Being" (ibid.).

The scope of this thesis is obvious. It first makes understandable why the neighboring-human is already a fellow-human, whereby this original with- and being-with-one-another is in no way derivable from a factical being together. Now an advocate of Levinasian ethics may object that being-*for*-another is still more original than being-*with*-one-another. This objection is to be taken extremely seriously. It should nevertheless not mislead one into false consequences, so that one would play the *for* against the *with*. The sole legitimate question in my eyes consists in asking oneself whether or not the ontological understanding of being-with-one-another blocks off the way to an *ethical* being-*for*-one-another, or conversely whether being-with-one-another can be derived from being-for-another. In any event, one must keep in sight the breadth of the Heideggerian "with," which is quite capable of containing the moment of abandonment and of being delivered over to the other, or of "being held hostage by the other" in Levinas' hyperbolic manner of speaking.

Nevertheless, it is to be admitted that from the outset, Heidegger's discussion of being-with-one-another does not at all move out upon the field of ethics. The reason for this is that the guiding question of the first part of the course is that of the original concept of truth, decisive for the determination of the relationship between philosophy and science. This explains why being-with-one-another first comes into focus as the "self-comportment of several to the same" (GA 27, 89). The thesis that being-with-one-another itself signifies "comporting in the same way to" will be regarded as a diversionary tactic by the contemporary ethicists sworn to alterity. Further still, it also poses for a modern ethics the problem of taking part or participation, as Ricoeur shows in the example of distributive justice, and which Heidegger investigates in a more aletheiological context. In this respect, one may rightly ask whether the insight that sameness in opposition to mere identity consists in something that "is the same for several" (GA 27, 97) cannot also be made fruitful in the field of ethics. Just as worthy of consideration is the manner and way in which Heidegger sets the thought of taking part (i.e. participation) over and against the splitting up of a thing (somewhat like the proverbial Sunday cake in the familial realm!): "To take part in something [*sich . . . teilen*] without it thereby being split into pieces [*zerteilen*] means: to leave something over for mutual use and enjoyment" (GA 27, 100). At most, one could object that in the field of business commodities at least, parting [*Teilen*] and dividing [*Zerteilen*] are inseparably bound up with one another!

For our considerations, the thought immediately following this one also is important; the just depicted leaving-over presupposes a definite composure [*Haltung*], which Heidegger determines as "the letting be of things," that is, "Leaving the things over to themselves" (GA 27, 102). This composure is grounded in what Heidegger calls the "original indifference [*Gleichgültigkeit*] of Dasein" (GA 27, 108) which, according to his view, belongs to the metaphysical essence of Dasein. Here, too, many ethicists will smell a misjudgment of basic ethical relations. For this reason it is especially important to take into consideration the statement in which Heidegger declares the ground of possibility for this indifference. Far from saying that it would be synonymous with carelessness or lightheartedness, that is, ethically understood, with a lack of responsibility—otherwise put, that it would add grist to the mill of the cynical cry "*Après nous le déluge!*" ("After us the deluge!")—it says exactly the opposite: it "is only possible in care" (GA 27, 102). For this reason Heidegger underlines that the "allowance [*Lässigkeit*]" which letting-be [*Seinlassen*] indicates is in no way to be equated to a reckless failure to commit oneself: "The allowance in this leaving over is no mere failure to do something" (GA 27, 102).

Of course, the question remains open as to how far this "metaphysical indifference to things" (GA 27, 103) can be carried over to the relationship with fellow-humans. Must one not here speak of a "metaphysical non-indifference [*Ungleichgültigkeit*] to the other"? Precisely with this question in view one should consider how Heidegger determines care in relation to the fellow-human: as *solicitude!*

Heidegger's account of being-alone furnishes an important reference for further considerations. The very experience of being-alone (of growing isolation in all material and psychical forms) shows just how little indifferent the other actually is for Dasein. "Being-alone always means being without others. In this without-others, one who exists alone is necessarily and by essence certainly in a definite sense related to others" (GA 27, 117). Only for this reason can solitary confinement in an isolation cell be perceived as a heightened punitive measure. Conversely, one can say: "If being-alone qua without another is essentially a being-with-one-another, then there also lies in solitary Being alongside the present-at-hand a being-with-one-another" (GA 27, 118). In this way, incidentally, Heidegger manages to found an intersubjective concept of truth—unconcealment signifies "necessarily and essentially a sharing [*Sichteilen*] in truth" (ibid.)—without thereby troubling himself over the concept of a so-called "communicative reason."

At the same time Heidegger's understanding of being-with-one-another makes possible an overcoming of that which he names the "fundamental error of solipsism." This consists in not taking the experience of being-alone seriously enough, or otherwise put, in overlooking that "every 'I alone' as solitary is already with-one-another. Only because the I is already with others is it able to understand an other. But it is not the case that the I would at first be an individual without others and then by some puzzling way would come to be with-another" (GA 27, 119).

What is striking in this expression is that here the question of being-with-one-another is immediately bound up with the question of understanding the foreign [*Fremdverständnisses*]. Can this statement be carried over into other contexts, where it concerns recognition, the acceptance of the other, or even the overtaking of responsibility from the other? Perhaps one could tie the question to the following already addressed alternatives—which suffix grants us the best access to the other: the "before" (Kierkegaard: *coram*), the "with" (Heidegger), or the "for" (Levinas)?

Heidegger's answer to this question we find in §18 of the *Einleitung*: "The 'with' is only there where a 'there' [*Da*] is," that is, "the one-another is a with-one-another" (GA 27, 137). Only ecstatically understood Dasein can actually found the relation to the other. How so? Because the "there" in Heidegger's understanding is equivalent to an "out of here [*heraus*]." "The way and manner that Dasein is by itself is essentially co-determined by the way that, as a being by itself, it is just as essentially stepping outside" (GA 27, 138).

This seems to me the crucial point for a confrontation with Levinas' critique of Heidegger. The picture that Levinas paints of Heideggerian Dasein is that of a being who is at first at home by itself and only later enters into relation with others. Against this, Levinas insists that the other breaks into the sphere of ownness of the self-masterful I, unasked and uninvited, and accusingly forces himself upon the I, putting the I into the accusative.

To this, I would like to bring two arguments to Heidegger's defense.

1. On the one hand, Heidegger himself emphasizes that every Dasein "as essentially stepping-out has also already stepped into the openness of the other" (GA 27, 138). A representative of the Levinasian thesis would surely object that Levinas' position is thereby stood on its head. For Levinas, the I is not the intruder in the sphere of the other. On the contrary, the other imposes itself upon the sphere of ownness. Further, one would have to ask how the idea of the "openness of the other" presents itself for Levinas: it is the "epiphany of the face." With this a different understanding of truth underlies the conflict between the two positions. However, one should observe how Heidegger precisely in this context accuses all philosophies of consciousness and reflection (including Husserlian phenomenology) with simultaneously under- and over-determining the essence of subjectivity. The under-determination is that the self-founding and self-determining autonomous subject of modernity does not require the other in order to achieve its self-understanding. At least at the level of understanding, it has enough in itself. The over-determination is that the lacking relation to the other must be compensated for, (i.e., overcompensated for) through a theory of intersubjectivity, or more modern still, of "communication." In my mind herein also lies Heidegger's most important objection against dialogical personalism: The I-you-relation comes too late if it must found that which is the basis of its possibility: the being-with-one-another, which at all times determines the self as a self with-and-for-the other.

2. Further, one can link the objection of self-relational being-by-oneself to yet another argument. Heidegger himself emphasizes that his metaphysic of Dasein finds its most important predecessor in the Leibnizian monadology. According to a well-known sentence, often cited by Heidegger, the monad needs no windows. Why so? Because it is a "living mirror of the universe." To demand that the monad should require windows in order to step into contact with the outer world is just as absurd as to demand that a mirror should put on glasses in order to see better. Heidegger's Dasein, too, has no windows, because

it needs none. Nevertheless, Heidegger's grounding is fundamentally different from the Leibnizian, because it is the "index of a totally other essential determination of the subject": human beings, understood in a manner appropriate to Dasein, require no windows, "not because they do not need to go out, rather because they are essentially already outside" (GA 27, 144). It is this "outside" which likewise forms the site of the true encounter of self and other. The way and manner that Heidegger and Levinas determine this "outside" (or this "exteriority") decide the possibility or impossibility of an encounter between the Heideggerian metaphysic of Dasein and the Levinasian conception of ethics.

Dasein As Transcending: What Type of Transcendence?

For our further considerations one should not overlook the fact that Heidegger's meditation upon Being-with-one-another ends in the admission that the "interpretation of the essence of Being-with-one-another [is] not yet exhausted" (GA 27, 148). A second important starting point for our inquiry is associated with considerations tied to the determination of letting-be as "originary practice [Urhandlung] of Dasein" (GA 27, 112, 183, 199). These are considerations of the transcendence of Dasein, which expresses itself in an understanding of Being [Seinsverständnis] (GA 27, 205). This connection has its basis in the fact that ontological truth is grounded in the transcendence of Dasein. Thus the meditation upon the relationship between science and philosophy likewise concludes with a modified version of the starting thesis: "The human Dasein as such philosophizes; to exist means to philosophize. Dasein philosophizes because it transcends. In transcending lies understanding of Being" (GA 27, 214). But what are we to understand by transcending?

We begin with a philological observation. The existential significance of the technical term transcendence is reflected in three expressions: "project, elevation, over-stepping" [Entwurf, Erhöhung, Überstieg]. "In the preceding project of Being we over-step beforehand, always already, the particular being. Only on the ground of this elevation, of such an over-stepping, are beings revealed as beings. But insofar as the project of Being belongs to the essence of Dasein this over-stepping of beings must occur, and occur in the ground of Dasein" (GA 27, 206).

We stand here before a central claim of Heidegger's that bears upon all further considerations. For this reason we must attend as carefully as possible to Heidegger's language, which reflects his understanding of what I call the "meta function." The triad Project—Over-stepping—Elevation requires a close reading. How is the association of the three terms justified? Is "project" necessarily and in all conditions equivalent to an "over-stepping"? Further, does the concept of over-stepping contain the thought of "elevation," that is, must the movement of transcendence be understood unconditionally as "trans-ascendance"? The latter concept was coined by Jean Wahl[2] and taken up again by Levinas in emphasized departure from Heidegger.[3] Particularly informative is the clarification of this principle that Levinas used to introduce the second edition of *Existence and Existents*, where the same concept appears again in slightly modified form. Here, in significant allusion to the Platonic thought of the superiority of the good over essence (*epekeina tês ousias*), the essence of transcendence is determined as "excendence" ("*excendance*"). In the context of our considerations, it is worth citing the corresponding passage. As an echo of the Platonic motif of the *epekeina tês ousias*, Levinas writes: "It signifies that the movement which leads an existent toward the Good is not a transcendence by which that existent raises itself up to a higher existence, but a departure from Being and from the categories which describe it: an *ex-cendence*. But excendence and the Good necessarily have a foothold in being, and that is why Being is better than non-being."[4]

A similar consideration in regard to the expressions "project" and "over-stepping" can likewise be made. The question bound up here can be very well illustrated by the problem of metaphor. It is not entirely by accident that this example urges itself upon me. As is known, Heidegger,[5] Derrida,[6] and Ricoeur[7] have each in his own way pursued the question of the affinity between the metaphysical meaning of the prefix "*meta*" and the rhetorical, as well as the poetical, determination of the "metaphorical" use of an expression. According to Aristotle, it is the carrying over of sense from a literal meaning to a figurative one that constitutes the essence of metaphor. It remains to inquire whether the surplus or expansion of meaning associated with this possesses a purely ornamental function or whether, on the contrary, metaphor here stands in the service of a better and deeper understanding of reality. In the former construal, "metaphor" serves only the purposes of beautification; it possesses no epistemological value but rather only a conversational value; in other words, it is a luxury of speech. The alternative to this is propounded by many more recent theorists of metaphor and followed by Ricoeur in his own hermeneutical determination of "metaphorical truth." From here, one could perhaps even throw a bridge to Heidegger's concept of "world-forming" [*Weltbildung*].

If one adopts this perspective, which opens the way for an ontological determination of metaphor, one is then able to clarify by the phenomenon of metaphor and without difficulty the meaning of the two first terms, namely, "project" and "over-stepping." In addition, it also is to be noted that there arises here the possibility of understanding metaphor not purely linguistically but also existentially. The capacity to over-step the literal meaning also has something to do with the understanding of freedom and the ways and means by which Dasein deals with reality. Either we submit to a monolithic understanding of the reality-principle or, in the light of a play-space, we understand our relationship to reality as indeed more limited, but not for all that as a set of possibilities codified once and for all.

Is the third basic meaning of transcendence, namely, elevation, also included in this existential and ontological understanding of metaphor? Otherwise put, does it suffice to understand the essence of metaphor as a broadening of sense, or are we permitted to speak of an over-heightening of sense [*Sinnüberhöhung*], that is, of a sublimation? This question is pursued by Stanislas Breton[8] in a meditation upon the medieval commentaries to the biblical *Song of Solomon*, and he has shown the significance in play here of an upswing onto a higher level of sense. In this manner, a philosophical interpretation of metaphor obtains not only an "ontological" but also a "metaphysical" dimension. Breton proposes a theory of metaphor that takes into account the aspect of elevation by marking the difference between the "metaphoric" and the "metaphoral."

After this excursus, I return to Heidegger's determination of transcendence. In his eyes, ontological truth, which stands under the sign of the previous project of Being, has for its part the ground of its possibility in over-stepping. Relying on a Kantian use of language, Heidegger adopts the concept "transcendental" as an indication of this state of affairs. Of course, one cannot overlook that Heidegger's concept of the transcendental claims to be "more basic, more original, and more expressive" than Kant's (GA 27, 207). Everything previously said can be summarized in the following thesis: "Ontological truth (unconcealment of Being) is for its part only possible if Dasein, according to its essence, is capable of over-stepping beings, that is, as factically existing has always already over-stepped the particular being. Ontological truth is grounded in the transcendence of Dasein; it is transcendental. The transcendence of Dasein however does not exhaust itself in ontological truth" (GA 27, 209). The closing sentence of this thesis is particularly noteworthy, insofar as it immediately forces the question as to which features of the transcendence of Dasein go beyond ontological truth. Does it merely concern recognizing on the pre-ontological level the transcendence of Dasein as already self manifesting, or does there open here, to take up the title of Levinas' second major work, a view onto the "beyond" of Being and essence?

However one answers this question as well, the way leads by necessity to a meditation upon the ontological difference, as Heidegger's eleventh summary thesis emphasizes: "The transcendence of Dasein is the condition of possibility for the ontological difference, that the difference of Being and beings can break open at all, that there can be this difference. But here too, the essence of transcendence does not exhaust itself" (GA 27, 210).

Looking back on the guiding question of the first part of the course—how can the relationship between philosophy and science be determined?—the following fundamental decision is also made: "What gives light to science, in the sense of the manifestness of beings, at the same time moves it into the dark—in the sense of the concealment of Being. The relative light of the scientific knowledge of beings is crowded around by the darkness of the understanding of Being" (GA 27, 213). Conversely, it holds for philosophy that precisely this darkness of the understanding of Being constitutes its life-element. The twelfth thesis, in which the first part of the lecture course comes to its close, deepens this insight: "Transcending is philosophizing, whether it occurs inexpressively concealed or if it becomes expressly grasped" (GA 27, 214). Or, more memorably: "The human Dasein as such philosophizes; to exist means to philosophize. Dasein philosophizes because it transcends. In transcending lies understanding of Being" (GA 27, 214).

The Great Game of Life and the Play of Transcendence[9]

What does the second part of the lecture course, which concerns the clarification of the relationship to world-view [*Weltanschauung*], provide for our question? To start with, the remark that world-view in comparison to science presents a complex phenomenon is important (GA 27, 200). The concept of world-view is inseparably bound up with life-view [*Lebensanschauung*]. Given this, the phenomenon cannot be handled at the level of pure representation but encounters at the very least the equally difficult problems of acting [*Handelns*] and value orientation [*Wertorientierung*]. Consequently, if world-view forms the background foliage for all acting and effecting, insofar as it is "the effecting and direction giving force of Dasein itself" (GA 27, 234), the question concerning its ethical implications immediately poses itself. The expression "view" [*Anschauung*], in the compound word "world-view," by no means indicates for Heidegger a purely theoretical or representational attitude but rather a "composure [*Haltung*] of Dasein, and indeed such a one that bears and determines Dasein from the ground up, in the way that Dasein sees and knows itself as posed in this composure to beings as a whole" (GA 27, 234). This also is the reason the determination of the concept "world-view" requires a "radical interpretation of Dasein's understanding of Being" (GA 27, 235).

Just as important is the shift in meaning that the concept "world" undergoes in the expression "world-view." It also requires an "original essential interpretation of the phenomenon of world" (GA 27, 239), so that behind the cosmological significance (recognized by early Christianity but later supplanted), an existential meaning must be rediscovered and newly considered.[10] The decisive hint for Heidegger's considerations is provided by a sentence from one of Kant's lectures on anthropology in which the "man of the world," well versed in "worldly knowledge," is designated a "co-player in the great game of life." For Heidegger there is no doubt that "the great game of life" refers to life-experience [*Lebenserfahrung*], that is, existentially understood to "the human Dasein as such." As a result there arises the possibility of a new existential determination of the concept of world: "World: the title for human Dasein, and this in regard to what is going on with Dasein, the play of the with-one-another of humans in their relation to the particular being. Word: title for humans, and precisely not as a member of the cosmos or a thing of nature, but rather in his historical connections to existence" (GA 27, 300). Does this new concept of world, which explicitly considers the play of the with-one-another of humans, that is, the "play and pursuits of humans as world" (GA 27, 303), grant new insights into the presuppositions of ethical action, or does the essential determination of Dasein as

"Being-in-the-world" (GA 27, 305) directly obstruct the horizon for the posing of ethical questions?

The answer requires a deeper working out of the concept of transcendence. Up until now the goal of the transcending step-over has remained undetermined. Now Heidegger says that in over-stepping Dasein does not step over the world but rather thereby first "comes to the world: Transcending means Being-in-the-world" (GA 27, 307). The reverse holds too; the selfhood of Dasein first constitutes itself in this movement of over-stepping: "This, upon which the essentially transcending Dasein transcends, we name world. In stepping-over, however, Dasein does not step out of itself such that it would equally leave itself behind, rather it not only remains itself, but precisely first becomes it" (ibid.).

This sketch of the genesis of selfhood appears at first glance to only strengthen the suspicion that not the other but rather the world is the womb of selfhood. Nevertheless, one cannot overlook that the "world," which is here spoken of, and that which the play metaphor indicates, is not that of nature cosmologically understood but the "world of Dasein" to whose essential constitution belongs "Being with others" (GA 27, 308). The other in Heidegger's understanding of world is thus no "spoilsport" ["*Spielverderber*"] in the "great game of life, entirely the opposite: without him this game loses all sense!"

Only proceeding from here is one able to properly understand why Heidegger in §38 of the course, which forms its heart, once again takes up the Kantian metaphor and gives it a Dasein analytical and even metaphysical significance. The transition from the anthropological-pragmatic application of the metaphor to its transcendental application is completed in three steps.

The Play Character of Dasein

One can only speak of a "game of life," as indicated by the human's colorful multiplicity of world behaviors [*Weltgebarens*], if one recognizes that a "play character" lies in the essence of Dasein (GA 27, 310). In passing, it is to be noted that a comparison with Gadamer's concept of play as developed in the first part of *Truth and Method* shows just how very far Heidegger is from a "natural" and romantic notion of play.[11] This "play character of Dasein" can be rightly understood only in a transcendental attitude, and not in a pragmatic one. In other words, "We play not because there are games, but rather the reverse. There are games, because we play, and indeed in a broad sense of playing, which does not necessarily express itself in a self-preoccupation with games" (GA 27, 312). The concept of play, so broadened, obviously circumscribes much more than the two basic anthropological characteristics of play: a determinate type of activity in compliance with the corresponding rules of a game. Herein lies the novelty of Heidegger's concept of play over and against the cultural-anthropological one of Johan Huizinga (*Homo ludens*) and the sociological description by Roger Caillois (*Les jeux et les hommes*).

The "Transcendental Play": The "Interpretation of Transcendence As Play"

The distance from the anthropological concept of play increases still further when one links play with the concept of transcendence, whereby it obtains a metaphysical sense: "'World' is the title for the game which transcendence plays. Being-in-the-world is this original playing of the game which every single factical Dasein must attune it-self to [sich einspielen muß] in order to be able to play itself, that which will be facti-cally so or so played with Dasein for the duration of its existence" (GA 27, 312).

In view of this statement, the bad Levinasian conscience of many a reader of Hei-degger will voice itself and ask whether precisely in this determination of transcen-dence every possibility is lost [verspielt] to recognize the relationship to the other as metaphysical originary fact [Urfaktum]. Otherwise asked: Is the fellow human as part-ner [Mitspieler] in the great game of life recognized in his or her radical alterity or straightway and completely misunderstood?

"Understanding of Being As Play": Beyond the Limit of "Onto-logic"

Before we pursue this question we must attend to a last consequence of the "interpreta-tion of transcendence as play" (GA 27, 323), which necessitates us to speak of a "tran-scendental play" (GA 27, 314). Heidegger is concerned at first to unhinge the usual opposition between play and reality. Understanding of Being now means so much as "to play the game, to game [erspielen], to be trained in these games" (GA 27, 315). Only in this manner is the ground provided for an ontology related to the understanding of Being, one not mistakable for a logical conceptuality. Of course, the attempt to over-come the "logical" narrowness of the understanding of Being by the concept of play ex-poses itself immediately to the suspicion of arbitrariness. For the logician, the just-mentioned formulation is a monstrous and an unreasonable demand; the fact that "the understanding of Being [is brought] upon the teetering ground of a game" (GA 27, 318) appears to amount to renouncing rationality. Nevertheless, in Heidegger's eyes, the overcoming of logical control neither signifies a defense of irrationalism nor leads to a falling back into life philosophy [Lebensphilosophie] (GA 27, 330).

Does not the thesis of "transcendence, qua understanding of Being, as game" also present an unreasonable demand for the ethicist? Heidegger parries the objec-tion of arbitrarity at first with the reference that the game is indeed a "free forma-tion," but at the same time is "the formative binding of oneself to and in the playing formation itself" (GA 27, 316). The development of the understanding of Being is therefore not entirely unbinding. Does this mean, though, that the suspicion of eth-ical obligationlessness is truly expurgated?

What Is at Stake in the Play: Self-Responsibility As Condition of Possibility for Ethical Responsibility

In order to find an answer to the question just posed, we must examine §37 more closely, where Heidegger sets as his goal the "winning of a concrete understanding of transcendence." This concretization of the concept of transcendence against the back-ground of the metaphor of play develops in many steps. In my eyes these steps are of particular importance, as they at least partially weaken Levinas' reproach that Heideggerian ontology is a philosophy of self-pronouncement, power, and injustice[12]: being-set-before-oneself, abandonment, and thrownness are the main characteristics that make possible a new determination of the concept of facticity in the frame of the "metaphysic of Dasein."

The Prize [Preis] of Selfhood: Abandonment [Preisgegebenheit]

The first positive result of the ontological deepening of the concept of play consists in the fact that it enables the essence of selfhood to be determined independent from the categories of philosophies of consciousness and reflection. When Kant determines the *personalitas moralis* as "the purpose [Zweck] of itself," this means for Heidegger that Dasein "is put into play" (GA 27, 325), that is, is "brought before itself and full selfhood" (GA 27, 324). With this the question immediately poses itself as to what belongs to "full selfhood" as its "guideline and task" (GA 27, 325). Heidegger emphasizes quite forcefully that an individualistic-egoistical understanding of selfhood, one that disregards Being-with-others, would be "the grossest misunderstanding of the problem" (GA 27, 324). Does this mean, to take up a formulation of Paul Ricoeur's, that alterity belongs to the innermost constitution of selfhood? Yes and no. Yes, insofar as Being-with others belongs to the "full severity of Dasein's being posed before itself." No, insofar as Heidegger does not take into consideration the more strident Levinasian hypothesis that Dasein first comes to itself by being posed before the other. In his eyes there exists an irreversible relation between *Being-delivered-over-to-oneself* [Selbstüberantwortung] and ethical responsibility [Verantwortung] for the other: "Dasein must essentially be able to be itself and properly [im eigentlichen] be itself, if it wants to know itself as borne and led by an other, if it is supposed to be able to open itself for the Dasein-with of others, if it is supposed to stand up for the other" (GA 27, 325). This statement pointedly shows that in Heidegger's understanding the self keeps the initiative in the "great game of life." The other comes into play only insofar as it bears and leads Dasein (in something like the forms of parental care or political responsibility) or as the object of the ethical "unfolding" of the self.

If in this context the talk is of a "severity of struggle" (GA 27, 325) then this means that "full selfhood" must be fought for: this is the primary and at the same time "ethical" task! Here Heidegger once again takes up the motif of an "accentuation [Zugespitztheit] of the self" from his early Freiburg lecture courses. For the confrontation with the Levinasian concept of ethics, the emphasis upon the motif of "the abandonment of Dasein to beings" (GA 27, 326) is particularly important, for with this the suspicion of a philosophy of power and a hidden *conatus essendi* is weakened. In abandonment (which obviously also includes being delivered over to the other!) the constitutive powerlessness of factical Dasein expresses itself "not in the sense of a mere knowledge [Kenntnis], but rather, since Dasein has essentially stepped out of itself, it is abandoned to the particular being and its overwhelming power [Übermacht], and indeed not only the overwhelming power of something like natural forces, but also the powers and violences which Dasein as a particular being harbors in itself" (GA 27, 326).

This ontological determination of abandonment is just as far from every pessimism as it is from every optimism. Nevertheless, Heidegger stresses, it is incompatible with a "universal kindness and honesty." It would be just as much an inversion to play the motif of struggle [*Kampf*] against love. In this context, Heidegger offers the following thought-worthy comments: "I doubt whether that which the philosophical men of convention [*Biedermänner*] secretly believe and what one there terms love encounters the metaphysical essence of the thing named. In the end, the petty feelings which one explains by this name are surely far from the mark. It remains to be asked whether every great love, which alone announces something of essence, is not at bottom a struggle—not first and foremost a struggle over the other, but rather a struggle for him—and whether love does not increase to the degree that sentimentality and the coziness of feelings decreases" (GA 27, 327).

Exposure and Thrownness

Up until now, the essence of abandonment was only considered from the extreme perspective of "being exposed." For Heidegger's understanding of selfhood, however, it is just as important that we take into consideration the internal perspective in which Dasein is thoroughly determined, defined, and "thoroughly ruled [*durchwaltet*] by the beings to which it is abandoned" (GA 27, 328). This internal aspect indicates the concept of "thrownness" by which the "powerlessness" of Dasein becomes still more poignant: "No Dasein exists on the basis of its own decisions and resolutions" (GA 27, 339). No one is stronger than one's attunements: no ethic can forget this basic fact, which prevents in advance every voluntaristic narrowing of conduct. Here, too, Heidegger deals more deeply with the ontological presuppositions than with the ethical consequences of the concept of thrownness. It concerns mainly the "nullity" [*Nichtigkeit*] and finitude of Dasein, which play a decisive role in the concept of a "metaphysic of Dasein."

The prominent point of our considerations, and at the same time the ultimate consequence of the transcendental expansion of the concept of play, lies in the recognition that being-in-the-world signifies an original "lack of bearing" [*Halt-losigkeit*]: "To be put into play, i.e., being-in-the-world, is in itself a lack of bearing, that is, the existing of Dasein must provide itself its bearing [*Halt*]" (GA 27, 337). This bearing-lessness is not to be mistaken for a moral judgment of value; on the contrary, everything depends on one's recognizing that Dasein, precisely because of the transcendental play, is not "factically, but rather metaphysically and according to its essence without-bearing [*Halt-los*]" (GA 27, 342). For this very reason, Dasein is fundamentally dependent upon bearing [*auf Halt angewiesen*]. Equally impossible to overlook are the ethical implications of this thesis: precisely that over which Dasein is not master—an illness, an accident, a physical handicap, or a stroke of fate—cannot be taken simply as a fact of knowledge; rather, it must be "worked through" and "survived": "Also that which does not arise of one's own express decision, as most things for Dasein, must be in such or such a way retrievingly appropriated, even if only in the modes of putting up with or shirking something; that which for us is entirely not under the control of freedom in the narrow sense, an illness or certain predisposition, is itself never something simply present-at-hand, but rather something that is in such or such a manner taken up or rejected in the How of Dasein" (GA 27, 337).

Here it becomes clear that the transcendental concept of play simultaneously and in an original sense constitutes the play space of ethics, that is, the space of freedom, without an oblivion of its limits: "that by its own decision Dasein has nothing to search for in the direction of its origin, gives an essential prod to Dasein from the darkness of its origin into the relative brightness of its potentiality-for-Being. Dasein exists always in an essential exposure to the darkness and impotence of its origin, even if only in the prevailing form of a habitual deep forgetting in the face of this essential determination of its facticity" (GA 27, 340).

Postlude [Nachspiel]: Dasein's Metaphysical Lack of Bearing and the Dependency upon Bearing [Angewiesenheit auf Halt]

Let us cast a concluding glance upon the closing part of the lecture course, in which Heidegger applies the concept of transcendence to the problem of the relationships between philosophy and world-view. Important for our considerations are the ways and means by which Heidegger knots together the concepts of transcendence and truth: "Bearing-lessness, which lies in transcendence, is . . . always dependant upon holding oneself [Sichhalten] in the truth" (GA 27, 342). With this it is clear from the outset that metaphysical bearing-lessness has nothing in common with a postmodern relativization of truth. Nevertheless, truth as "making manifest" shows different faces in accordance with each type of being that it concerns: in relation to the present-at-hand, it means "dominance," in relation to existing-with, "acting" [Handeln], in relation to being a self, "resoluteness to one's self" (GA 27, 343). "Dasein . . . is world-view, and this necessarily" (GA 27, 345). In Heidegger's presentation, everything depends on the recognition of how two fundamental possibilities of world-view are rooted in the play character of transcendence.

On the one hand, the experience of being delivered over to the overwhelming power [Übermacht] of beings, that is, of being thoroughly mastered by this overwhelming powerfulness [Übermächtigkeit] (GA 27, 358), corresponds to the mythic conception of Being. Never was unconcealment more sharply experienced than here. For this very reason, the experience of concealment or of a sheltering in beings as a whole must overcompensate for this unconcealment: "Bearing is found in the overwhelming power of the particular being itself; it is that which grants both bearing and concealment" (GA 27, 360). Heidegger indicates that from here decisive insights open up into such essential phenomenological contexts [*Wesenszusammenhänge*] as veneration, rites and cults, prayer, morals and customs, and the need for protection. At the same time Dasein proves itself as the place of the unconditioned, or otherwise put, of the divine. "Dasein always has in itself in its existence a determinate idea of the divine, even if it be only of an idol" (GA 27, 360).

On the other hand, a second fundamental possibility of world-view is contained in the "play character of transcendence" (GA 27, 367): equiprimordial with the experience of bearing [*Halt*] as a sheltering is there the possibility of bearing as composure [*Haltung*], which has its bearing "primarily in self-possession [*Sichhalten*] itself" (GA 27, 366). If everything up until now stands under the sign of "mightiness [*Mächtigkeit*] as holiness," the expressed comportment now leads to overwhelming powers [*Übermächten*], to the "Dasein's confrontation with these in everything within its essential relations."[13] Only against this background is the possibility given for a "choice of itself in resolution to itself and to the corresponding activity" (GA 27, 371), that is, the possibility for an "ethical" world-view. That Heidegger in fact has this thesis in mind belies a philological reference to the original and the later philosophical meanings of the concept of *eudaimonia*. As long as he refers to holding oneself [*Sichhalten*] in the overwhelming power ("daimonic") of beings, world-view is predominantly a sheltering. As soon as *eudaimonia* is sought for in *praxis*, in free activity giving itself its own goal (*prohairesis*), the stepping over to world-view as composure follows (GA 27, 372).

The so understood "composure" achieves its deepest expression in philosophy, the primary task of which is the "overcoming of the overwhelming mightiness [*Übermächtigkeit*] of beings" (GA 27, 381) and, one with this, the "waking up to the problem of Being" (GA 27, 382). From the mythic (i.e., religious) point of view, such a composure can only be understood as a Promethean rebellion, as a "raising up of the arm against the particular being and its still dawning overwhelming mightiness" (GA 27, 383). This, however, in no way means that the transition from the first to the second possibility of world-view must be understood as an emancipation process or process of enlightenment in the usual sense. Similar to Schelling, Heidegger emphasizes that "philosophy as a basic composure [*Grundhaltung*] is necessarily a nuisance for every world-view as sheltering" (GA 27, 399). Nevertheless, philosophy remains essentially and necessarily related to myth.

For Heidegger, there is no doubt that philosophy as composure fulfills, in an exceptional sense, the original meaning of the Greek word *êthos*, but precisely this prohibits the proclamation of a determinate ethics (GA 27, 379). This shows just how inadequate the numerous attempts are that present Heidegger's ontology as something opposed to an ethics (i.e., charge it with a misrecognition of the ethical). In truth, the metaphysic of Dasein has the possibility conditions of an ethics in view from the start, even if it does not concern a ground-laying of morals in the usual sense. The concluding thesis also indicates that, in Heidegger's understanding, the act of philosophizing itself has an "ethical" sense: "Philosophizing as the letting occur [*Geschehenlassen*] of transcendence is the freeing of Dasein. . . . The original letting be [*Gelassenheit*] of Dasein lies in the letting occur of transcendence as philosophy . . . the human's confidence [*Vertrauen*] toward the Da-sein in him and its possibilities" (GA 27, 401).

Notes

This chapter was translated by Andrew Mitchell.

1. *"Das große Spiel des Lebens und das Übermächtige,"* in Paola-Ludovico Coriando, ed., *«Herkunft aber bleibt stets Zukunft»*, *Martin Heidegger und die Gottesfrage* (Frankfurt am: Main. Vittorio Klostermann, 1998), pp. 45–66.

2. Jean Wahl, *Existence humaine et transcendance* (Neuchâtel: Ed. de La Baconnière, 1944).

3. Emmanuel Levinas, *Totality and Infinity: An Essay on Exteriority*, translated by Alphonso Lingis (Pittsburgh: Duquesne University Press, 1969), p. 35.

4. Emmanuel Levinas, *Existence and Existents*, translated by Alphonso Lingis (The Hague: Martinus Nijhoff, 1978), p. 15.

5. PR, 41–49.

6. Jacques Derrida, "White Mythology: Metaphor in the Text of Philosophy," in *Margins of Philosophy*, translated by Alan Bass (Chicago: University of Chicago Press, 1982), pp. 207–71; "The *Retrait* of Metaphor," translated by Frieda Gasdner, et al., *Enclitic* 2:2 (1978): 5–33.

7. Paul Ricoeur, *The Rule of Metaphor: Multidisciplinary Studies of the Creation of Meaning in Language*, translated by Robert Czerny, with Kenneth McLaughlin and John Costello (Toronto: University of Toronto Press, 1977), pp. 280–95. For a discussion of their respective positions, I refer to my study *"Les mots et les roses. La métaphore chez Martin Heidegger,"* in *Revue des Sciences Philosophiques et Théologiques* 57 (1973): 433–55.

8. Stanislas Breton, *"Sur l'ordre métaphoral,"* in J. Greisch and R. Kearney, eds., *Paul Ricoeur: Les métamorphoses de la raison herméneutique* (Paris: Ed. du Cerf, 1991), pp. 373–80.

9. Translator's note: In the pages that follow, Heidegger plays on the two senses of the noun *"Spiel,"* both "play" and "game," and I render it as one or the other according to context. The verb *"spielen"* is translated throughout as "to play."

10. See Rémi Brague, *La Sagesse du Monde* (Paris: Fayard, 1999).

11. See my essay *"Le phénomène du jeu et les enjeux ontologiques de l'herméneuique,"* in *Revue Internationale de Philosophie* (forthcoming).

12. Levinas, *Totality and Infinity*, pp. 44–48.

13. GA 27, 368. Characteristically, this motif also emerges again in the interpretation of the Platonic myth of the cave that Heidegger sketches during the following semester (GA 28, 353–54).

8

"Homo Prudens"

Miguel de Beistegui

Somewhat provocatively, and from the very start, I would like to suggest that, in the work of Heidegger, it will have been a matter of nothing other than man. And yet, in no way and at no stage can Heidegger's thought be mistaken for a straightforward anthropology, even if, beginning with Husserl himself, there has been a long history of anthropological (mis) interpretations of Heidegger's early thought.[1] What renders this straightforward anthropological reading of Heidegger impossible is Heidegger's fundamental intuition according to which what constitutes the human as such, its essence, if you will, is itself nothing human. This, however, does not take the question concerning the essence of man in the direction of either the infra-human (*animalitas*) or the superhuman (*divinitas*), for the *essence* of man is indeed the essence of *man*, that which belongs to man most intimately, but in such a way that, through it, man is from the very start and always something more than just man. As soon as it is a matter of man, it is a matter of something other than man. And it is precisely through this excess, through an originary openness to a constitutive and non-human otherness, that man as such emerges. So the history that Heidegger recounts, the genesis that he sketches, is not that of the species "man," in its slow and progressive differentiation from other species, nor is it, for that matter, the story of the creation of man by a supersensible being whose being and power by far exceed those of man himself. Heidegger's discourse concerning man must be rigorously distinguished from anthropology, biology, and theology.[2] Rather, the history that Heidegger recounts is man's relation to his essence, the history of the *essence* of man, in which the concepts of "man," "essence," and "history" come to be reformulated radically. How, exactly? In such a way, first of all, that the concepts of essence and of history are no longer simply opposed to one another, but implicate one another: the concept of essence mobilized here does not refer to an extratemporal and ahistorical realm, one that would define man in its necessary and permanent being, independent of the vicissitudes and contingencies of its becoming, but to time itself, understood as the ecstatic-horizonal temporalizing

117

whence history itself unfolds. This, in turn, allows one to identify a history of man as the history of man's relation to his own essence. Also, and by the same token, it is vital to note that even if man is what and who he is on the basis of an essence that exceeds him, he also becomes who he is through the repetition of this essence. It is in the very movement of returning to his essence, in the opening to the opening of being that he himself is, or exists, that man *becomes* man. And if this particular repetition of his essence, this particular opening to that which always and from the very start has begun to open itself in him is itself historical, in the twofold sense of having a history and of making history, of being historical by being an epoch-making principle, it is also, I would like to suggest, ethical. For Heideggerian ethics—and I believe there is such a thing, implicitly at work in *Being and Time* and particularly in the category of *Entschlossenheit*, to which I shall limit myself here—is the demand to become what one already is. It involves a repetition of oneself, or of one's being, as the being that is disclosed (*erschlossen*) to the very event or disclosedness (*Erschlossenheit*) of being. If man, then, as Heidegger will have insisted throughout, is essentially ek-sistence, or openness to the truth of being,[3] then ethics will signify nothing other than the ability to exist this essence to the full, to open oneself to it as to that which allows one to be this being that one is, and thus to realize fully one's ontological potential. And the repetition involved in the moment of ethics is the very operation in which something like a self, or a singularity, comes to be affirmed in the human Dasein for the first time. If ek-sistence is characterized in terms of disclosedness, then ethics will designate just one way in which Dasein can be its own disclosedness, one mode of truth, alongside these other modes, which Heidegger describes at length throughout the 1920s (production, fabrication, and manipulation; investigating, researching, representing; philosophising, etc.). Yet ethics also is a distinct mode of truth in that, in it, ek-sistence discloses itself to itself as disclosedness, becomes transparent to itself as this primordial operation of truth that it is. In thus turning to itself as to the self that is turned toward the world, or turned outward, Dasein does not become other, but appropriates what is most proper to it, its essence. This is where ethics begins to take place, namely, in the movement of appropriation, whereby one becomes what one already is, in the peculiar doubling of truth that ek-sistence *is*. And in this doubling, in this turn back onto itself as the self that is turned outward, Dasein moves deeper into being, persists in it, in such a way that it now exists its own being to the full, thus increasing its own ontological *potentia* as the power to be being, thus elevating to another power. And it will not come as a surprise, then, that Heidegger, in a remarkable proximity with Spinoza, will celebrate the feeling of "joy" that overwhelms him or her, as this redoubling elevates his or her being to another power.

The analysis of *Entschlossenheit* is preceded by a number of preparatory analyses. The moment of ethics is progressively introduced. It is not even recognized by Heidegger as such, for reasons that have to do with the phenomenological commitment to the pure description of phenomena. But, against the letter of Heidegger's own warnings, I would like to affirm the spirit of "resoluteness": implicit in it is an injunction, not just a description (unlike anxiety, or boredom, or fear—who can claim to have experienced "resoluteness" prior to reading *Being and Time*?), and it is as such that it liberates its ontological potential, it is with this call that Heidegger's philosophy becomes, once again, a philosophy of life, for life.

Anticipation

The analysis of *Entschlossenheit*, or of resolute disclosedness, is first announced in the analysis of "anticipation" (*Vorlaufen*) as marking the possibility of a genuine or proper relation to death as to this own-most, uttermost, and singularizing possibility. In anticipating death, it is neither a matter of running ahead toward one's death, of actualizing it (for, as pure possibility, it can never be actualized); nor is it a matter of thinking about death, of "brooding over it" (SZ, 261;BTa, 305), or of developing a morbid relation to one's life in the expectancy of one's demise. It has little to do, then, with a death drive, or with the demand to die the right death. I would like to suggest that it is quite the opposite, that the holding in view of one's mortality amounts to an increase in one's life potential, in one's ability to open oneself to life, or to one's being as potentiality (*Seinkönnen*). To envisage oneself as mortal, to see oneself as this being whose being is essentially finite, is not to learn to die, but to live: it amounts to an intensification of life. To allow death to come to bear on life itself is not conducive to a morbid or a somber mood; it entails neither resignation nor passivity—in other words, it does not lead to a "sad" passion in the Spinozistic sense of the term—rather, it is joyful and sober: "Along with the sober anxiety which brings us face to face with our singularized ability-to-be, there goes an unshakable joy in this possibility" (SZ, 310;BTa, 358). Joy is not to be mistaken for this bourgeois contentment that too often we identify with happiness; rather, it is the feeling linked to the increase and the "acting out" of our power of being. To anticipate one's death, to envisage oneself as mortal, is to live oneself in the mode of anticipation, as this being which is itself (which is a self, singular and yet multiple, triply ecstatic) only by being ahead of itself and which, in returning to itself from beyond itself, eksists being. Such is the privilege and the joy of being human: to be able to be (being): *Sein-können*. And if there is a single Heideggerian injunction, it is in the continuation of this *Können* into a *Sollen*: *Seinkönnen-sollen*, a having to be, or to act one's own ability to be. Since one *can* be it, one *must* be it. Yet since this being which we can be is the being which we always already are, it becomes a matter of elevating it to another power, the nth power.

Death, then, is not the negation or the opposite of life but the condition of its affirmation, the freeing of its potential. So, in anticipation, it is a question of comporting oneself to death as a possibility, and as a distinct possibility, in that it is a possibility of which we do not expect that it be actualized. And it is on the basis of the anticipation of this non-actualizable possibility that Dasein as such has the general structure of anticipation, or of projection of itself into a realm of possibilities which themselves can be actualized, which are indeed projects in the ordinary sense of the term. Death is not a project, but the horizon from out of which Dasein projects itself and frees possibilities for itself, frees itself as freedom for this or that possibility, this or that future. It is with "anticipation" that Dasein reveals itself to itself fully, that is, becomes transparent to its own being as the fundamental and originary operation of truth whence things appear in truth, disclosed in this or that way:

> Being-towards-death is the anticipation of a power-to-be on the part of that being whose kind of being is anticipation itself. In the anticipatory revealing of this power-to-be, Dasein discloses itself to itself as regards its uttermost possibility. But to project itself on its ownmost power-to-be means to be able to understand itself in the Being of the being so revealed—namely, to exist. Anticipation turns out to be the possibility of understanding one's *ownmost* and uttermost power-to-be—that is, the possibility of authentic existence. (SZ, 262-63;BTa, 307)

What anticipation does, then, is to shift the focus from the result of the operation of truth—the disclosedness of things with the world—to the very operation of truth, that is, to the ecstatic clearing whereby things are made manifest. Such is the reason Heidegger insists that "authenticity" is just a "modification" of Dasein's being (SZ, 267;BTa, 312): it does not amount to a change of Dasein's being but to a different way of being this being, that is, no longer on the basis of its lostness or alienation within the anonymity of the One, but on the basis of itself as this absolutely singular disclosedness, as the happening of truth. In and through anticipation, then, Dasein is revealed to itself in truth, as truth. And so, in thus relating itself to its own self, in becoming itself through the appropriation of that which is most proper to it, that which constitutes it as Da-sein or as the being that "is" or ek-sists Being, existence exists more existingly. By existing differently, that is, by existing explicitly the ground or the origin from out of which existence exists, man exists more intensely; for now it is existence itself that is existed, it is the very disclosedness that characterizes existence, which becomes the explicit possibility of existence. But to exist more authentically naturally means to be in the world more authentically, to be turned back into the world, returned to the world, yet on the basis of one's ownness; it is thus to relate to oneself, to the world and to others again and anew; it is a repetition of that which always and already is, and yet, through this repetition, this always already comes to be differently.[4] Heidegger does not venture into any detail concerning what this proper mode of relation to the world and others would be. Perhaps such a description did not belong in the analysis of existence as the average or everyday existence. But if there is an ethics that follows from the existential-ontological description, this is where it begins: at the point where, returning from itself as this self which is the site of truth, as this self which discloses on the basis of a radical and an inescapable finitude, Dasein turns back to the world and to others in a way that no longer resembles the kind of relation that prevails in the One: "As the non-relational possibility, death individualizes—but only in such a manner that, as the possibility which is not to be outstripped; it makes Dasein, as Being-with, have some understanding of the *Seinkönnen* of Others" (SZ, 264;BTa, 309). Solicitude takes on a different form; language becomes more discrete, almost silent (*Verschwiegenheit*)⁵; the ordinary, manipulable relation to the world as the world of things there for me is suspended. Existence is now held in view as the ecstatic happening of truth, and one's Being as being toward death is allowed to bear on how we see the world. And the look onto the world has shifted. It is no longer the technical look that guides the handling of things and practical affairs but the more hesitant and altogether briefer glance, in which existence catches a glimpse of itself. To anticipate is to see oneself as such, or as existence, from the very limit of existence: it is to see oneself come or arrive from a distance, to see oneself approaching, and, in this approach, to witness the birth of the world, the burgeoning of Being. For death is indeed there, absolutely real and yet entirely virtual, purely possible, and it is the presence of death that presides over the birth of the world and grants it value and intensity. It is by pressing against the present that death is able to inject it with a sense of fragility and urgency, thus turning it into a moment that matters, wresting it from evanescence and the destructive flow of time. By pressing against the today, as if the today were without tomorrow, death transforms the contingent into a necessity. Then, I am not the only one who is finite but the world is too, this world from which I cannot dissociate myself: this landscape, this love, this friend, or this smell—all are here as if for the last time. Death clarifies and brings all things into their proper light. In its wake, the false problems tend to vanish, and only the peaks and points of existence remain.

In anticipation, existence frees itself *for* its own death, and this means for itself. It becomes free—free for its own freedom, free to *be* its own freedom. Its world is freed anew, and so are the possibilities contained therein. For existence has now "liberated" itself from its lostness in those possibilities that normally thrust themselves accidentally over it; and "one is liberated in such a way that *for the first time* one can authentically understand and choose among the factical possibilities lying ahead of that possibility which is not to be outstripped" (SZ, 264;BTa, 308; emphasis added). This liberation is a release, the release of a power or a potential linked to a giving up of itself as an absorbed self: to anticipate, in the case of a possibility that is irreducibly so, does not mean to intend in the traditional phenomenological sense; it does not mean to expect, to look forward to; it does not reveal a certain impatience; for that which is coming is not something present-at-hand. It is something that exceeds the form of the present altogether. For what is coming is Dasein itself, the event or the happening of truth: a reversed intentionality, in which the I is summoned and comes to be as such on the basis of something that happens to it. And to comport oneself to

truth does not mean to await or expect; it means to hand oneself over to it. "Anticipation reveals to Dasein its lostness in the they-self, and brings it face to face with the
possibility of being itself, primarily unsupported by concernful solicitude, but of
being itself, rather, in an impassioned *freedom towards death*—a freedom which has
been released from the illusions of the "One" (SZ, 266;BTa, 311).

Resolve

The phenomenon that designates the operation through which existence decides itself for its own being, for itself as singular existence, Heidegger calls *Entschlossenheit.*[6] To be "resolute," or disclosed resolutely, amounts to nothing other than to a
mode of being, in which one is, or rather *I* am, necessarily and unavoidably, open
to my own disclosedness: it amounts to living at the tip of existence, at its extremity, where it gathers itself and "is" truly, where its power is most visible and most
penetrating. Thus existence is itself sharpened to a point, its extremity both at the
end and at the beginning. It is an arrow thrown into the free space of being, which
it discloses as it penetrates it. And so "resoluteness" amounts to nothing other
than a sharpening of existence, as a result of which existence becomes more inci-
sive, penetrates deeper into its own capacity and power to be, deeper into the flesh
of being. If Dasein, as being-in-the-world, designates man's relation to being, resoluteness, in turn, designates the operation through which one, or rather, *I*—but it
is in that very operation that *one* is turned into an *I*—become disclosed to this very
relation that Dasein always and necessarily is. It is therefore a double relation: a re-
lation to one's relation to being. In this relation, which is not a relation to something other, or even a new relation, but a relation to that which, in and of itself, is
always in relation, and thus a relation of relation, existence is as it were doubled, or
repeated. It is reentered and affirmed as such. And in this reentering, it comes to
be *properly*. What is being reentered there is not the everyday existence, not the
anonymous existence that is oblivious of itself, but existence as such, the existing of
existence. This existence is thus at once the same and an other. It is the same, insofar as it is existence as such, and not this or that existent that is in question. And
yet it is other, insofar as, in repeating itself, existence repeats only its own disclosedness as existence, only this very disclosing that it *is*. In this repetition, existence is brought to another power, for it has freed for itself its own (ontological)
power, it has freed within itself this power that it has and is, this power of being or
existing being as such.

   Thus existence is resolute when, turning back on itself *as* disclosedness, it decides itself in favor of existence, and thus lives its relation to the world, to others
and to itself in the mode that is proper to it, that is, possibility or freedom. So far
from designating a withdrawal into some pure interiority, in which *I* would no
longer be concerned with others and with the world as such, resoluteness signifies

a different way of being in the world, a way which is an essential modification of our everyday way of being in the world, and in which something like an "I," something like a first-person singular, first becomes possible. And insofar as this way of being takes its point of departure in Dasein's own-most power to be, it also designates the possibility of a proper or an authentic relation to others, of a solicitude that is genuine insofar as it is itself centered around the own-most possibility of who one is relating to:

> Resoluteness, as *authentic being-one's-self*, does not detach Dasein from its world, nor does it isolate it so that it becomes a free-floating "I." And how should it, when resoluteness as authentic disclosedness, is *authentically* nothing else than *being-in-the-world?* Resoluteness brings the Self right into its current concernful being-alongside what is ready-to-hand, and pushes it into solicitous being with Others.
>
> When Dasein is resolute, it can become the "conscience" of Others. Only by authentically being-their-Selves in resoluteness can people authentically be with one another—not by ambiguous and jealous stipulations and talkative fraternizing in the "One" and in what "One" wants to undertake. (SZ, 298;BTa, 344–45)

To the being-together of everyday existence in which one forgets oneself as singularity and lives according to the mode of the empty majority, we thus need to oppose the community of singularities, the *being*-together of which would precisely be the meaning of existence as such, the community of mortal, factical existents.

Augenblick

Yet resoluteness, as the specific mode of being in which the very being of Dasein is held in view, or as the doubling of existence in which existence comes to be as singularity, also and primarily defines a mode of temporalizing. Let us not forget that the operation of truth or clearing with which Dasein coincides (and it is as such, i.e., as clearing, that it is Da-sein) is a function of the meaning of the being of Dasein as "ecstatic" or "rapturous" temporality. As every instance or mode of truth, then, resoluteness clears a space and opens up a present from out of an originary and a twofold throw: the projected future of Dasein that approaches from the death of Dasein as its own-most and uttermost possibility; the thrownness of Dasein, in which Dasein finds itself as the being that has always already been, and that has no other choice than to be this been-ness as long as it is. Thus from this twofold throw, and like every other mode of truth, resoluteness marks a site, a spatial and temporal clearing that is experienced and seen as presence in the present: resoluteness is a way of being "there," present to the world and to oneself.

But which present is opened up in resoluteness? How is Dasein *there* when resolute? The term that Heidegger reserves to designate the present of resolute Dasein is *Augenblick*: when resolute, Dasein is there in the "moment." Now the present or the time that is thus opened up is to be radically distinguished from the present of this or that particular situation. It is to be distinguished from the kind of present that is linked to a punctual and practical situation, in other words, from the mostly "concerned" and "absorbed" present of our everyday life, the present of needs and ordinary dealings with the world. Furthermore, it also is to be distinguished from the abstract present (the "now") of the theoretical attitude, which we now unquestioningly consider the very form of the present, unaware of the spatial, and specifically linear understanding of time that such an attitude presupposes, the ontological-existential ground of which can be traced back to the ordinary or fallen nature of our relation to the world in everyday life. Rather, the present that is at issue in the "moment" is that present in which existence is present to itself as the very operation of disclosure, or as the very *there* of being. In the moment of vision, or the *Augen-blick*, Dasein "brings itself before itself" (GA 29/30, 247;FCM, 165): it *sees* itself for the first time for what it is, that is, for the originary clearing, the truth or the "there" of being. Thus the Moment is not linked to the disclosure of a particular situation but to the disclosure of situatedness as such. It is the present or the time of truth's disclosedness to itself as the originary event of being. Thus the *Augenblick* designates a different relation to time and to the present in general: it marks at once a rupture or a caesura (*Gebrochenheit*) in the continuum and the fascination or the entrancement of "fallen" time, and a return to the essence of time as ecstatic and rapturous, as finite and horizonal. This, then, does not mean that the Moment marks the possibility of a flight from time into eternity.[7] On the contrary: it means that existence becomes *all the more* open to the world and to the situation in the essential modification that takes place in resoluteness. For the situation is now disclosed from out of Dasein's disclosedness to itself as originary disclosure:

> When resolute, Dasein has brought itself back from falling, and has done so precisely in order to be "there" in the moment all the more authentically for the situation which has been disclosed. (SZ, 328;BTa, 376)

A few pages further down, Heidegger adds the following:

> That *present* which is held in authentic temporality and which thus is authentic itself, we call the "*moment*." . . . The moment is a phenomenon which in principle can not be clarified in terms of the "now." The "now" is a temporal phenomenon which belongs to time as within-time-ness: the "now" "in which" something arises, passes away, or is present-at-hand. "In the moment" nothing can occur; but as the authentic present [*als eigentliche Gegen-wart*], the moment

makes it possible to encounter for the first time [*läßt er erst begegnen*] what can be "in a time" as something at hand or objectively present. (SZ,338;BTa, 387–88)

Nothing occurs *in* the moment: no single thing, no concrete situation, but the sheer power of occurrence which Dasein itself is. In the moment, time itself occurs as the suspension of the impersonal, anonymous, and objective dimension within which things, events, and situations are believed to take place. For these, as things to be handled or as objects to be contemplated, are first encountered from out of the event of time itself, which presents itself in the Moment. Unlike the "now," as the empty form within which events and facts take place, the Moment marks the very advent or gathering of time, the fold at which and within which past and future are folded into one another, thus transforming the present into a site of intensity, so that Dasein reenters the world or repeats its own existential facticity with a renewed and heightened sense of itself as the power, and thus also the freedom to be (Being), as the power and the freedom of Being itself:

> Dasein is not something present at hand alongside other things, but is set in the midst of beings through the manifestness of the full temporal horizon. As Dasein it always already maintains itself in this threefold perspective. As that which rests in time it only is what it can be if in each case at its time—and that simultaneously means in each case here and now, with reference to these beings that are precisely thus manifest—it is there, that is, opens itself up in its manifestness, that is, resolutely discloses itself. Only in the resolute self-disclosure of Dasein itself, in the moment of vision, does it make use of that which properly makes it possible, namely time as the moment of vision itself. (GA 29/30, 224;FCM, 149)

In resoluteness, existence liberates itself from its own entrapment in the absorbed life of everydayness. It frees itself for itself, as this ability to be or disclose being. Thus the modification or conversion brought about by resolute disclosedness also is at the source of a renewed understanding of what it means to *act*, of the very possibility of action in the most essential sense, and, yes, of what I would be tempted to call, albeit under erasure perhaps, the very possibility and beginning of ethics: "The moment of vision is nothing other than the *look of resolute disclosedness* [*Blick der Entschlossenheit*] in which the full situation of an action opens itself and keeps itself open" (GA 29/30, 224;FCM, 148). Thus, in the moment, Dasein has an eye for action in the most essential sense, insofar as the moment of vision is what makes Dasein possible as Dasein. And this is what man *must* resolutely disclose itself to. Man must first create "for itself *once again* [emphasis added] a genuine knowing concerning that wherein whatever makes Dasein itself possible consists." And this, Heidegger tells us, is the "fact that the moment of vision in which Dasein brings itself before itself as that which is properly binding must time and again stand before Dasein as such" (GA 29/30, 224;FCM, 148). Thus, in the moment of vision, existence resolves itself to itself, to itself as Da-sein, thus allowing it to become free for the first time—free not to *do* this or that, at least not primarily, but free to be its own being, free to *be* in the most intense and generous sense, that is, free to be for its own freedom or its own ability to be. Thus "the moment of vision must be understood, and that means seized upon [*er-griffen*], as the *innermost necessity of the freedom of Dasein*" (GA 29/30, 248;FCM, 166). And this, Heidegger adds, is tantamount to "liberating the humanity in man, to liberating the humanity of man, that is, the *essence* of man, *to letting the Dasein in him become essential.*" (GA 29/30, 248;FCM, 166). With resoluteness, then, as the mode of disclosedness in which Dasein is presented to itself according to its essence, that is, as this power and freedom to be, are we not also de facto presented with the essence and the possibility of action? In the light of a possibility of existence itself, in which existence grasps itself as pure possibility, does action, and the demand to act in a certain way, or rather, the kind of demand that can be made of Dasein so that it will activate its own-most and uttermost ontological potential, come to be redefined radically? With Heidegger, can we not begin to articulate an ethics that would not be of alterity, but of the self (which does not mean an ethics of selfishness), or of the essence of man as power and freedom to act Being? Is this not what Heidegger suggests when he writes that:

> As resolute, Dasein is already *acting (Als entschlossenes* handelt *das Dasein schon)*. However, the term "acting" (*Handeln*) is one which we are purposely avoiding. For in the first place this term must be taken so broadly that "activity" (*Aktivität*) will also embrace the passivity of resistance. In the second place, it suggests a misunderstanding in the ontology of Dasein, as if resoluteness were a special way of behavior belonging to the practical faculty as contrasted with one that is theoretical. Care, however, as concernful solicitude, so primordially and wholly envelops Dasein's being that it must already be presupposed as a whole when we distinguish between theoretical and practical behavior; it cannot first be built up out of these faculties by a dialectic which, because it is existentially ungrounded, is necessarily quite baseless. *Resoluteness, however, is only the possible authenticity of care itself, that is, the authenticity which, in care, and as care, is the object of care itself.* (SZ, 300-01;BTa, 347-48)

Thus were it not for the classical opposition between theory and praxis, were it not for the way in which praxis and ethics are traditionally understood in opposition to thought, as action in opposition to contemplation, resoluteness could come to designate the origin of proper action, and thus to delimit the sphere of ethics itself. Were it not that the very operation whereby existence as such, or care, becomes the very concern of care itself, simply takes place before any distinction can be made between the theoretical and the practical, between thought and action, resoluteness could indeed be seen as the movement that opens existence to itself to the site or place of its singularity, to its *proper* place. And so, despite Heidegger's warnings in *Being and Time*, but keeping them in mind, we shall offer to reactivate the old Aristotelian word of φρόνησις (prudence) to designate the mode of disclosedness in which Dasein comes face to face with itself as the site or the truth of being: at that moment, the ἀληθηεύειν and the ἀληθής, the disclosing and the disclosed, coincide absolutely, in what amounts to a doubling of truth. And we shall also offer to reactivate the ancient and noble word "ethics" to designate the kind of relation—to others: to the world, to men, to things and to Dasein itself—that characterizes the man of prudence thus redefined. But this, of course, as we now know from the 1924-25 lectures on Plato's *Sophist*, is something that Heidegger himself suggested, in an effort to translate Aristotle's analyses concerning πρᾶξις, φρόνησις, and βουλεύεσθαι back into their existential-ontological ground. In that text, which in many respects announces and provides a context for the analysis of *Entschlossenheit* in *Being and Time*, Heidegger suggests that the ἀληθηεύειν, or the mode of truth that is at stake in φρόνησις, involves the being of Dasein itself: it is an ἀληθηεύειν where the human Dasein tries to wrest itself from its own coveredness, tries to become transparent to itself through a constant struggle against its tendency to cover itself over. For, Heidegger argues, the human Dasein is for the most part concealed to itself in its proper being. It is so wrapped up in itself that it cannot even "see" itself for who it is. And so, it must learn to *see*. This apprenticeship in seeing its own being, and in *being* it in the right and proper way, is what φρόνησις is about: it is primarily a matter of seeing through, and thus of clarity (*Durchsichtigkeit*), and, subsequently, of considerateness (*Rücksicht*) (SZ, 146; BTa, 186). It is only as phronetic or prudent that man can act accordingly, for only thus is the situation fully disclosed to him. And action itself, which, according to Aristotle, is the ultimate goal of the process of deliberation (βουλεύεσθαι) that characterizes the prudent man, presupposes this seeing as guiding the right and proper way to be Dasein. It is this seeing (also characterized as an *Erblicken* and a *Blick des Auges*, a "catching sight" and a "blink of the eye") in which Dasein catches sight of the momentary situation and decides or resolves itself (the Aristotelian βουλή is translated as *Entschluß*) for it on the basis of itself. All of this happens in a moment, in the blink of the eye that defines the moment, the time of action and ethics, and which Aristotle is careful to distinguish from the time of those beings who are forever, the time of eternity:

> Φρόνησις is the inspection of the this here now, the inspection of the concrete momentariness of the transient situation. As αἴσθησις, it is the blink of the eye (*der Blick des Auges*), a momentary look (*der Augen-blick*) at what is momentarily concrete, which as such can always be otherwise. On the other hand, the νοεῖν in σοφία is a looking upon that which is ἀεί, that which is always

present in sameness. Time (the momentary and the eternal) here functions to discriminate between the νοεῖν in φρόνησις and the one in σοφία. (GA 19, 163-64;S, 112-13)

Thus, in Heidegger, there always will have been a place for ethics, a space for the properly human time of action and decision, as the fragile and always threatened time within which man lives. There always will have been a place for the affirmation and the enacting of man's essence as the ecstatic disclosedness to the truth of being. There always will have been a place on earth for man as the mortal and, for that very reason, the most alive of all beings. Indeed, ethics no longer gestures toward a morality of good and evil, of the will as a capacity to choose between good and evil, or even as the ability to obey a law as the universal law of reason. Freedom is here entirely disconnected from the will and rearticulated along the lines of an ontological power, which one always already is, and which can nonetheless be related to in such a way that it is increased, in such a way that it amounts to a general increase of one's beings as this *power to be* (being).

Notes

1. See Husserl's marginal annotations to his copy of Heidegger's *Being and Time*, originally published in *Jahrbuch für Philosophie und Phänomenologische Forschung*, vol. VII (Halle & Saale: Niemeyer Verlag, 1927), and *Kant and the Problem of Metaphysics* (Bonn: Cohen Verlag, 1929), as well as the lecture entitled "Phenomenology and Anthropology" (*Husserliana*, vol. XXVII, *Aufsätze und Vorträge* [1922-1937], edited by T. Nenon and H. R. Sepp), delivered on three occasions in June 1931.

2. So in raising the question of man as the question concerning his essence, Heidegger simply refuses to think of man on the basis of some history, some narrative that would account for his birth, for his emergence from out of the realm of animality, or *ex nihilo*. Thus Heidegger refuses to think of the origin of man in terms of a mere branching off, of a differentiation of a unique, singular process called "life." If man as such, or man according to his essence, is alive—and indeed he is—it is in quite a different sense: already the Greeks, and Aristotle among others, made a distinction within the human between the life of needs and necessities (ζωή) and the life that can become an object of pursuit, debate, and argument (βίος). Similarly, and after Husserl, one must here distinguish between the body that lives according to such necessities, the body that survives (*Körper*), and the body that lives ontophenomenologically, the existing body (*Leib*). If man lives, it is not simply as an organism; but nor is it, for that matter, as an organism with something specific and nonorganic in addition to the organic, a soul, for example, or an

intellect. The metaphysical representation of man as "rational" is essentially complicit with the biological representation of man. Thus Heidegger wishes to wrest the question of man from the grip of representation by bypassing the classical determination of man with respect to its animality, or with respect to the problematic of organic life, on the one hand, and with respect to the problematic of the supersensible, on the other hand, which locates the origin of man in the representation of a higher being. For further details concerning the issue of life and Heidegger's problematic attempt to distinguish the life of Dasein from that of animality, see GA 29/30, part 2, particularly §45.

3. In his "Letter on Humanism," for example, Heidegger writes: "Man occurs essentially in such a way that he is the 'there' [*das 'Da'*], that is, the clearing of being. The 'being' of the *Da*, and only it, has the fundamental character of ek-sistence, that is, of an ecstatic inherence [*Innestehens*] in the truth of being" (GA 9, 157;P, 248). And in his "Introduction to 'What is Metaphysics?'" from 1949, Heidegger writes: "The proposition 'the human being exists' means: the human being is that being whose being is distinguished by an open standing that stands in the unconcealedness of being" (GA 9, 203;P, 284).

4. Insofar as the repetition involved here brings existence to a greater level of intensity, it is not a mere reiteration but the very beginning of ethics. Repetition as an ethical, that is, life-enhancing, concept must therefore be distinguished from a purely mimetic, ontologically redundant concept of repetition, which reiterates the same.

5. Heidegger describes the mode of discourse that is at work in anticipation as "the call of conscience" (§56), in which Dasein is summoned [*aufgerufen*] to itself, that is, to its own-most *Seinkönnen*, precisely by remaining silent, by not telling anything, by not disclosing any content, any information regarding the world: "in the content of the call, one can indeed point to nothing which the voice 'positively' recommends and imposes" (SZ, 294;BTa, 341). It is a call, then, which is literally empty, speechless, and the very silence of which is precisely such as to bring Dasein face to face with itself; it is a call that resonates from within, but also from afar, that is, from ahead of and beyond everyday existence, from that very limit or end whence existence is disclosed. It is interesting to note here that the authentic mode of speech, in which the singular existence calls Dasein back from its lostness in the One and into the truth of existence, takes on the form of silence; the alien voice that bespeaks silence is the mode of discourse that coincides with Dasein being wrested from its ordinary and familiar relation with the world, normally expressed in "idle talk." Also, this is the point at which Heidegger locates the possibility of praxis in the genuine sense of the term, resisting anything like a prescriptive ethics in favor of an existential one, in which the true object of action, that which needs to be enacted, is existence as such, that is, as disclosedness, or truth. That which needs to be

enacted or liberated is the power or the capacity that is proper to Dasein; this is the point at which Heidegger's treatment of the call of conscience comes close to Spinoza's ethics: it is, after all, a matter of persevering in one's Being, of freeing one's power to be. Man is first and foremost a power of disclosedness, a power of letting things be within the Open, a capacity to open itself to the Open as such, to comport itself to truth as such. It is an ethics of the self, which does not mean a "selfish" ethics, but an ethics for which a true concept of action can only be derived from a genuine understanding of what it means to be for man (of the essence of man as existence), and from an appropriation of the proper thus understood. It is a matter of self-appropriation. De facto, it is not just a description but also an affirmation and a celebration of the essential finitude of human existence as condition of possibility of existence as the site or place where truth happens. Heidegger says it all quite explicitly in the following passage:

> We miss a positive content in that which is called, because we expect to be told something currently useful about assured possibilities of "taking action" [*Handeln*] which are available and calculable. This expectation has its basis within the horizon of that way of interpreting which belongs to commonsense concern—a way of interpreting which forces Dasein's existence to be subsumed under the idea of a business procedure that can be regulated. Such expectations (and in part these tacitly underlie even the demand for a *material* ethic of value as contrasted with one that is "merely" formal) are of course disappointed by the conscience. The call of conscience fails to give any such "practical" injunctions, *solely because* it summons Dasein to existence, to its ownmost capacity-to-be-its-Self. With the maxims which one might be led to expect—maxims which could be reckoned upon unequivocally—the conscience would deny to existence nothing less than the very *possibility of taking action*. But because the conscience manifestly cannot be "positive" in this manner, neither does it function "just negatively" in this manner. The call discloses nothing which could be either positive or negative as something with which we *can concern ourselves*; for what it has in view is a Being which is ontologically quite different—namely, *existence*. On the other hand, when the call is rightly understood, it gives us that which in the existential sense is the "most positive" of all—namely, the own-most possibility which Dasein can present to itself, as a calling-back that calls Dasein forth [*als vorrufender Rückruf*] in its capacity-to-be-its-Self every time. To hear the call properly means bringing oneself into a factical taking-action. (SZ, 294;BTa, 341)

6. No matter how one decides to translate this term (resolution, resolve, resoluteness, decision, etc.), the intimate connection with the term of which it is an essential modification, to wit, *Erschlossenheit*, is lost. Yet this connection is what matters most here. *Entschlossenheit* designates first and foremost a mode of disclosure, or a mode of truth: specifically, the mode whereby existence discloses itself to itself as

disclosedness. It is thus a mode of disclosure in which the whole and the essence of existence are at issue, and not just this or that aspect or concern that belongs to existence.

7. This is where, despite Heidegger's acknowledgment of his debt to Kierkegaard's concept of the moment on page 338, footnote 1 of *Sein und Zeit*, the Heideggerian *Augenblick* becomes irreconcilable with the Kierkegaardian Moment.

Part III

The Question of the Political

9

In the Middle of Heidegger's Three Concepts of the Political

THEODORE KISIEL

Dagegen ist ein scharfer Kampf zu führen im nationalsozialistischen Geist, der nicht ersticken darf durch humanisierende, christliche Vorstellungen, die seine Unbedingtheit niederhalten. Es genügt auch nicht, wenn man dem Neuen Rechnung tragen will, indem man alles mit etwas politischer Farbe bemalt. Vom großer Gefahr sind die überall auftauchenden unverbindlichen Pläne und Schlagworte, die nur zur Selbsttäuschung führen, ebenso wie der "*neue*" *Wissenschaftsbegriff*, der weiter nichts als der alte ist, den man etwas anthropologisch unterbaut hat. Auch ist das viele Reden vom "Politischen" ein Unfug, denn altem Schlendrian wird nicht das Treiben gelegt. Zum wirklichen Ernst des Neuen gehört die Erfahrung der Not, die zugreifende Auseinandersetzung mit den wirklichen Zuständen. Nur das Tun ist berechtigt, das in innerem Einsatz für die Zukunft erfolgt.

> —"*Die Universität im neuen Reich*" (der erste Vortrag eines politischen Erziehungs-programms, von Professor Martin Heidegger)

An *intense struggle* must be waged [in the community of the university] in the national socialist spirit, and this spirit must not be suffocated by humanizing Christian ideas that suppress its unconditionality. Nor is it enough to want to accommodate oneself to the new Reich by touching everything up with some political color. Of great *danger* are the *noncommittal plans and slogans* popping up everywhere, which merely promote self-deception, and so too is the "*new*" *concept of science*, which is nothing more than the old one with some anthropological underpinning. A great deal of the talk of the "political" is also mischief, for it does nothing to put an end to the old routine of doing things. The true gravity of the new situation brings a sense of emergency and a contentious engagement with the actual conditions. Only that *deed is justified* that is performed with an *inner commitment to the future.*

> —"*The University in the New Reich*" (speech held at the University of Heidelberg on June 30, 1933)*

Rektor-Führer Heidegger first gave this talk launching a "program of political education" at the University of Heidelberg in order to bring the revolution then taking place throughout the German nation (*Reich*) into the university itself. For it, like all other German institutions, "has to be reintegrated into the people's community [*Volksgemeinschaft*] and joined with the state. The university must again become an educational force that draws on its knowledge in order to educate the class of leaders in the state toward knowledge" (GA 16, 762;HC, 44). The university's educational task in the new Reich would be enormous, and in fact total in its revolutionary character and service to the state: "The national socialist revolution is and will become the total reeducation of the people, the students, and the coming generation of young instructors" (Ott, 231/243). But would this be a totally political education? Would the educational contribution of the universities to the admittedly political revolution begun by the National Socialist Party under the leadership of Adolf Hitler be itself political, or something more basic than the "political," even more radically revolutionary, thus something else entirely?

Exactly two months after the constitutional—and popular—transmission of political power to the German National Socialist Labor Party, its so-called "*Machtergreifung*," thus even before the very prospect of the rectorship that would empower him to implement his own long-incubating ideas on university reform for the Third Reich, Heidegger, in a revealing letter to Elisabeth Blochmann, with whom he had an ongoing frank discussion on German party politics, expresses his enthusiasm over the sudden surge of historical events on the political front, to the point of regarding it as an ontological *Ereignis* full of opportunity and potential, a veritable καιρός:

> It intensifies the will and the confidence to work in the service of a grand mission and to cooperate in the building of a world grounded in the people. For some time now, I have given up on the empty, superficial, unreal, thus nihilistic talk of mere "culture" and so-called "values" and have sought this new ground in *Da-sein*. We will find this ground and at the same time the calling of the German people in the history of the West only if we expose ourselves to being itself in a new way and new appropriation. I thereby experience the current events wholly out of the future. Only in this way can we develop a genuine involvement and that *in-stantiation* [*Inständigkeit*] in our history which is in fact the precondition for any effective action.[1]

On the other hand, Heidegger, who with his fellow Germans had suffered through the post–Versailles Weimar years of increasing political frustration to the most current economic crises, can well understand the purely political enthusiasm of many of his conservative compatriots over the new turn of events, to the point of

> taking each and every thing as "political" without considering that this can be only *one* way of the first revolution. To be sure, this can for many become, and

has indeed become, a way of first awakening—provided that we at once sense the need to prepare ourselves for a second and deeper awakening [revolution]. The argument with "Marxism" and the "Center" [Catholic party] will actually make no proper headway if it does not ripen into a contestation of the alien spirit of communism and the perishing spirit of Christendom. [. . .] We must of course not allow such fears to diminish the momentum of today's historic events nor to regard it as an assurance that our people have already grasped its hidden mission—in which we have faith—and has found the ultimate operative powers for its new course.[2]

Party politics understood as competing powers within the history of the Western "spirit" were now coming to a head in this unique historical moment of opportunity for the powers indigenous to the "German spirit": one begins to sense Heidegger's deeper "philosophical" reading of the *Realpolitik* of post–Versailles Europe and the geopolitical situation of a defeated Germany struggling for survival in a series of crises devastating the global economy in general and cultural-political Europe in particular, wracked as it was by a widespread pessimism portending the "demise of the West." Even before this letter was written, Professor Heidegger, in his involvement in a "Working Group of German University Teachers on Cultural Politics," was already on record in concurring with the new regime's demand that the German university must include, as one of its basic tasks, the "political education of a select class of leaders. It is in this collective task that research and teaching, faculty and student body, fulfill their common meaning."[3]

But all of the above citations already suggest that Heidegger has a somewhat different sense, more "authentic" and "originary," of what constitutes a "political education" at the university level than what the regime had in mind and many of his colleagues were proposing "in non-committal plans and slogans." Already in 1923, another year of economic and political crisis for the Weimar Republic, at the time that he was developing his protopractical phenomenological ontology of Dasein, Heidegger had been prompted to find a place for the phenomenon of the "political" in the protopraxis of Dasein. The new indigenous challenge—or "promise"—ten years later of the "national socialist spirit," in its dissociation from competing metaphysical "-isms" such as the international "specter" of communism and the Christian "spirit" of Centrist conservatism, eventually led Heidegger into an equally complex and more public in-depth analysis of the revolutionary political situation in which he found himself deeply involved. This analysis would borrow from both the constructive and deconstructive elements of his earlier analytic of Dasein as it proceeds to deepen the site of the political beyond the metaphysical into its German Da-sein, understood as a prepolitical πόλις that is at once the source and end of the political. We thus find three distinct levels of the political in Heidegger's analytic of the Dasein of the German people—the phenomenological, metaphysical, and *seynsgeschichtliche*—as it were, three "concepts of the political," borrowing Carl Schmitt's favorite expression. For

Schmitt, as one of National Socialism's first self-professed political philosophers, will provide one of the more metaphysical challenges to Heidegger's own deepening sense of the political in his temporal ontology and history of be-ing. Schmitt, with whom Heidegger was in correspondence at this time, in part because of their common official duties in the new regime, had even before 1933 spoken of the "total state" in his prolific tracts on political theory, by which he meant the thoroughgoing politicization of all sectors of society in the service of the state.[4] The state, as "the political" par excellence, has the potential and propensity to embrace all hitherto ostensibly "neutral" domains of society: the economy, culture, religion, education, and thus that domain reserved by the research university for itself, science (knowledge). It is this "new" concept of politicized science, "which is nothing but the old one with some anthropological underpinning," that would become the special focus of Rektor Heidegger's resistance, calling for the "self-assertion of the German university," over against the increasingly absolutist regime's campaign of total coordination or "bringing into line" of all the institutions of German society under National Socialist rule. His repeated talks and lecture courses at this time on the "essence of truth," as the ever-unique historical unconcealment for which errant humans must provide an equally unique historical opening, are a tacit expression of this resistance, since this particular "essence of truth" is the originating ground of the essence of science, which in turn is the ground of the essence of the university. Is that opening for the historic mission of the German people to be granted solely by the state and understood purely as a political mission, or do not the nation's "thinkers and poets," especially in Germany, have an equally primordial role in outlining the "leeway of freedom" that would release the indigenous "spiritual" powers of the *Volk*, both on the domestic and the larger European scene?

The Phenomenological Concept of Rhetorical Politics

Heidegger's first concept of the political begins to take shape in 1923 against the historical backdrop of a viciously internecine party politics made more rabid by the increasingly rampant inflation brought on by the Weimar parliamentary government's fiscal responses to the French occupation of the Ruhr industrial region. It was out of this political and economic turmoil that the Munich-based Nazi Party and its chief rhetorician, Adolf Hitler, first came into national prominence. It also was a time in which Heidegger was developing his protopractical ontology of Dasein by a wholesale confrontation of the phenomenological and practical Aristotle.[5] Aristotle's several definitions of man are being interpreted in close conjunction with his practical works, including his *Rhetoric*. The three Aristotelian definitions of the living being called human are in fact understood as equally primordial: a living being that has *and is had* by speech (λόγον ἔχον, understood as middle voiced), a political life (ζῷον πολιτικόν) that expresses itself by speaking in community and in concert with others, and a practical being-in-the-world pervaded by speech. The human being both occupies the world and is occupied by it, practically, politically, and most basically, discursively. The understanding human being in its practical and political world accordingly has hearing, responsiveness to speech, as its most fundamental mode of perception. The animal possessed by speech is through and through political and rhetorical, gregarious and loquacious.

For the early Heidegger, therefore, the more ontological Greek *Urtext* of political philosophy is Aristotle's *Rhetoric* rather than Plato's *Republic*, which will play its fateful role ten years later in Heidegger's Rectoral Address. Aristotle's *Rhetoric*, "the first systematic hermeneutics of the everydayness of being-with-one-another,"[6] depicts for Heidegger a speech community, a being-with that is at once a speaking-with, whose basic goal is coming to an understanding of agreement (*Verständigung*) with one another, ἑρμηνεία, the protohermeneutics of communication and the accord that it brings to the public sphere, the πόλις. The communication of a community ultimately has as its practical aim the agreement that allows for living in concert and getting along together. The basic aim of everyday natural discourse, the business of speaking to and with one another, accordingly listening to one another, is not knowledge but understanding. The speech in question is public, not private; its judgments are not scientific, but practical; its discursivity is not just linguistic but extends to the nonverbal articulations of action and passion; its truth resides not in the clear and distinct λόγος of statements, but in the chiaroscuro λόγος of δόξα, the partial truth of opinions. Rhetoric is the very first "logic," the primitive logic of everydayness dealing with the more practical and crucial kinds of judgment (κρίνεις) at issue or in abeyance in everyday speech situations. Understood as the hermeneutics of everyday life of the Greek πόλις, classical rhetoric has classified three peak moments of discourse that have generated three genres of civic speech making—the deliberative, the judicial, and the festive or epideictic. It is by way of Heidegger's rehearsal of these three genres of phenomenological rhetoric that a rudimentary protopolitics begins to take shape and to seek its site in his emerging fundamental ontology.

1. The properly political speech seeks to persuade or dissuade a popular assembly or deliberative body toward a certain decision on a course of action that would resolve a communal crisis, say, in matters of war or peace.

2. The judicial speech before a court of law in prosecution or defense is directly addressed to the audience of a judge and jury. As a matter of right and law, it is also a matter of the πόλις. A current politicized example that Heidegger could have given was Hitler on trial for treason at this time, where the already masterful rhetorician from Munich played to the media of newspapers and radio and thus made the entire nation his audience and jury.

3. The festive speech is designed to bring the audience into the presence of something admirable and noble, though it may involve not only the praise of the noble but also the censure of the ignoble, (e.g., of the police spies who betrayed Albert Leo Schlageter, whose death in 1923 by a French firing squad provoked a spontaneous solemn epideixis of the entire German nation).

Deliberating on a future course of action, passing judgment on a past action, reviving the presence of an inspiring action—the simple temporality of the three genres of speeches of the πόλις, understood as peak moments of response to an everydayness "exponentialized" by crisis (e.g., war, rampant inflation, general strike), spells out and punctuates the rhythms of its public life.

The basic aim of all three types of political rhetoric is not didactic but dispositive. The speaker aims to sway his audience over to his view of things by forming a receptive disposition and arousing an appropriate mood in the audience. The πάθος of the auditor is therefore the most central of the three classical means of *persuasion*, the three πίστεις, the "trusts" that inspire "confidence" in the credibility of the speaker and his speech. Nevertheless, the other two confidences, the ἦθος (character = resolute openness) of the speaker and the demonstrative power of the speech itself, (λόγος), are equally primordial to πάθος in the speech situation. (The three are destined to become, in *Sein und Zeit*, the triad of *Befindlichkeit-Verstehen-Rede*, which formally indicates the situated disclosedness of Da-sein, the "clearing" of its be-ing.)

Demonstration in the everyday speech situation is not a matter of logical proof or scientific procedures but instead is conveyed by enthymemes, the abbreviated syllogisms of rhetoric, literally curt speech that goes directly "to the heart" (ἐνθύμιος)—striking examples, memorable punch lines, emotionally charged but pithy tales (e.g., "the November betrayal" of 1918), narrative "arguments" that hit home quickly and cleanly. The public speaker draws upon popular prejudices and current opinions to develop the seldom-stated major premises of δόξα that found his abbreviated but striking conclusions about how things look and what seems to be the case. For the thinking of the crowd is short-winded, having absolutely no interest in the lengthy process of getting "at the things themselves." Even for Aristotle, the human being is first of all not the rational animal but the being living in ordinary language and its idle talk, who, inured by its habit, has neither the time nor the inclination to speak primordially about the things themselves. Socrates and Plato in particular took arms against this prevalence of talk "in idle," which Heidegger here identifies as one of the inescapable concealments of truth, the concealment of and by opinions in which daily life on the average first and foremost operates. But Aristotle, the rhetorician, had a much greater appreciation of the δόξα of his native language, its "folk wisdom," as it were, and so its partial truth when properly authenticated by a native orator who uncovers it in appropriate speech situations that aim at the preservation and advancement of the πόλις. His common front with Socrates and Plato was rather against sophistic phrasemongering, which deliberately perpetuates and exploits idle talk to self-advantage. Through the use of the catchphrase and cliché, through the glib polish of concepts, the pseudo-philosophical Sophist takes the originally disclosed matters of the philosopher and puts them forward in the guise of obvious matter-of-fact self-evidence, parading his pseudo-knowledge as a familiar possession that is in no need to be returned time and again to its original sources, in a constant interrogation of its authentically original concealment, its "mystery."

Thus, in his very first listing of the three modes of truth's concealment, Heidegger attributes two of them directly to the language of rhetoric, and so enlists not only the philosopher but also the rhetorician-statesman into the gigantic struggle (*Kampf, Titanenkampf, gigantomachia*) of "wresting" truth from its concealment, which always begins with the struggle of tearing away the disguises of the concealing catchphrase, the surface cliché, the "sound bites" of popular jargon, in order to expose the more telling "enthymeme" befitting the particular speech situation of a native people, more in keeping with the ἔθος (custom, usage, tradition) of its "folk wisdom."

In *Sein und Zeit* (hereafter SZ), this authentic dimension of rhetoric as an unconcealing process is obscured by the all-pervasive predominance of the existential category of *das Man*, according to which I am one-like-many in an average being-with-one-another. The true bearer of the peculiar universal of averageness, called the Anyone, is our language, in the repetitive prevalence of "what one says" that circumscribes the self-evidence of public opinion. As many readers of SZ, such as Pierre Bourdieu, have long suspected, *das Man*, the Anyone, οἱ πολλοί, "the many" understood not as a loose sum of individuals but as a public kind of power of apathy and indifference built into the repeatability of language, is the baseline category or "existential" of Heidegger's properly political-rhetorical ontology. But what "many" have not noticed is that Heidegger also formally outlines a path out of the leveling impersonal anonymity of the masses, whereby a "being-with-one-another in the same world . . . in *communication* and in *struggle* [*Kampf*]" (SZ, 384, emphasis added) finds its way to an authentic grouping by actualizing the *historical uniqueness* and self-identity of its community. In the leveling of its essentially *general* state (SZ, 300), the Anyone "itself" is not historical, just as the "masses" are rootless, homeless, and stateless, stripped of all uniqueness and credentials of historical identity. The everyday Dasein is infinitely scattered in the average with-world and in the multiplicity of the surrounding world (SZ, 129, 389). The groupings of the Anyone are endlessly dispersed and manifold—businesses, circles, classes, professional associations, political parties, bowling clubs, robber bands—"such that no one stands with anyone else, and no community stands with any other in the rooted unity of essential action. We are all servants of slogans, adherents to a program, but none is the custodian of the inner greatness of Dasein and its necessities. . . . The mystery is lacking in our Dasein" (GA 29/30, 244; FCM, 163). The authentic grouping of being-with-one-another can never arise "from the ambiguous and jealous conspiracies and the garrulous factions of clans in the Anyone. . . . Authentic with-one-another first arises from the authentic self-being of resolute openness" (SZ, 298). The passage to authentic coexistence "in the rooted unity of essential action" proves to be a historical rite of passage to a concerted historical action in first finding that one's own unique fate is inextricably rooted in the historical destiny of a unique historical people acting in community. "The fateful historical happening of unique Dasein as being-in-the-world is thereby a co-happening which is defined as destiny. This is how we define the happening of a community, of a people. . . . The power of destiny first becomes free in communication and in struggle. The fateful destiny of Dasein in and with its 'generation' constitutes the full authentic happening of Dasein" (SZ, 384f).

The Metontological Concept of the Political—A Fragment

"Who are we then? Do we know who we are? Who are we *ourselves*? Are we in fact a community and a people?" This fateful question of definition of the historical uniqueness and self-identity of the community that is the German folk is first posed by Heidegger in the microcosm of the university lecture hall toward the end of 1929 (GA 29/30, 103;FCM, 69), with the world financial crisis in full swing, and finds its first public political denouement in the rectoral statement of "self-assertion of the German university" in 1933: "But do we know *who we ourselves* are, this corporate body of teachers and students of the highest school of the German people?"[7]

The communal circle of the we becomes ever more comprehensive as Heidegger thinks more nationally: a teacher and his students engaged in their common study, the "fighting community" (*Kampfgemeinschaft* = struggle in common, a more benign translation) of the university, the German state university system, the German people among the Occidental peoples, each struggling for historical self-identity, usually by statehood. In the logic course of Summer Semester (hereafter SS) 1934, the question "Who are we?" is answered by "We are a people," and the selfhood of a people is defined in terms of decision, mission and vocation, historical character, and common tradition and language, since this selfhood, the unique character proper to a people, is basically the proper-ty of the properizing event of be-ing, *das Eigen-tum des Er-eignisses*. In the Hölderlin course of the next semester, the German people discover their original time of tradition in the poetic words "fatherland" and "home," the native senses of the "national." In SS 1935, German Dasein, the metaphysical people landlocked and squeezed in Europe's middle, is called upon to assume the mission of saving the West from its impending demise. In these contexts, Dasein no longer refers to the individual human situation, as in SZ, but to the unique historical situation of a people, German Dasein, Greek Dasein. For Heidegger and for Germany, it is now the "time of the we" (*Wirzeit*) of national socialism, and not the time of the I, characteristic of democratic liberalism. The characteristics of Dasein are thus transposed from the individual to the communal totality, the πόλις. Just as a generation is thoroughly temporal and historical and thus mortal, so is a people and a community. Like a mortal generation, a people also undergoes a rise, a peak, and a fall (GA 39, 51). Pushed to its extreme by "total" worldviews such as capitalism and communism, the perspective of finite Dasein makes the people itself and not God "the aim and purpose of all history" (GA 65, 24;C, 18, 40f/28f).

Heidegger's analysis of the Dasein of a people is clearly an application of his fundamental ontology in the direction of what he variously called a metontology, metaphysical ontic, and metaphysics of existence, where "the [ontic] question of ethics [and so politics] can first be posed" along ontological lines (GA 26, 199;MFL, 157). This is the level at which Heidegger then wishes to enter into the public "battle of worldviews" arising from German party politics and debated in the German press by ideologues and intellectuals of every stripe, often with regard to the question of which worldview is most in keeping with the "German spirit" or German self-identity in the then-current European situation. It is only after the world depression of 1929 that Heidegger feels compelled and empowered to bring his situation-oriented philosophy to bear on the "higher journalism of our age," whose interpretations "are in part borrowed second- and third-hand and configured into an overall picture" in order to "create the spiritual space" which immediately defines the moods and shapes the decisions of German Dasein at a particular time (GA 29/30, 106;FCM, 71, 114/77). Two of the four examples of the higher journalism that Heidegger reviews in his late 1929 course, Oswald Spengler's *The Decline of the West* (1918) and Max Scheler's "Man in the World Epoch of Balance and Compromise" (1927), will have a direct impact on Heidegger's own ventures into "higher journalism," such as the famous "pincers passage" of 1935, of a landlocked Germany in Central Europe being squeezed from both sides by the alien global worldviews of American capitalism and Russian communism, which are "metaphysically the same." Nietzsche's cultural diagnostics and Ernst Jünger's insights into "total mobilization" are also well-documented influences on Heidegger's political vocabulary and rhetoric at the time.

But other philosophical influences have yet to be brought to light, especially as Heidegger is brought closer to his fateful pact with National Socialism. One that should be named here is the political-theological pamphleteering carried on by the national-conservative, anti-capitalist Protestant "Tatkreis" (Action Circle). A copy of one such pamphlet, "Where Is Germany Heading?," written under the penname "Leopold Dingraeve," was dedicated to Rudolf Bultmann by Heidegger on December 20, 1932. This political Christmas present perhaps serves to justify Heidegger's admission to Bultmann that he had voted for the National Socialist "movement" in the recent elections while denying the "outhouse rumor" that he had joined the National Socialist "party" (letter dated December 16, 1932). The pamphlet praises National Socialism for its leadership in promoting a nationalism and an indigenous socialism appropriate to German circumstances and concludes by calling for a broad coalition of all rightist conservative forces with centrist elements to "establish a socialistic people's community," first by the formation of a firm and clear public opinion which would unequivocally and unconditionally represent the basic national and anti-capitalist will of the overwhelming majority of the nation, so that it itself becomes a politically formative power. The creation of such a public opinion is nothing other than what Martin Luther calls the "public truth that makes us free."[8]

Heidegger has only one qualm with the interpretive philosophical journalism of the "Action Circle, which I eagerly follow," and it is a major one, as he observes to Blochmann (December 19, 1932: 55/568):

It has now become the fashion to let loose *against* Greek antiquity, even by people whose work and will deserves every affirmation: I am thinking of the Action Circle [*Tatkreis*]. As much as I'd like to, I cannot believe in this purported renewal of Protestantism. And when it comes to antiquity, these people—almost comically—confuse the later pre-Christian Roman antiquity, which then later defined the "world" of the German secondary school, with primordial antiquity.

The same return to the "great inception of the Greeks" is invoked in another pet political peeve of Heidegger's, one "that I experienced directly on my own body from my earliest youth" (June 22, 1932: 37/567): "All the recent political discussions basically concerned with Brüning and the Catholic Central Party took on the appearance of party politics. But *this* is precisely not the way I see the Center. Instead, I see *Rome-Moscow* and—yes, "and" is what I want to say—the *Greeks*, to whom, as Nietzsche put it, the *Germans* alone are equal."

This regress from 1) a geopolitical position to 2) spiritual postures (= worldviews) besieging the "metaphysical folk," such as the spirit of capitalism epitomized by "Wall Street," the specter of communism sweeping Europe from its shifting geographical centers, and the "demon" of Jesuitism or Catholicism that Heidegger would exorcise from his very being, culminating finally in the return to their ultimate measure in 3) German Da-sein in its close kinship with Greek Da-sein, the two most philosophical of the European languages: such a regress is most evident in Heidegger's Eurocentric analysis of the various geopolitical responses to technological globalization in his notorious course of SS 1935. The two latter regresses respectively, constitute Heidegger's second and third "concepts of the political."

Space does not permit more than a partial elaboration of Heidegger's second concept of the political, the one concerned with competing metaphysical "-isms" and their correlative competing concepts of the political in their bearing on concrete German Dasein between the world wars. For one thing, much of the documentation bearing on this aspect of the "Heidegger case" is still being withheld. Attention here will therefore be directed to just one of these still-unknown texts in which, in the context of reviewing some of the competing metaphysical concepts of the political,

Heidegger develops his own metontological concept of the political by the "ontological difference" between the people and the state, which predominates in the most public years of his career, when his philosophy resorts deliberately to hortatory journalism as well as the factual history of Germany. This in turn has of late generated a spate of journalistic rhetoric in the epideictic mode over the "Heidegger case," where notoriety serves to supplant the blatant lack of adequate supporting documentation.

The last half of Heidegger's seminar of Winter Semester (hereafter WS) 1933–34, "On the Essence and Concept of Nature, History, and the State,"[9] focuses its attention on the relationship between a *people* and its *state*, which constitutes the essence of the political. The seminar thus ends as an exercise in the political education of the "future leaders of the nation," as Rektor Heidegger construes this mandate imposed on the German universities by the Third Reich.

The political, which is a basic human possibility, a distinctive mode of being human, is the reason a state comes to be and is. The be-ing of the state is rooted in the political be-ing of human beings, who as a people decide for this state and support it. This political (i.e., historically fateful) decision requires clarification of the essential connection between the people and its state. Connecting the two constitutes the political education of a people, an introduction to its political being. A statesman or a leader is a leader insofar as he understands and examines and actualizes, in the vital disclosure of his true being, what a people and a state are, whence the need for a "political education" of the future leaders of the nation, which Heidegger will discharge in the last four hours of the seminar.

Every state, and every knowledge of a state, unfolds in a political tradition. Without this nourishing historical ground, the best idea of the state will not take root, grow, and develop out of the sustaining womb of the people. Otto the Great founded the First Reich upon the spiritual princes, obligating them to political and military service and knowledge. Frederick the Great educated the Prussian nobility to be guardians of his state. Bismarck personally supervised the planting of his idea of the state in the firm and fertile soil of the political nobility, and when his sustaining arm let go, the Second Reich collapsed. Today we cannot oversee the grounding of a political tradition nor the education of a political elite. Rather, each individual must come to meaningful terms with himself or herself in order to come to a knowledge of the people and state and to achieve self-responsibility. The state now rests on our watchfulness and readiness and on our life. Our way of be-ing marks the be-ing of the state. Every people takes a position toward the state, and no people lacks the drive toward a state. A people that rejects the state and so is stateless has not yet found the gathering of its essence. It still lacks the composure and strength of obligation to its fate as a people. (In the language of SZ, it has still not achieved its authentic and proper historicality.)

Clarification of the essence of a people and its state thus hinges on the clarification of the political as a mode of being of the human being, which makes the state possible. Against this essentially ontological conception are other concepts of the political, such as Carl Schmitt's. He situates the concept of the political in the friend-foe relationship, which in turn is grounded in the intuition that combative struggle (*Kampf*), that is, the real possibility of war, is the presupposition of all political comportment. It entails the possibility of a decisive battle, a struggle for decision that can also be fought without military means. Existing oppositions, whether moral, confessional, or economic, become acute to such a degree that they link friend and foe in a radical unity. All political existence rests on this unity and totality of opposition of friend and foe. It is crucial for us to note that this political unity of adversaries does not have to be identical to the state and people. (The single extant letter from Heidegger to Schmitt at this time hinges on the Heraclitean concept of the comprehensiveness of πόλεμος (*Kampf, Auseinandersetzung*), which Heidegger is already developing in an ontological direction at this time.)[10]

Another conception of the political is expressed succinctly in Bismarck's words, "Politics is the art of the possible." This does not refer to any conceivable possibility whatsoever, but rather to what is uniquely possible and only possible concretely. Politics for Bismarck is the capacity to see what has to arise essentially from a historical situation accompanied by the skill (τέχνη) to bring about what one at first merely envisions. Politics thus becomes the creative project of the great statesman, who surveys the comprehensive happening of history far beyond the present and sets a goal for his idea of the state, which he firmly keeps in sight despite all of the chance variations of the situation. This view of politics and the state is closely tied to the person of the genial statesman. The be-ing of the state is dependent on his essential vision and energy and persistence. When this power and vitality leaves off, the impotence of the state sets in. Once again we see that a state that is to have durability and to be able to come to maturity must instead be grounded in the be-ing of the people. The people are related to the state as a being is to its be-ing.

PEOPLE: STATE: BEING: BE-ING. The kind of be-ing in play in this relationship can only be understood through the be-ing of the human being, which can be characterized in terms of its consciousness and conscience. Just as the entity human being is conscious of his or her human be-ing, of how he or she comports to it and cares about it, so does the entity people have a basic cognitive relation to its state. The entity called the people in its be-ing brings about the state, knows about the state, cares about it, and wills it. Just as each human wants to live and to be there as human, just as she or he tenaciously holds onto it and loves her or his Da-sein in the world, so does a people love and will the state as its way and manner of being a people. The people are dominated by the drive or ἔρως toward the state. Insofar as this ἔρως is a superlative way of being human, the will toward the state cannot be understood merely in biological terms and compared to the instinct of bees and termites for their "state." The life (ζωή) of animals differs fundamentally from the life (βίος) of humans. As in the word "biography," βίος for the Greeks means the course of a life, its story, and thus the history and existence of human beings. Aristotle distinguished two noble kinds of human life, the active and the contemplative, where βίος πολιτικός strives for honor, fame, and good repute, and βίος θεωρητικός" is dedicated to pure beholding, philosophy.

The love, desire, and will of a people for the state are expressed in taking a position, rejection, dedication, service, and sacrifice, in brief, in a concern for the essence and form of the state. The form and constitution of the state is the essential expression of what the people posits for itself as sense, as meaning for its be-ing. The constitution is not a rational contract, an order of law, a political logic, or some other arbitrary absolute. Constitution and law are instead an actualization of our decision for the state, the factual testaments for what we hold as our historical task as a people and seek to live. Knowledge of the constitution and law is not something that only concerns "politicians" and jurists. It belongs to the Dasein of all individual human beings who take it upon themselves to struggle for the responsibility for their people. Our task in this historically decisive moment (καιρός) includes the cultivation of, and reeducation in, the thought of the state. Each and every man and woman must learn that his or her individual life, however faintly and unclearly, decides the destiny of the people and the state, supports or rejects it.

ORDER AND RANK. This knowledge includes a binding commitment to the order of the state. The order of the state is expressed in the domain of tasks designated for individuals and groups. This order is not merely organic, as one might assume and has assumed from the fable of Menenius Agrippa; it is human and spiritual, which means that it is voluntary. It is grounded in the relationship of governance and service among humans. Like the medieval order of life, the order of the state is today sustained by the free and unadulterated will to lead and to follow, to struggle and to be loyal and true. For when we ask, "What is governance? What is its basis?" and answer it in a truly essential way, we learn nothing of power, slavery, repression, and force. We learn rather that governance, authority, service, and subordination are grounded in a common task. Only when the leader and led bind themselves through commitment to a *single* destiny, and struggle for the actualization of *one* idea, does a true order emerge. Spiritual superiority and freedom then make themselves felt as a deep devotion of all forces to the people and state, as stringent discipline, as engagement, as a firm and steady hand, solitude, and love. The existence and superiority of the leader is then rooted in the be-ing, the soul of the people, and thus binds it to the task with originality and passion. And when the people sense this devotion, they will allow themselves to be led into the struggle, willing it and loving it. With every new moment of decision, the leader and his or her people will bind themselves ever closer together in order to bring about the essence of their state, and thereby of their be-ing. Growing together and apart, they will oppose the two ominous powers of death and the devil (i. e., of transience and decline) from their own essence, from their meaningful historical be-ing and willing.

Consider once again the internal reasons for the failure of Bismarckian politics. We heard that, in addition to a leader, a people need a tradition borne by a political elite, the nobility. The Second Reich collapsed after Bismarck's death, not only because he did not succeed in creating this political nobility, but also because he did not come to regard the proletariat as a phenomenon in its own right and so did not bring it into the state through appropriate concessions. But the real reason for the collapse was the popular character of the Second Reich exhausted itself in what we call patriotism and fatherland. These elements of the federation of 1870–71 are not in themselves negative, but they are totally inadequate for a true people's state, since they were not ultimately rooted in the people.

The state is a mode of being of the people and cannot simply be projected by a theoretician of the state. The people constitute the being whose be-ing the state is. There are two ways of considering this ontological relation. We can proceed from above, from the universal, from be-ing to beings. Since be-ing is not a being, an abyss of nothing opens between the two, and we must run the gauntlet of a nihilism in order to apprehend the sense of this be-ing. The universal approach should not be confused with the attempts to deduce the state in the seventeenth and eighteenth centuries. Rousseau believed for example that the state is a social contract concluded solely on the basis of each individual's striving for welfare. This is no longer the state in the sense of the political as a basic character of Occidental humanity, which exists on the basis of philosophy. It is instead a subordinate means, an association whose purpose is to serve the development of the individual personality in the liberal sense of that word, one domain among many.

SPACE AND PLACE. The second possibility is to proceed from below, from ourselves as a people and a state. Since the state as the be-ing of a people is manifestly historical, we might inquire into the historical character of a people. But since it is still undecided whether every deed of a people is from the start "stately" or political, we shall proceed from another direction. We have already seen that all processes of nature and happenings of history run their course in space and time. Since antiquity, space and time have been regarded as principles of individuation and determination, the moments that define beings in their uniqueness, individuality, and one-time-only character. They determine beings, including a people, in their concretion.

When we speak of a people in space, we first think of the slogan currently in circulation of a "people without space." But this already goes too far. What the catchphrase really means is a people without enough "living room" or space [Lebensraum], sufficient to permit their positive development. Literally, there is no such thing as a "people without space," which would mean a people without their concrete being. Every people has its own space over which it rules and by which it is marked. This of course is not to be taken in a purely geographic sense, which means the quasi-geometric, two-dimensional surface prescribed to a people on a "geopolitical" map. Even animals are not related to their space in such a two-dimensional way but rather in an "ecological" way, according to their locale or vital locus. A fish is defined by the water in which it lives, which gives it "living room," and so its life possibilities. Animals accordingly "accommodate" and "adjust" themselves to the space in which they at any given time find themselves. A crab transposed from a pond to a larger body of water itself also grows larger.

For the human being, accordingly, space is not simply its surroundings as an indifferent container. Each people—sea, mountain, valley, desert people—has its distinctive space over which it rules and by which it is marked. Both mastery over its space and being marked by its space reciprocally belong to the essence and way of being of a people. History teaches us that nomadic peoples are not nomadic because of the desolation of deserts and steppes, for they often leave deserts behind where there was once fertile cultivated land. It is not correct for a people to regard its single ideal to be in autochthony (*Bodenständigkeit*: nativity, rootedness) and long-standing residency, rootedness in its native soil, as peasants develop a sense of having sprung from an earth (*Bodenverwachsenheit*, a common primal myth) and of belonging to an earth as a result of the stubborn persistence required in cultivation, propagation, and growth. Equally necessary is the extension of range through interaction [*Verkehr*] that ventures abroad: trade, traffic, commerce, communication, and so on. The concrete way in which humans operate in space and shape it necessarily includes both autochthony and interaction.

What, then, is the space of a state? For the state is not a construction of spirit, nor a sum of laws, nor a verbal constitution, but it is essentially related to and marked by space. The space of a state is in a certain sense the space of the autochthonous people, understood as the operative range of its interaction in trade and traffic, commerce and communication, thus the "reach" of its power (*Be-reich*), the "realm" of its regime and rule (*Reich*). We call this space a land, territory, sovereign domain, dominion. It is in a sense the fatherland, which is not to be confused with a home. Viewed externally, home is in most cases a narrower region of the state's space, and it need not have anything at all to do with the state. Each involves entirely different relations. We can speak of the state only when the will to extension, the interaction generally called traffic and trade, is added to autochthony. I have a home because of birth, I am tied to it by natural powers. Home finds its expression in the nativity of autochthony and the sense of being bound to a place. But nature makes man autochthonous only when it belongs to the people as an environment, a surrounding world of which that man is a member. A home becomes the mode of being of a people only when it enters into the wider interaction of trade and traffic, commerce and communication, when it becomes a state. Peoples or their offspring who do not move beyond their home ties to their proper mode of being, the state, are in constant danger of losing their status as a people and entering into decline. This also is the great problem of those Germans who live outside the borders of the Reich. They have a German home but do not belong to the state of Germans, to the Reich, and so they are without their proper mode of be-ing. In summary, we can thus say that the space of a people, the people's ground, reaches as far as the branches of this people have found a home and have become autochthonous, so that the space of the state, its territory, arrives at its boundaries through traffic and trade, through its interaction at a distance, in the expanse of the world.

The state is the superlative be-ing of the people, whereas a people in its be-ing is not bound to the state in its various forms, and so outlasts the state. Folkish be-ing and stately be-ing are thus separate. But what a people is in its essence or in its prestately stand is not an easy question to pose. Since it always appears in a particular stately be-ing, it is always already political. The political and philosophical inquiry into one or the other moves in the polarity of the difference of people and state as a being to its be-ing.

But what is a state? We have already noted that a universal characteristic of the state is "order," but this abstract concept of order as a formal direction of thinking easily allows a discussion of the state to go astray, as the doctrines of the state of the nineteenth century bear witness. What kind of order is meant here? The order of rule, control, and mastery, thus the order of power, the order of superordination and subordination, of leadership and its following. The will of the one is succeeded by the will of the other, who therefore becomes the ruled, but this approach of ruler and ruled is accompanied by the idea that the people from the start and necessarily are the ruled, thereby denying in principle the self-will of the people. Here we have a rule that knows nothing about itself, it assumes the status of sovereignty, the highest power apprehended as the essence and expression of the state. From this circumstance, in which the state as this highest power accrues to one or a few, arises the tendency to transfer this sovereignty to the other partner, to the people, thus going to the other extreme. Only from the idea of the sovereignty of absolutism can we in fact understand and explain the essence of the French Revolution as a counter phenomenon.

WILLPOWER. Rule is power in the sense of the prevailing of a will, enforcing it, carrying it out to full enforcement. This presupposes a certain mightiness and command or control of power that first guarantees such an enforcement. Since rule and sovereignty are modes of being of a people, always imposed from a particular stately be-ing of a people, the question of the origin and grounding of power is always already politically defined. The will of the state enforces itself in a number of ways (e.g., in governance and administration).

But what is will? Will, in contrast to a wish, is a striving that puts itself into action, engages itself. In this engagement, will is directed at something important and definite, a goal or an end, with a clear sense of the ways and means to actualize that goal. The will grasps the situation in the fullness of its time, in it the καιρός is at work, calling for resoluteness and action in the full sense.

Action can be practically technical, directed toward the realization of a thing, or practically moral, directed toward the actualization of the will of another or of an entire group, a community of will. The will of an individual and the will of a people are not the same. A people's will is not free in the way an individual's will is free. It is a people's will, which is not the sum of individual wills, that a leader has to contend with and carry through. The question of the volitional consciousness of a community is a problem of all democracies. The question can become fruitful only after the leader's will and the people's will are known in their essentiality. Today it is a matter of orienting the basic relationship of our communal being to this inseparable reality of folk and leader. Only when this basic schema is transformed into its essentiality is a true schooling of leaders possible.

SPEECH AND ACTION. The relationship of ruler to ruled does not necessarily mean that the ruled are the oppressed. True rule, which has the power to create rank order, and true power, which points out and assigns means and ends to the ruled, do not oppress the ruled. Will as committed engagement in any goal it pleases is the will of an adventurer. True rule requires true knowledge of the goal, the wisdom of a statesman, as well as engagement, the leap toward its fulfillment, and the perseverance, the staying power, to bring this commitment of action to its conclusion. There are two ways of carrying out a will, putting it into effect, enforcing it (*Durchsetzung*)—*persuasion* and *coercion*.

Persuasion can occur by speech or by deed. The Greeks in particular recognized the power of speech as a political power. Their political instinct made the persuasive power of the speech into a paradigm of politics, like the unforgettable speeches of Thucydides. If nowadays the speeches of the Führer give the impression of "drumming" their points across, in his inimitably forceful style of "propagandizing" (*Trommelnder*), such an impression is but an unconscious acknowledgment of the power of speech that the Greeks had already uncovered politically [cf. the three forms of πίστεις of rhetorical politics, discussed above]. But the active will "persuades" most forcefully through deeds. The doer of deeds and the man of action are at once the "power in authority," the "ruler," whose Dasein and will are determining through "persuasion," that is, through the knowledge and acknowledgment of the superior governing will of the Führer.

Carrying out the will also can be done by *coercion*, executed in the form of a command. This form is not creative. Nevertheless, a command can be an occasion for the release of conviction, as it was in 1914. Can coercion generate a will? What is the attitude of the coerced in an action performed under coercion? The "counterwill" of antipathy [*Widerwille*] is a form of willing and not just a non-willing. Willing-in-counterwilling is a relationship of privation, a superlative form of negation.

POLITICAL EDUCATION. True effectuation of a will does not come by coercion but by awakening the same willing in the other (i.e., the same goal in its engagement and fulfillment). It in effect brings about the recreation of the man to accord with the mood and temper of the ruling will. It comes about not by a momentary yes-saying but by a decision on the part of the individual. Important here is not the number of individuals but the qualitative value of the individual decision. This is the way in which the present requirement of "political education" is to be understood: it is not a matter of learning maxims, opinions, and forms "by heart," but of creating a new fundamental attitude of a willful kind.[11]

The will of the leader first of all recreates the others into a following out of which a community arises. It is out of this vital solidarity of followers to leader that sacrifice and service arise, and not from sheer obedience and institutional coercion. Political education is a superlative form of the effectuation of the will of the leader and of the state's will, which is the people's will. Other forms of rendering the will of the state effective, such as the administration of governance and justice, were noted above only in context.

CONCLUSION. Today's development of the state as a becoming of the people is once again emphasized, along with one of the essential concepts of the modern theory of the state, namely, the concept of sovereignty. First formulated precisely in Johannes Bodinus's *Republica* (1576), this power is made subject to the superior obligation to God. Today we say "people" instead of "God" when we invoke this ultimate bond of obligation. It produces the highest freedom, whereas the breach of this bond is negative freedom. Political freedom often has been misconstrued as negative freedom, which has led to the claim of sovereignty for the people, just as the omnipotent God has been secularized into the sovereignty of the state. This line of thought led to three great modern solutions in the face of the dissolution of the universal duties and obligations inherited from the Middle Ages. Descartes'—declaration of the independence of the various regions of being thus alludes to the three regions thematized by our seminar discussions—nature, history, and the state. Of the three, the state is the narrowest in scope, and yet it is the most actual of actualities, which must give a new and an original sense to all of be-ing. The highest actualization of the human be-ing happens in the state. The leader state [*Führerstaat*] that we have signifies a completion of historical development: the actualization of the people in the leader. The Prussian state, as it was brought to completion under the tutelage of the Prussian nobility, is the preliminary form of the present state. This relationship generates the elective affinity and congeniality that prevailed between Prussiandom and the leader. We come from this great tradition and stand in it when we confess to its sense in the words of the royal elector, spoken in the spirit of Luther: *Si gestamus principatus ut sciam rem esse populi non unam privatam* [To assume the mantle of leadership is for me to understand that the affairs of the people are not a private matter.]

The Archaic Concept of the Political

The regression to German-Greek Da-sein that generates the third concept of the political, the archaic (poietic, *seynsgeschichtlicher*) concept, is facilitated especially by Hölderlin's poetic German translations of Greek tragedy. It is a return to the great beginning and first inception of ontology in the Western language which, "next to German, is at once the most powerful and the most spiritual of languages (in regard to its possibilities of thought)."[12] In the example that we shall now quickly track in its historical sense (*Be-sinnung*), it is a matter of restoring the originative power of one of the most influential words in the Greek language, πόλις, the root of the political, its politics, polity, policy, police, and so on, in so many Western languages and overly exploited in the politicized time of 1935 (EM, 102). In the context of the tragic fate of humanity drawn in the foreboding lines of the chorus of Theban elders in Sophocles's *Antigone*, Heidegger finds that πόλις is not merely a geographically located state (*Staat*) or city (*Stadt*) but, more basically, a historical site [*Stätte*] (EM, 156), virtually identical to the ontological site of Da-sein, in which a unique humankind (e.g., Greek being-here, German being-there) "takes place" (*statt-findet, statt-hat*), is "granted stead" (*gestattet* = permitted), and in this "leeway" (*Spielraum*) of allotted time and historical place makes its unique "homestead" (*Heimstatt*) befitting its historical destiny.

> The πόλις is the site of history, the There, in which, out of which, and for which history happens. To this site of history belong the gods, the temples, the priests, the celebrations, the games, the poets, the thinkers, the ruler, the council of elders, the assembly of the people, the armed forces and the ships. All this does not first belong to the πόλις, is not first political, because it enters into a relationship with a statesman and a general and with the affairs of state. Rather, what we have named is political, that is, at the site of history, insofar as, for example, the poets are *only* poets, but then are actually poets, the thinkers are *only* thinkers, but then are actually thinkers, the priests are *only* priests, but then are actually priests, the rulers are *only* rulers, but then are actually rulers. Are—but this says: to use their power as violence-doers and to rise to eminent stature in historical be-ing as creators, as doers. Rising to a supreme stature in the site of history, they also become ἄπολις, without city and site, lone-some, un-canny, with no way out amidst beings as a whole, at the same time without statute and limit, without structure and fittingness, because they as creators must in each of their situations first ground all this. (EM, 117)

The creators of the political are not only the politicians but also the apolitical. Poets and thinkers statesmen and prophets are gathered together in unity and lonely, untimely, tragic, and contentious dialogue at this core of history, Da-sein. The very example, Heidegger's choice of Hölderlin's translation of Sophocles's *Antigone* itself, illustrates this unity and peculiar interchange among the creators of the πόλις. To be truly political is to be at the site of history, Da-sein in its root facticity and possibility, which in each of its epochal instantiations is ours here-and-now. The epochal history of the West begins with the ancient Greek Da-sein retrieved incipiently above from the Greek tragedy of conflict between family piety and royal ediction and is now ending in the global epoch of technological geopolitics, which Heidegger, in this course of SS 1935, depicts from the here-and-now instantiation of the German homeland in

contention with the global, technological powers of Russia and America. In each in
stantiation of Da-sein, "the human being is then related in an exceptional sense to this
pole [of the πόλις], insofar as human beings, in understanding be-ing, stand in the
middle of beings and here necessarily have a 'status' in each of their historical instantiations, a stance in their states and their circumstances. Such a 'status' is the 'State'"
(GA 53 100;I, 81). Geopolitics is now to be regarded neither geographically nor metaphysically, but in its purity as a "site" within the *seynsgeschichtliche* politics of Dasein
as it instantiates itself in the epochal history of archaic be-ing, now on the verge of the
revolution to a new and radically different inception. This "'politics' in the supreme
and authentic sense" (GA 39, 214) thus takes place at the supreme site of radical historical transition displayed by the Greek tragedy, as the above recital shows, which
glosses the oxymoronic status of the tragic heroine (Antigone) as ὑψίπολις ἄπολις,
at once far beyond and without home and site, unhomely, lonesome, uncanny, singled
out for lofty greatness by creating a new home for her people, as well as for the precip-
itous destruction which also was the fate of Heidegger's more contemporary heroes:
Hölderlin, Nietzsche, van Gogh, and Schlageter. Throughout this "Greek-German
mission of transmission [*Sendung*]" (GA 39, 151) across the history of be-ing by
Hölderlin's translation of Sophoclean tragedy, Heidegger repeatedly alludes to the
counteressence of the tragic hero, his hubris in arrogating power (GA 53, 116;I, 93),
but without ever truly confronting the inhuman possibilities of this lonesome superiority and uncanny "greatness" that yields another kind of hero, or anti-hero (Creon,
Hitler). The Greek-German mission focuses instead on a repetition of Hölderlin's
transmission of a poetic sense of the "fatherland" and the "national" and "home" that
Heidegger had originally hoped to find resonating in the folkish mythos of a uniquely
German National Socialism, guiding the decisions of its statesmen in the "land of
poets and thinkers." Politics (or better, statesmanship) here finds its origins in poetizing and thinking. "It is from these two prior activities that the Dasein of a people is
made fully effective as a people through the state—politics" (GA 39, 51).

It is from this archaic vantage of Da-sein that Heidegger now criticizes the Nazi
claim of the totalitarian character of the political. "These [Nazi] enthusiasts are now
suddenly discovering the 'political' everywhere. . . . But the πόλις cannot be defined
'politically.' The πόλις, and precisely it, is therefore not a 'political' concept. . . . Perhaps the name πόλις is precisely the word for that realm that constantly became
questionable anew, remained worthy of question, and necessitated certain decisions
whose truth on each occasion displaced the Greeks into the groundless or the inaccessible" (GA 53, 98f;I, 80). Aristotle saw clearly that man was a political animal, because he was the animal possessed by speech. But he did not see the full uncanniness
that membership in the πόλις brings, far outstripping the rhetorical as well as the
political (GA 53, 102;I, 83) of a people's state. Hölderlin's poetic words, "Since we
are a conversation/and can hear from one another," refer to the thoughtful dialogue
among solitary creators (poets, thinkers, statesmen) at the very abysses of be-ing. Language here is the original institution of be-ing in the violent words of poetic origin

and not just a means of communication for the sake of quick and easy agreement, rhetoric. The community of creators is a combative community of struggle over the extreme issues of be-ing. Hearing from one another, listening to one another, reciprocally involves radically placing each other in question over the radical issues at stake. Rapprochement here is contention, contestation, war. Coming to an understanding is combat. "Conversation here is not communication, but the fundamental happening of radical exposure in the thick of beings" (GA 39, 73).

Notes

Heidelberger Neueste Nachrichten 150 (July 1, 1933):4. This old newspaper article was republished in Guido Schneeberger, *Nachlese zu Heidegger. Dokumente zu seinem Leben und Denken* (Bern: private circulation, 1962), pp. 73–75, and recently reprinted in the Appendix to GA 16, 761–63 (hereafter cited as GA 16, followed by the German and English pagination). Translated as "The University in the New Reich" in Richard Wolin, ed., *The Heidegger Controversy: A Critical Reader* (Cambridge: MIT Press, 1993), pp. 43–45, (hereafter cited as HC). A similarly entitled talk, "Die Universität im nationalsozialistischen Staat," was delivered by Rektor Heidegger at the University of Tübingen on November 30, 1933, and reported the following day in the *Tübinger Chronik* (article reprinted in GA 16, 765–77). It was extensively paraphrased by Hugo Ott in *Martin Heidegger. Unterwegs zu seiner Biographie* (Frankfurt/New York: Campus, 1988), p. 231, and translated by Allan Blunden as *Martin Heidegger: A Political Life* (London: Basic Books, 1993), p. 242f, (hereafter cited as Ott, followed by the German and English pagination). The November talk, however, touches only lightly on the concept of the political and restricts itself to a single sarcastic remark on "political education": "The new docent writes pamphlets about the new concept of science, there is talk about political students and political faculties . . . but this is simply old wine in colorfully re-labeled bottles [*das übermalte Alte*]" (231/242). Clearly, Heidegger felt that he was underway toward developing a new philosophical concept of the political, albeit steeped in traditional, and therefore comprehensible, language. See the seminar of WS 1933–1934 below.

1. Letter dated March 30, 1933, in Martin Heidegger/Elisabeth Blochmann, *Briefwechsel 1918–1969*, Joachim W. Storck, ed. (Marbach am Neckar: Deutsche Schillergesellschaft, 1989), p. 60. and translated by Frank W. H. Edler in "Selected Letters from the Heidegger-Blochmann Correspondence," *Graduate Faculty Philosophy Journal* 14:2–15:1 (1991):557–77, esp. 570f.

2. Ibid.

3. Directive 5 of "*Richtlinien für die Kulturpolitische Arbeitsgemeinschaft deutscher Hochschullehrer,*" document drafted by Ernst Krieck and signed on March 3, 1933, by

Heidegger and other charter members of this "working group" at its organizational meeting. The group held its first conference in Frankfurt on April 22-23, 1933, with Heidegger scheduled to speak on "The Concept of Science in Research and Teaching." Documents deposited in the Central State Archive of Potsdam.

4. Heidegger's letter to Carl Schmitt, dated August 22, 1933, is published in bilingual form in *Telos* 72 (summer 1987): 132. Hans Frank founded the Academy for German Law in June 1933. Shortly thereafter, its Committee for Philosophy of Law was formed, with Rector Martin Heidegger and State Advisor Carl Schmitt as charter members. It is not clear whether in the course of these common activities the two ever met, for example, at its meeting in the Nietzsche Archive in Weimar on May 3-5, 1934. At least Hans Frank and Albert Rosenberg came from Berlin to hold the major addresses in the presence of Elisabeth Förster-Nietzsche, and Heidegger and Erich Rothacker and others were given a tour of the archive.

Schmitt's concept of the "total state" as the identity of the state with all of society, to which Heidegger frequently refers in his oral and written works of the mid-1930s, first surfaces in Carl Schmitt, *Der Hüter der Verfassung* (Tübingen: Mohr [Siebeck], 1931), pp. 78-79. Cf. also the Preface to the 1934 edition of *Political Theology*, translated by George Schwab (Cambridge: MIT Press, 1985), p. 2; *The Concept of the Political*, translated by George Schwab (New Brunswick: Rutgers University Press, 1976), pp. 22-23, 29, passim; total state distinguished from totalitarianism, pp. 38-39. Schmitt arrived at the "total state" by the common understanding of WW I as a "total war" and the "total mobilization" (Ernst Jünger's phrase, 1930) that enters into it. Cf. Carl Schmitt, *Briefwechsel mit einem Schüler*, Armin Mohler, ed., with Irmgard Huhn and Pied Tommim (Berlin: Akademie, 1995), pp. 417-18.

5. A more detailed account is to be found in Theodore Kisiel, "Situating Rhetorical Politics in Heidegger's Protopractical Ontology (1923-1925: The French Occupy the Ruhr)," *Existentia* 9 (1999):11-30. A more accessible version under the same title is to be found in *International Journal of Philosophical Studies* 8:2 (2000): 185-208.

6. Martin Heidegger, *Sein und Zeit* (Tübingen: Niemeyer, 1927; 17th ed. 1994), p. 138.

7. Martin Heidegger, *Die Selbstbehauptung der deutschen Universität: Das Rektorat 1933/34*, Hermann Heidegger, ed. (Frankfurt: Klostermann, 1983), p. 9., translated by Lisa Harries as "The Rectoral Address," in Günther Neske and Emil Kettering, eds., *Martin Heidegger and National Socialism: Questions and Answers* (New York: Paragon House, 1990), p. 5.

8. Leopold Dingraeve (alias of Ernst Wilhelm Eschmann, member of the Action Circle), *Wohin treibt Deutschland?* (Jena: Diederichs, 1932), p. 79.

9. The title constituted a last-minute change by Rektor Heidegger, who had announced instead a seminar on Fichte's *Wissenschaftslehre*, or perhaps Leibniz's *Monadologie*. "Every week, beginning on Friday, November 3, from 17 to 19 hours." See *Heidelberger Neueste Nachrichten*, pp. 137–38. The seventh to the tenth (concluding) weeks were devoted to the concept of the state in accord with the seminar title. I am grateful to Marion Heinz, Alfred Denker, and Klaus Stichweh for transcribing and deciphering the extant protocols of this seminar.

10. See note 4 above.

11. At about the same time as his philosophical seminar of WS 1933–34 was illustrating the nature and purpose of political education at the university, Rektor Heidegger's public (local) speeches and statements began to address the same issue in more popular forums. "The university is becoming the highest political school for the people of this scenic region" (January 6, 1934; *Heidelberger Neueste Nachrichten*, p. 171, reprinted in GA 16, 227). "Anything that is political does not consist in sermons on statements of principle but in action that accords with the situation. As soon as the rising new generation of teachers is in place, the university will acknowledge its political task" (January 29, 1934; ibid., p. 197). "The new university must be the bridge between the people and its leadership. Every science is political; political in the sense that knowledge in every question, in every answer, is grounded in the people" (February 21, 1934; ibid., p. 214).

12. Martin Heidegger, *Einführung in die Metaphysik* (course of SS 1935) (Tübingen: Niemeyer, 1953), p. 43, (hereafter cited as EM). Newly translated by Richard Polt and Gregory Fried as *Introduction to Metaphysics* (New Haven, Conn.: Yale University Press, 2000), which gives the German pagination of the Niemeyer edition in the margin.

10

The Baby and the Bath Water
On Heidegger and Political Life

DENNIS J. SCHMIDT

> If one knew the facts, would one have to feel pity even for the planets? If one
> reached the heart of the matter?
> —Graham Greene, cited by Vernon, in *A Book of Reasons*

T o speak about "Heidegger and political life" is still exceedingly difficult, and the proximate reason for this is painfully obvious: we have precious few texts in the enormous body of works by Heidegger that clearly address themes that one would expect in the matter of political life, and most of the texts that we do have where there is some direct acknowledgment that the character of political community is indeed worthy of philosophical reflection are those entangled in some manner in the most monstrous politics of the twentieth century. For this and other more subtle reasons, I believe that it will be quite some time still until the question posed by the topic of Heidegger and political life can be addressed productively and creatively.

The details both large and small, which seem to preempt any effort to speak about political life from out of the horizons opened by Heidegger, are amply documented and well known.[1] It is unlikely that there remain facts that are to be unearthed and that might illuminate the issues for us. Rather, it is our inability to *think* these facts that needs to be addressed; it is the noncoincidence of the facts and the forms of judgment that we have inherited that deposits us in this difficult impasse. It is the fact that *we still do not yet understand* that is most disturbing. And yet it is precisely this impasse, this exceeding difficulty we face in any effort to think the conjunction between what Heidegger's work signals and the task of thinking the enigmas of our shared life in time, that makes this topic all the more urgent. It also is indicative of the situation out of which we might address this topic, namely, that in truth we have not yet moved beyond the forms of thinking that Heidegger has shown in need of overcoming. The aporias of our history and our failure to grasp this history philosophically have absorbed into themselves some of the most creative philosophizing of our age, and in this regard, Heidegger is preeminent. Consequently, we find ourselves unable to answer even the most basic questions raised by the theme of Heidegger and political life. And so, almost before we can begin to truly address this theme, we must put some questions to ourselves that pry open this difficult nut. How are we to situate Heidegger's own political error with respect to the history that he argued must be overcome, as well as the history that he would open up? What will it take for us to think the situation of political life from the point of view articulated by Heidegger, in other words, from out of a future that does not rely on the forms of thinking that have stilted and ossified our conception of shared life in history? Why is it that the political character of what must surely be regarded as one of the most creative and provocative minds of our era has yet to be unfolded and discussed? Why is it that we have not yet been able to come to any clear understanding of just what it means that such a mind could, in some sense, understand itself in collusion with the one of the most distorted political movements in the history of the West? In the end, what becomes most clear in this matter is that *we* have not yet come clear about the proper measure that might justly assess the political significance of philosophical reflections that require us to think outside of the framework of assumptions that have come to be taken for granted. What should be clear from the outset is that the one put to the real test by the topic of Heidegger and political life is *us*.

Perhaps there are two reasons the current state of reflection on this topic is so complicated: one is to be fought against, and one is to be reflected upon. One reason we have yet to come to terms with the awkwardness announced by the conjunction "Heidegger and political life" is simple: there is an effort to discredit Heidegger by tarring him whole cloth with the worst features of his political blunder in the 1930s. This is the argument that Heidegger was and remained a Nazi, and we need to recognize that his thought bears an essential relation to Nazism. Such an argument is one that proposes we throw the baby, Heidegger, out with the bath water of National Socialism, because here the baby drank the bath water.[2] Those making this argument based on moral grounds simply slow the process, whereby we will eventually truly come to think the issues we must confront. However, one feature of this argument is worth noting and preserving, namely, the claim that Heidegger's work cannot be thought independently of history, that it cannot be surgically removed from the tendencies of the times (this means, of course, that the photographic negative of this argument that dismisses Heidegger as a whole—namely, the argument that passes over the dilemma of politics in the matter of Heidegger—is itself thoroughly specious, since it relies on such a surgical strategy). But, generally, the argument to dismiss Heidegger's contributions to philosophy as a whole on political and moral grounds, an argument that would bring to a close without reflection the critique of Western culture that Heidegger has shown to be crucial to our age, needs to be unmasked as itself an obstacle to progressive political reflections. Such arguments, which are simply dismissive of Heidegger and which typically tend to be fueled by a self-righteous moralizing, need to be fought. We need to ask whether *moral* grounds are the proper grounds upon which the difficulty of politics in the matter of Heidegger is to be thought.

But the other reason that we have yet to come to real terms with the issues broached by the topic of Heidegger and politics is found in specific character of Heidegger's thought itself. There we find a complicated argument that claims that the crisis of the historical present is first and foremost rooted in the nature of metaphysics; in other words, that *the crisis of culture is, at bottom, a philosophic crisis* and so must be addressed as such. Heidegger's project of overcoming metaphysics, the effort to shift philosophic reflection to a new register, must be seen, in part at least, as an effort to overcome the props of Western culture and the politics possible in such a culture. Of course, Heidegger is not alone in formulating a radical critique of Western culture that links the unfreedoms of that culture to its metaphysical character. The tradition of this argument is a long one begun by Hegel and accelerated by Nietzsche, but what must be acknowledged is that perhaps the greatest leap in this tradition, the moment of its most extensive synthesis (the wedding of the critiques of technology, values, metaphysics, substance, and humanism, to name just a few of its features), is accomplished by Heidegger. But what is puzzling is that this leap, this dramatic effort to open forms of thinking that might lead to a different kind of future, comes, horribly enough, at the precise historical moment that the seeds of the culture Heidegger is criticizing blossom hideously. But *this is no accident*, and when it is finally properly addressed, Heidegger's political thought, both its implicit and explicit features, will need to be thought in conjunction with the historical rupture defining the moment of its first real formulation. Revolutionary to the core, Heidegger's work wants minimally to displace the fundamental terms that have long served to define the goals of political reflection, and even the very definition of political. Here the political is thoroughly subordinated to the philosophical, so that a transformation in the character of philosophy presents itself as a revolutionary act.[3] Strangely, incomprehensibly, Heidegger's self-understanding of that revolution linked it, for a while at least, to what was paraded about as the National Socialist revolution. But nothing could be more remote from the truly revolutionary character of Heidegger's thought.[4]

There have been promising efforts to think creatively from a perspective more or less shaped by the horizons opened by Heidegger (namely, to think from out of a profoundly altered sense of our relations to, and the meaning of, time, history, and language).[5] But even the most innovative efforts to liberate Heidegger from his brief but unrepented political self-interpretation in 1933 still must confront that self-interpretation, especially as it is expressed in Heidegger's address as the Rector of the University of Freiburg.[6] In the end, for the present at least, any reflection on the topic of Heidegger and political life must begin by confronting the Rectoral Address. We must do this not because it represents the best text for understanding how we are to think political life in the wake of Heidegger, but because it is so thoroughly compromised by its own place in history and because it is precisely this entanglement that Heidegger has long argued needs to be thought.

The modest remarks that follow are divided into two parts, each designed to in-dicate some strategies that might open the paths down which the topic of Heidegger and political life becomes a theme that challenges us in creative ways. In the first part, my intention is to situate the Rectoral Address in a tradition that might let us see more clearly how it is to be read. One purpose of this part is to call attention to what I take to be the serious questions that Heidegger tries to raise in that address. Though frequently discussed, the Rectoral Address seldom seems to be *read*.[7] In the second part of this chapter, my intention is simply to outline some of which I take to be Heidegger's real contribution to a possible politics. My intention in this part, largely programmatic in nature, is to widen the horizon of texts that we recognize as pertinent to the question of political life in Heidegger. Here I want to argue—very much against Heidegger's explicit declarations to the contrary—that Heidegger's work, especially the work of the decade or so immediately following the debacle of the Rec-toral Address, exhibits a profoundly political character.

Two extremely different texts forming bookends in the history of Western phi-losophy and a closely knit tradition of texts dedicated to the nature of the university help us place Heidegger's "Self-Assertion of the German University" in an interesting context. The two texts to which I refer are Plato's 7th Letter and Fichte's *Addresses to the German Nation*. The tradition of texts concerning the nature of the university to which I refer begins with Kant's *The Conflict of the Faculties* and moves through Schelling's "Lectures on the Method of Academic Studies," Hegel's "On Lecturing on Philosophy in Universities, amd Schleiermacher's "Some Remarks on Universities in the German Sense," and ends with Nietzsche's "On the Future of Our Teaching Institutions." While one can never deny the historical moment in which this address is composed and delivered (and delivered more than once, always to great effect, thus compounding the problem), we do this text a disservice if we only read it against its historical moment. The following remarks are intended to serve as a preliminary ef-fort to unfold and legitimate the suggestion that, while never forgetting its historical moment, we also read the Rectoral Address in the context of these other texts.

Reflecting on Heidegger's political involvement in the 1930s, Gadamer makes the following remark: "That Heidegger's revolution in the universities failed, and that his involvement in the cultural politics of the Third Reich was a sad story we watched at a distance with anxiety, has led many to think about what Plato came up against in Syra-cuse. Indeed, after Heidegger resigned from the rectorate, one of his Freiburg friends, seeing him in the streetcar, greeted him: "Back from Syracuse?"[8] No more pointed, and appropriate, question could be put to Heidegger. No greater parallel can be found in the history of philosophy to serve as a sort of model for understanding Heidegger's astonishing political naivete than the case of Plato. The reference to Plato's involve-ment with Dion of Syracuse is perfectly on target, and it must be said that the kinship between Heidegger and Plato is never greater than in the Rectoral Address. It is a kinship found both in the circumstantial parallels to Plato's dealings with the tyrant at Syracuse and the philosophical argument that Plato makes regarding political life.

One sees this kinship with Plato in the way that the Rectoral Address makes the thoroughly Platonic move of tacitly suggesting that the philosopher should be the spiritual leader of the people. Here, in thinly disguised form, we find a repetition of the argument that Plato makes in the *Republic*, that thinking, defined according to an image ruled by the privilege of theory, has prerogatives in all matters of politics and shared life. In other words, here Heidegger succumbs to the ultimate metaphysical self-understanding, namely, that the philosopher should be king.[9] Behind this self-aggrandizement of philosophizing lies a forgetting of the relation of truth and *praxis*, a forgetting of the riddle of judgment that is masked by the absolutism of the idea. And yet it is precisely this relation and this riddle that Heidegger had so powerfully disclosed and made the leitmotiv of his work from the earliest years, when Heidegger had exposed the finitude of truth and the hermeneutic obscurity of every judgment as so deep that he could say "*Das Leben ist diesig, es nebelt sich selbst immer ein.*"[10] Nothing could be more remote from the presumptions of the infinite and absolute claim of the idea than the enduring and finite starting point for thinking that Heidegger formulates.

With Plato, the matter is different, and his 7th Letter, which is an effort to come to terms with his own political misjudgment, struggles to hold onto the conviction that the idea is the proper vantage point of thinking's relation to truth, and thus is privileged in all forms of reflection.[11] That letter, written as a reflection upon his efforts to educate the tyrant and his hope that he might lead a revolution, thus constructing a real polity on the basis of the idea, is a protracted defense of the most basic metaphysical conviction about the relation of philosophy to politics, namely, that political decision be submitted to philosophical control. Such a view is founded in the notion that the idea, the real currency of metaphysics, is itself free precisely because of its detachment from practical life.[12] In the 7th Letter, Plato says this quite clearly: "Hence I was forced to say in praise of the correct philosophy that it affords a vantage point from which we can discern in all cases what is just for communities and for individuals, and that accordingly the human race will not see better days until either the stock of those who rightly and genuinely follow philosophy acquire political authority, or else the class who have political control be led by some dispensation of providence to become real philosophers."[13] Plato writes that he was quickly disillusioned by the truth of the situation, and that he soon found himself at odds with the assumptions and habits that animated the culture of Syracuse. Nonetheless, fueled by the conviction of the rightness of philosophy for the tasks of shared life, he persisted in trying to educate the tyrant and thus to change the conditions of the culture. His lack of judgment in this matter almost cost him his life, but in the end he simply comes to the conclusion that, "Some fate too strong for man made havoc of our plans."[14] Though perhaps shaken (one sees this somewhat in the contrast between the tone of the *Republic* and the *Laws*), Plato's faith in the idea as the element of truth and in the resulting conception of truth as the determining ground of political life holds fast. It will be Aristotle to whom Heidegger is beholden in so many ways who will first propose something like a genuinely philosophical acknowledgment of the limits of the idea in matters of practical life. And it is precisely this Aristotelean insight, this rejoinder to Plato's conception of the relation of philosophizing and political life, which will be so decisive for Heidegger in *Being and Time*.[15] Though he seems to argue otherwise, I would suggest that the Rectoral Address gives voice to a conception of political life that finds its solutions in the possibilities of thinking defined by both the idea and the relation to the idea found in *technê*.[16] In other words, the Rectoral Address is the most Platonic of Heidegger's texts.

But the parallel to Plato is circumstantial as well as substantial in this case. Like Plato, Heidegger consorts with the tyrant for awhile, and like Plato, it is not with the hope of enlisting himself to the ends that the tyrant has laid out, but with the intention of serving as the spiritual leader of the tyrant, that is, *"den Führer führen."*[17] Insofar as this failure to appreciate the limits of theoretical reflection, of the idea, defines the logic and spirit of the Rectoral Address, it must be said that, rather than being an expression of the revolutionary move to overcome metaphysics and the culture built upon its presumptions, this address stands as the epitome of a metaphysical conception of the relation of thinking to political life. If this is so, then we would do well to read Heidegger's subsequent remarks on the Rectoral Address, the remarks found in the small text *"Tatsache und Gedanken"* (1945), as Heidegger's own 7th Letter. Sadly, something more is needed than even this, and yet it must be said that Heidegger's remarks of 1945 never reach the philosophical level of the 7th Letter.

Interestingly, and tellingly, the conclusion of the Rectoral Address is made with a citation from Plato's *Republic*. The final words of Heidegger's text appear without context, first in Greek, then in Heidegger's translation. The Greek line runs "τὰ . . . μεγάλα ἐπισφαλῆ"; Heidegger's translation reads *"Alles Grosse steht im Sturm."*[18] The translation is telling, but even more telling is the context of this citation, a context that Heidegger does not provide. This line, which Plato presents as itself a citation (of a proverb), occurs in Book VI when, in a conversation about the twin themes of how philosophy is slandered by those who do not understand its role in the city and the risks to philosophy when philosophizing about political life, Socrates answers a question by saying that it is necessary to understand "How a city can take philosophy in hand without being destroyed. For surely all great things carry with them the risk of a fall, and, really, as the saying goes, *fine things are hard* [τὰ . . . μεγάλα ἐπισφαλῆ]."[19] Plato, whose teacher was executed by the state, thought he knew well the risks for his understanding of the task of philosophizing in matters of political life. Heidegger would learn this too, or at least if he did not learn this lesson, he would stand as a reminder to us about this risk. What we still might need to understand is the true nature of this risk; above all, we need to understand that the risk is not (as Plato presents it) only *to* philosophy but *comes from* philosophy and places the city itself in jeopardy.

But lest the Rectoral Address be misunderstood as a work genuinely concerned with matters of the community rather than a text enlisted for political purposes, it should be said that Heidegger never really conceived of the Rectoral Address as a statement on political life or on the character of community or justice. Rather, his concern here is first and foremost with the nature of the university, and with the role of the university in the political community. Saying this brings me to the second point I would like to make about the context for a reading of the Rectoral Address, namely, that we should read it as yet another contribution to a long line of addresses found in German philosophy about the nature and role of the university. This point also needs to be seen in light of the aforementioned reference to the Platonic character of the address: the turn to the university, the call for its "self-affirmation" or "self-assertion"(a bold claim at this historical juncture),[20] is the specific form that Heidegger's affirmation of theoretical life takes. When we permit the text to define its own horizons, then we must say that the concerns of this address are remarkably narrow in scope and, while one might justly be troubled by the blindness at work here and by the academic tunnel vision that frames what is said here, we should not on that account read the text too far beyond the borders of its own announced context. If we do let the text define its own context, in part at least, then the question of the wider cultural mission of the university should be recognized as the central axis of this context. The politics driving Heidegger in this text tend to be the lowest form of politics, namely, what we refer to now as "academic politics." Issues within the university, and issues at stake in professional associations, are more on Heidegger's mind than the national and international questions shaping world history at this moment.[21] One can only be stunned by the role that such small matters played at a moment that such very large matters were clearly at stake; nonetheless, one should acknowledge the smallness of what is at play in the Rectoral Address as Heidegger conceives it.[22] But there are some larger, and genuinely philosophical, concerns at stake here, and Heidegger is self-consciously joining a tradition that had long sought to understand the spiritual mission of a people, here specifically "the" German people by a set of reflections on the task of philosophy. It is a long tradition, one that finds its most extensive expression in Fichte's *Addresses to the German Nation* (a text to which Heidegger's Rectoral Address owes so much that one must wonder why Heidegger does not acknowledge a debt to it[23]).

Heidegger's real concern in this address is to renew the university by calling it out of its increasing commitment to professionalization and to a specific conception of science and the role of technology in knowledge. Professionalized and technicized, Heidegger argued that the university had lost its unity and inner articulation. More precisely, his view is that philosophy has lost sight of its privileged role, in other words, that it had lost its metaphysical preeminence, and that for the university to recover its cultural task, philosophizing must recover its central place in the university. The university is thought on the model of a living organism, and philosophizing gives expression to the special nature of its unity. It is an old argument, one made clearly by Kant and Schelling, and it is an argument still made frequently (and in significant measure justly) today.[24] However, what must be stressed here is that Heidegger links this project of renewing the *university* to a renewal of the German *nation*. No longer is the university thought of from a cosmopolitan point of view (as Kant at least tries to do); rather, here the concern with the national is conflated with a concern with the university. This text, which wants to lay out the terms of a renewal of the university and which wants to defend philosophizing from the threats of the present age (largely the threats of the technologization and scientization of knowledge), misunderstands its own task by seeing it wedded to the concerns of nationalism. But it is crucial that we recognize that there are no philosophical grounds for this misunderstanding in Heidegger's thought, either before or after this text. One can easily see the operation of nationalism in Heidegger's thinking at this stage, and it will be evident in subsequent works such as the *Introduction to Metaphysics* and in several of the lecture courses (most notably, those on Hölderlin).[25] However, what one does not see in these works is a philosophical justification of these operations; in other words, this insertion of a nationalistic element does not come from Heidegger's thought and finds no basis there. The "Self-Assertion of the *German* University" by all rights should have simply been the "Self-Assertion of the University." Still problematic in many ways, the address would nonetheless carry a very different significance were it shorn of its nationalist element, an element that intervenes without any philosophic validation. When the Rectoral Address is finally read, it will mean, among other things, that we have finally philosophically learned to raise the question of the national. But it must be said that we remain a long way from genuinely reading this text, which places us in an exceedingly difficult position.

But, as I have suggested, there are far better and far more productive texts for addressing the question of the possibility of a progressive (must it really be said that the questions of political life concern emancipation, the amelioration of suffering, and the extension of justice in the world?) political understanding from Heidegger's work. In what follows I simply propose to indicate, in a schematic manner, what I take to be some of the most relevant texts for this question and some of the key issues that emerge from those other texts.

The common image of Heidegger's work, especially in the English-speaking philosophical community, where the availability of translations has proven a powerful determinant in how Heidegger is regarded, has it that his work never touches upon political themes. But as new texts are released—and here three are especially relevant: *Beiträge* (1936–1938), *Besinnung* (1938–1939), and *Reden und andere Zeugnisse eines Lebensweges* (1910–1976)—we not only are presented with works that make a more direct effort to confront the problems of the historical present, but we also come to see other texts, texts we have known for a long time, in a new and far more politically charged light—here one thinks especially of *Einführung in die Metaphysik* and *Brief über den Humanismus*, as well as the bulk of Heidegger's work on poetic language.[26] While I do not agree with Otto Pöggeler's judgment that the *Beiträge* is Heidegger's "true magnum opus,"[27] I do believe that this hermetic and opaque book might prove to be the entry into Heidegger's real contribution to a possible politics.[28] What makes this text so pertinent for the questions of political life is that here one finds a critique of what Heidegger refers to as "machination," which is his designation of the deepest logic of Western culture that has absorbed metaphysics into its own character, and this "critique" (a thoroughly problematic word, since every normative ground has been removed in advance by Heidegger's own arguments) is clearly aimed at overcoming existing political structures. One also finds there the effort to take up the question of race, a topic clearly directed against National Socialist dogma by demonstrating that it stands as the final form of machination and the obliteration of history.[29] What one finds expressed most clearly in the *Beiträge* is the view that the *philosophical forms of thinking* that animate culture are criticized, and that this critique is carried out according to the form in which Heidegger genuinely believes any transformation of political life must first happen. There one sees most clearly that his criticisms of the forms and practices of Western culture are not based on *moral* grounds but on the failure of those forms to set truth free.

While the *Beiträge* contains an extensive (and often a Nietzschean-flavored) critique of Western culture, it is, for the most part, rather silent about the shape of the postmetaphysical cultural forms and practices. This is so because Heidegger does not exercise this critique on normative grounds that take constant reference to an imagined future of culture. But some themes and concerns do become evident in the *Beiträge* and elsewhere. Six themes in particular need to be noted: (1) the insistence that political and ethical reflection be understood as working in a region *beyond good and evil*; (2) the shift away from the idea as the determining ground of the character of the common; (3) indeed, the shift away from the idea of the common as the governing conception of political reflections to a conception of community formed upon the *vitality of differences*; (4) a deepened sense of *the singularity of the human being*; (5) a basic recognition of the fundamental need for *freedom* to be alive in the world; (6) a commitment to thinking the operations of *history* as the deepest element of the shared life of mortals. A few remarks about each of these themes might help point to some of the details that need attention as we move forward with these matters.

Like Nietzsche, Heidegger is committed to the view that the Western ideals of "good" and "evil" only serve as props of power and the legitimation of existing forms of its distribution, and that consequently any advance in our understanding of political and ethical life needs to move beyond these notions. This, in part at least, entails a critique of moral theology (the need for a critique of Christianity is especially clear in the *Beiträge*) but, more importantly, it means overcoming all forms of thinking that rest upon the image that there is a war of good and evil to be fought. Heidegger, again like Nietzsche, argues that this conception of the character of the struggle of shared life is simply mistaken. As Greek tragedy never ceased to remind us, there might well be evil, even the evil of a suffering that we call down upon ourselves, but there is no "good" that might defend or war against such a possibility. The grounds on the basis of which we seek justice are different than the grounds formed by the idea or image of the good. That is why, troubling as this feels to us, Heidegger never tried to condemn the Nazi atrocities on moral grounds, and why he was able, in a now infamous remark, to equate the extermination camps of Nazi Germany with mechanized agriculture.[30] For him, they both remain symptoms of the same basic failure of Western culture to open itself to its own relation to history and freedom. It is the failure of the West, indeed, the very *idea of the West* that would assert itself that Heidegger persists in naming. All of the particular manifestations of this failure get thought as expressions of it.

Hand in glove with this need to get beyond good and evil as the measures of political and ethical life is the need to get beyond the notion of the idea as the determining ground for thinking. This means as well that the notion of the common and the universal, both features of the idea itself, and both long regarded as the sacred cows of political thought, needs to be overcome. Heidegger's hostility to the notion of communism, a hostility that drove him to place his hopes for the future in National Socialism, comes from this point.[31] Against the idea of the common, of an identity that would serve as the ground of the just community, Heidegger argues on behalf of a more differentiated conception of the political world. Overcoming the hegemony of the idea means opening up shared life in history to a more varied conception of how it is that we belong together. No idea overarches thinking. No ground guarantees its security. No common ground absorbs pluralities into itself. Rather, when alive thinking, and what it opens up as possible, never ceases to be open and, like the movement of truth that it opens, it is infinitely self-differentiating.

That is, in part, what it means to suggest, as I did above, that what also emerges from Heidegger's thought for an understanding of political life is a deepened sense of the singularity of human beings. This is an understanding of political life that has mortals as its central "category."[32] The "realm [at issue] is through and through not human, i.e., not determinable nor sustainable by *animal rationale* and even less by the *subjectum*" (GA 65, 490). It is a starting point that entails, as its most evident consequence, a deepened sense of the enigma of the other. Such a conception of the beings who stand at the center of political and ethical reflections also has two further important, and yet still unthought, consequences: first, the human being is no longer defined by an image of autonomy and individuality. Heidegger's conception of the singularity of mortal being does not permit itself to be translated into an Enlightenment sense of the autonomy of individual beings and, even more importantly, perhaps, the human being is no longer able to be regarded as the defining center of political and ethical concerns; rather, animal life and nature now come to be recognized as having a central place in such concerns.

With this translation of the center of political and ethical reflection away from the claims of the human subject Heidegger opens up the realm of such reflections to the full force of freedom in such matters. Once we truly begin to appreciate the direction in which Heidegger takes political reflections we will, I believe, find it necessary to think, in a manner reminiscent of Schelling, the essence of freedom as the essence of being itself. This sense of freedom is one not grounded in any ontology of the subject, not governed by any sense of agency or the will, indeed, it does not even coincide with anything that we might call a subject. It is this obscure yet elemental freedom that needs to be thought if we are to move forward with understanding what might be said of political life after Heidegger, since it is this sense of freedom that dispenses history and the possibilities of relation. Out of it emerges the possibility of any form of community. Out of it emerges as well the risk of evil.

Finally, it is history that will require our attention as these matters finally come to be thought, since it is the most extensive and elemental arena within which political life is to be thought for Heidegger. Here matters become most complicated, because here freedom emerges in time and sets our shared lives in motion. In the end, this is where the theme of Heidegger and political life takes us: to the realities at stake in history. It takes us to the dispensations of freedom that are proper to mortals, and to that which exceeds what we define and can control. In other words, this thought of history awakens in us a sense of the *limits* of what we can know and control in the matter of our shared life, and it breeds in us a profound sense of the *respect* which, as Kant so persuasively demonstrated, is always the moral and political meaning of the limits we encounter.

Notes

1. Three of the best sources in this regard are: Rüdiger Safranski, *Ein Meister aus Deutschland: Heidegger und seine Zeit* (München: Hanser Verlag, 1994); Hugo Ott, *Martin Heidegger: Unterwegs zu seiner Biographie* (Frankfurt: Campus Verlag, 1988); Hans Sluga, *Heidegger's Crisis* (Cambridge, Mass.: Harvard University Press, 1993).

2. One of the first of such attacks is Farias' *Heidegger et le nazisme*, translated by Myriam Bennaroch and Jean-Baptiste Grasset (Lagrasse: Éditions Verdier, 1987). There are numerous other examples of such unreflective judgment regarding Heidegger and politics. It also should be acknowledged that those who would simply evade the difficulty of the question in order to defend Heidegger succumb to the same unreflective tendency. It is a tendency capable of gripping even great and large minds: see, for instance, Adorno's judgment that "Heidegger's thought is fascist right down to its innermost core" (Letter in *Diskus*. January 1963). One of the most balanced and judicious attempts to actually *think* the riddle of politics out of Heidegger as a *philosophical* problem is found in John McCumber in *Metaphysics and Oppression* (Bloomington: Indiana University Press, 2000). I do not, however, agree with McCumber's opening comment, which has it that Heidegger was a "life-long Nazi"

(p. 1). Equally worth attention, but thought from a different point of view, is Miguel de Beistegui, *Heidegger and the Political* (London: Routledge, 1998). See also my "Changing the Subject," in *Graduate Faculty Philosophy Journal* 14:2, 15:1 (1991):441–64. That issue of the *Graduate Faculty Philosophy Journal* is a valuable addition to the literature on this theme; it also contains a rather thorough bibliography of pertinent works.

3. Here see de Beistegui, *Heidegger and the Political*, p. 33ff.

4. On this, see Frank Edler, "Philosophy, Language, and Politics: Heidegger's Attempt to Steal the Language of the Revolution in 1933-1934," in *Social Research* vol. 57, no. 1 (1990) 197-238.

5. Here one thinks of Giorgio Agamben, *The Coming Community* (Minneapolis: University of Minnesota Press, 1993), and of Jean-Luc Nancy, *L'experience de la liberté* (Paris: Editions Galilée, 1988). One might rightly argue that the bulk of Jacques Derrida's work needs to be seen in this light, that is, as an effort to open the political to thinking in a time after Martin Heidegger. It is noteworthy just how much French philosophy has taken the lead on pioneering the issue of a post–Heideggerian politics.

6. On the topic of Heidegger's refusal to confront the questions posed by his own political activities, see Berel Lang, *Heidegger's Silence* (Ithaca, N.Y.: Cornell University Press, 1996).

7. Some notable exceptions to this are Charles Scott, "Heidegger's Rector's Address: A Loss of the Question of Ethics," and Christopher Fynsk, "But Suppose We Were to Take the Rectoral Address Seriously," both in the previously cited issue of the *Graduate Faculty Philosophy Journal*; also see Gérard Granel, "Appel à tous ceux qui ont affaire avec l'université," in *De l'université* (Mauzevin: Trans-Europ-Repress, 1982), pp. 75–96.

8. Hans-Georg Gadamer, "Back from Syracuse," translated by John McCumber, in *Critical Inquiry* 15: 2 (winter 1989):429.

9. On this, see Jacques Taminiaux, *The Thracian Maid and the Professional Thinker: Arendt and Heidegger*, translated by Michael Gendre (Albany: State University of New York Press, 1997).

10. "Life is misty, it always shrouds itself in fog." See the discussion of this in my Introduction to Hans-Georg Gadamer, *Heidegger's Ways* (Albany: State University of New York Press, 1994).

11. A full treatment of this theme in Plato should take up the (often neglected) *Laws*, which is the dialogue Plato writes while wrestling with the fallout of his own interventions in Syracuse. The longest of his dialogues, it also is significantly different from the better-known *Republic*.

12. This is something we see dramatized in the opening scene of the *Republic,* which has Socrates standing apart from the festival that is being celebrated by the community he is observing.

13. "The 7th Letter," translated by L. A. Post, in *Plato: The Complete Dialogues,* edited by Edith Hamilton and Huntington Cairns (Princeton, N.J.: Princeton University Press, 1980), lines 326a-b.

14. *Ibid.,* line 337e.

15. See, for instance, SZ, 68.

16. On this point, see my "Changing the Subject," p. 453ff. Also see Philippe Lacoue-Labarthe, *La fiction du politique: Heidegger, l'art et la politique* (Paris: Christian Bourgois Éditeur, 1987).

17. Heidegger's words to Jaspers, quoted in Willy Hochkeppel, "Heidegger, die Nazis und kein Ende," *Die Zeit* (May 6, 1983).

18. Martin Heidegger, *Die Selbstbehauptung der deutschen Universität* (Frankfurt: Klostermann Verlag, 1983), p. 19. The citation is from the *Republic,* line 497d9.

19. The translation here is Bloom's (emphasis added).

20. There are other remarks that have a sort of boldness about them; for instance, Heidegger's claim that, "But all forms of following carry within themselves resistance" (Heidegger, *op. cit.,* p. 18).

21. Sluga does a very good job of clarifying the details of these academic politics in his *Heidegger's Crisis.*

22. This remark should in no way be construed as an excuse or an apology for Heidegger. It is simply part of my effort here to ask about what is really said and thought in the Rectoral Address. That Heidegger would squander the opportunity to address the larger issues of history beginning to play out at that moment is itself a true failure of the philosophical imagination.

23. Two of the elements of Fichte's text that find a clear resonance in Heidegger are the emphasis on language and the assertion of the role of the Greeks for the Germans. On this, see my *On Germans and Other Greeks: Tragedy and Ethical Life* (Bloomington: Indiana University Press, 2000).

24 On this, see de Beistegui, p. 36ff.

25. Here one thinks, for instance, of the celebrated remarks about Europe standing between the "pincers" of America and Russia in *Einführung in die Metaphysik* (Tübingen: Niemeyer Verlag, 1966), pp. 28–29.

26. On this, see my "Poetry and the Political," in *Festivals of Interpretation*, edited by Kathleen Wright (Albany: State University of New York Press, 1990), pp. 209–28.

27. Otto Pöggeler, "Heidegger und die hermeneutische Theologie," in *Verifikationen: Festschrift für Gerhard Eberling* (Tübingen: 1962), p. 481.

28. Details of this argument can be found in my "Strategies for a Possible Reading," in *Reading Heidegger's "Beiträge,"* edited by Charles Scott et al. (Bloomington: Indiana University Press, 2001).

29. On this, see the work of Robert Bernasconi.

30. The remark to which I refer is the following: "Agriculture is now a motorized food industry, the same thing in its essence as the production of corpses in the gas chambers and the extermination camps, the same thing as blockades and the reduction of countries to famine, the same thing as the manufacture of hydrogen bombs." It is found in the 1949 lecture published in Wolfgang Schirmacher, *Technik und Gelassenheit* (Freiburg: Karl Alber, 1984).

31. See his *Die Geschichte des Seyns* (Frankfurt: Klostermann, 1998), especially p. 191ff.

32. On this, see my "What We Owe the Dead," in *Research in Phenomenology* XXVI (1997):190–98.

11

Heidegger's Practical Politics
Of Time and the River

CHARLES E. SCOTT

> Peace, if it ever exists, will not be based on fear of war, but on love of peace. It will not be the abstaining from an act, but the coming of a state of mind. In this sense the most insignificant writer can serve peace, where the most powerful tribunals can do nothing.
> —Juliet Benda (quoted in the Foreword to Wouk's *The Winds of War*)

Heidegger's one foray into national politics during his short tenure as rector of the University of Freiburg was a multiple failure. A combination of tribal emotions, ideology, and mythology constituted his German nationalism and distorted horribly his efforts in the early 1930s toward revitalizing Western thought. It enmeshed him in a larger politics of brutality that embodied what he later identified as "technology," a rampant technology informed by foolish myths of German blood and earth and a spiritually immature desire for a charismatic hero. He appears now to have had no idea of the force, the sheer political power with which he aligned himself—he seems to have thought that he could subtly redirect German National Socialism toward an emerging era in which thought would replace ideology, and a new sense of time and destiny would transform the politics of world domination. If ever a man were captured by mere illusion in the form of political ideals, Heidegger was that man. His thinking at that time was in the sway not only of German nationalism but also of the optimism that Husserl expressed in *The Crisis*: a culture can be turned decisively by those thinkers who are able to provide a historically based unity for diverse and combative endeavors within that culture. Heidegger wanted to revolutionize German political culture whose power he did not understand.

When I am able to get beyond the emotions of revenge, beyond a sense of profound disappointment and outrage over what I consider to be his political stupidity, I am able to confront in a way that seems preferable to me what I will take as the subject of this discussion: the positive and practical implications of Heidegger's thought for our lives. With that sentence I have already engaged the subject, for if I am to engage what is practically efficacious and affirmable in his thought, I feel obliged to get beyond, if I can, revenge, disappointment, and outrage. I feel this obligation partially because I think that those feelings are among the ones in the German National Socialist movement that misled Heidegger politically, and I want to avoid an orientation that recognizes things on the basis of revenge, personal disappointment, and outrage, even if the outrage seems morally justifiable to me. Or, I should say, especially if the outrage seems morally justifiable to me. Rage is certainly appropriate in situations where a certain kind of violence is called for, and where a frenzy of aggression is the best mode of protection. But such violence is highly susceptible to brutalization in the name of what is to be protected and advanced, and the advantage of outrage lies in its lack of measure and good sense. In spite of what Heidegger says about the everyday, I want to affirm good sense. But I want to recast the orientation out of which good sense often arises and show the practicality of a good sense that is oriented differently from the good sense that often operates in our Western cultures. In order to have a chance at good sense, I need to move on from outrage and monomania that usually accompany its episodes, move to a different base of feeling and attitude from which thinking might derive, one that is affirmative in its power of direction while it encounters differences before which it departs.

If I consider practical matters on the basis of disappointment, I not only elevate that personal emotion, for all practical purposes, to a position of arbitration and evaluation, I also take a position that is oriented by a reactive relationship and by negative, personal discontent. *Discontent* is a soft word for what I at times feel when I picture Heidegger showing respect for the Reich's swastika, but if I change to the words disgust and repulsion, I nonetheless designate a state of mind that I expect to further rancor, the privilege of personal expectation, and a prioritization of the kind of struggle that looks for victory and defeat. Do I not want victory over fascism? Indeed I do. But I do not want to set a direction that makes very likely the enforcement of another fascism. That perplexity will help define this discussion, and for now I note that an attunement of disappointment, discontent, and disgust can have such consequences as repression, discouragement, and prioritization of personal preference, none of which can serve well as constructive motivators as we look for life without fascism.

As far as revenge goes, I understand it all too well. I come out of a lineage of revenge that has its instantiation in religious wars and an intense family loyalty that seeks injury for those who injure a member of the clan. I too have fantasized about what I would do if the beach bully kicked sand in my face and walked off with my girlfriend, and I have dreamed of torturing the torturer. What I mean is that I know well the emotions that seek to answer torment with torment and oppression with oppression. Revenge happens as a way of overturning a dominant and repressive power, and Nietzsche is right: it is a state of mind to which one is most likely to be subject when he or she suffers oppression, rejection, or the infliction of pain without effective recourse. People seldom seek revenge against a power with which they are a near or superior match—unless they are given to generalized hatred toward whatever opposes them or acquiesce to traditional habits of revenge on opponents.

I do not intend to attempt to establish biographically that Heidegger was moved by revenge, disappointment, and outrage but only to note that he joined a political movement that showed clearly and with mythological, ideological force those characteristics. I speculate that his availability to such an institutionalization of these attitudes had its own private motivators. What seems more important now, however, is noting that a state of mind significantly governed by those attitudes will not be able to see, much less appreciate, the positive, practical dimensions of his thought. Such a state of mind still finds its satisfactions in condemning or criticizing him and his work. I would rather deal with some aspects of his thought that are not under the control of such hostilities and that compose important differences from them—so different, in fact, that we can understand those "differences" well only if we turn in directions that are not related affectively or dialectically to the other hostile or disappointing aspects. And that means, in part, that I need, as best I can, to let go of my anger, resentment, disappointment, revenge, and outrage regarding Heidegger's tragic episode with German National Socialism.

But a significant problem remains. If his one major practical political foray was "tragic," "stupid," and "spiritually immature," how are we to approach his thought in terms of practical implications without landing squarely in the middle of an incipient (at best) fascism? This is not a question that I intend to address by separating politics and "the political" and showing that while Heidegger's politics were bad, there is a redeeming aspect in his thought that gives us insight into citizenship or governance generally. I do not want to work on the basis of such a separation, because thinking seems to me to compose practical, political space and activity, to compose an event of politics, however momentary, as thinking brings to bear an orientation of communal living in the affections, recognitions, and arrangements of things in their appearances as they are thought. I shall hold in mind that thinking is quite different from ideology, and in that difference we will find important political and practical aspects of Heidegger's thought. It is not that his politics were bad and his thought's implications for "the political" might be good. It is rather that some of his political engagements were bad and others rich in positive value—just as, in retrospect, I can say that some of my political judgments and activities have been bad (although I do not think that they were as bad as Heidegger's), and some have been and are constructive and seem good to me. This observation about thought and politics also means that when people are thoroughly engaged in *Being and Time*, for example, they can indeed find themselves inclined to find a great hero and find as well that they distinguish both the ontic and the ontological in ways that lend support to the distinction between politics and "the political," whereas in the Rectoral Address, when they are following its movement well, they can find a joining of the ontological and the ontic in the figure of national mobilization under the control of a charismatic leader. Thoughtful readers can find themselves in mourning over departed gods in

Heidegger's Hölderlin lectures. And in other parts of the same writings they can feel and think in movements of thought that release them from the hold of ideology, mourning over lost gods, and a strictly conceived distinction of the ontic and onto-logical. Heidegger's thought during the over half a century of his writing is composed of many different movements, many different nuances and implications. Any effort to unify it under a dominant concept (as distinct to guiding or leading questions) will impose a kind of unification that I fear is far closer politically to a totalization than the diverse movements of his thinking allow. That move toward totalization is a po-litical activity that stands against an important freedom that can be found in the sweep of his work. It also constitutes a politics of a kind of unification to which I would like to find viable alternatives.

I am saying that a manner of thinking comprises at once a kind of politics. The ways in which words are arranged, the manners in which things appear in thought, the functions, attitudes and hierarchies of recognition, the employment of certain signs for particular things, the kind of images that give texture and mood to think-ing, the evaluations that pervade, often unnoticed, a way of thinking, the beliefs, anx-ieties, and desires that inhere in a body of thought and, above all, the lineage that bestows identity on things—this complex texture of appearances in thinking com-poses all manner of connections, adherences, and divisions with people and things, with histories, present circumstances, and future developments: such dynamic tex-turing constitutes a politics. To think and to experience another's thinking are to en-counter a politics and be politically engaged. I believe that this is one implication in the claims of some of Heidegger's harshest critics when they say that *Being and Time*, far from an innocent phenomenological essay, is a quasi-fascist document. And while I disagree with that claim, I affirm their recognition that thinking, far from innocent of politics, constitutes a political action that engages us corporally and socially and that can influence us decisively. When thinking happens, a politics takes place.

I have thus begun with a preliminary affirmation of the political import of Hei-degger's account of being-in-the-world in *Being and Time*. The effect of that group of descriptive claims is an alertness to the worldly extensiveness of human perceptive-ness and thought and to their disclosive dimension. Both the extensiveness and dis-closiveness have the effect of turning a supposed interiority of thought inside out. An individual does not "do" the externalizing or disclosing. Neither does a universal sub-jectivity. As human awareness happens a vast and, for all practical purposes, unen-compassable range of nonvoluntary influences takes place, plus something else that is not an influence. That plus—mortal, temporal disclosiveness—comprises the event of appearing, the coming to light, as it were, of whatever is apparent, and before I come to the end of this chapter I will elaborate this account of disclosive "coming to light" as a process of making lighter in the sense of less heavy. "Being-in-the-world" not only has an enormous impact on the concepts and images of subjectivity that have governed Western perspectives and evaluations for a long time, it also suggests a commonality of people in the fragility of their being and sets aside those immortal bases by which we can find an uncompromisable authority for making miserable people who are very different from us or only useful to us. In the thought of *Being and Time*, there is no sustained basis for thinking or believing that any one grouping of concepts and their interconnections, any one dominant image, any one body of beliefs and feelings have authority over the eventuation of mortal, temporal disclosiveness. For such disclosiveness, as Heidegger describes it, has being-in-the-world as its site of occurrence; and since such disclosiveness is only occurrence, without being-in-the-world it would not occur.[1]

This sustained turning of interiority inside out and the unseating of the priority of subjectivity constitute one of Heidegger's primary philosophical accomplishments. It—this accomplishment—requires a severe rigor, for the power of images of interiority and the valorization of subjectivity in modern thought could be exaggerated only with difficulty. They have figured not only such laudable values as the dignity and rights of individuals and the importance of representative government, they also have figured a regrettable sense of private aloneness, the fundamental importance of autonomous actions without external influence or constitution for evaluations of integrity and freedom, the priority of the power of individual mastery (including figurations of the great leaders) and, as I intend to show in greater detail, the immense power of ideological orientations. But the required rigor has as part of its composition a transformation of many ingrained and traditional concepts, feelings, and beliefs—so ingrained that I expect that our best hope can project no more than alertness to the figurations of interior subjectivity as they operate in attempts to marginalize their influence. Indeed, Heidegger shows the power of such predispositions in his effort to overturn it in his vulnerability to the heroic subjectivity of the leader, who embodies not only a virtual, transcendental destiny for a people but also an identity to which people are to commit themselves in an all too typical structure of activity and passivity. Such power also appears in the language he uses to describe authenticity and in the externalized metaphor of horizon that plays an important role in *Being and Time*. These instances of a "metaphysics of subjectivity," however, and many other instances are in a larger context of transformation in which authenticity, for example, means an openness to mortal, temporal disclosiveness and not primarily an accomplishment within the boundary of individual identity or universal subjectivity. Authenticity, according to *Being and Time*, is an openness in being with others that is without a definitive, determinate basis; it composes an appropriated occurrence of mortal disclosiveness. And while this thinking cannot tell people prescriptively what to do, it is attuned to a way of being that values the *appearances* of differences more highly than it values a disposition toward universal enforcement of a people's morality or posting a universal basis for a formal ethics. Even in Heidegger's most insistent period of German tribalism in the period 1933–1934, with its imagery of blood and earth, or in his attachment to Hölderlin's equally (to my mind) regrettable mythological romanticism during the mid-1930s and early 1940s, his thought was moved by a sense of ungrounding ground that undercuts the authority of a great leader, a unique Greco-German destiny, or the singular achievements of individuals.[2]

What strikes me as having the most practical value in his thought is found in its movement that overturns any possible, final authority that a person might give to his specific claims. Even in his Rectoral Address of 1933, with its emphasis on willpower and individual adherence to the state, he places emphasis from the beginning on an essence that, in its priority, displaces individual selves, an essence that also purports to relativize Heidegger's own particular interests as rector; and with this emphasis he opens the door to the ungrounding ground of being that will unseat parochial interests as well as universal prescriptions. I find his relegation of the essence of the mission of German higher education to a Greek tinctured German history, under the circumstances, most disturbing, but in the midst of that limitation he prepares the way dimly for the bottom to drop out from under this authority and its elevated history. He clearly intends to begin a process of transformation in German education that will make Bismarck's changes to the educational system seem pale, and with that goal in mind the reader can see that the essence of the German university cannot remain long within the limits of an ideology. Indeed, this intention on Heidegger's part can be carried out only if he attends to something borne by German history that is neither his nor Germany's. The educational system will bear out the destiny of the people by a thorough and revolutionary attunement to the questionableness of being, a questionableness that is neither possessable by a people nor translatable into an ideology of tribal nationalism.

❧

By the time Heidegger gave his lectures in 1942 on Hölderlin's poem *Der Ister*, he had moved a considerable distance from his Rectoral Address. But I believe that some aspects of the address are carried out in that study and indicate the meaning of both "essence" and "displacement."[3] The earlier emphasis on mobilization and people's will is mercifully diminished.[4] Now the words "originary," "destined," and "decided," all of which carry direct reverberations of authenticity, question, and temporality, as he describes them in *Being and Time*, refer to poetic attunement to the essence, the *Wesen*, the coming to pass of events of disclosure. Such events are in no one's and no people's possession. They "sustain all relation to whatever is coming" and compose the shining singularity of what appears (I, 14).

"Shining singularity" might sound esoteric and a little precious, especially in the context of a practical politics that has in its background the devastation of war and the eradication of "different" people. Heidegger's lecture on the Ister river addresses, in part, homelessness, passage, and flow in the midst of a homeland and what is most familiar. In gentle terms, he also is addressing a state of cultural mind that is attuned by the *tisis*, the devastation, in being's coming to pass.[5] It elaborates the question of being and the formations of Heidegger's thought by that question. "The question of being" refers to the early and shaping language in our Western lineage by which the event of life itself appears questionable. It is not a matter only of good things dying and disappearing. It is one of being itself appearing to pass, its essential questionability—in "The Ister" lectures, Heidegger follows Hölderlin's metaphor of the sun's rising and setting daily with a recognition (that could please Hume) that its regularity does not have behind it a clear law of inevitability. Its regularity and familiarity seem suspended with nothing regular and familiar behind it. The question of being means that being, the *appearing* of things, comes to pass, that the mortality of all that appears discloses the possibility of no being at all, that being seems to happen by disappearing as appearing takes place. Being does not appear to be "transcendentally" necessary. It is not a subject that takes things away. It rather composes the event of appearing-disappearing. The happening of being comprises the loss of being, and the loss of being seems to compose a temporal space for being's coming in events of appearing. It is, in its event, in question. Being happens as "temporal self-deferring," as enacted self-displacement, and that figures being's mortality.

Attunements are basic to political convictions, and attunement to this continuous, mortal self-displacement, this questionableness, has as one of its possible effects an exceptional alertness to things in their present passage—quite different from those attunements that engender the holding patterns of ideologies and compose fascist values. Heidegger valorizes this alertness in his consideration of Hölderlin's use of the word "now," a dimension of tone that gives an originary, this-once, shining dimension to what appears, a time in which a person can find what appears in an almost unspeakable freshness and singularity, not as something that one processes and categorizes but before that as something that one encounters with prejudgmental astonishment in its happening. In attunement to the questionableness of being, a person encounters a thing as it shines in its singularity, much like a person's encountering freshly and by welcoming intensity the very moment of the sun's rising or the appearance of bright Venus in coming twilight. Or, as when one sees another person and is struck by the person's being there at all, sees the freckles as though for the first time, as if he or she were witness to a birth. In such attunement, when it composes a person's comportment, the violent passions of a Nazi regime—or those of ethnic cleansing, infliction of unnecessary pain, or political manipulation—seem crude and stupid, even if astonishing in their appearances.[6]

When I say that such a transformation of comportment and mentation is politically practical, I am aware of the practical limits of such transformation. I do not think that we can expect a transformation like that to invest our worldly life and times with a force that causes inevitably vast cultural conversion. I can think of few things more fragile and less subject to the demands of everyday physical survival, and I have no doubt that with effective compartmentalization a person can experience at times the shining singularity of things in the midst of a life many aspects of which I would consider very bad. But this mindfulness does compose an interruption in a wide range of manipulative and ideological behaviors. In Heidegger's thought it

displaces a predisposition to controlling aggression, a dominance of subjective spontaneity, contexts of conceptual certainty, tribal absolutes, transcendental justifications for specific cultural practices, instrumental interpretations of language, and the
bland familiarity of routines and accustomed social environments. This mindfulness
accents singular differences, destabilizes generalizing categories, invests thought and
recognition with wonder, and finds a commonality of homelessness in the space and
time of the homeland. Blood and earth as well as the axioms of a state are displaced
within their own occurrences (i.e., in their finite, mutable coming to pass) by their
own dimension of being's loss.

The rivers of which Hölderlin speaks vanish, "they go away," they "designate a
Here and abandon the Now" (I, 15). They are given poetic expression in a mood of
celebration that has no intention to make them hold still, to explain them, justify
them, or recast them in human form. The intent of Hölderlin's language—and of Heidegger's language in his celebration of Hölderlin—is to allow without disturbance what
neither can say explicitly, capture in words, or accurately depict. The, as it were, flowing, bestowing, abandoning, home-giving, home-devastating river moves on. This is
not, I believe, in the direction of a mysticism, unless attending to what is not directly
expressible is mystical. The thought is rather that we can attend to the arising, flowing
passage of life's occurrence in its instances—we can celebrate it (or shrink from it)—
without being able to hold it in any of the forms by which it comes to presence. A further point is that we are on the verge of ways of speaking and thinking that can allow
what is never familiar by the manner in which we allow our familiar words and concepts to undergo their own transforming displacement. In the process of displacement
lies the possibility for attunement that is quite distinct to activities that attempt to hold
things in required places of uninterrupted familiarity. The river thus composes an
image—Heidegger would never say image, but might well say a poetic unveiling—an
image of uncapturable destiny, such as the destiny of (I would say) being's loss in the
coming of things—Heidegger might say, an uncapturable destiny of concealing-uncon-
cealing in being's temporal gift.[7] But however else the river appears in Hölderlin's poetry, it "'is' the locality that pervades the abode of human beings upon the earth,
determines them to where they belong and where they are homely (heimisch). The river
thus brings into their own and maintains them in what is their own" (I, 21).

I note that Heidegger is turning to the poet and to his poetry, not to a state or a
state's leader, to find the place and the language for being's destiny, and he is finding in
Hölderlin's language a "poetic telling" in which the essence—the temporal and non-
possessable disclosiveness—of what is named is "called" (I, 21). The preposition that is
usually associated here with "called" is, I believe, "to"—called to. But one could also
say "called forth," in the sense that this poet's language makes apparent an overlooked
and unappropriated dimension of German language and culture, a dimension of their
"home" that they have pretty much excluded from their active recognition and cultural understanding. Hölderlin is "naming" "what is before your eyes," and the "your"
in this case indicates those who belong to "Germania" (I, 22). He wants to name

something that should be apparent to the Germans, that is not apparent and, now that it is named and spoken, will remain no longer an unspoken mystery (ibid.).

Heidegger is looking for a language and thought that can open "the world as a whole . . . to human beings in general" (I, 23). He finds in Hölderlin's poetry a way of speaking that provides that opening. Or, in the context of his discussion, I would say that he finds in Hölderlin's language a political site that effectively (if in a very limited way—see his caution on p. 23) provides an opening— a threshold, I would say—to something essential but unappropriated in his people's history and culture. And this availability is to "something" that, when appropriated, could have a huge and salutary effect on and affect in that society.

But Hölderlin cannot make that noticing and mindful move directly, because the meanings that constitute the familiar forms of directness are based on the loss of what Hölderlin makes available in his language, Hölderlin's (and presumably Heidegger's) "hearing" of what has remained unspoken and of what cannot be fitted to the disclosing event that comprises this unspokenness—that hearing requires, in its practical effect, a changed linguistic locale and a reconsideration of the ways in which language can say things. Hölderlin's poetry provides for Heidegger a "Now" that is at once the locale for saying and naming what does not fit the linguistic practices common in German culture. In other words, Heidegger finds *in* Hölderlin's poetry a revolutionary transformation of German language, understanding, values, and practices. And *this* "here and now"— Hölderlin's extraordinary language—is where "we wish to build" (I, 27).

In this context, Heidegger finds most significant these lines concerning rivers, ". . . vanishing/Full of intimation, hastening along not/ My path"(I, 28). The rivers "rush still on" and are "unconcerned with our wisdom" (I, 27). And in this vanishing and difference they are full of intimation. This intimation comes as rivers tear "human beings out of the habitual . . . so that they may be in a center outside of themselves, that is, be extrinsic" (I, 28). A river's path is "like an abandonment of the realm of the human landscape" (ibid.). And the threshold that is provided by rivers and Hölderlin's noticing them in the way that he does is vis-à-vis a space and time that is at once centering and self-displacing. Neither an orthodoxy nor an ideology nor anything else habitual survives unchanged the moment of such divestiture, and that composes one of the most powerful and practical effects in Heidegger's consideration of Hölderlin's poetic writing. In this way of speaking and thinking, shining singularities come to pass. The coming to pass belongs to the shining, and attentiveness with such ungrounding composes the best possibility of German destiny. I believe that means in part that German culture should lead the way in unseating the force and priority of ideological thinking, in overturning highly determined nationalism, in removing doctrine from the aim or basis of thinking, and in displacing transcendental grounds in interpretations of language's suspended historical fragility.[8]

The kind of mentation that Heidegger is both considering and carrying out is one of "journeying" (*Wandern*). If readers of Hölderlin understand him to be speaking primarily of the Danube or the Rhine in their factual actuality, they will miss the force of his language. What he means by "river" (*Strom*) happens in the river poems (*Stromdichtung*), and this language composes a manner of dwelling and being at home—composes a practical accomplishment— that is not fixed by any specific, determinate formation. The factually actual rivers are like images of a language that flows as a current of displacements, wandering in many carrying strands, runs, and rhythms. It is not that rivers do not constitute important political entities. It is rather that Hölderlin's language and Heidegger's language regarding Hölderlin compose a different kind of political event in which the currency *is* a manner of attendance to fluid issues, passages of connection, and temporal extension, in which an ungrounded homeland begins to emerge. A manner of language and thinking runs through holding fixations and carries the passage that gives stabilities to vanish. What this language does hold is a source of streams and passages that is not *a* determination but one that issues in beginnings through losses and its own concurrent withdrawal. Such language composes both a memorial to and an anticipation of its own passage, a continuous flooding of its own predisposition to ossification. It is a language that knows—Heidegger says "intimation" in this context—that it extends back and also toward, simultaneously, the flowing that gives it to name itself river journey (I, 28–31). One's home is then found in journeying, and not in the stasis of an overpowering governance or of a dry-landed and sun-baked law. "The river is the locality for dwelling" (I, 31).

Heidegger speaks of "river" in this book we should hear at first "the Danube" or "The Rhine," their watersheds and their sources. When he speaks of "home," we should hear at first German culture, and when he speaks of "human being" we should hold in mind that he means people in the West and, I assume, primarily Western Europeans, and still more specifically, Germans (see I, 42–43). In the poetic turn, when this culture is turned through itself to its hidden river quality, we should hear first and foremost, I believe, German culture, especially its language. I have emphasized the enormity of Heidegger's dissatisfaction with this culture as he finds it. It is for him the site of instances of the West's most thorough nihilism (Nietzsche's and, not far behind, Hegel's), the place where the traditions of Plato and Aristotle come to the standstill that their thought seems to make inevitable. And if he still views America and Russia as the primary demonic carriers of technology's domination, he does not say so. He seems, rather, to locate the dominance of willpower in the German culture (I, 43–45). German culture is largely blind to its river dimension, and it is the site in which Hölderlin most likely will not be heard, as well as the place where he might be heard.

I find in this orientation at least two edges. On the one hand, Heidegger struggled with exceptional rigor to let his "metaphysical" fixations flow away, and failing that, he did what he could to let Hölderlin's language, concurrent with his own, undercut those fixations that interrupt the river journey. He locates the problems where he is and, outside of Hölderlin, he does not make German idols into the river's measure.

But as he thinks historically, he also adopts Hölderlin's romantically tinged imagery, into those essential relations within which this humankind stands: the relation to the world, the relation to the earth, the relation to the gods and to alternative and false gods. These relations are not, however, simply added on to "human beings" in addition to "their" being human; rather, to be human is in itself to be the unity of this configuration. (I, 43)

When I put together "this humankind," which seems to refer primarily to German culture, with "human in itself," and when I add to that combination a Hölder-linian law that earth is divine (at least in Heidegger's reading, see p. 28), and that certain ephemeral gods, especially in their ephemeral departure, are essential for human being—when I l look from this angle I am clear that Heidegger has a way to go to free himself from a German orientation that, from my point of view, romanticizes the Greek lineage and German culture's relation to it—even in his effort to flow with the river as he locates his and Hölderlin's language in a German tradition, in "that history to which we ourselves belong." And while the river figures "the essence of Western humankind" and performs powerfully in dissolving universalized, local ideas and values, Hölderlin and he nevertheless give rise to a distinctly Germanic hope for a German-Greek revitalization in a context of nostalgia for a culture of now-disappeared gods. This drift of imagery and affection takes on a cast of universaliza-tion ("human in itself") from which I believe Heidegger never freed himself.

And why should he? He was German. My hopes are largely informed by Amer-ican culture. I presume that I articulate that American history and culture as I pause before the threshold that Heidegger enacts. The response that I find from his thought as I engage it is that my divergence is not a problem, that Heidegger's language is not formed by a goal of agreement, that what counts are noticing, at-tending, pausing, listening again, exploring, entertaining, celebrating in one's own way, allowing the words and thoughts to flow through my mind: that the practical import of Heidegger's language is found in a lack of insistence that accompanies his firmest hopes and his strongest loyalties. I do not find in my engagements with his thought resentment toward my differences. I do find him often going on a different way from mine—there are many tributaries, and at times we can speak, if at all, only at a considerable distance. But always I find turning in his thought, a turning prob-ably best expressed in the fugal formations of his *Contributions to Philosophy*, and one that I have found turns out from this thinking as well as turns in—there are ed-dies and whirlpools that can send a person engaged in the flow of his work in other directions.

I believe that he presented himself and his spirit well when he wrote to a young and worried Karl Löwith, who was afraid that his departure from and criticism of his *Doktorvater's* (Heidegger's) work would upset him:

What is accursed in my obligatory work is that it has to operate in the realm of ancient philosophy and theology, and I have to do it critically, with a view to inconsequential matters like "categories." It seems as if something's *having a corresponding content* is supposed to be contrasted by critique with what is negated. And as if my work were something for a school, a particular persuasion, continuation, supplementation![9]

I find no hesitation in Heidegger's thought in his affirmation that enigma invests what he most wants to think, that enigma is never resolved by right belief or correct conceptuality, that the establishment of schools of persuasion, interpretation, and certainty resists their own historical flow, and that before an enigma, people can find that their solutions, as solutions, are ill suited to an ungrounding dimension in their daily lives. That means that while he did not find freedom from one kind of quasi-mythological, romantic nationalism (in my language), he also thought and wrote in a way that shows performatively and most practically the limits and, perhaps, foolishness of such affections.[10]

Although the practice of unseating a mind set upon ideological correctness, static and universal values, and the dominance of subjectivity is richly accomplished in Heidegger's thought, the practical advantages of humor are missing from his readings of Hölderlin as well as from his other works, and humor is one of the best devices I know to keep the river flowing in our thought and practice. I turn now to a strangely similar and also very different orientation before a German river myth. Mark Twain's account provides an interesting instance of connecting with river folklore in which are prominant nonbelonging and transformation without mythological seriousness or cultural lionization. In his account the myth does not define the departure of its own force, and a language does not hold in force its own destiny.

Twain's manner of retelling the Lorelei, "an ancient legend of the Rhine," presents an alternative, and to my mind salutary, attitude in comparison to Heidegger's when one confronts that seriousness bred of last gods, national myths, and images.[11]

> Lore (two syllables) was a water nymph who used to sit on a high rock called Ley or Lei (pronounced like our word *lie*) in the Rhine, and lure boatmen to destruction in a furious rapid which marred the channel at that spot. She so bewitched them with her plaintive songs and her wondrous beauty that they forgot everything else to gaze up at her, and so they presently drifted among the broken reefs and were lost. (I, 87)

The young count Hermann fell head over heels in love with her without having seen her—she was indeed an "enigmatical Being" (I, 88). He doubtlessly lost weight and became drawn as he skipped meals and wandered about lost in his sweet-sad reveries, playing upon his zither and "Expressing his Longing in low Singing" (I, 88).[12] The extent of his ardor is contained in poignant lines that Twain himself translated, in the third verse of his love song: "how willingly thy love to part!/With delight

I should be bound/To thy rocky house [!] in deep ground."[13] Then Hermann saw her! "An unintended cry of Joy escaped the Youth, he let his zither fall to the ground,"and he called to her with open arms. She seemed to "call his name with un- utterable sweet Whispers, proper to love. Beside himself with delight the youth lost his Senses and sank senseless to the earth."[14]

Seeing things turn considerably for the worse with his swooning son, Her- mann's father decided to send him away,[15] but Hermann was determined to have a departing encounter, this time by boat, which, we can imagine, was exactly what Lore had in mind. He wished to "offer to the Nymph of the Rhine his Sighs, the tones of this Zither, and his Songs." As he approached Lore's high perch, "the moon shed her silvery light over the whole country; the steep bank mountains appeared in the most fantastical shapes, and the high oaks on either side bowed their branches on Her- mann's passing." And lo, he sang to her a song of his own composition, which turns out to be the very folk song now handed down from generation to generation. That entire boating, singing gambit, Twain says, "was a serious mistake. The Lorelei did not 'call his name in unutterable sweet Whispers' this time. No. That song naturally worked an instant and thorough 'changement' in her; and not only that, but it stirred the bowels of the whole afflicted region round about there." [16] And, in a phrase, all hell broke loose; while still beckoning to the love-besotted Hermann with one hand, with the other "she called the waves to her service. They began to mount heaven- ward; the boat was upset, mocking every exertion; the waves rose to the gunwale, and splitting on the hard stones, the Boat broke into pieces. The youth sank into the depths."[17] The Nymph not only destroyed the lovesick Hermann, but she was, I be- lieve, never seen again with such proximity. For this culminating and mercifully sui- cidal as well as homicidal finishing accomplishment, Twain says, "One feels drawn tenderly toward her and is moved to forget her many crimes and remember only the good deed that crowned and closed her career." In that crowning and closing event she killed not only the poor, romantically crazed, ecstatic youth but her own presence as well. No more songs from him! And, as Twain says at the end of the chapter, "the raft moves on."[18]

I have said that our ways of speaking and thinking compose political events, that they provide the images of possibilities and options that attract or repel us, that they are practical occurrences, that as ways of thinking change, people change. I have said that people often overlook or obscure the temporal and displacing dimension of thinking in their desire to establish the right, lasting values, images, and ideas. In such obscurity we can ignore the eventful and questionable quality of our own think- ing and speaking, especially when we are fired by outrage or intense disappointment, and reinvest our ideals and prescriptions with movements that reinstate, for example, the kind of totalization that universalizes local values and turns thought into a cata- logue of accurate inscriptions and steers political decisions toward communities of collective conformity. I have found that Heidegger's encounter with Hölderlin often displaces such movements in thought and language, that both his thinking and his subject matter provide an alternative kind of alertness when they are compared to the ideological or judgmentally based mentation to which he also fell prey. I have emphasized the transformational quality of the intimation and evocation that Hölderlin provides in his poem *The Ister*, a quality that Heidegger also gives in his reading of that poem. And because of this politically important accomplishment, I have said that the ideology and emotions of German National Socialism or other forms of fascism not only do not have a safe harbor in Heidegger's thought but experience radical transformation in it.

On the other hand, there is in the language and thought of Hölderlin and Heidegger a persistent and highly nationalistic mythological element that is far from politically innocent. One of the practical effects of that mythology is found in exaggerating and romanticizing German language and culture. That exaggeration and romanticizing could be mitigated if one were clear that the myths compose part of a specific lineage, and that they are subject to the river's vanishing aspect—as distinct to myths being definitive of the vanishing aspect—if one could think without their invocation, could let go of their "call" and think in gratitude for their crowning achievement of flying away and leaving room for things without their benefit (or curse). But Heidegger, at least, is not always clear about that, and he also lionizes Hölderlin's poetry, making it into a disclosive event of heroic proportions. He turns that brilliant and crazed young man's writing into a form of linguistic heroism with epic and seemingly universal implications. And there seems to be no effective Lore to self-destruct while saving us from the exaggerations—although on Heidegger's own, river-informed terms, there could well be such a Nymph. (She would express, I hope, "Germany" at her self-displacing best.) Nor do we find a saving sense of humor—as quite distinct to a saving body of gods. For this we owe an inestimable debt of gratitude to Twain in the midst of an equally inestimable debt to Heidegger's thought, for the practical benefit of their combination could be differential ways of thinking and writing that are attuned to the shining singularity of what appears, and that do not take themselves with that overblown mythological or tribal seriousness that creates edifices of destruction in the name of destinal truth and right.[19]

Notes

1. I could spend the rest of this chapter qualifying, refining, and textually supporting the remarks of this paragraph. There are many different ways of interpreting being-in-the-world, disclosiveness, and mortal temporality. Each has subtle or not so subtle implications and evocations that compose its own politics. I will provide more support for my initial observations later. Presently I want to indicate a direction of

reading and acknowledge that my account of some of Heidegger's practical implications is indebted in part to my reading of *Being and Time*, in spite of the fact that I understand myself to engage Heidegger sympathetically with a kind of pluralistic democracy that I believe he could not affirm. One of the political effects that I have found in Heidegger's thought is the stimulus and allowance it has for departure from it. His thought is not designed so much for repetition as for encouragement of continuing and differentiating thought, and we will find this aspect coming to expression in his reading of Hölderlin's river poetry. In that quality, I find a common ground with Heidegger that goes beyond our considerable differences concerning all manner of values.

2. By use of *romantic* and *romanticism*, I do not mean that Hölderlin is fully a member of the eighteenth- and nineteenth-century literary manner called Romanticism. I mean that he and Heidegger had a kind of romance with German culture, that both were drawn by certain kinds of mysterious remoteness, that heroic figurations appealed to them, and that both tended to visionary excess at times. These characteristics suggest caution, irony, and satire now and then, and other remedies for overseriousness and inclination to ecstatic flight. Heidegger's ungrounding thought is one of these remedies.

3. See Heidegger's discussion of *polis* as site in Hölderlin's Hymn *The Ister* (pp. 79–83), a section that I will not discuss directly, but one in which he describes the site of politics in terms of displacement, groundlessness, and inaccessibility as distinct to a static formation. "Perhaps the *polis* is that realm and locale around which everything question-worthy and uncanny turns in an exceptional sense." I will not address his remarks concerning Greek thought and literature in order to limit the focus of this discussion. But one of my preoccupations, complementary to this section, will be with the way in which his considerations of Hölderlin's river poem undercut any tendency, Heidegger's included, toward the establishment of a regime of totalitarian doctrine and manners of thought.

4. A history of this development in Heidegger's thought in his lectures on Hölderlin during the mid-1930s, in his lectures on Nietzsche, and in his meditations on *Being and Time* in his *Contributions to Philosophy* could detail this important change of emphasis. But that is more than I can do in this chapter. What he says of his lectures on *The Ister* in 1942 applies to my work here, that his remarks proceed from his interests and are thus selective, arbitrary, disjoined from the primary writing; they come from outside the writings he is considering. They compose the limits of what a relatively short and contained set of observations can accomplish. On the positive side, however, such limitations point toward the singularity of the attended work and provide possible encouragement for us to attend still more intensely to the primary "Dichtung" (I, 14).

5. "The Anaximander Fragment," in EGT, 13ff.

6. I am reasonably sure that in sadomasochistic situations a person can experience astonishment in the shining singularity of the victim or the tormentor, and this possibility considerably qualifies any implication that the mood of astonishment in a sensibility that is governed by the question of being provides a way out of cruelty. I doubt that any kind of comportment or attitude can be completely free of the danger of cruelty, which is surely one of the most subtle of people's possibilities. But occurrences of the attunement that Heidegger is accounting are nonetheless ones that seem to lead to a profound affirmation of differences, to esteem for the appearing of a passing now, and to lead as well away from cruelties of totalization and oppressive hierarchies. I will say in a moment that it can lead to cultivation of a nonlegalized kind of compassion that is politically significant. Such attunement, however, is not sufficient for any politics, even when it makes a significant and practical contribution.

7. I am well aware of how inappropriate *image* is here, particularly since Heidegger goes to such length to disassociate Hölderlin's language, as well as Heidegger's own reading, from any hint of symbolization and image making. Indeed, he explicitly rejects the idea of image (see, e.g., pp. 30, 43). The emphasis falls on noticing: Hölderlin's language gives notice to "what" it cannot say directly and to "what" does not fit into the sensuous-supersensuous distinction that is necessary for the idea of symbolization. See Section 3 of the book for Heidegger's elaboration of this point. I, on the other hand, would like to retain *image* with the full play of its ambiguity as a way of noticing what cannot come to direct expression. It may well be the case that I am placed squarely within a context of Platonism with a heavy dose of Kantian qualification when I use the word, but I do not think so, because I believe that I can use the word in an ordinary way without suggesting either a transcendental grounding or a transcendental faculty of imagination. And I would like to serve notice to a reservation that I have regarding a habitual and an uninterrupted appeal to the language of disclosure.

8. Heidegger says, "Thus there is indeed a belonging to the rivers, a going along with them. It is precisely that which tears onward more surely in the rivers' own path that tears human beings out of the habitual midst of their lives, so that they may be in a center outside of themselves, that is, be extrinsic. The prelude to inhering in the extrinsic midst of human existence, the 'centric' of 'central' abode in existence, is love. The sphere proper to standing in the extrinsic middle of life is death. The vanishing rivers, full of intimation, do not take the path of human beings . . . and what is most intrinsic to human beings become limitless." (I, 28). The complicated paragraph from which these lines come could be read with many emphases. The one that I am underscoring pays attention to "vanishing" and to the radical unsettlement of transcendentally justified teachings and perceptions.

9. Löwith quotes this 1924 letter to him from Heidegger in "The Nature of Man and the World of Nature: For Heidegger's 80th Birthday," *Martin Heidegger: In*

Europe and America, edited by E. Ballard and C. E. Scott and translated by R. Phillip O'Hara (Nighhoff, 1973), pp. 37. The next quotations are also from this article (pp. 38, 39), and were written by Heidegger in 1927 and 1929. "Whether one goes along with *Sein und Zeit* is a matter of complete indifference to me." And, "Whether or not you materially agree with me is for me no reason for acceptance or rejection [of your dissertation]." Writing of Löwith's sharp criticisms of his work, Heidegger says, "How could I take offense with you over such matters as these. In that case I could have most comfortably and without much difficulty thwarted your inauguration into an academic career. Try and find one among the governing bigwigs who has inaugurated one of his students into an academic career who wrote such an antithetical dissertation! I do not reckon that to my merit, but I am surprised . . . how little you . . . understand me in my conduct when you suspect an irritation such as your comments suggest."

10. As Mark Twain wrote at the end of his account of the Lorelei and of literal and hence misshaped translations that he found in a museum catalog: "But in the meantime the raft moves on." See *A Tramp Abroad* (New York: Penguin, 1997), p. 95.

11. Ibid., chapter XVI. Page numbers will be included in the text.

12. Twain, in this sentence, the one preceding, and those that follow, is quoting with obvious and ironic delight "the wildly gifted Graham, Bachelor of Arts," who translated the legend into awkward, overwrought English. Twain recounts Graham's translation, "to refresh my memory . . . for I have never read it before."

13. These sexy lines conclude his final love song to the Nymph which, as we shall see, enflamed her in a manner unexpected by Hermann. Or at least she took parting from her love and letting him be bound to her rocky house, lying in (her?) deep ground, in a decidedly nonerotic way.

14. I am sure that a "serious" interpreter could do much with the naming of the earth (Earth?) at this crucial point in the legend, but I will forego that opportunity in the interest of keeping the narrative moving.

15. In our religious heritage, we could do a lot with that allusion too.

16. In the context of this chapter, *region* would be important for a "serious" and thorough reading of this passage, especially with the adjective that precedes it!

17. Again, these are the words of the wildly talented Graham. Notice the interpretive possibilities of "heavenward" and "sank to the depths."

18. Op. cit.

19. When preparing this chapter I was helped through conversations with Julia Davis and Tom Davis, and by the following works: Dominique Janicaud, *The Shadow of This Thought*, translated by Michael Gendre (Evanston, Ill.: Northwestern University

Press, 1996); Hugo Ott, *Martin Heidegger: A Political Life*, translated by Allan, Blunden (New York: Basic Books, 1993); Jean-Francois Lyotard, *Heidegger and "the Jews,"* translated by Andreas Michel and Mark Roberts (Minneapolis: Minnesota University Press, 1990); Hans Sluga, *Heidegger's Crisis* (Cambridge, MA: Harvard University Press, 1993); Véronique M. Foti, *Heidegger and the Poets* (Atlantic Highlands, N.J.: Humanities Press, 1992); David Farrell Krell, *Intimations of Mortality* (University Park, PA: Pennsylvania State University Press, 1986); Miguel de Beistegui, *Heidegger and the Political* (New York: Routledge, 1998); Jacques Derrida, *Of Spirit*, translated by Geoffrey Bennington and Rachel Bowlby (Chicago: University of Chicago Press, 1989); Jean Patocka, *Heretical Essays*, translated by Erazem Kohak (New York: Open Court Press, 1996); Jean-Luc Nancy, *The Inoperative Community*, translated by Peter Connor, Lisa Garbers, Michael Holland, Simon Sawbeney (Minneapolis: University of Minnesota Press, 1991); Philippe Lacoue-Labarthe, *Heidegger, Art and Politics*, translated by Chris Turner (New York: Blackwell, 1990).

12

Heidegger and Arendt
The Birth of Political Action and Speech

PEG BIRMINGHAM

In *The Human Condition*, Hannah Arendt explains that her thought is a thought of natality rather than dying; it is a thought of the joy of beginnings rather than the anxiety of endings. Such thinking, Arendt claims, avoids a metaphysics of death and in doing so allows for a thought of the political insofar as to think beginnings is to think action. With this Arendt seemingly implicates Heidegger's thought with its emphasis on being-towards-death as both metaphysical, insofar as death provides the limit that allows a grasp of the whole, and nonpolitical, insofar as it is a thought of endings and, thereby, a thought of passivity rather than of activity with its sense of beginnings. I wonder, however, whether Arendt's self-understanding of her work as offering an antidote to Heidegger's is not itself partially blind to her debt to Heidegger in her thinking of natality and, partially blind at the very place that makes her own thinking most problematic, namely, the separation of political life (*bios politikos*) from biological life (*zôê*).[1] The separation of the *bios politikos* from *zôê* is the basis for Arendt's subsequent strict distinction in *The Human Condition* between the political and the social. This partial blindness, I submit, prevents Arendt from developing her understanding of natality and action as fully as she might if she had acknowledged that Heidegger's analysis of being-towards-death in *Being and Time* is at the same time an analysis of natality and the possibility of new beginnings. Moreover, it would have prevented her from making the strict distinction between the social and the political, which has the consequence of seeming to make the political devoid of any material or embodied content.

Yet, I submit, this blindness is only partial insofar as those few references that Arendt makes in her work to Heidegger suggest that she is aware of her debt to him and that the relationship of these two thinkers is much more nuanced and complicated than a first glance might suggest. Three references especially suggest that Heidegger's thought provides at the very least an implicit frame for Arendt's thought of

natality: two references to Heidegger in *Men in Dark Times* as well as a reference to
his reading of Nietzsche's eternal return in *Life of the Mind* reveal the ways in which
Heidegger's thought is present in Arendt's understanding of the way language is at
work in the event of natality, how it is that a space of action could be darkened, if not
altogether foreclosed, and finally, the temporality of the event of natality.[2] These references suggest that key terms in Arendt's thought, such as *action* and *speech*, are far
more indebted to Heidegger than even she explicitly admits.

In what follows, I will outline briefly Arendt's understanding of action and
speech as a "second birth," showing how this second birth requires an account of
the "first birth," an account I submit that Arendt develops. I then want to ask
whether Heidegger's understanding of natality in *Being and Time*, itself always already
bound up with fatality, allows us to better grasp the "first birth" out of which the
Arendtian second birth emerges. I would like to suggest that reading Arendt and Heidegger together on the issue of natality allows us to see how materiality and embodiment are necessarily at work in Arendt's second birth, and at the same time allows us
to see that thinking together the first and second birth confounds any simple distinction between *zôê* and *bios politikos*, the social and the political.

I

In *The Human Condition*, Arendt states, "With word and deed we insert ourselves
into the human world, and this insertion is like a *second birth*, in which we confirm
and take upon ourselves the naked fact of our original physical appearance" (HC,
176; emphasis added). This second birth, argues Arendt, allows human beings to appear, and without this birth humans would literally be dead to the world: "A life
without speech and without action . . . is literally death to the world, it has ceased to
be a human life because it is no longer lived among men" (HC, 176). Through this
linguistic birth, humans become political kinds of beings. Arendt cites Aristotle's definition of man as *zôon logon ekhon*, one for whom exists, ". . . a way of life in which
speech and only speech made sense" (HC, 27). This linguistic birth is the birth of
the "who," the unique self, insofar as the event of linguistic natality is the being-born
of the unexpected and the new. In other words, the birth of the political self is the
birth of the unexpected word.

Arendt's understanding of the birth of the self in terms of the unexpected word reveals that she understands action (that which allows for the appearance of the self) as
inseparable from the event of linguistic natality. It is speech that constitutes the self at
the very moment of its utterance. The self is not a consequence of speech: the "who" is
born in the very speaking itself. For Arendt, therefore, the unexpected word is performative; it is *inaugurative* and not descriptive. This explains why Arendt continuously
refers to the theater when attempting to grasp the appearance of the self. Indeed, in *On
Revolution*, she refers to the Greek notion of the self as *persona*, the voice that speaks

through the mask in ancient tragedy. For Arendt, the important point is that there is no one behind the mask—the self is the persona, the voice that shines through.[3] The self as the unexpected word is the performance of the new. This self, therefore, is never representational or positional. Linguistic natality is the birth of the singular unique self, "before whom there was nobody" (HC, 177).

It would be easy, but also a mistake, to think of this second birth as the birth of a kind of heroic individuality, distinct in the sense of being "a word unto itself."[4] Arendt, however, rejects any notion of the self as a "singular word," arguing that the unexpected word is always already immersed in a web of relationships and plurality of enacted stories (HC, 181). The Arendtian notion of a "web" reveals that the unexpected word erupts from within a plurality of discourses entangled and interwoven in their sedimented histories. At the same time, Arendt makes only a brief reference to the unexpected word as tied to an *embodied* web: "To be sure, this web is no less bound to the objective world of things than speech is to the existence of a living body, but the relationship is not like that of a facade or, in Marxian terminology, of an essentially superfluous superstructure affixed to the useful structure of the building itself" (HC, 183). Although largely unexplored, this passage reveals that Arendt's all too tidy distinction between the first birth, the birth of the living body, and the second, linguistic birth is eventually undone in her thought. Linguistic natality cannot be "laid over" physical natality, suggesting that both births must be thought of as intimately connected. This entangling of speech and the living body problematizes her distinction between *zôê* and *bios politikos*, as well as her distinction between the social and the political. I return to this shortly.

Arendt's notion of a public space, understood through this "second birth," is larger, therefore, than simply a set of laws and institutions. The public space, as a space of action and the possibility of new beginnings, is one of possibility for inaugurative speech. In other words, the *polis* understood as a space of appearance is a "performative polis" wherein what appears is the unexpected word that marks the self. Only in this way, Arendt argues, can Pericles' words be understood: "Wherever you go, you will be a *polis*":

[These words] expressed the conviction that action and speech create a space between the participants which can find its proper location almost any time and anywhere. It is the space of appearance in the widest sense of the word, namely, the space where I appear to others as others appear to me, where men exist not merely like other living or inanimate things but make their appearance explicitly. (HC, 198–99)

The *polis* finds its proper location anytime and anywhere there is the appearance of the unexpected, unpredictable word.

The space of action as a place of inaugurative speech allows us to understand Arendt's claim that both the use of clichés and the rise of ideology foreclose the space of action. The use of clichés discloses nothing or no one; it is a cliché precisely because it says nothing. Indeed, it is worse—saying nothing, the cliché darkens the public space by making it more difficult, if not impossible, for the unexpected word to appear. Arendt's reference to Heidegger's claim in *Being and Time* is now clear: what ought to be illuminating, namely, the appearance of speech, darkens and obscures whenever it is the case that speech has become a cliché. Arendt thinks that Heidegger got it "entirely correct" when, when in his analysis of *das Man*, he notes the absence of authentic speech and the resulting loss of a truly public space. Far from denigrating the realm of *doxa*, Arendt argues that Heidegger understands correctly that the widespread use of clichés (*Gerede*, according to Heidegger) renders action impossible, precisely because it deadens the possibility of the appearance of the unexpected word.[5] Still further, clichés are the speech of *das Man*, the Anyone, whose speech covers over the uniqueness of the "who." Indeed, Arendt's *Eichmann in Jerusalem* could be read as a long reflection on the use of clichés, and how it is that their use stands at the very basis of the "banality of evil." This allows for a different emphasis on what Arendt understands by this phrase, pointing not only how it is that "thoughtlessness" is evil in its banality, but also how the absence of action, that is, the absence of the unexpected and unpredictable word, also contributes to the "banality of evil."

The rise of ideology forecloses a space of action, precisely because it systematically sets out to destroy any possibility of the unexpected word by insisting on "strident ideology." Here again, Heidegger's influence is felt. For Arendt, "strident ideology" that replaces the unexpected word is tied to a notion of truth as productive and technological rather than as disclosive in Heidegger's sense:

> If Western philosophy has maintained that reality is truth—for this is of course the ontological basis of *adequatio rei et intellectus*—then totalitarianism has concluded from this that we can fabricate truth insofar as we can fabricate reality; that we do not have to wait until reality unveils itself and shows us its true face, but can bring into being a reality whose structures will be known from the beginning, because the whole thing is our product.[6]

"Strident ideology" appeals to the inherent worldlessness and lack of speech that for Arendt characterizes the modern world of technology. Rather than action, there is only atomization and a "perfect functionality." At its extreme, perfect functionality becomes terror, the elimination altogether of the unexpected. In place of the unexpected, there is "the tranquillity of the graveyard."[7] In other words, only by eliminating entirely the event of natality could terror meet with success. Following Heidegger, Arendt suggests that this is possible, because the modern stance toward the world is one of *Gestell*, a technological enframing in which everyone and everything is understood in terms of a worldless functionality. Lacking a sense of belonging to the world, these functionaries are imbued with a sense of being superfluous, and, therefore, with a mixture of gullibility and cynicism they are more than ready to substitute reality with a fictive ideology. And Arendt agrees with Heidegger that the modern world of enframing is accomplished through a technological language that attempts to foreclose the possibility of the unexpected word. In other words, the understanding of truth as logical, rooted in *adequatio rei et intellectus,* is one of the crystallizing elements of totalitarianism. It is noteworthy that Arendt looks to a notion of truth as unveiling or disclosive (*Unverborgenheit)* as providing a way out of ideology.

The possibility of the unexpected word reveals the vulnerability and infelicity at the very heart of language. But how can we think this infelicity, this vulnerability that allows for the unexpected word, the new beginning? Or, more precisely, how can we think this vulnerability of language that is the vulnerability of the newcomer, the stranger? And further, what is the relation between the second birth, that is, the unexpected word, and the first birth, that which Arendt calls "the naked fact of physical appearance"? Certainly Arendt claims an inseparability between the first and second birth, pointing out that that is because of the *fact* of the beginning that the self is able to be born again as the unexpected word. Yet it is striking that Arendt does not develop her account of the first beginning and how it is the possibility of the second. It seems to me that this lack of account allows Arendt to separate far too neatly the political (the realm of free speech and action) from the social (the realm of coercive bodily needs). It is my suggestion that Heidegger's understanding of natality does give an account of this first birth and at the same time further illuminates the second. In other words, Heidegger's account of the birth allows for a more developed understanding of "linguistic natality" and the possibility of a recommencement, another beginning. At the same time, Heidegger's account does not allow for a strict distinction between the social and the political.

II

In Section 72 of *Being and Time,* Heidegger takes up the beginning and end of Dasein: "Factical Dasein exists as born; and as born, it is already dying, in the sense of Being-towards-death. As long as Dasein factically exists, both the "ends' and their "between' *are,* and they *are* in the only way which is possible on the basis of Dasein's Being as *care*" (SZ, 374;BTa, 426). Dasein's natality is inseparable from its fatality, and both are as care (*Sorge*): "As care, Dasein is the "between"; it is between its no-longer and not-yet." And yet, the no-longer and the not-yet are not to be understood as external, as bookends to this between that is Dasein's care. The "between' is permeated with the ends:

> Understood existentially, birth is not and never is something past in the sense of something no longer present-at-hand; and death is just as far from having

the kind of Being of something still outstanding, not yet present-at-hand but coming along. (Ibid.)

Dasein's "who," its self-constancy, therefore, can be grasped only by understanding a "specific temporalizing of temporality" (SZ, 375;BTa, 427). This leads Heidegger to an analysis of Dasein's authentic historicity which, he shows, is the temporality of the *Augenblick*. In what follows, I would like to point to two important aspects of this discussion that illuminate the beginning inherent in Dasein's being-born and in turn allow for the possibility of a recommencement, another beginning, or what Arendt calls a "second birth." The first aspect of the discussion is Dasein's being-born as *Sorge*, and the second is the temporality of being-born understood as the temporality of the *Augenblick*.

Significantly, in *Being and Time* the first discussion of Dasein's being as care is given in the discussion of *Fürsorge*, a solicitude that frees. There is an inseparability between freedom and solicitude. *Fürsorge* does not leap in and dominate the other, but instead it is the solicitude that lets the other be "who" he or she is. Most important for our discussion, *Fürsorge* compounds any easy distinction between receptivity and agency or, in other words, between passivity and activity. Indeed, Heidegger shows that no distinction can be made: the act of freeing is receptive, solicitous. What interests us here is how natality, inseparable from fatality, allows for the possibility of Dasein's being as care. In other words, it is my suggestion that the event of being-born allows for the freeing solicitude that marks the very being of Dasein.

Heidegger is careful to show in Section 41 of *Being and Time* that this act of freedom is not located in the individual will:

Care is always concern and solicitude, even if only privately. In willing, an entity which is understood—that is, one which has been projected upon its possibility—gets seized upon, either as something with which one may concern oneself or as something which is to be brought into it Being through solicitude (*Fürsorge*). . . . In the phenomenon of willing, the underlying totality of care shows through. (SZ, 194;BTa, 238–39)

It is in this discussion of authentic care and solicitude, a solicitude that frees rather than dominates, where Heidegger first formulates what he will much later think as *Gelassenheit*, "the will not to will." The activity of freedom is the activity of receptivity; it is not an act of the will but of the word—the finite word that receives, that is, welcomes the newcomer and the stranger; it is the initial power of the welcoming address that inaugurates and sustains linguistic existence, conferring singularity in time and place. The facticity of the self is given through the welcoming word. In other words, the event of natality, Dasein's thrownness (*Geworfenheit*) is always bound up with a welcoming. The self, set free through the address of the other, becomes a self capable of addressing others. One comes to be through the welcoming word.

To be named is to be welcomed—this is the entrance into language. And it seems to me that this is precisely what Arendt suggests when she refers to Heidegger's statement that "man can speak only insofar as he is the sayer."[8] The possibility of saying is the welcoming. And, furthermore, Heidegger suggests that this entrance into language is an *embodied* entrance. Indeed, Heidegger's analysis sheds light on Arendt's undeveloped claim in *The Human Condition*, namely, that speech is not merely an essentially superfluous superstructure affixed to embodiment. In this section of *Being and Time*, Heidegger suggests that the first birth, the being-born, is never simply the naked fact of physical existence but is already infused with language. In fact, *Fürsorge* carries with it the sense of "prenatal care," rendering impossible a distinction between the word of welcome and the fact of physical birth. Being-born is always already immersed in discourse, prenatally. In Arendtian terms, *zôê* is always already *zôon logon ekhon*. Naked facticity is always already the site of language, that is, the address that calls one into existence.

Moreover, Heidegger's discussion of *Ent-fernung*, that is, Dasein's embodiment as always at a distance with itself, suggests that embodiment, "naked facticity," is never fully present—it is itself permeated with a lack and a loss that mark the event of natality. This is extremely important insofar as it would seem that one reason Arendt separates *zôê* from the *bios politikos* is in order to ensure that the political space is not understood in terms of some organic or naturalistic fantasy that allows for the totalitarian attempt to make this fantasy present. However, in his discussion of *Raumlichkeit* (better translated as embodiment), Heidegger offers a way to think the materiality of the political body that avoids some organic fantasy. *Raumlichkeit* is Dasein's spatiality, and it is bodily. Dasein, therefore, is an embodied being, always already immersed and involved in the world. The question of the place of Dasein's embodiment, however, is not a question of a corporeal thing present-at-hand. Being-alongside is an embodied "here" that is also "there": "Dasein understands its "here" in terms of its environmental 'yonder.' The "here" does not mean the "where" of something present-at-hand but rather the "whereat" (*Wobei*) of de-severant Being-alongside together with this de-severance" (SZ, 107;BTa, 142).

Deseverance (*Entfernung*) brings close, but never eradicates, the difference between the here and there of circumspective concern. Moreover, Dasein's embodiment is never the "where" wherein Dasein stands. The place of embodiment is the whereat (*Wobei*); it is a region given in the body's directionality: "To free a totality of involvements is equiprimordially, to let something be involved in a region, and to do so by de-severance and directionality" (SZ, 110;BTa, 145). Directionality allows for orientation, for example, the difference between the left and right. The difference, Heidegger maintains against Kant, is not given in a subjective feeling; rather, orientation is always already given in an involvement whose basis is the deseverance and directionality of embodiment. The point here is that Dasein's embodied stance (*Wobei*) is within a region of involvements wherein Dasein is always immersed, finding itself from a there. Most importantly, however, the there is never crossed out completely, and therefore there is never any possibility of an embodied presence-at-hand. In other words, Dasein's embodiment is the place of difference and dislocation. Significantly, Heidegger offers a way to think of *zôê* and *bios politikos* as inseparable, while at the same time avoiding any notion of an organic, totalizing fantasy.

Returning to our discussion of the address that always already suffuses the naked facticity of the event of natality, Heidegger shows that this address, this hearkening, is always to that which is without why, to the being-born and the dying that are without place or representation; it is to be addressed or called at the moment when we do not or no longer have possessions or identity cards to present. Still further, it is a saying that says nothing other than the lack or loss out of which its saying is articulated. This is *Verschwiegenheit*, the silence that articulates Dasein's potentiality-for-being. (SZ, 165;BTa, 208). *Verschwiegenheit*, the articulated silence that is the voice of the friend, the welcoming that every Dasein carries with it. There is nothing so other than being born and dying, the indices of all alterity. There is nothing that makes clearer my gratitude for being received: *Fürsorge*. And is it not the gratitude that marks Arendt's own thinking of gratitude as "*amor mundi*"? And is this not also the gratitude that Heidegger speaks of, the thankfulness at the very heart of *Denken*?

Being-born and being-toward-death, the indices of all alterity, reveal that Heidegger's notion of fatality is not metaphysical and furthermore has important implications for thinking the space of the political. Natality and death are limits in the sense of an opening—an opening not only of Dasein's authentic possibilities of itself but an opening that is never at the disposal of Dasein, whose advent does *not* take place *within* Dasein's history. There is an experience of a limit that relates Dasein to its possibilities but at the same time means that these possibilities are not self-contained. Dasein cannot set its own limits, and it cannot absorb its beginning and end into those limits. In short, Dasein is open to its own possibilities by being held in an opening it did not create and can never appropriate. From this analysis, it is clear that Dasein's authenticity, that is, the appropriation of one's ownness, is impossible. Indeed, as the stretch between natality and fatality, a stretch that is itself permeated by these nonappropriable ends, Dasein is permeated with loss. Moreover, Dasein's inability to appropriate its ends illuminates why Heidegger insists that Dasein's being-toward-death is *nonrelational*. Being-toward-death brings one face to face with radical alterity: that to which there is no relation. Although Heidegger does not explicitly say so, the same is true of our being-toward-birth. The stretch between, therefore, is an endurance saturated with loss, characterized by an openness to that which is always other and cannot be owned. The significance of this politically is that the political space, the space of beginning something new, despite the attempt of terror, is always open to something other than itself.

Finally, Heidegger's discussion of authentic care, that is, the temporality of the *Augenblick*, allows us to see how the temporality of this first birth allows for the Arendtian second birth. As mentioned above, Arendt, in her reading of Kafka, is influenced by this discussion as evidence in her reference to Heidegger's notion of the *Augenblick* in *Life of the Mind*.[9] Arendt invokes Heidegger's notion of the *Augenblick* as well as Nietzsche's notion of the "eternal return" to illuminate the temporal duration of the gap wherein the "who" stands, arguing that this is the moment of the "untimely." Arendt, however, does not link Heidegger's discussion of the *Augenblick* to her concept of natality. It is my suggestion that if she had done so, she would have been faced with the way in which our "naked facticity" is always already imbued with linguistic natality.[10] Indeed, this is precisely what Heidegger shows in his discussion in *Being and Time*.

Heidegger's discussion of the *Augenblick* emerges in an analysis of Dasein's thrownness, its immersion in its destiny and the taking over of this destiny as fate. Significant to our discussion is that Heidegger prefaces his remarks on fate and the temporality of the *Augenblick* by stating that Dasein's freedom and finitude are at the very heart of this temporality of the *Augenblick*:

> Only an entity which, in its Being, is essentially *futural* so that it is free for its death and let itself be thrown back upon its factical "there" by shattering itself against death—that is to say, only an entity which, as futural, is equiprimordially in the process of *having-been* can, by handing down to itself the possibility it has inherited, take over its own thrownness and be *in the moment of vision* for "its time." Only authentic temporality which is at the same time finite, makes possible something like fate—that is to say, authentic historicality. (SZ, 385;BTa, 437)

Within the moment of insight (*Augenblick*), Dasein grasps its historical, factical possibilities. At the same time, the moment of insight is a site, a historical conjunction of the temporal and spatial. Dasein's resolute authentic response to its historicity is possible only at this moment of insight in the taking over of *repeatable* historical possibilities. It is the notion of repetition that I wish to explore here—what kind of repetition is at work in the *Augenblick*? Heidegger insists that the repetition cannot be understood as "mere repetition," a simple taking over of historical possibilities. The term Heidegger uses is *Erwidert*. This term must be heard from its preposition *wider* meaning "contrary to or against":

> The repeating of that which is possible does not bring again (*Widerbringen*) something that is "past," nor does it behind the "present" back to that which has already been "outstripped." . . . Rather, the repetition makes a critical reply (*Erwidert*) to the possibility of that existence which has-been-there. But when such a rejoinder is made to this possibility in a resolution, it is made in a

moment of vision; and as such it is at the same time a disavowal of that which in the "today" is working itself out as the "past." (SZ, 385-86;BTa, 437-38)[11]

The "between" that marks the temporality of the *Augenblick* is the time of this repetition that takes the form of a reply that is at odds with what has been handed down. Indeed, repetition understood as "critical response" (*Erwidert*) is precisely what allows for the unexpected and unpredictable, precisely because it disturbs and disrupts, the critical response that dissolves any authorization of repeatable possibilities based on a myth of being tied to a beginning. The critical response is possible, because that "between" that marks the temporality of the *Augenblick* (and let us not forget that this is the "between" that marks the "who" of Dasein) is a gap between the no-longer and the not-year, a gap that is permeated with this loss or lack that marks both ends. Thus the moment is untimely and out of order.

This means that the break with context and destiny is always possible. The fate of Dasein as the fate of a "*unique* who" is possible, insofar as there is the possibility of a critical reply. Paradoxically, the temporality of the *Augenblick* reveals that the constancy of the self is always becoming *undone* in the moment of the critical reply. As the "between," the "who" is untimely, out of order, there is a gap where the self is. And this is because the lack, the loss that marks being-born and dying, permeates every moment of the being.

The significance of this loss at the very heart of speech for Dasein's freedom and finitude is now clear. The first beginning, being-born, makes possible a second beginning, if the latter is understood as the possibility of saying something new, that is, the Arendtian second birth. At the beginning of saying there is a loss, a lack at the very heart of the reply, which means that the possibility of a different reply is never foreclosed. In other words, while speech is always historically situated and delimited, it also is open to further and unexpected delimitations, and this is because of Dasein's natality and fatality. The loss or lack that permeates the reply can work in counter-hegemonic ways. The *Augenblick* is the moment in which a speech without prior authorization nevertheless can assume authorization in the course of its saying. In still other words, the loss or lack that permeates the reply reveals that the word always has the possibility of being unmoored. The force of the critical reply is derived precisely from its decontextualization, from its break with a prior context and its capacity to assume new contexts. Limited by natality and fatality, speech is bound to nothing. In other words, although materially entangled, it is bound to no context in particular. Thus there is an infelicity, a vulnerability to all enacted speech—an inherent independence from any of the webs in which it appears. There is always the possibility of the unexpected word.

Although largely ignored by readers of both Heidegger and Arendt, Heidegger's notion of being-toward-birth, particularly when thought through his discussion of *Fürsorge*, offers therefore a corrective to Arendt's discussion of natality. To summarize, Heidegger shows how the "naked fact of physical birth" is always already linguistically bound. To be born, to be a mortal, is to have been welcomed, to have been given a name. And only because the "who" is named is he or she able to die. More precisely, it is the welcoming through the name that renders one mortal. At the same time, Heidegger's account of natality complicates Arendt's strict separation between *zôê* and *bios politikos* with the subsequent distinction between the social and the political. Heidegger's account of *Fürsorge* and being-toward-birth articulates how it is that the "second birth" is never simply laid over the "first birth," but instead both births happen at once. This is the wonder of appearance, that is, the miracle of natality.

Notes

1. Hannah Arendt, *The Human Condition* (Chicago: University of Chicago Press, 1957). Hereafter cited as HC, followed by the page number.

2. Hannah Arendt, *Men in Dark Times* (New York: HBJ, 1955). The first reference is to Heidegger's statement in *Being and Time*: "*Das Licht der Offentlichkeit verdunkelt alles*" (The light of the public obscures everything), and the second reference, found in her essay on Walter Benjamin, is to Heidegger's statement: "Man can speak only insofar as he is the sayer" (pp. xi, 204, respectively). The third reference is in *Life of the Mind* (New York: HBJ, 1971), p. 212.

3. Hannah Arendt, *On Revolution* (New York: Penguin, 1963), pp. 106–07.

4. Seyla Benhabib, for example, argues this in *The Reluctant Modernism of Hannah Arendt* (London: Sage, 1996).

5. This is Jacques Taminiaux's argument in *The Thracian Maid and the Professional Thinker: Arendt and Heidegger,* translated and edited by Michael Gendre (Albany: State University of New York Press, 1997). I disagree with his argument.

6. Hannah Arendt, *Essays in Understanding* (New York: HBJ, 1994), p. 354.

7. Ibid., p. 348.

8. Arendt, *Men in Dark Times,* p. 204.

9. Indeed, Arendt's reading of the Kafka parable "He," which is explicitly indebted to Heidegger's notion of the *Augenblick,* plays a prominent role throughout her work. Arendt discusses this parable in which she illustrates the gap between the past and the future, the gap of both thought and action, in at least six different places in her work.

10. Certainly in her many readings of this parable, Arendt does show how the gap between the past and the future is made possible because of the insertion of the

human being in time, an insertion that breaks up the continuum of time and deflects the present from both the past and the future. This "deflected present" is what allows for the new. Arendt, however, does not link the event of natality to her account of the linguistic natality.

11. I have translated *Erwidert* as "critical reply" rather than Macquarrie's and Robinson's "reciprocative rejoinder," because the latter terms give too much of a sense of the reply as reciprocity that continues the past into the future rather than a critical rupturing of the past.

Part IV

Responsibility, Being-With, and Community

13

Heidegger and the Origins of Responsibility

François Raffoul

The concept of responsibility has traditionally been associated, if not identified, with accountability, under the authority of a philosophy of free will and
causality, itself resting upon a subject-based metaphysics. Responsibility, as
accountability, designates the capacity by a subject to be the cause of its acts, and ultimately to appropriate and "own" its acts and meaning. In such an enframing, it may
well be the case that the phenomenological and ontological sources of what is called
"responsibility" have remained obscure and neglected. The ambition of this chapter
is to begin unfolding what I would call here "the origins of responsibility." I will
argue that Heidegger's thought provides key features to allow for a rethinking of
what being-responsible as such could mean, a meaning missed in the thought of accountability. I will pursue this effort by identifying and focusing on two of these features—facticity and alterity—with the hope of showing that Heidegger's thought of
Dasein helps us think a primordial, factical, and finite responsibility, one that manifests the essential exposure to alterity of human beings. The sense of responsibility
that will then emerge can no longer be confused with *accountability* but will signify
instead the very movement of a radically finite existence having to come to itself, and
to itself as other, from an inappropriable (and thus always "other") ground.

The Facticity of Responsibility

We know the crucial place that the motif of facticity—factical life, hermeneutics of facticity—occupies in the early work of Martin Heidegger. Heidegger has stressed that
facticity is an *irreducible* phenomenon for philosophy. For instance, in the 1921-22
winter semester course (GA 61) on Aristotle, he writes that the determinations of factical life "are not indifferent qualities that one notices trivially as when I say: that

thing there is red. They are alive—in facticity—this means, however, that they include factical possibilities and are never (and thank God never [*Gott sei Dank nie*]) to be freed from them; consequently, a philosophical interpretation that aims at what is most important [*die Hauptsache*] in philosophy, that is, facticity, such an interpretation, insofar as it is authentic, is factical" (GA 61, 99). The very element of philosophizing, then, is facticity. It remains for us to reflect on the philosophical significance and relevance of facticity for the task of rethinking responsibility. More precisely, what is the import of the thought of facticity for *ethics*, and more particularly for our thinking or rethinking of *responsibility*, of the senses of being-responsible? This project might seem at first paradoxical: the very motif of facticity could indeed be seen as a challenge to the very possibility of responsible agency, as it opposes the traditional values and ideals of modernity, its model of the absoluteness and transparency of subjectivity. More precisely, does facticity, with its senses of opacity, finitude, and expropriation, not challenge the very *possibility* of a free self-assumption of subjectivity in responsibility, since it represents precisely not only what I am not responsible for but also what I cannot in principle appropriate? I will try, however, to argue that facticity, although it represents for Heidegger an irreducible opacity and even expropriation for the human being, should not be understood as an obstacle or an external limit to the possibility of responsibility and freedom but in fact as its very condition. I hope to show as well that the traditional senses of both facticity and responsibility are radically transformed in such a thought: there is a sense of responsibility that does *not* amount to accountability and that is *not* necessarily a simple appropriation and thus a reduction of facticity. Facticity, in turn, is not what opposes the position of a consciousness, but the "throw" of an existence that is called from such a throw to appropriate what will always remain inappropriable. I will thus argue that one is responsible *from* out of the facticity of existence and ultimately *for* it. What I hope to demonstrate, ultimately, is that ethics pervades through and through our factical existence and therefore does not need to be founded in some problematic "beyond," after having been first taken out of existence: on the contrary, facticity reveals the responsibility of the existent and the finitude and alterity of such responsibility.

Responsibility and Dasein

The first point that we need to bear in mind in any discussion on Heidegger and responsibility is that if there is a notion of responsibility in Heidegger's work, it will not be, and it cannot be, *accountability* in the classical sense. Accountability—which has defined the traditional concept of responsibility, if exhausted it—rests upon the notions of agency, free will, and subjectivity. One is accountable as a subject who is the cause of his or her actions through the freedom of the Will. Accountability, as a concept, assumes the position of a subject-cause, an agent or an author who can be displayed as a *subjectum* for its actions. Such is, for instance, Kant's definition of accountability or imputation in the first *Critique* (CPR, A 448/B 476). Now we know that Heidegger does not think the human being in terms of subject, and we also know that he does not think freedom in terms of free will. The basis for an identification of responsibility with accountability thus seems to disappear in the thinking of Being, which does not mean that it does not harbor *another* thought of responsibility.

Indeed, at the same time that the concept of accountability is deconstructed, Heidegger consistently maintains that Dasein—a being who as we know is neither a subject nor an ego, a consciousness, a person, a rational animal, or even a man—is to be thought in terms of responsibility. In at least three respects, responsibility defines the essence of Dasein, it constitutes selfhood, and finally, it defines man's relationship to Being, that is, his very essence. One could go so far as to say that the very concept of Dasein *means* to be a responsibility of and for oneself. It is Heidegger who says that, for instance, in *The Basic Problems of Phenomenology*: "Only in responsibility does the self first reveal itself" (GA 24, 194); in the 1930 summer semester course (GA 31, 262), *On the Essence of Human Freedom*, he states that responsibility for oneself (*Selbstverantwortlichkeit*) represents the very essence of the human being: "*Responsibility for oneself* then designates the *fundamental modality of being* which determines all comportment of the human being, the *specific and distinctive human action, ethical praxis*" (GA 31, 263). This "ethical," or "practical," dimension of the concept of Dasein appears early in *Being and Time*, in fact, as early as we are told that Dasein designates that entity for whom Being is at issue. Dasein is that entity for which and in which Being is at issue. Being is given in such a way that I *have* to take it over and be responsible for it. I am not myself as if I "had" myself in the sense of a possession or a predicate; rather, I have being *to be* as my own, because such a being is addressed to me as a possible way of Being, as a way to be, and not as a "what." "To be": the being that I am is to be taken over. This determination of Dasein from the outset defines the self as a responsibility of itself. What else can the expression of Care (*Sorge*) mean if not that primordial responsibility of oneself that Dasein, as *Zu-sein*, is? For man, this is the "ultimate demand," Heidegger explains in the 1929–30 course on *The Fundamental Concepts of Metaphysics*, namely, that he "takes upon itself again, explicitly and expressly, its own Dasein and be responsible for it" (GA 29/30, 254).

We see from the outset that responsibility is not thought as a consequence of a subject "owning" his or her actions but is instead approached in terms of a response to an event that is also a call, the call of Being. Such a call individuates Dasein, constitutes its selfhood. Responsibility is not based on subjectness but constitutes the self as the one who is called. (1) The call does not give us some universal potentiality-for-Being to understand: on the contrary, it reveals the one called "as that which has been individuated at a given time and which belongs to that particular Dasein" (SZ, 280). Not in some external or superficial way, but in the sense that "in the claim (*Forderung*), each Dasein must always conceive of this necessity for itself, from the ground of its essence" (GA 29/30, 255). By itself, the call singularizes the existent. (2) The definition of Dasein as existence implies having-to-be. In this "having-to-be," I am *called to be*, and to make this Being my own. Dasein can only be as called. Indeed, I do not posit myself as a transcendental subject but am called *to be* the being that I am. Dasein has itself "announced" to itself, so to speak, by the call of existence, as having-to-be in its two senses of future and obligation. It is the call in the sense of the temporal rhythm of an "each time" that individuates the I: each time, the I is thrown into existence, into existing; each time, Dasein is delivered over to itself. This is why the call also is that which I have to *answer*. There lies the hidden source and resource of responsibility: to be responsible means, before anything else, to respond, *respondere*. (3) "Having to be oneself": such is the originary responsibility of Dasein. "Become what you are," Heidegger also said, a proposition that is not to be understood ontically, as "Realize your potential!" but ontologically, that is, what you are, you can only "become it," because Dasein's being is . . . to-be. In this "to-be" resides the ontological sense of responsibility, and it is thus a responsibility that defines the self.

Dasein, from the questioning/questioned entity of *Being and Time*, will in the later works of Heidegger be referred to more and more as the "called one," *der Gerufene*, having to answer for the very openness and givenness of Being and having to be its "guardian." In the lecture "What Is Philosophy," for example, Heidegger refers *antworten*, to answer, to *ent-sprechen*, to correspond, to indicate that the "response" to the call or the *Anspruch* of Being is an attuned listening, a responding as corresponding that "listens" to the voice of Being, and to that extent is a keeping or a sheltering of the givenness of Being. The response, we should stress, does not follow the call but is already given in the call, always already corresponding to the Saying (*Zusage*) of Being. In fact, Dasein *cannot but answer it, it has each time already answered, already said "yes" to this call of Being, it has always-already gained access to itself in such an answer.* To be responsible here means to have been struck, always already, by this event. Heidegger writes in *On the Way to Language*: "[The Saying's] vow is not empty. It has in fact already struck its target—whom else but man? For man is man only because he is granted the promise of language, because he is needful to language, that he may speak it" (GA 12, 185;OWL, 90). Responsibility then refers to that event by which Being "enowns" humans. It therefore represents human beings' very belonging to Being, as well as their essence as humans.

Responsibility thus defines the very essence of man. Yet by emphasizing that facticity is the element of philosophy, and the root and horizon of philosophizing, Heidegger decisively breaks with all hopes for an integral, idealistic reduction of phenomena; facticity then indicates the impossibility of a total appropriation of meaning in thought. The stress on facticity thus seems to represent an essential limit, if not a failure, of the project of appropriation that seems to be an integral part of the concept of responsibility. I will identify such a limit by stressing three moments: the enigma of facticity; the question of birth; facticity as expropriation.

The Enigma of Facticity

Whenever Heidegger describes facticity in *Being and Time* (i.e., mostly in terms of thrownness), it is to emphasize the element of opacity and withdrawal that seems to break and foreclose any possibility of appropriation. For example, in the paragraph devoted to "moods" and "affective dispositions," which exhibit Dasein's being-thrown, Heidegger explains that moods are beyond the reach of both will and cognition. They are like the "enigma," he says, of Dasein's pure "that-it-is," that is, Dasein's facticity. For instance, Heidegger states that in being-in-a-mood, "Being has become manifest as a burden." He then adds: "Why that should be, one does not *know*" (SZ, 135). In fact, he continues, as to this "why," Dasein "*cannot* know anything of the sort" (ibid.; emphasis added). Cognition reaches "far too short." Now this phenomenon is not due to some weakness of our cognitive powers that somehow could be improved; rather, it has to do with the peculiar phenomenon of moods as they exhibit the facticity of Dasein. For in moods, which is a mode of disclosure, Dasein is said to be able to "burst forth as a naked 'that it is and has to be'" (ibid.). Moods disclose the Being of the there in its "that it is. Heidegger states: "A mood makes manifest 'how one is, and how one is faring'. In this 'how one is,' having a mood brings Dasein to its 'there'" (ibid.). And what is peculiar with this phenomenon is that the "that it is" of our being is given in such a way that "the 'whence' and the 'wither' remain *in darkness*" (ibid., emphasis added). This is why cognition falls short: in the phenomenon of facticity, there is this "remaining in darkness," which is irreducible: it is, Heidegger says, a "characteristic of Dasein's Being" (SZ, 135). Against this darkness, or opacity, any enlightenment is powerless, whether theoretically or practically. Facticity is "beyond the range of disclosure" of both cognition and volition, beyond their possibilities of mastery. This explains, incidentally, why only a "counter-mood" can master a mood, as Spinoza had already shown. This indicates that "against the phenomenal facts of the case," all of the ideals of rational enlightenment "count for nothing," "for the mood brings Dasein before the 'that-it-is' of its 'there,' which, as such, stares it in the face with the inexorability of an enigma" (SZ, 136). Moods thus reveal the opacity and inappropriability of our origins. In the course "Introduction to Philosophy" (*Einleitung in die Philosophie* (GA 27)), Heidegger claims that the fact "that by its own decision Dasein has nothing to search for in the direction of its origin, gives an essential prod to Dasein from the darkness of its origin into the relative brightness of its potentiality-for-Being. *Dasein exists always in an essential exposure to the darkness and impotence of its origin, even if only in the prevailing form of a habitual deep forgetting in the face of this essential determination of its facticity*" (GA 27, 340, emphasis added).

The Question of Birth

There is, therefore, a dimension in our being that resists appropriation, whether practical or theoretical. That dimension is nothing other than our very coming into being, and the sheer inappropriability of it. This, of course, mobilizes the question of birth. It is often said, following Hannah Arendt, that Heidegger has neglected the phenomenon of birth, that he privileged being-toward-death. Notwithstanding the fact that thrownness *is* the ontological name for birth (and that in the later work his reflection on *phusis* can be seen as pertaining to birth understood in a nonbiological or naturalistic way), and that any discussion of thrownness and facticity already includes a reflection on birth, we should stress that the question of birth is addressed explicitly in paragraph 72 of *Being and Time*. Dasein is said to exist *between* birth and death, not in the sense that Dasein would occupy an actual place between two external limits. Rather, Dasein exists as stretching itself *between* birth and death, which means Dasein *is* the between of birth and death. Being that between, Dasein exists toward each of them. In other words, Dasein exists toward death, *and Dasein exists toward birth*. This is why Heidegger speaks explicitly of a "Being-towards-the-beginning" (*Sein zum Anfang*) (SZ, 373). Dasein is also said to exist "towards-the-end." But there are *two* ends: birth and death. So principally, birth is an integral part of the existential analytic, and it is not entirely accurate to say that Heidegger ignored this dimension. Further, the charge that he privileged death over birth rests upon a questionable philosophical assumption, namely, first, that birth and death are somehow to be opposed as phenomena, and second, that one leaves birth "behind," so to speak, to only relate to death. But Heidegger shows that in a sense birth and death should be thought of as part of the *same* phenomenon, or that at least they are not to be opposed. And he also stresses that I am not born once in order to leave that event behind, so that I now only exist toward-death (the basis of Hannah Arendt's critique of Heidegger in *The Human Condition*); rather, the event of birth is happening each time as I exist stretching between birth and death, as being-toward birth and toward death. I am thus each time beginning, each time coming into being anew. Heidegger explains that very clearly: "Understood existentially, birth is not and never is something past in the sense of something no longer present-at-hand; and death is just as far from having the kind of Being of something still outstanding, not yet present-at-hand but coming along" (SZ, 374). As beginning, I am already dying. I exist as born, I exist as dying: the same event. I am born into death. "Factical Dasein exists as born; and as born it is already dying, in the sense of Being-towards-death" (ibid.). So Dasein exists as born, that is, "in a natal manner" (*gebürtig existieren*), which immediately means "always already dying."

We thus exist both in a "natal" way, and in a "mortal" way, in the sense that we relate to both ends, "our" ends. But are they really "ours"? In fact, they remain for Heidegger inappropriable: I can no more go back behind my coming into being than I can appropriate death by making it somehow actual. Facticity, understood as thrownness, reveals that Dasein can never go back beyond this "throw" to recapture its being from the ground up. Dasein can never become master of and appropriate its own ground and origins. As Heidegger put it: "'Being-a-basis' means never to have power over one's ownmost Being from the ground up" (SZ, 284). I am thrown into existence on the basis of completely opaque (non)ground that withdraws from all attempts at appropriation. It would then seem that in facticity I am depropriated from my own being, thereby rendering any meaningful sense of responsibility impossible. Facticity seems to represent a radical expropriation for the human being. In a rich article, "The Passion of Facticity,"[1] Giorgio Agamben underlines that facticity entails an element of nonoriginarity, and therefore of non-propriety, which is the very mark of finitude. Drawing from an etymological analysis of the term, Agamben shows that "originally," facticity, or *facticius*, is opposed to *nativus*, and signifies "that which is not natural, that which did not come into being by itself," but rather was produced or made. The factical then means what is made (Descartes, in the third meditation, speaks of those ideas that are "produced" by me; the Latin term is *factae*) and therefore the nonoriginary, if not the nontrue (as in the English "factitious"). Facticity, according to Agamben, indicates "Dasein's constitutive impropriety" (p. 72). He then concludes by stating that the place of facticity in Heidegger's thought of Being leads to affirming a "primacy of the improper" (p. 74).

Facticity As Expropriation

Does this not indicate the failure and impossibility of responsibility as the capacity to be properly one's own? And is it not what Heidegger called Dasein's being-guilty (*Schuldigsein*), the essential "nullity" (*Nichtigkeit*) in Dasein's being? We should not be too quick to come to this conclusion, and I fear that Agamben's reading suffers from an oppositional (i.e., nonphenomenological) account of the proper and the improper, which does not allow him to see that the "inappropriable" is in fact the secret resource of appropriation, and that therefore facticity is perhaps the secret resource of responsibility. In *Introduction to Philosophy*, Heidegger thus explains that precisely that over which Dasein is not master must be "worked through" and "survived." He writes: "Also that which does not arise of one's own express decision, *as most things for Dasein*, must be in such or such a way retrievingly appropriated, even if only in the modes of putting up with or shirking something; that which for us is entirely not under the control of freedom in the narrow sense . . . is something that is in such or such a manner taken up or rejected in the How of Dasein (GA 27, 337, emphasis added). Finitude and facticity are not objections to existence. They are instead its very constitution, and our being-responsible, if it is at all, will have to be both factical, and finite. We should not attack existence (or the philosophers who try to think it!) in order to make it conform to a preset norm of accountability and subject-based thinking; we should instead drop the latter in order to start thinking responsibility phenomenologically. It is therefore that sense of responsibility (i.e., as existential, finite, and factical) that needs to be brought forth.

The inappropriable in existence (facticity), as we saw in the phenomena of moods, is primarily felt as a weight or a burden. What weighs is the inappropriable. The being of the there, Heidegger writes, "become[s] manifest as a burden" (SZ, 134). But, interestingly, the very concepts of weight and burden reintroduce, as it were, the problematic of responsibility. In a marginal note added to this passage, Heidegger later clarified: "Burden: what one has to carry; man is charged with the responsibility (*überantwortet*) of Dasein, delivered over to it (*übereignet*)." The expropriation manifested by facticity, the fact that Dasein is always "late" with respect to its being, reveals a certain withdrawal in the gift of being: Being withdraws in the very "throw" that brings Dasein into existence. But it is this withdrawal itself that calls Dasein, which summons it to be this being-thrown as its own and to be responsible for it. It is the withdrawal that calls, to be and to think, and to be "responsible" for it.

What Dasein has to be, and what it has to be responsible for, then, is precisely its very facticity, its being-thrown as such. What I have to make my own is thus what can never belong to me, what evades me, what will always have escaped me. Heidegger underscored this incommensurability when he claimed that: "The self, which as such has to lay the basis for itself, can never get that basis into its power; *and yet, as existing, it must take over being-a-basis*" (SZ, 284, emphasis added). It appears—and this is why facticity is not factuality—that Dasein is not thrown like a brute fact and is not thrown only once and for all (it "is constantly, as long as it is, its 'that-it-is'" [SZ, 284], it exists as born each time). Rather, it is thrown (born) in such away that it has to be this being-thrown (this birth) each time, in the sense of carrying it or of assuming it as its own.

Thus what I have to appropriate, ultimately, is the inappropriable itself. This shows that responsibility is in a sense identical to finitude. I am not responsible, as Kant argued, because I am a subject as that which begins absolutely (CPR, A 448/ B 476), and therefore as a subject to which actions can be assigned. Rather, I am responsible because I am thrown in an existence that I have to answer for. So that to be thrown (facticity) and to be called (responsibility) are one and the same phenomenon; hence the expression "Facticity of Responsibility" (SZ, 135). Heidegger made that very point in his "Letter on Humanism." There he explained that the phenomenon of thrownness and the call of being are one. For it is from the call (throw) of being that Dasein discovers itself to be thrown. He writes: Man is "called (*gerufen*) by being itself into the preservation of being's truth. The call (*Ruf*) comes as the throw (*Wurf*) from which the thrownness (*Geworfenheit*) of Da-sein derives" (GA 9, 339;BW, 221f). Ultimately, then, the motif of facticity shows that I am responsible for finitude itself. With facticity, responsibility is brought back to its limit as to its most essential resource, if it is the case, as Heidegger puts it, that "a limit is not that at which something stops, but, as the Greeks recognized, the limit is that from which something begins its presencing" (*sein Wesen beginnt)* (PLT, 154, tr. slightly modified).

The primordial sense of responsibility is hence: the appropriation of the inappropriable, *as inappropriable*. And this is what weighs. The weight, the assignation to a call that precedes me, the infinite task of owning up to it, all of this indicates that ontological responsibility implies the exposure to an irreducible otherness. It is in this perspective that Paul Ricoeur, in his recent work *Oneself As Another* (Chapter 10), investigates the notion of responsibility in connection to the categories of passivity and otherness. The facticity of responsibility reveals the alterity of Dasein. In that sense, factical responsibility could no longer be taken as solipsistic, or egoistic, but needs to be unfolded in its essential relation to alterity.

The Alterity of Responsibility

It often is argued that Heidegger privileged the "pole" of the self over the inscription of the other at the heart of selfhood, so that responsibility would primarily be for oneself, and existence unfold (un)ethically as the infamous "struggle for existence." Jean Greisch cites a passage from *Einleitung in die Philosophie*, in which Heidegger seems to accord priority to the self over the other. Heidegger writes: "Dasein must essentially be able to be itself and properly [*im eigentlichen*] be itself, if it wants to know itself as borne and led by an other, if it is supposed to be able to open itself for the Dasein-with of others, if it is supposed to stand up for the other" (GA 27, 325). One would seem justified in concluding from such statements that, as Greisch points out, "the other comes into play only insofar as it bears and leads Dasein (in something like the forms of parental care or political responsibility) or as the object of the ethical 'unfolding' of the self" (HPP, 111).

A Responsibility for Self?

Heidegger often has stressed that Dasein's being for the sake of itself should not be identified with an egoistic struggle for existence. In the *Beiträge*, for instance (par. 48, 178, 179, 197), he rejected firmly such a misunderstanding. But already at the time of *Sein und Zeit*, and in the years immediately following it, Dasein's being-for-the-sake-of-itself, its being-responsible, was from the outset said to be beyond or outside of the opposition of the ego and the alter-ego. It is rather to be thought, as Heidegger explains in the 1928 course, in its "primordial metaphysical import," that is, as an ontological statement and not in its ontical or existentiell sense. Being-for-the-sake-of-oneself is the presupposition of ontic relations to oneself and for this reason cannot be taken as a "solipsistic" or "egoistic" statement about Dasein's self-interest to the exclusion of others, that is, within the subjectivist sphere. Because of its ontological scope, *Dasein's for-the-sake-of-itself in principle includes the possibility for Dasein to concern itself for others in their Being*. Heidegger is then able to claim that Being-for-the-sake-of-oneself is the "metaphysical ground of the possibility" that Dasein be "with others, for them and through them" (GA 26, 240). Being-responsible-for-oneself is a Being-responsible-for-others. Heidegger writes: "Being with Others belongs to the Being of Dasein, which is an issue for Dasein. Thus as Being-with, Dasein " is" essentially for the sake of Others. This must be understood as an existential statement as to its essence" (SZ, 123). There is thus little sense in opposing a "care for others" to a "care for oneself," or in opposing examples of "humane" sacrifices to Dasein's Being-for-the-sake-of-itself. The authentic existence that is chosen in resoluteness is not a solipsism of the isolated I (GA 26, 244) and could not be an exclusion of others and the world, which, as *Mitsein* and *In-der-Welt-Sein*, are constitutive of Dasein. This is why Heidegger explains that "in choosing itself Dasein really chooses precisely its being-with-others and precisely its being among beings of a different character" (GA 26, 245).

The constitutive alterity of Dasein's Being appears in *Sein und Zeit* in the phenomenon of the call of conscience, which often is interpreted by commentators, on the contrary, as a closure of the self upon itself. Certainly Heidegger writes: "Conscience, in its basis and its essence, is each time mine" (SZ, 278). It is so in two ways: on the one hand, because it is each time my own-most Being-a-self that is "called" and, on the other hand, "because the call comes from that being which each time I am" (ibid.). It would then seem that "I" am at once the origin and destination of the call, for Heidegger himself writes that Dasein "calls itself" (SZ, 275), and also that "Dasein is at the same time both the caller and the one to whom the appeal is made (*Das Dasein ist der Rufer und der Angerufene zumal*)" (ibid.). And yet, before we rush to conclude that Dasein is closed upon itself in a solipsistic way, in a kind of "soliloquy" that would reproduce within the Self the Platonic "dialogue of the soul with itself," or even that there is here something like an "auto-affection," "auto-interpellation," or even "auto-nomy," we should note that Heidegger does not state that the call of conscience, of responsibility, comes "from me." Rather, the call is said to come from the being "which each time I am." Now I am this being only in the mode of a having-to-be, that is, in the manner of a possibility to be. It does not therefore "belong to me," if what is meant by this is that the call is proffered by me. Nonetheless, I have to answer it as my own. To call oneself here means to make the call one's own, to answer (for) it, take it on one's shoulders, so to speak. Because there is no pregiven subject or self-identity on the basis of which the call would be initiated, we understand why the "author" of the call, in a certain sense, escapes all attempts at identification (SZ, 274). There is no "author" of the call: no ego, no subject, no other person. There is an origin to the call, but no author. This agent is "other," not an anthropological other, for it does not let itself be identified as a person. It is instead the very movement of the call in its sheer alterity, which brings a self-to-come, the pre-personal (if not impersonal) event of Being that precedes and exceeds the one who will have to assume it as his or her own: *it* happens, before me, without me, without stopping at me, and even without ending with me, but nonetheless, "it" happens only to me, because it calls me: *Es ruft mich*. The call cannot be referred to any entity, be it divine, because it is the event and advent of presence itself.

We should therefore nuance our earlier statement: the call certainly comes from the being that I am, but as something that falls upon me, thus in a sense, as something that does not come from me. These are the very terms that Heidegger uses: "The call comes *from* me and yet from *above and beyond* me, falling on me (*Der Ruf kommt aus mir und doch über mich*)" (SZ, 275). In Jacques Derrida's words, "it falls upon [Dasein] from inside,"[2] and conscience is therefore, as Françoise Dastur writes, "the most intimate alterity." This paradoxical statement is presented by Heidegger as a "phenomenal finding," from which proceed the usual representations of the voice of conscience as an "alien power" arising "within Dasein," and also as a source of autonomy, which is here founded upon a certain alteration of the self: the self as other than itself, "oneself as another." Thus it is correct to say that the caller and the called are "at the same time one's own Dasein themselves" (SZ, 279), if one recognizes that this sameness is not a simple identity, that there is a "thin wall" between the "authentic" self and the They (SZ, 278). I do not call myself: it calls me (*"es ruft mich"*) to myself. The call of conscience is thus above all a call *of* the Self, in both senses of the genitive. The Self is not the author of the call, but comes to be in and *as* the call. I am called to myself, from "afar." In that respect, *the self takes place at the place of the other*. Paul Ricoeur makes this point in *Oneself As Another*. With respect to the alterity of the voice of conscience, he writes: "Unlike the dialogue of the soul with itself, of which Plato speaks, this affection by another voice presents a remarkable dissymmetry, one that can be called vertical, between the agency that calls and the self called upon" (p. 342). This verticality, or dissymmetry, prevents all autonomous closure of the self. The call of conscience is a hetero-affection and manifests the otherness that lies at the heart of Dasein's self-appropriation. For as Heidegger puts it, hearing the call, the very capacity to hear the call, "is Dasein's existential way of Being-open as Being-with for Others" (SZ, 163).

The Otherness of Responsibility

That otherness of Dasein, the fact that, as Heidegger says, "Dasein in itself is essentially Being-with" (*wesenhaft an ihm selbst Mitsein*) (SZ, 120), that Being-with is co-extensive with Dasein's Being-a-self, that Being-oneself is a Being-with, that, finally, the "with" in Being-with is "something of the character of Dasein" and is "to be understood existentially" (SZ, 118), in short, the place and the necessity of the other in the existential analytic can be situated properly only if one understands from the outset that it cannot be framed within an anthropological or an egological enclosure. In short, and characteristically with Heidegger, the question of the other cannot be posed on an ontical but rather an ontological level. The question of the other could only take the form of a question on the *being-with*-others. This is why, one should note from the outset, the other cannot be approached in the context of egohood (as alter-ego), for instance, in the schema of the "intersubjective" relation between the ego and the alter-ego. The other is not the alter-ego, it is not exterior to the ego. Heidegger explains very clearly in the 1925–26 winter semester course on *Logik. Die Frage nach der Wahrheit*: "The other, the Thou, is not something like another ego to which my ego would be opposed" (GA 21, 236). One cannot therefore object to the absence in Heidegger of this figure, no more than the I can be reduced to egohood. This obviously does not mean that the figure of the other is missing from the thought of Being; as Heidegger put it, "Many times, even *ad nauseam*, we pointed out that this being *qua*

Dasein is always already with others and always already with beings not of Dasein's nature" (GA 26, 245).

Such an otherness, which is inscribed in the nonpunctual coming to itself of Dasein, or in the structure of self-affection, which necessarily implies hetero-affection, is referred in the 1928 course on the *Metaphysical Foundations of Logic* to a transcendental dispersion. This originary "dissemination" (*Zerstreutheit*) or "bestrewal" (*Streuung*) belongs to the essence of Dasein: "In its metaphysically neutral concept, Dasein's essence already contains a primordial bestrewal (*ursprüngliche Streuung*)" (GA 26, 173). The multiplicity that arises from such a dispersion affects primordial Dasein itself, and such a primordial dispersion represents a general and of course an irreducible structure of Dasein. Dasein can consequently never get hold of itself outside of this primordial dispersion in some simple unity or identity. Even in the unity that is proper to it, Dasein cannot be thought outside of this (existential) stretching, which primordially disseminates its Being. This accounts for Dasein's Being-with: it is not that there is Being-with, because there are others, but on the contrary, there are "others" only because Being-with essentially belongs to Dasein. And there is no Being-with except on the basis of this primordial dispersion and dissemination, to the extent that "Being-with is a basic metaphysical feature of dissemination" (*das Mitsein eine metaphysische Grundbestimmung der Zerstreuung ist*) (GA 26, 175). It is this primordial dispersion that accounts for the essential openness and exposure of Dasein to the other.

Paradoxically, Heidegger's rejection of empathy (*Einfühlung*), understood as an identification with the other, is due to this primordially open character of Dasein. Heidegger takes issue with empathy as a model for the relation to others, precisely because that representation remains trapped within the egoistic understanding of selfhood. Thus, in the 1929–30 winter semester course, *The Fundamental Concepts of Metaphysics*, he firmly states that empathy, understood as the possibility to transpose oneself in another human being in the sense of identifying with an other, is a question "empty of content," "impossible," "meaningless," "absurd," and ultimately "superfluous" (GA 29/30, 301). Why? Simply because empathy is a possibility that *already* belongs to the essence of Dasein as Being-with, an essence that empathy inadequately designates. The question of knowing how the ego could come out of itself in order to then "enter" into the other is an absurd one, for Dasein is always already "in" others, that is, open to them. Empathy is thus derived from Being-with, and presupposes it. Heidegger writes in *Being and Time*: "'Empathy' does not first constitute Being-with; only on the basis of Being-with does " empathy" become possible" (SZ, 125). This Being-with is so essential that it includes as deficient modes the difficulty in understanding others, to genuinely accompanying them, loneliness and isolation, conflictual relations in which one "walks away from one another," or "against one another," unless it is "next to one another" (GA 29/30, 302). In short, through this critique of *Einfühlung*, Heidegger violently challenges the "dogma that man would exist for himself as an individual, and that the individual ego would be, with its own sphere, precisely that which first and with most certainly is given to itself" (ibid.). Starting with the correlation I-Thou solves nothing: The I-Thou correlation as the correlation of two egos is a "solipsism for two" (GA 24, 394), he writes severely.

This critique of egohood in all of its forms opens as we know onto an appropriation of the concept of Dasein as being-in-the-world, that is, precisely, no longer a self-enclosed ego but an openness to beings as a whole. Dasein relates to itself not as an isolated individual but as openness to the whole of beings. "Man's soul is, in a certain way, all entities" (*hê psychê ta onta pôs estin*), said Aristotle, whom Heidegger cites (SZ, 14). Heidegger often specifies this openness in the following way: Dasein is opened to intraworldly entities, to the other Dasein, and to the entity that I am. *The very concept of Dasein thus includes a responsibility to the other*: to the other entity, to the other Dasein, and to itself as another: Dasein is Care. It should therefore come as no surprise if one of the forms of care (*Sorge*), as we know, is "care for" others, or solicitude (*Fürsorge*). This "care for" others includes even those deficient modes that are "inconsiderateness" (*Rücksichtlosigkeit*) and "indifference" (*Naschsehen*): as deficient modes, these actually confirm Dasein's openness to others. Heidegger distinguishes two fundamental modalities, or "extreme possibilities," of this Being-for-others: one kind of solicitude will consist in taking over the care of the other by substituting oneself to him or her: it consists in leaping in (*Einspringen*) for him or her, that is, in taking his or her responsibility of Being *away* from him or her. This solicitude is clearly inauthentic, in at least three respects: first, because it treats the other Dasein as something ready-to-hand, a *zuhandenes*, as Heidegger notes (SZ, 122); second, because it consists in taking the place of the other, such a substitution representing for Heidegger an inauthentic relation to others; and third, because it disburdens the other Dasein of his or her care and responsibility. Now the latter is for Heidegger inauthenticity par excellence, if it is the case that inauthenticity consists of a fleeing of Dasein in the face of its own existence and of its weight. I can never be the other, though; in turn, I can never be without the other. Heidegger explains clearly in the 1929–30 course that to transpose oneself in another cannot mean taking the other's place, that is, for Dasein, taking his or her responsibility. I can at most *accompany* (*Mitgehen*) the other, and this is how Dasein is *with* others, this is how we are together. No identification, then, but accompaniment. In fact, everything takes place as if it was precisely the *disruption* of this commonality between the I and others, as Jean-Luc Nancy has emphasized, which provided the basis for the very emergence of the other *as other* and therefore for the very possibility of an ethics of responsibility. Heidegger mentions such an ethics of responsibility toward the other: the other kind of solicitude will not unburden the other of his or her responsibility, will not leap in for him of her, but rather leaps ahead (*vorausspringt*) of him of her, so as to free the other for his or her own responsibility; "it helps the Other to become transparent to him/herself in his care and to become free for it" (SZ, 122). It frees the other for his or her own Being-toward-death and his or her own potentiality-for-Being: it therefore lets the other be *as other*. Authentic solicitude does not attempt to appropriate the other but does justice to the infinite alterity of the other. Only in that sense can Dasein become, as Heidegger put it, the "conscience of others." It then appears that responsibility, once it is understood away from the tradition of subjectivity, causality, and free will, signifies an essential exposure to the other and cannot simply be reduced to a responsibility for a self asserting itself. Returning to the origins of responsibility thus allows one to reveal its facticity and otherness, which are in fact its very possibility. It is in such a nexus of responsibility, facticity, and otherness that the site of ethics, of an "originary ethics," is to be situated in Heidegger's work.

Notes

1. In *Heidegger: Questions ouvertes* (Paris: Osiris, 1988).

2. *Donner la mort*, in *L' éthique du don, Jacques Derrida et la pensée du don* (Paris: Métailié-Transition, 1992), p. 49.

14

Reading Heidegger Responsibly
Glimpses of Being in Dasein's Development

DAVID WOOD

> To be sure, that distress varies in the essential beginnings and transitions of man's history. But this distress should never be taken superficially and reckoned with summarily as a lack or misery or something like that. This distress exists outside any "pessimistic" or "optimistic" valuation. The grounding-attunement that attunes unto necessity differs according to the inceptual experience of this distress.
> —Heidegger, *Contributions to Philosophy* (*From Enowning*)

Introduction

My aim here is somewhat experimental—to engage Heidegger's encounter with the question of being to reopen the issue of time's horizonality in a way licensed by the accounts Heidegger himself gives of reading other philosophers. I will try to show that Heidegger's problematic can be effectively developed through a consideration of the complex temporality of human maturation and development. I will comment on the various difficulties that this proposal runs into and will try to show, nonetheless, how it helps us make sense of Heidegger's other concerns—the saving grace in the danger of technology, philosophy as a *way* of thinking (or performativity), that philosophy begins with distress (*Not*). Finally, I will offer a somewhat speculative account of why this particular reading suggests itself, indeed presses upon us, today.

Heidegger's General Remarks about Reading Others

I have proposed to read Heidegger in a way licensed by his remarks about reading others and, indeed, his practice. Why is this a relevant consideration? Put simply, Heidegger raises the stakes of reading in a way that cannot be ignored. But ultimately, not to ignore them means to take them seriously, which would mean "going to Heidegger's encounter," however we might come to construe that. I present what I am doing in this way to make it more challenging to those who see themselves as defenders of Heidegger's legacy. That very legacy is concerned with the transforming legacies.

There are in this chapter traces and echoes of two previous works—one in which I try to connect Heidegger's quest for the originary to a lost memory of the mother, via a detour through Freud's account of the uncanny,[1] and the other,[2] in which I deal with the question of repetition in Heidegger and allude to some of the same texts. I trust that anyone who notices these overlaps will find them productive. A larger project is underway.

The first track I pick up begins in Heidegger's *Kant and the Problem of Metaphysics*:

> [A]n interpretation limited to a recapitulation of what Kant explicitly said can never be a real explication, if the business of the latter is to bring to light what Kant, over and above his express formulation, uncovered in the course of his laying of the foundation. To be sure, Kant himself is no longer able to say anything concerning this, but what is essential to all philosophical discourse is not found in the specific propositions of which it is composed but in that which, although unstated as such, is made evident through these propositions [. . .] in order to wrest from the actual words that which these words "intend to say," every interpretation must necessarily resort to violence. This violence, however, should not be confused with an action that is wholly arbitrary. The interpretation must be animated by the power of an illuminative idea. Only through the power of this idea can an interpretation risk that which is always audacious, namely, entrusting oneself to the secret *élan* of a work, in order by this *élan* to get through to the unsaid and to attempt to find an expression for it. The directive idea itself is confirmed by its own power of illumination.[3]

Heidegger claims to have been inspired here by Kant's own formulation of the principle of interpretation:

> The fundamental purpose of the present interpretation of the *Critique of Pure Reason* is to reveal the basic import of this work by bringing out what Kant "intended to say." Our interpretation is inspired by a maxim which Kant himself wished to see applied to the interpretation of philosophical works and which he formulated in the following terms at the end of his reply to the critique of the Leibnizian Eberhard: "[T]hey do not understand the intentions of these philosophers when they neglect the key to all explication of the works of pure reason through concepts alone, namely, the critique of reason itself (as the common source of all concepts), and are incapable of looking beyond the language which these philosophers employ to *what they intended to say*." (K, 206, emphasis added)[4]

Heidegger here distinguishes two kinds of interpretation: recapitulation and real explication, and he emphasizes the need for the risk, violence, and daring needed for the latter. But, curiously, this "real explication" is no less directed by what we might call the truth than recapitulation. The claim, however, is that the truth at this level can only appear through the illuminative power of a directive idea, which the reader brings to the work.

This claim, developed later by Gadamer,[5] helps resolve what otherwise looks like a difficulty in Heidegger's use of Kant here. For it seems as though Kant writes everywhere of what the *author* intended to say, while Heidegger, in contrast, speaks of what the words intend or, in the passive voice, of what "is made evident through these propositions." Is Heidegger here deploying a certain interpretive violence at the very point at which he is crediting Kant with being the source of his inspiration? Turning again to Kant himself, this time to the first *Critique*, we find Kant's deployment of the famous words (italicized below) in the context of a discussion of Plato, and of the importance of Plato's understanding of the Idea, precisely for not being a purely subjective property or merely a creature of the understanding. It is here that Kant writes:

> I need only remark that it is by no means unusual, upon comparing the thoughts which an author has expressed in regard to his subject . . . *to find that we understand him better than he understands himself.* As he has not sufficiently determined his concept, he has sometimes spoken, or even thought, in opposition to his own intention. (CPR, B 371–72, emphasis added)

These remarks in a way reproduce within themselves the difficulty in reconciling Heidegger's version of what is at stake in a real explication with Kant's. I am tempted to say that what Kant really means here by the sufficient (or full) determination of a concept is close to what Plato really meant by an Idea. And that while for Kant an intention, or at least the kind of guiding intention that informs a philosophical work directs itself, knowingly or not, toward an Idea, Heidegger adds that we need to provide an illuminative idea to be able to crystallize at least something of the right order. What is put into play here, in other words, are two principles, potentially pulling in different directions: (1) the need to recognize that philosophers are typically onto something without their being precisely aware of what it is; and (2) that a "real explication" is required to try to get at *something of the order of* what a philosopher is onto. Heidegger's solution to the possible divergence of these two desiderata is validation through the illuminative power of a directive idea. And here, it has to be said, Heidegger is endorsing, in a completely serious and rigorous form, a certain experimental orientation.[6] The seriousness and rigor prescribe, however, a certain quality to a successful reading.

In *What Is Called Thinking?* Heidegger distinguishes between going counter to thinkers and going to their encounter.[7] On the one hand polemics, on the other hand, thinking. In the end, we have to conclude that, as Nietzsche said about friendship, we cannot exclude *polemos* from thinking. To think with someone is quite as much to struggle with him or her over or about what matters. The point is that the struggle is quite as much that of entering a space in which any struggle would be significant, rather than just missing the point. Heidegger makes this claim at the very end of *Being and Time*:

> We must look for a way [footnote: * "Not the 'sole' way"] to illuminate the fundamental ontological question, and *follow* it. Whether that way is at all the *only* one or even the *right* one can be decided only after we have followed it. The strife in relation to the question of being cannot be settled *because it has not even been started*. (SZ, 437;BTb, 398)

If I may now capitalize on my initial selectivity, I would like to make some remarks on the specific responsibility of Heidegger's readings of Kant and Nietzsche, namely, his pursuit of the question of time. Each in different ways, these two readings will enable me to open up the possibility of a further reinterpretation of Heidegger himself. I apologize for my brevity here.

The central thrust of *Kant and the Problem of Metaphysics*, in the terms we have already announced, is that Kant cannot just be read as an epistemological thinker, that the question of knowledge is subordinated to the question of man's relation to the world, a relation that is ontological in character, not just in the traditional metaphysical way but in the sense of our having constantly to deal with the strangeness of this relation. Kant's failure to grasp the full extent of his own thinking has to do, in Heidegger's view, with his inability to divest himself of the traditional model of time:

> Rather . . . the laying of the foundation and even in its conclusion . . . are presented according to the provisional conception of the first point of departure. And because Kant, at the time of his presentation of the transcendental schemata, had not worked out an interpretation of the primordial essence of time, his elucidation of the pure schemata as transcendental determinations of time is both fragmentary and obscure, for time taken as the pure now-sequence offers no possible means of access to the "temporal" interpretation of the notions. (K, 206)

Now what is interesting from our point of view is the temporal model implicit in Heidegger's own analysis of Kant's failure to determine the concept (of time) with which he was working. I do not mean the full-fledged doctrine of ecstatic temporality and being-toward-death in *Being and Time*, I mean the model actually employed in making sense of Kant's failure. It is Heidegger's claim that Kant's failure was to revisit the temporary provisional model of time with which he started off, in light of the subsequent vistas of understanding that he had opened up. Kant, in other words, has failed to rework, to work through, the model that did indeed allow him to begin and

progress. The "fragmentariness and obscurity" of his account of the schematism itself reflects a temporal deficiency, namely, having failed to update his provisional
starting point, while precisely acknowledging the necessity of provisional starting
points. This is, of course, quite a different account from that in *Being and Time*, where
Heidegger insists on the need for a *Wiederholung*, a repetition that would give us access to "Those primordial sources from which the categories and concepts handed
down to us have been in part quite genuinely drawn" (SZ, 21;BTb,).

My second focus will be on Heidegger's reading of Nietzsche in *What Is Called
Thinking?* Pursuing the theme he had already worked on in *Contributions*, that the necessity (*Notwendigkeit*) of philosophy lies in it being a response to *Not*, to distress, to
difficulty, Heidegger fastens here on Nietzsche's lament—that the wasteland grows.
The essence of Heidegger's reading of Nietzsche here can be spelled out in four steps:

1. Nietzsche locates the "spirit of revenge" as a critical dimension of this
   our wasteland;

2. What drives the spirit of revenge, "time and its it was," is "time itself," time construed as passing away, as transitory, that condemns
   every now to extinction;

3. But this is not time as such, but "the representational view of time
   . . . standard through the metaphysics of the West" (WCT, 99);

4. Nietzsche's project of overcoming the spirit of revenge, willing the
   Eternal Return, needs to be reevaluated in light of this fundamentally unthought through but fateful conceptualization of time.

It might be suggested that Heidegger's subsequent thinking about time in *Time
and Being*, of space-time, the "*es gibt*" and *Ereignis*, succeeds in precisely such a way as
to dispel the possibility of loss, mourning, revenge, and so on, and the kind of thinking that follows from those fundamental evaluations.[8] But is this correct? And if so,
what kind of an advance could it be?

For my own "illuminative idea" to stand a chance of striking root, some preparatory remarks are in order, and I try here to bear in mind the following: that Heidegger's method concerns itself with problematic, impeded repetition, suggesting that
the past is not readily available to us, and that Heidegger is right to think of the model
of time as a leveled-off succession of now points as a hopeless basis on which to open
up the question of being. It flattens the dimensionality that opens up the possibility
of freedom, authenticity, and transcendence. Heidegger is quite right to insist that
man's being is essentially temporal, that the ontological grammar of our ecstasis is
distributed in three dimensions, that the economy through which we acknowledge
our being-toward-death is critical to any judgment of authenticity, that being is historical in the sense of suffering epochal transformations, that we misunderstand what

it is to think if we believe it is possible to complete philosophy or to return to the beginning, and that linear time constantly leads us down the wrong track.

The refusal to think of time either as a succession, or as a teleological directedness to an end, a future present, a completion, has consequences for philosophical practice itself, given that philosophical texts appear at least to begin and end and arrive at conclusions. Add to this the refusal to think of language as a mere means of expression or communication or naming and philosophy is inexorably drawn toward the question of performativity, in which the very shape of its practice embodies these claims. These concerns are evidenced by Heidegger's insistence that "our task is to cease all overcoming" (TB, 24), that he does "not want to get anywhere. We would like, only, for once to get to where we are already" (PLT, 190), and that these have just been "a series of propositions [what matters is] rather to follow the movement of showing" (TB, 2). The question I will pursue shortly is whether a certain understanding of performativity, which seems required by a certain responsibility, might itself be a dangerous seduction.

More immediately, I want to begin to declare my hand, to explain how I would like to say "yes, but" to Heidegger. If we ask what was at stake in his raising anew the question of being, my response would be that Heidegger was trying to create or recreate an immanent basis for transcendence, in the face of the otherworldly mystifications of theology, and the one-dimensional threat of science and technology. As the very idea of Man is caught up in a hopelessly entangled matrix, opposed to God and to Nature, it is better dropped. The recovery of the question of Being is the recovery of a dimensionality within existence that makes truth, freedom, and responsibility possible. It is, as he says in *What Is a Thing?*, the strange space of the in-between.[9] Why does time seem like the key to such a transformation? First, the experience of strife within our experience of time is common currency—common, for example, to Kant, Nietzsche, Bergson, and Husserl. But equally, time has already been put at the service of a certain transcendence in its religious partition into the "temporal" and the "eternal," life on earth and life after death. Heidegger is essentially reclaiming the power of this distinction from the traditional model of time that it presupposes. Another dimension of time cannot be thought of as following the first, except with the greatest naivete. Heidegger's distinction between everyday and authentic temporality is an attempt to totally secularize the resources made possible by transformations in our relation to time. And not surprisingly, this centers around our relation to death. Different modes of being-in-the-world can, so to speak, coexist, as different possibilities of existence, and do not need to be thought of successively.

There has been a certain interest in recent years in Heidegger's relation to questions of sexual difference, especially from Derrida and Irigaray, and mostly it is the neutralization of Dasein's sexuality that has been discussed. There has been a struggle for a certain primacy between the ontological difference, sexual difference, and just plain difference.[10] The key to this interpretive entry is to show how what may just appear as an empirical difference (sexuality) is (quasi) transcendental in its function, in other words, that it serves to distribute other values and concepts. I mention this because at least as strong a case can be made for childhood and indeed human "development" in general. And what is more, although it is possible to give a temporal index to sexual difference, one does not need to make a case for this in the area of child development. Of course, many phenomena can be given a temporal index. The rings of a fallen tree function in that way. The question in each case is what kind of constitutive role is played by the temporality in question. In child development, that is, human development, through childhood, it is hard to imagine a more powerful constitutive role. What I will try to argue now is that what Heidegger calls the question of being is intimately tied to our condition as beings who are essentially the product of development. My main focus will be on individual human development, but some of these remarks apply to history too. I propose to offer a rather abstract account of human development that will free us from a particular allegiance to particular theories (though I will give some specific illustrations). I will argue that with this directive idea, we can illuminate many of the claims Heidegger wants to make, and that this developmental perspective gives Heidegger's thinking a new future.

Dasein, for the most part, seems to mean adult Dasein.[11] And there is clearly a significant difference between a human who has developed through a series of stages, both physically and psychologically, and the infant crawling on the ground. The adult has acquired capacities—motor skills, capacities for empathic relatedness, survival skills, language and communication, knowledge, critical skills, judgment, and so on. The adult has acquired a complex mix of independence and new forms of dependency. The adult has perhaps come into her or his own, become free. And in introducing these kinds of concepts, we are making it harder to confine what is at stake to the realm of the empirical. When we talk about skills, we are tacitly supposing a constant bearer of such skills. But we know that this is not how it is. We know that these developments involve wholesale transformations in our way of being-in-the-world, dramatic changes in the ways we negotiate the in-between. The kinds of changes I have in mind here are those marked, for example, by Lacan, as the mirror stage, and the entry into the symbolic. These each involve a transformation in what we could call the economy of being. In the first, we accept the synthetic power of the image in giving us, albeit at this specular level, a sense of ourselves as a unity. In the second, we accept a position in language, an identity through naming, in exchange for accessing the powers of language. I am not here arguing for Lacan's particular account. What it offers us, however, is a glimpse of what is at stake from a structural point of view, in development.[12] Heidegger's later discussions of language are precisely of this order—transforming not our theory of language but our relation to language. And it is hard not to see this as a further step, building on the achievements of childhood development. If for a moment we were to glance at history more broadly, we find in Heidegger's account of the epochality of being one with at least some analogous features. These epochs are not commensurable, and what qualifies as an epoch is something like an economy of being. And the way he describes technology as the era dominated by *Gestell* is not wholly different from the spectrality of the mirror stage.

So far, then, I have tried to show that there are at least candidates for stages of human development that would qualify as different modes of Being-in-the-world.[13] What significance would Heidegger give to such stages? We know that in the case of the evolutionary steps marked, however complexly, by animal existence, he treated their alterity as a form of impoverishment or, indeed, absence of world. This uncharacteristic reemergence of a kind of teleological ordering principle suggests a kind of urgency or emergency to the question of the animal.[14]

There is every reason not to do the same with the child, or the infant, if we are really concerned to move thinking forward.

There are two extreme versions that one might give of the development of a certain complexity through a series of stages. The first is that the early stages fall away having done their work, like booster rockets, having no further role. They are simply a means to an end. The second is that all of the early stages remain transparently available at the later stage, which nonetheless grasps its own privilege in relation to them. Neither of these models seems appropriate to human development. So let us suggest a third option—that some kind of memory of earlier stages may be available, but that access to these stages is extremely difficult not the least because the very way in which "experience" was formatted has changed. Moreover, the other variable to be considered in each case is whether the transitions from one stage to another have been wholly and successfully completed.[15] Let us assume, in the way that Freud understood neurosis (a universal phenomena only writ large in neurotics), that what is standard is that these transitions are never quite completed.

If all of this were true, what would adult human experience be like? First, it would be riddled with the being question, as well as with normalizing pressures to deny the significance of such questions, because even the marginal availability of other modes of being in the world, activated, reactivated, and transformed within adult experience, makes the question of being visible. Second, our experience would be haunted by the possibility of something like self-fulfillment, even as that very idea is being made problematic. Third, the experience of *Angst*, the uncanny, and the anticipation of death (and even what Freud calls the fear of castration) would become closely linked. Such interconnectedness, as I see it, argues in favor of our proposal. If we see all of these as variants of *das Nichts*, we have found a source for such experiences in the incomplete transitions from one economy of being to another. From the vantage point one is leaving, the new economy can easily appear as death, and from the new economy, the prospect of slipping back into the previous regime can seem like death too.

We may not, as Derrida reminds us, be in any better position than an animal to experience or know death *as such*[16] but we are strangers to the experience of the horror or fear of extinction, of our relation to the world breaking down completely, only if we have completely sealed ourselves off from childhood. My basis point here is that when "beings as a whole slip away,"[17] the experience is not that of the loss of the world but the loss of a certain grasp of the world as a whole, which is exactly what is at stake in our developmental transitions. In this way, we find an oddly inverted reprise of

Plato's doctrine of anamnesis. In that story, we recover, if we are lucky, the soul's transitional preterrestrial glimpse of the forms. Also, if we are lucky, we are neither wholly shut off from those transitional experiences nor reflectively incapacitated by them, and they give us access not to the Forms but to being, precisely at the moment of its being put into question. I would claim too that it is our access, and sometimes our ability to escape, from such experiences that allows us to think, or at least grope toward thinking, what Husserl described as "that there might no longer be any world" (i.e., that it might cease to have any meaning),[18] or what Blanchot calls disaster.[19]

If this is right, then, the secret connection between time and being is indeed through Dasein's existence, and it does indeed become visible through a transformation of our grasp of Dasein's temporality, and ecstatic being toward death points to what is at stake here. But the truth about Dasein's temporality lies in its developmental incompleteness, and the way in which a complex of different economies is nested in our being-in-the-world. I would like to have shown how these different economies are themselves different ways of economizing time. It is a cliché, of course, that maturity and education bring about a capacity to cope with delay and the frustration of immediate gratification, hence, a different economy of time. And to the extent that overcoming metaphysics involves moving away from the privilege of presence, and that ceasing all overcoming involves a recognition that something like presence still survives as the telos underwriting the desire to overcome, then we can see that Heidegger's sense of the subsequent possibilities of thinking continues to involve transformations in the economy of time.

All of this would suggest that Dasein's temporality cannot be thought without this grasp of our having each inherited not just a tradition but also an ontologically ingrained complex of incompatible and unintegrated temporalities. If the word "economy" grates on the ears of those used to Heidegger's "horizon," "dispensation of being," or "time-space," what is true in each case is that there is a certain uneasiness about whether what is fundamental is time or *a certain horizonality of time*, that is, a certain dimensionality that might not be quite separable from space.[20] The relation between time and economy repeats that uneasiness.

How specifically does this account graft onto Heidegger? Let me give just two examples: first, it gives us better access to why Heidegger was so obsessed with Nietzsche. For Nietzsche's whole thought of *ressentiment*, of the spirit of revenge against time, and of the affirmation of the eternal return is precisely an attempt to overcome both the sense of loss associated with the past and the crippling psychologies we develop to deal with that loss.

This account is isomorphic, at least, with much of what Heidegger says about the need to retrieve the past (and the difficulty of doing this), about reanimating the tradition, and about our (and Kant) getting stuck with provisional versions of things.

And if I had more time I would try to rope into this account all that Heidegger has to say about pain, the threshold, distress, and so on, and I would suggest that it has its place in the kind of account I am pointing to.[21] For the moment, let me suggest that this is a good place at which to return to our opening quotation:

To be sure, that distress varies in the essential beginnings and transitions of man's history. But this distress should never be taken superficially and reckoned with summarily as a lack or misery or something like that. This distress exists outside any "pessimistic" or "optimistic" valuation. The grounding-attunement that attunes unto necessity differs according to the inceptual experience of this distress. (C, §17)

When Heidegger says that there is distress [*Not*] "in the essential beginnings and transitions of man's history," he means, of course, not an individual biography but our involvement in the history of being. It is not my claim that Heidegger is really saying what I am claiming about individual development. But what these remarks show is that Heidegger is more than open to the shape of this thought—that philosophy is born from the pain of transition and renewal. My claim, if you like, is a loose version of the claim that ontogeny repeats phylogeny,[22] that individual human development exhibits the same *kind* of traumatic transformations as are to be found in human history, that our own memories give us access to the difficulty of access to the past. And all of this makes it understandable why Heidegger should speak of the need for and the difficulties of a new beginning. The need for what Nietzsche called overcoming is precisely, as Nietzsche thought of, and Heidegger agrees, the need for a new economy of being, which for Heidegger, contra Nietzsche is thought in terms of *Gelassenheit*. And the idea that we must cease all overcoming is precisely an attempt to not allow our practice of thinking to bear with it the seeds of transformative failure, hence, performativity.[23]

Finally, what follows are remarks on this experimental interpretation of Heidegger that lend a little credence to our directive idea and encourage us to dwell awhile on the strangeness and unwelcome aspects of this thought.

Performativity

As I have said, the temptation of performativity is obvious, natural, and in some ways surely productive. If a philosopher comes to see the possibilities of transformation tied to one's taking up a new relation to language,[24] it is hard to resist the idea that the difficulties of bringing about, or even adequately articulating, that change might be tied up with the fact that in one's very announcement of these possibilities one may be perpetuating the very relation that one is trying to overcome. Performativity would be the attempt to put that right. And the idea that pursuing the question of being is most successful if it follows up the connection with time, and then with shifting economies of time and being, gives a clear direction to such performativity.

To be brief here, I suggest

    1. that the performative dimension of Heidegger's own trajectory of philosophical experimentation is driven by the need to come to terms

with this nestedness of times and economies that we inhabit, and that inhabits us;

2. that the insistence and persistence of these economies may make opening a new beginning an infinite task;

3. that there will naturally arise a certain temptation, one to which Nietzsche was more sensitive than Heidegger, of striving for a certain *coincidence* between, say, the what and the how and the content and the style. This may seem obvious. Surely the opposite of coincidence would be a certain dissonance, sowing the seeds for failure by reproducing just what one is trying to move beyond;

4. and that, nonetheless, it may be wise to raise the performativity to another level, not to try to mirror in one's writing some pure coincidence between the what and the how but rather to deploy a whole range of styles and strategies, accepting, at each point, both opportunities and liabilities. We cannot, for example, do without making propositional claims, comparative judgments, and critical remarks—in other words, we cannot just allow language to speak itself. Whichever way we turn we take risks, we enter territory in which we are not entirely in control, and it is through failure that we may find success. This is not only unavoidable, it is something we could celebrate. And that would be a second level of performativity—affirming the risks, dangers, and impurities associated with thinking anew, without aiming at a pure coincidence. It is fair to say that I have learned from Nietzsche and Derrida to seek more of this in Heidegger, and sometimes to find it.

Psychoanalysis

Does this reading simply open the way to a psychoanalytical absorption of Heidegger?

No. But we are moving to a point at which what psychoanalysis indicates—that structural transformations are inherent in human development, that humans are essentially developmental creatures, and that these developments are essentially incomplete—are truths independent of a specifically psychoanalytic interpretation.

Furthermore, there is something of a parallel between the way in which Husserl's phenomenology grew out of Frege's charge of psychologism, and the way in which Lacan transformed and reworked the biologistic basis of Freud's thinking in light of a certain structuralist logic. This said, there remains the question of whether Lacan completes this process of transformation, or whether he too gets stuck at a certain point. Thus, while in *Of Grammatology* (1967), Derrida specifically mentions psychoanalysis as the place, outside linguistics, in which the "deconstitution of the founding concept-words of ontology" is most likely to see a breakthrough,[25] by the time of *Le Facteur de la Vérité* (1975), Derrida is claiming that for all of its radicality, psychoanalysis in Lacan's hands is committed to the mastery of truth. "Abyss effects are severely controlled here."[26] Derrida sees Lacan as finding in castration a new site of truth. The question then for Derrida would perhaps be this—could there be a disseminative psychoanalysis? For us, the question is a little different. The picture we are developing is one in which human development is marked by a movement through a series of structures of psychosomatic organization, or economies.[27] These economies would each constitute different regimes of truth, different ways of distributing self and other, man and world.

To the extent that *dissemination* captures the dynamic (associative and substitutive) consequences of the differential basis of meaning and identity, the restlessness of any presence, it would operate *within* any economy, and as a principle of leakage or permeability between economies. In these ways, dissemination operates, as I see it, as a principle that prevents closure.

But it cannot itself account for the differences *between* the economic organization of different stages. Derrida's remarks about Lacan attempting the mastery of abyssal effects infer a parallel suggestion about Heidegger and death. I have offered that developmental identity transitions are, or are potentially, abyssal in quality, that they are reexperienced as *angst*, and that such experiences provide us with the lived experience of extinction, or death. I think Heidegger's own thinking of death, and of the possibility of an authentic being-toward-death, is precisely caught up in this struggle for mastery over the abyssal dimension of death, and even a struggle with the desire for and value of mastery.

So the short answer to the question about psychoanalysis is that the question of the relation between philosophy and psychoanalysis is a reprise of the situation that brought about the birth of phenomenology. We have to trust that whatever empirical content we pursue philosophically will eventually yield a logic, or an economy; the question of being can be constantly refreshed and reworked only by these forays into the *sache selbst*.[28]

Speculative Conclusion

I will conclude, in a speculative way, with a story that I would graft on to Heidegger's discussion of the danger and the saving grace of technology, a story that supplies the answer to a question. I have offered here a way of thinking about the relation between time and being that obviously makes common cause with all of those interested in trauma, in mourning, in nonlinear and problematic understandings of memory, and so on.[29] Is this just a fashionable thing to be doing, or does it reflect some deeper shape of our times? A long time ago, I read Marcuse's *Eros and Civilization*, in which he introduced the idea of repressive desublimation. This term captured Marcuse's vision of the psychic innovation that is America, and perhaps especially California. If sublimation involves an internalizing and enculturing transformation of those desires for gratification that the external world will not meet, desublimation occurs when a new world tells us that these desires are good, and that they will be satisfied. This is repressive, because with this Faustian acceptance of consumerism, we end up sacrificing the very internality that rooted our freedom. *Eros and Civilization* operates a little like Volume 2 of *The Genealogy of Morals*, with some help from Freud and Heidegger. As an immigrant from the Old World myself, I am still taken by Marcuse's analysis but would like to suggest another version that bears directly on our topic. If I may, I will explain this position informally and indirectly. I recently had the opportunity to comment extensively on the work of Richard Kearney who, after Paul Ricoeur, promotes the power of narrative imagination as a way of supplying both personal and national identity with sufficient substance to be able to bear ethical responsibility.[30] Theoretically, this project seems to be threatened by attacks on the status of narrative from postmodernism, threats of which Kearney is well aware and to which he responds. I propose to read this debate symptomatically, in the following way. Suppose we bring together Heidegger's diagnosis of technology (as a kind of enframing that prepackages the real in ways that conform to its own principles of relationality) and Deleuze's and Guattari's accounts of deterritorialization, and our commonsense grasp of the way in which economic relations (of exchange) increasingly dominate, that is, ultimately *define,* the real for us. We can now understand Nietzsche's account of our cultural and moral wasteland as a diagnosis of our failure to answer a question posed to us by history. If individual human development is quite standardly a traumatic journey, in which different stages are incompletely traversed, one which leaves each of us with a nested bundle of modes of being, times, and economies, then we may ask ourselves how people typically have dealt with this constitutive personal legacy. I suggest that in the past the central coping mechanism has been the work of narrative at every level, that what we are witnessing today is a crisis in narrativity as it becomes displaced by technological, calculative modes of explanation and legitimation, and that this has the effect of exposing the incomplete work of human development, as a high tide exposes the shipwrecks buried under the sand.

This is at least one lens through which we can glimpse the shape of our distress, and this distress supplies the historical pressure under which we are coming to see that time does indeed operate as the horizon of the question of being. This is a secret locked in the heart of the human soul.[31] However, it is not nature but history that is unlocking it for us.

Heidegger's confrontation with Nietzsche could be said to have culminated in Heidegger's transfiguration of the will-to-power into performativity. The will-to-power is not just a vitalistic critique of truth as representation, because it puts into question, even as it draws on it, the very idea of life. Heidegger could be said to have found the truth of the will-to-power in the ineliminable performativity of philosophy, that philosophy cannot ultimately be about it must itself eventuate. And it eventuates as a form of self-transformation, one marked by "life," "affirmation," and "creativity," precisely to the extent that it draws one back into the truth of *Ereignis.* This is the shape of Heidegger's reenacting responsibility toward Nietzsche. This responsibility requires that we sacrifice truth as (mere) accuracy for truth as a kind of living in relation to disclosure. Responsibility requires that one live with risk. I myself have taken up this challenge by bringing a particular illuminative idea—that of human development as a fundamentally incomplete ontological journey—to the interpretation of Heidegger's fundamental question. Such a story not only allows a certain "naturalization" of ontology, it permits us to stage again the whole question of the relation of the ontic to the ontological. In our view, which Heidegger at times shares,[32] the ontological is already in the ontic, rightly construed. But such a construal constantly falls away. Finally it might be asked—what is the specific responsibility of choosing this "illuminative" or "directive" idea rather than another? That it continues the thematic of time and temporality is not unimportant. What gives it in some ways a distinct advantage over the ways in which Heidegger will develop this question (toward time-space, the truth of *Ereignis*, and a possibility to come) is that the whole issue of human development is like a courtyard opening onto, and opened onto by, the most pressing concerns of our time—historical, political, educational, and environmental. Our continuing responsibility consists in the willingness to keep exploring these passages, opening these doors, and not resting reductively on the attractions of any single account.

Notes

Presented to the Heidegger Conference, Huntington, West Virginia, May 2000.

1. "Between Phenomenology and Psychoanalysis: Embodying Transformation," in *Interrogating Ethics*, edited by Jim Hatley and Chris Diem (Evanston, Ill: Northwestern University Press, 2001).

2. See my "Heidegger and the Challenge of Repetition," Proceedings of the Heidegger Conference, DePaul University, Chicago, 1999.

3. *Kant and the Problem of Metaphysics*, translated by James S. Churchill (Bloomington: Indiana University Press, 1962), pp. 206-07. Hereafter, this edition is cited as K, followed by the page number.

4. *Uber eine Entdeckung* (1790), in *Immanuel Kant's Werke*, edited by Ernst Cassiver et al. 11 vols. (Berlin: Bruno Cassiver, 1912; reprinted, 1922; reissued, Hildesheim: Gerskuberg, 1973), vol. 1, p. 71.

5. See Gadamer, *Truth and Method*, translated by William Glen-Doepel (London: Sheed and Ward, 1975), p. 238ff., where he discusses Heidegger's development of the forestructure of understanding, the enlightenment's prejudice against prejudice, and the positive and negative values of prejudice.

6. I say "experimental" despite Heidegger's own association of the experiment with *Machenschaft*. See, for example, C, §§77-80.

7. We may, as he puts it, "go to their encounter" [*Entgegen gehen*], or "go counter to them" [*Dagegen angehen*] (WCT, 77).

8. And this is surely just what is going on in pursuing the connection between thinking and thanking. Thanking certainly has the potential for an affective expansion and connectedness that will rule out understanding thinking in any narrow, calculative way. But what is more important, I think, is that it is one of the planks in a general strategy of resistance against dwelling on the past as a site of loss, even as Heidegger is articulating structures of withdrawal (of Being). Indeed, we could understand the demonstration that withdrawal is a necessary structure as another of these planks, as too the whole way in which for Heidegger we are "called upon to think." Answering this call is a responsibility, not lamentation or mourning.

9. See C, §§217, 227. See also Heidegger, *What Is a Thing?*, translated by W. B. Barton and Vera Deutsch (Chicago: Gateway, 1967), p. 244.

10. See Derrida's *Spurs/Eperons* (Chicago: University of Chicago Press, 1978) and "Choreographies" (interview with Christie McDonald), in *Feminist Interpretations of Jacques Derrida*, edited by Nancy Holland (University Park: Pennsylvania State University Press, 1997).

11. Of course, the situation is more complicated than this. In his *Contributions to Philosophy*, Heidegger begins in effect to identify Dasein with Nietzsche's *Ubermensch*, suggesting that ordinary adult existence is only on-the-way toward Dasein. I also am grateful to Lawrence Hatab for drawing my attention to §15 of GA 27. This section is entitled "*Entdeckendsein beim Fruhzeitlichen und fruhmenschlichen Dasein*," discussing both primitive Dasein and childhood, albeit somewhat schematically. Heidegger does here seem to treat childhood not as a state with its own positivity but as a process of growing into the light.

12. Given Lacan's hostility to the very idea of development, it might be thought rash to use him as an example, but it is precisely my point that "development" occurs by transformations that preserve discontinuities.

13. I believe that Freud's distinctions between oral, anal, and genital stages, as well as the stages identified by Melanie Klein, and the fundamental distinction between what Kristeva calls the semiotic and the symbolic, can all be understood to mark out different economies of being. In saying this, I do not mean to underplay the differences between these different theoretical positions.

14. See my "Comment ne pas manger," in *The Animal As Other*, edited by Peter Steeves (Binghamton: State University of New York Press, 1998).

15. Freud's discussion of mourning and melancholia depends on this distinction.

16. See Derrida, *Aporias*, translated by Thomas Dutoit (Stanford, Calif.: Stanford University Press, 1993). This responds, for example, to such remarks of Heidegger's as "Mortals are they who can experience death as death. Animals cannot do so." See "The Nature of Language" (OWL, 107).

17. See "What Is Metaphysics?" (BW, 102).

18. See Husserl, *Ideas*, translated by W. R. Boyce-Gibson (London: George, Allen & Unwin, 1931), §49.

19. See Blanchot, *The Writing of the Disaster*, translated by Ann Smock (Lincoln: University of Nebraska Press, 1986).

20. Heidegger makes this explicit, for example, in *Contributions*, §98. "Time as what removes-unto and opens up is thus in itself simultaneously what *spatializes*; it provides "space." What is ownmost to space is not the same as what is ownmost to time, but space belongs to time—as time belongs to space."

21. In his essay "Language" (1950), in PLT, Heidegger offers an astonishing interpretation of Georg Trakl's poem *Ein Winterabend* [*A Winter's Evening*], especially the line "*Schmerz versteinert die Schwelle*"/"Pain has turned the threshold to stone." Pain is understood as a marker of difference, the rift, the mutual bearing/granting of world and things. See also "Language in the Poem" (PLT, 180–84, 189–90). Heidegger insists that this is not normal physical or psychological pain, but perhaps this is just what should be said about the pain, distress, and anxiety associated with transitions between one economy of being and another, and our residual memory of such transitions.

22. The original claim, Ernst Haeckel's biogenetic law (1866), may have been something of an exaggeration.

23. See, for example, my "Performative Reflexivity," ch. 8, *Philosophy at the Limit* (London: Unwin Hyman, 1990); and also see Karen Feldman, "The Performative Difficulty of Being and Time," *Philosophy Today* (forthcoming).

24. This is the central theme of "The Nature of Language" in OWL, pp. 57–108. It is clearly both thematized and practiced in *Contributions*.

25. *Of Grammatology*, translated by Gayatri Spivak (Baltimore: Johns Hopkins University Press, 1976), p. 21.

26. "Le Facteur de la Vérité," in *The Postcard*, translated by Alan Bass (Chicago: University of Chicago Press, 1987), p. 467.

27. This would add a temporally layered dimension to Nietzsche's remark (in the second Preface to his *Gay Science*, translated by Walter Kaufmann (New York: Vintage, 1974), pp. 34–35) when he asks himself "whether, taking a large view, phi-

losophy has not been merely an interpretation of the body and a misunderstanding of the body."

28. We do not need to retreat from beings to pursue being. A certain material-ist history (I am thinking of Marx, Nietzsche, a certain reading of Lacan/Freud, and even aspects of Derrida in "Eating Well") is still perhaps both possible and necessary. In each case we find a logic of materiality, or (perhaps) different economies or organizations of beings. Must the question of being be lost sight of if we pursue beings? Perhaps it is precisely in seeming to be willing to give up the question of being that it can be returned to us!

29. See, for example, Charles E. Scott, *The Time of Memory* (Albany: State University of New York Press, 1999).

30. At the Stony Brook meeting of the International Association of Philosophy and Literature, May 2000. Kearney's many writings include *Poetics of Imagining* and *The Wake of Imagination*.

31. I allude here, of course, to Kant's remark in the *Critique of Pure Reason*, that the "schematism of our understanding . . . is an art concealed in the depth of the human soul, whose real modes of activity nature is hardly likely ever to allow us to discover" (B180).

32. There is a particular move that Heidegger makes that leads him to abjure beings, one tied to the limits of transformative movement present *within* beings. And his sense that what is not there or at the beginning cannot be there later. All discovery is an uncovery or a recovery. This may be an unhelpful generalization of the claim that there can be no linear departure from the logic of the beginning. But everything depends on how we proceedited by It is true that attempts at recovery often lead to blind repetition—a reawakening of the same mistake! This is a vital insight when thinking about renewal, and the force of the new, and it suggests the need for a systematic engagement with Deleuze, who understands philosophy to be in the business of creating concepts, Derrida, who champions invention and chance, and indeed, Donna Haraway, who seems to have found a way of undermining Heidegger's claim that science does not think. Finally, Lyotard's complex position on the inhuman (see *The Inhuman* (Cambridge: Polity Press, 1993) suggests that far from technology being essentially repressive, it is contradictory, and the contradictions need feeding to be creative.

15

The Community of
Those Who Are Going to Die

Walter Brogan

I will argue in this chapter that *Being and Time* provides, in several essential respects, the appropriate philosophical basis for a contemporary, postmodern understanding of ethical relationships and political community. This formulation of a new basis for community that does not erase the singularity and alterity of those who participate is further developed and radicalized in Heidegger's later work, *Contributions to Philosophy*, inasmuch as in this work Heidegger eradicates the last vestiges of a fusion model of community found in his earlier analysis of horizon and world and develops instead a model of community that also, even more strongly, decenters subjectivity while at the same time emphasizing difference, cleavage, and nonreciprocity at the heart of the community of singular beings. My primary contention is that death as understood in Heidegger's analysis, which indeed is the constitutive existential mark of Da-sein, is the precondition for a philosophy of community that remains faithful to the utter singularity and finitude of each of the members of the human community.

The claim that being-toward-death is the site of Heidegger's more radical conception of community is of course ironic, since Heidegger appears to insist, contrary to the overwhelming emphasis on Da-sein's situatedness in the rest of the text, that in the end Da-sein remains inescapably caught in its projection back onto itself. Death, Heidegger claims, is the "*ownmost non-relational possibility not to be bypassed*" (SZ, 250). But this apparent denial that death forms the basis for community is only apparent. Heidegger's account of being-toward-death does argue against the notion of community based on a fusion theory that cedes the separateness of the other's being from one's own for the sake of unity and togetherness. But Heidegger's claim that "*no one can take the other's dying away from him*" (SZ, 240) shows being-toward-death as the limit condition that prevents the co-optation and appropriation of the being of another. In other words, the analysis of being-toward-death provides a basis for a conception of being together and friendship that has as its condition the acknowledgment of the otherness of the other.

Yet precisely this unshareability and aloneness of death have led many critics to accuse Heidegger's ontology of being unable to give a strong account of either alterity or community. In the view of these critics, Heidegger's account of being-toward-death leaves no room for an existentially rich encounter between Da-seins. For this reason, Heidegger's ontological account of alterity, they say, ends up reducing the other to an aspect of the being of the ontologically isolated individual, or otherwise, in one's search for an understanding of Heidegger's sense of community, one must rely on Division I of *Being and Time*, where one finds an ontic, tool-centered encounter with other beings in the world of concern.

For example, Jacques Taminiaux argues in *Heidegger and the Project of Fundamental Ontology* that implicit in *Being and Time* is a Platonic bias that leads Heidegger to read Aristotelian *praxis* as though it were an intellectual *phronêsis*. He claims: "This is why in fundamental ontology transcendence prevents us from conceiving *praxis* in connection with a common realm of shared deeds and words, as did the Greek city and its Aristotelian account."[1] In Taminiaux's reading, *Being and Time* is fundamentally solipsistic, offering a concept of world that, he says, is empty of things and people. The only contact Da-sein has with others, in Taminiaux's analysis, is through the inauthentic life of fallen Da-sein, who allows its being to be determined by the tool-world in which it is involved. To state Taminiaux's position, as I understand it, in the strongest terms authentic Da-sein is a being unto itself, self-enclosed in a way that fundamentally isolates it from any genuine access to the other. In contrast, inauthentic Da-sein is mired in the everyday world of concernful absorption in others and suffers a concomitant loss of self. The retrieval of authentic selfhood is possible only because Da-sein does not truly belong with others. I hope to show that this reading, which is feasible only if one relies on a bifurcation of the theoretical and practical life, misses an important aspect of Heidegger's treatment of Da-sein's own-most, authentic being-itself, namely, that relationality also is at the basis of the authentic experience of self analyzed in Division II of *Being and Time*. Were this acknowledged, then authentic, resolute Da-sein would be seen to be at the same time *both* the moment of existential solitude and the ecstatic openness to the other as other.

Taminiaux's reading that ascribes *poiêsis* and Da-sein's involvement with beings other than itself to Division I of *Being and Time* resembles, ironically, the reading of Hubert Dreyfus in his book *Being-in-the-World: A Commentary on Heidegger's "Being and Time," Division I*.[2] Both Dreyfus and Taminiaux share a similar assumption, namely, that there is a dichotomy between existence and facticity in the structure of *Being and Time*, a dichotomy that parallels a distinction between transcendence and entanglement. Both fail to see the centricity of Heidegger's treatment of the movement between facticity and existence, a "movement" that opens up the space of being in the world. As a result, each reads Heidegger in such a way as to collapse the distinction between the two. Taminiaux sees Heidegger's fundamental category as existence and therefore accuses Heidegger of a philosophy of transcendence that shares with Plato a disdain for involvement. Dreyfus, on the other hand, reads *Being and Time* primarily as a treatise on factical life, and he subsumes Heidegger's treatment of authentic existence into the world of everyday concern by positing the thesis that authenticity for Heidegger amounts to the realization that one's existence is a nullity, and thus as Da-sein one's being is nothing other than what one does.

Dreyfus is largely responsible for what seems to me to be an overemphasis on Division I of *Being and Time,* and the assumption that it is in Division I that can be found Heidegger's sense of community. Thus Dreyfus writes: "Heidegger seeks to show that the shared public world is the only world there is or can be."[3] Dreyfus argues that Division II of *Being and Time* makes explicit the primacy of Division I by demonstrating that Da-sein has no other self than the one that it finds when it encounters itself as immersed in everydayness. "Anxiety reveals that the self has no possibilities of its own, and so Da-sein's response to anxiety cannot be to find some resource in *itself* . . . . there is no human potential." Dreyfus goes on to claim that, "Heidegger holds that (1) all for-the-sake-of-whichs are provided by the culture and are for anyone, and (2) Da-sein can never take over these impersonal public possibilities in a way that would make them its own and so give it an identity."[4]

Dreyfus wants to accomplish something for Heidegger, which I also want to argue, namely, that in *Being and Time* Heidegger overcomes the modern concept of isolated subjectivity and provides a basis for understanding the fundamentally communal and relational character of Da-sein. But the overcoming of modern subjectivity does not require one to deny the main point of Division II of *Being and Time,* which is to show that the possibility of being whole and of being a self, far from being destroyed by the destruction of subjectivity, for the first time authentically comes to the fore. Moreover, Heidegger's sense of human community is not bound to his analysis of the world of equipmentality, outlined in Division I. Indeed, this world belongs to inauthentic Da-sein, precisely the Da-sein that tends to take itself as a subject and who encounters other Da-sein only through the public realm of shared economies and enterprises. Genuine community is founded not out of this public realm of the "they," a realm in which other existential Da-sein are never authentically encountered, but rather on the basis of a way of being together that itself creates the possibility for a kind of public sharing of oneself that is authentic and existentiell. I believe this is what Heidegger means when he emphasizes in Division II that "*only on the basis of the ecstatic and horizonal temporality is it possible for Da-sein to break into space*" (SZ, 369), the space of circumspective taking care (*Besorgen*). If even the world of concernful involvement, the work world and this way of connecting to others, is founded upon Da-sein's own potentiality of being (*Seinkönnen*), then this does not indicate that significance-relationships belong to a worldless subject, but rather that Da-sein is not a worldless subject at all.[5]

In a discussion of death that occurs in Heidegger's 1922 "Introduction to Aristotle" essay, one finds the following statement: "Existence becomes understandable in itself only through the making questionable of facticity, that is, in the concrete *de-struction* of facticity."[6] I call attention to this point in order to highlight the close connection Heidegger draws between existence and facticity (fallenness). Existence is described in this essay as a counter-movement against the tendency toward falling; existence, he says, occurs precisely in the concrete movement of dealings and concern. Though co-primordial with facticity in the being of Da-sein, existence always arises out of a recovery from one's absorption in the they-self, thus existence is founded in a way of being together with others that it resists. The question, then, is whether existence, which puts facticity entirely at risk and makes Da-sein's factical life entirely questionable, whether this imminent possibility of not-being that moves against concrete factical being, destroys Da-sein's fundamental way of being related to others or transforms it and makes the relationality that essentially belongs to Da-sein utterly unique. Heidegger emphasizes that "the counter-movement against the tendency towards falling must not be interpreted as flight from the world" (PIA, 11). Existence does not constitute Da-sein's being as outside the world or as in any way isolated, by its authentic being, from belonging with others. In *Being and Time*, Heidegger says: "[E]xisting is always factical. Existentiality is essentially determined by facticity (SZ, 192). If one severs the relationship between Division I and Division II of *Being and Time* and fails to pay attention to the middle-voiced character of the movement of repetition between existence and facticity that binds the two divisions together, then any discussion of Da-sein and community will inevitably miss the radical dimension of Heidegger's thought. On the one hand, one understands being-with-others only in terms of specific factical ways of being thrown together. The concept of community that inevitably grows out of this is based on my being the same as the others I encounter; in other words, it is a community based on the they-self, a community based on actualized, concrete relations in which Da-sein finds itself and to which it gives itself over. It is a community that remains bound by an economy of exchange. The tendency to allow oneself to be defined by what is outside oneself is at the heart of the modern concept of community, the community of those who are the same.

Fundamentally it also is the same tendency that is at work when one understands Da-sein's being as existential to the exclusion of facticity. Heidegger's emphasis on the existential as being toward a possibility is then seen as tearing Da-sein away from every actuality and from any genuine involvement with practical life. In such a reading, Da-sein's mineness and radical individuation are interpreted as a fundamental solipsism, a return to the notion of Da-sein as an isolated subject devoid of any substantive connection to an objective world. In this reading, the nonrelational character of Da-sein's existential being makes any notion of community implausible, especially a notion of community and being-with that is intrinsic to the very being of Da-sein. A community of radically subjective beings can only be established from outside, by a principle of universal law and divine authority.

Both of these accounts of Da-sein's community cloak a theological bias that insists on the need to have the human being defined by a principle outside of its own being in order for the human being to encounter that which is radically other than it-self. But in his 1922 "Introduction to Aristotle" essay, Heidegger specifically criticizes this theological bias and declares that any authentic, philosophical understanding of Da-sein must be fundamentally atheistic and draw its understanding of human life from that life itself (PIA, 12, n. 2). This is especially significant in that in this essay Heidegger defines philosophy as a way of standing within the movement of existential facticity (PIA, 14). The phenomenologial commitment to the facticity of human life provides Heidegger with both the structure of human involvement and world and the singularity of the existential moment. In the space of this double movement of facticity and existence, a space of repetition marked by Heidegger through his emphasis on the *je* in *Jemeinigkeit*, in this repetition that individualizes, I believe, can be found an argument for plurality in human community, a plurality of utterly singular individuals, defined by their relationships to death. This "between" opens up the space of community, a community of differing beings.

I now will turn to an explication of certain passages from Heidegger's analysis of Being-toward-death in *Being and Time* in an attempt to outline a basis one may find there for an authentic, existential community of possible beings, a community that in a fundamental sense can never be completely actualized but is not for this reason either otherworldly or utopian but rather fundamentally mortal.

The entire analysis of death is governed by the question of whether Da-sein can in any sense have its being as a whole. Heidegger shows that Da-sein's way of being is in some sense fundamentally not accessible and ungraspable. This inability to be held in a grasp is essential to an understanding of the problem of human community. This basic point demonstrates that the kind of community to which Da-sein would belong cannot be one based on appropriation and ownership. The *Jemeinigkeit* (mine-ness) and *Eigentlichkeit* (properness) that belongs to Da-sein in being-toward-death are at the same time the impossibility of ownership and appropriation. Da-sein's being cannot be had or owned, not even for itself; disowning is Da-sein's own-most way of being itself. Also implied in these statements on Da-sein's death, and made explicit elsewhere, is the fact that were ownership to be taken as Da-sein's authentic way of being itself and being toward others, this would presuppose that Da-sein is a subject that takes what it encounters as objects and enowns them. Surely this way of establishing community can be instituted, and often is, but it is not, according to Heidegger, an authentic basis for human community. Only a lack of imagination would lead us to draw the conclusion from this that therefore no authentic community is possible. But we can conclude that any such genuine human community would have to be premised on an understanding of relationality that does not presuppose taking over the other or the place of the other. It would have to be a community where the other remains other, in this sense, a community of singular beings. One can imagine such a community in a culture that did not require assimilation. One can imagine a principle of negotiation that acknowledged the other as stranger and saw a breakdown in negotiation as the beginning of communication. One can imagine personal relationships that celebrate the other as necessarily different from oneself. But what are the philosophical indications in Heidegger's thinking that would find there support for such an imagined community?

Heidegger argues that one Da-sein cannot in any fundamental sense represent or take the place of another, an analysis that also may be read as a critique of representational democracy. Heidegger writes: "This possibility of representing gets completely stranded when it is a matter of representing that possibility of being that constitutes the coming-to-an-end of Da-sein, and gives it its wholeness as such" (SZ, 240). The fact that one Da-sein cannot substitute for another, and is fundamentally not like any other, places demands on our understanding of being together, especially if we are trying to develop an understanding of a community of those who stand in relation to each other as a whole, who recognize each other in the whole of their being—an existential community, so to speak. When Heidegger says "No one can take the other's dying away from him" (SZ, 240), this does not mean that being-toward-death makes community impossible. It means rather that Da-sein's being cannot be appropriated, and that the possibility of exchange and expenditure between such beings cannot be thought in these terms.

If we were to look back from Heidegger's analysis of being-toward-death to his earlier treatment of solicitude and care, we would find collaboration for the argument that the unshareability that defines human being not only does not preclude community but is the foundation for any truly human being together. According to Heidegger, the analysis of care shows that for Da-sein its being is for it *at issue*, that is, its being is always ecstatic, ahead of itself, uncapturable. Then Heidegger says: "Being-ahead-of-itself does not mean anything like an isolated tendency in a worldless 'subject,' but characterizes being-in-the-world" (SZ, 192). Care is said to be "the existential and ontological condition of the possibility of *being-free for* authentic existentiell possibilities" (SZ, 193). Because Da-sein's being is always possible and not actualizable in its whatness, because Da-sein is always in the throes of death, its being is *free* in its relations with others, in what Heidegger calls its existentiell possibilities. Death constitutes the possibility of *free* beings.

Heidegger's analysis of truth as disclosedness rather than as embedded in the language of assertion, where truth is the predication of properties as owned by a subject, also confirms that Heidegger's thought in *Being and Time* is after a new sense of community. Heidegger says: "*Disclosedness in general* belongs essentially to the constitution of the being of Da-sein" (SZ, 221). The "in general" here does not indicate that there is no content, but rather that the disclosedness is of the sort that comes in advance and does not take over the being of what is there.[7]

The language of existential community is more primordial than the language of shared properties and common interests. It is fundamentally the language of the unsayable, if by language is meant the predicative language of subjects in relationship to objects. Existential language establishes a community of beings whose speaking acknowledges a fundamental untranslatability as the basis for human conversation.

This kind of disclosive relationality also is at work in Heidegger's analysis of solicitude (*Fürsorge*), where he says it is not a matter of leaping in for the other but of leaping ahead and returning (giving back) to the other *for the first time* its care, its free possibility (SZ, 122). The peculiar character of the exchange that occurs here needs to be appreciated. How can one give something back, and yet also give it for the first time? What kind of exchange is this that gives the other what it already is—its being as possibility?

Heidegger offers us a similar paradox in his discussion of the understanding of death as something still outstanding in Section 46 of *Being and Time*. Here it is more clear that the notion of possibility is transformed by death and cannot be understood as simply saying that our being is not yet actualized and present at hand for us. *Ausstehen*, we are told, usually refers to a debt that has only partially been paid and is still outstanding, but indebtedness belongs to our very being. This means we *owe* our being; we never own it, and it, can never be owned. There is something always to be settled, and no closure is possible. The community of such beings is one that does not aspire to closure and one in which there is always a lack of totality. The Da-sein community is never without a relationship to what is outside, to otherness. But Heidegger quickly translates this discussion into one of the impending character of death and says in being-toward-death: "[A]ny being-with the others fails when one's ownmost potentiality-of-being is at stake" (SZ, 263). Death is nonrelational and thus loosens the grip that others have on our being and that we have on others, letting each be the being it is. In this sense, being-toward-death is the basis for the possibility of a community of singular beings. Being with others in the sense of the "they" and the "we" fails us in being-toward-death, and death, Heidegger says, "individualizes Da-sein down to itself" (SZ, 243). Da-sein must be on its own. Da-sein is free from the tyranny of the they. Heidegger says: "Being towards this possibility, as a being which exists, is brought face to face with the absolute impossibility of existence" (SZ, 262). The community of possible beings stands face to face with the impossibility of all community.

In the sections of *Being and Time* on being-toward-death that seem more and more to me to speak of mortal community, the passages on anticipation (*Vorlaufen*) are particularly telling. Heidegger says: "Anticipation discloses to existence that its uttermost possibility lies in *giving itself up*, and thus it shatters all one's tenaciousness to whatever existence one has already reached" (SZ, 264). Being-toward-death teaches us not to hold onto ourselves. But in doing so, Heidegger says, it also frees us from the grasp of others and frees others from our grasp. Thus Heidegger continues: "As the non-relational possibility, death individualizes—but only, as the possibility not-to-be-bypassed, in order to make Da-sein as being-with understand the potentialities-of-being of the others" (ibid.).

Throughout the *Beiträge*, Heidegger attempts to relate his discussion of Da-sein and the enowning event of the truth of be-ing to the issue of Da-sein's selfhood and community. It becomes clear early on in the text that this work attempts to enact an even more radical separation from metaphysics than occurs in *Being and Time*. "In the domain of the other beginning there is neither 'ontology' nor anything at all like 'metaphysics.' No 'ontology,' because the guiding question no longer sets the standard or determines the range. No 'metaphysics,' because one does not proceed at all from beings as extant or from object as known (Idealism), in order then to *step over to* something else" (GA 65, 59). In the *Beiträge*, Heidegger declares that "in *Being and Time* Da-sein still stands in the shadow of the 'anthropological,' the 'subjectivistic,' and the 'individualist,' etc." (GA 65, 295). Nevertheless, the direction of *Being and Time* is transitional, from the guiding question toward a transformation of this question into the grounding question of be-ing. The turning from metaphysics that is accomplished in *Being and Time* here is radicalized in the direction of another beginning. Heidegger now says that, "Da-sein is the *crisis* between the first beginning (the whole history of metaphysics) and the other beginning" (ibid.). Da-sein then is no longer the human subject per se, but the one that holds itself steadfastly in reservedness at the moment of the de-cision that imparts and thereby also shelters the truth of the enowning event (*Ereignis*) of be-ing (GA 65, 96).

But then, who are these Da-seins? How are we to understand Da-sein in its non-subjectivistic selfhood? And is this decision a solitary one, or one that is shared in a community of those who stand resolutely in the opening of the between that founds truth (GA 65, 101)? Heidegger first of all clarifies the sense in which Da-sein is yet to come, indicating a futural character that is never overcome in the completion of its being; Da-sein is fundamentally ecstatic, outside itself, exposed in its being, and thus inherently transitional and apart from itself, the site of a fissure that, though finite, is not determined by closure. This tear in the being of Da-sein is thematized over and over again in this text, and becomes finally, as we will see, a way of understanding being-toward-death in the *Beiträge*.

Contributions to Philosophy clarifies Heidegger's thought on the kind of being together that might exist among Da-seins who are open to the truth of be-ing. Heidegger calls Da-sein, precisely on the basis of Da-sein's singularity, the "ground for a people" (GA 65, 98). "A people first becomes a people when those who are its most singular ones (*Einzigsten*) arrive and begin to intimate (*ahnen*)" (GA 65, 43).[8] The community of Heidegger's later thought, the community of those to come, is one of singular beings. Its people are historical in the sense that they resist the uprootedness of the technological age and thus return to the originary, founding experience, but they also simultaneously herald an opening to a new site for enduring the strife of earth and world (GA 65, 62). Among the characteristics of Da-sein in its singularity, as Heidegger depicts them in the *Beiträge*, are reticence, reservedness, and the solitude that attends Da-sein's stillness in the face of the withdrawal of be-ing. Keeping in mind that Da-sein is no longer thought in terms of ontology and existence in this text, an examination of these traits will help one understand the peculiar character of Da-sein's way of being related to the other. This holding back and keeping still and holding in reserve its being, this drawing back in a way that constitutes selfhood, also is the condition for a communication and community that is founded upon the leaving open of a space for what is other, the opening up of the between.

Sorge is the fundamental ontological characteristic in *Being and Time* for Da-sein's being, and the unity of Da-sein's existentiality and facticity. In the *Beiträge*, Heidegger says, "Reservedness (*Verhaltenheit*) is the ground of care" (GA 65, 35), that is, the ground of Da-sein's being with and concern for others. In reservedness, Hei-degger says, the words fails; it is the source of the temporality of the deep stillness. Yet precisely in the failure of language, Da-sein's poetic openness to the withdrawal of the other, and thus to the possibility of the leap at the heart of communication, is sus-tained. "Reticence (*Erschweigung*) in silence stems from the essential origin of lan-guage itself" (GA 65, 79). The two key terms to Heidegger's sense of community in the *Beiträge* are sheltering and withdrawal. In an even deeper sense, Da-sein is now conceived of as a questioner, because seeking and holding in question is Da-sein's way of gathering and being together with what is other than itself.

The community of singular beings is grounded in its attunement to the play be-tween this granting and refusal of be-ing. Heidegger names the togetherness of shel-tering and withdrawing a jointure (*Fügung*). A jointure both unites and holds apart what it gathers. The coming community that Heidegger envisions sustains its being in common precisely by holding in question the closure of its own unity and holding its unity out toward and open to what has remained unsaid in its history. "Reserved-ness attunes each grounding moment of a sheltering of truth in the future Dasein of man. This history, grounded in Da-sein, is a hidden history of deep stillness. In this stillness alone there can still *be* a people" (GA 65, 34). This formation of a people that is here grounded in reticence and reservedness is a far cry from the idle chatter and commodification of reality that Heidegger bemoans in his description of machi-nation and calculative thinking. At the heart of this community is a strife and an ex-perience of lack and negation, but the negation is no longer conceived of in negative terms as what is in need of sublation and dialectical overcoming. The negation and lack belong to the fullness of possibility of this coming community. It is the very con-dition of holding back and keeping silence that makes possible the sovereignty (*Herrschaft*) of the singular beings Heidegger describes as the future Da-seins.[9]

In the section of the *Beiträge* entitled "The Leap," Heidegger declares that "sov-ereignty is the necessity of the free to be free" (GA 65, 282). It is the complete oppo-site, he says, from a concept of power that is rooted in coercion and the co-optation of the space of the other. Coercion breaks into things, is powerless to leap, and has no relationship to possibility (ibid.). Coercion operates as force and brings about change by forcing itself onto its objects. Sovereignty is neither coercion nor the power to resist coercion, that is, neither the community founded in tyranny nor the com-munity founded in the social contract is the community to come. Neither of these forms of community power is truly originary. These formations of power among peo-ple are of course altogether important to the health of a community, but Heidegger is attempting to think something different in his notion of sovereignty. The mastery at work here is not power over beings. Rather, Heidegger says, it is the bequest of empowerment (*Vermächtnis*): "It is not itself bequeathed (*vermacht*) but rather bequeaths the continuing originariness" (GA 65, 281). Sovereignty is not self-promotion; it is the gift (outside of the economy of exchange) of empowerment that recognizes the originary power of the other. This is why Heidegger associates mastery with the fissure, which he says is characteristic of the coming community and why the leap is required. "Splitting this cleft and thus parting it in togetherness as *mastery*, that is the origin that leaps forth" (ibid.). The ones to come, the sovereign ones, belong to this togetherness that parts and imparts the space of singularity.

In many crucial ways, the thinking of the *Beiträge* on community and the formation of a people situates itself beyond that of *Being and Time*, although, as I have tried to show, *Being and Time* is itself an advance in the direction of the *Beiträge*'s notion of community in comparison to the traditional metaphysical theories rooted in subjectivity and a notion of community as fusion. In both texts, however, the analysis of being-toward-death is crucial to understanding Heidegger's notion of a community of finite beings. In both texts, Da-sein forms a community of those who are going to die.

Heidegger indicates in his treatment of being-toward-death in the *Beiträge* that this notion, and its relationship to anticipatory resoluteness, which must be thought together, is the connecting point between the thinking in the *Beiträge* and in *Sein und Zeit*. He says: "What is sheltered here is the essential belongingness of the not to being as such (to the truth of be-ing, he says later)" (GA 65, 282). Being-toward-death does not, he says, negate be-ing and hold itself only in relationship to a nullity, but is "the utmost corroboration of be-ing" (GA 65, 284).[10] In being-toward-death, Heidegger argues that we recover an essential relationship to time-space, "not in order to negate 'be-ing' but in order to install the ground of its full and essential affirmability" (ibid.). Being-toward-death is the most affirmative concept in *Being and Time*. It is the utmost affirmation of being. Those who accomplish and take up this relationship toward their being as being-toward-death are the sovereign ones who are prepared for the coming community (GA 65, 285).

Notes

1. Jacques Taminiaux, *Heidegger and the Project of Fundamental Ontology* (Albany: State University of New York Press, 1991), p. 131.

2. Hubert Dreyfus, *Being-in-the-World: A Commentary on Heidegger's "Being and Time," Division I* (Cambridge: MIT Press, 1991).

3. Ibid., p. 301.

4. Ibid., p. 305.

5. This is not to deny the importance of a further analysis of Heidegger's notion of being-in-the-world and the extent to which worldliness needs to be put into question as the basis for a community of those who are going to die. It seems to me that Heidegger's *Contributions to Philosophy* provides an account of the relationship of being-toward-death and community that does not rely on a horizontal understanding of Da-sein's relationality.

6. Martin Heidegger, "Phenomenological Interpretations with Respect to Aristotle (Indications of a Hermeneutical Situation)," translated by Michael Baur, *Man and World* XXV (1992):11. Hereafter cited as PIA, followed by the page number.

7. "To care belongs not only being-in-the-world, but being together with inner-worldly beings. The being of Da-sein and its disclosedness belong equiprimordially to the discoveredness of innerworldly beings" (SZ, 221).

8. "Intimating (as grounding attunement of another beginning) does not at all aim only at what is futural, what stands before—as does the intimating that is generally thought in a calculative way. Rather, it traverses and thoroughly takes stock of the whole of temporality: the free-play of the time-space of the 'there.'" (GA 65, 22). This presentiment of the other beginning is an indication of the community of Daseins who stand decisively in the transition between "the no longer of the first history *and* the not—yet of the fulfillment of the other beginning" (GA 65, 23). The community of singular Da-seins is therefore radically transitional and indeterminate and never constituted by the fixed horizon or closure in which it dwells.

9. Here I think one can invoke the work of Georges Bataille and Giorgio Agamben who, in their own way, have developed this notion of sovereignty as the very condition of community in the postmodern age.

10. This passage seems to go against the interpretation of being-toward-death offered by Dreyfus.

16

Heidegger and the Question of Empathy

Lawrence J. Hatab

E mpathy has played an important role in moral philosophy, given that some thinkers (e.g., Hume, Schopenhauer, Rousseau) have maintained that sympathy or compassion is essential to ethics, as a kind of shared affect that is prior to rationality, principles, or rules. Empathy signifies a central concern in ethics: a sensitivity to the weal and woe of others, a caring about and for others that can both prompt beneficence and stave off harm and abuse. Modern moral philosophy, however, in its subject-centered orientation, has generated a variety of problems surrounding empathy and its implications. With the presumption that the self is an isolated individual consciousness, there has arisen a general skepticism about empathy and its concomitant altruistic expressions: empathic concern is a puzzle along the lines of the problem of other minds; empathic altruism is either a fiction (psychological egoism) or morally dispensable (ethical egoism). With the presumption that feelings and emotions are merely internal psychic states, there has arisen the concern that an affective ethics would collapse into egoism; in response to this concern, the subject has been bifurcated into rational reflection and emotional self-interest, and ethical norms have been formulated in constructions of disinterested reason (utilitarianism and deontology).

The aim of this chapter is to address these questions in light of Heidegger's thought. I will consider the following themes: the ekstatic nature of Dasein's finite being-in-the-world; the ekstatic conjunction of being-in and being-with; the primacy of *Befindlichkeit* and *Stimmung*; and Heidegger's occasional remarks on empathy (*Einfühlung*). In this analysis I hope to establish the following: (1) empathy is a genuine possibility in human experience and cannot be understood as a "subjective" phenomenon; (2) empathy is "natural" in a way that can trump psychological egoism and open alternatives to ethical egoism; (3) the role of empathy in ethics shows the limits of reason and the structural defects in utilitarian and deontological theories; (4) findings in social psychology can reinforce Heidegger's phenomenological findings, and the latter can help surmount flawed assumptions in the former; and (5) the alteric features of Heidegger's thought help surmount exclusive reductions in ethical thinking, including an overemphasis on empathy.

It is important to establish at the outset that empathy cannot be sufficient for an ethics, but I hope to show how empathy is crucial in understanding and enacting ethics, how it may be originary from the standpoint of human moral development, and how, via Heidegger, it can provide a meta-ethical analysis of background existential conditions that make ethical life possible and can guide the course of various avenues of moral philosophy.[1]

The Ekstatic Nature of Being-in-the-World

In *Being and Time*, Heidegger undermines the subject-object bifurcation and the notion of an isolated, unencumbered self by showing how human Dasein is being-in-the-world, is ekstatically *there* in its circumstances, is involved and immersed in its concernful dealings and social relations, prior to reflective distance that instigates various divisions between mind and thing, self and Other. In this regard I will give a brief sketch of three aspects of being-in-the-world: (1) its basic ekstatic element; (2) the "there" of Da-sein; and (3) the "with" of *Mit-sein*, followed in the next section by a coordinating sketch of the "in" of being-in—all of which is meant to show that Dasein's primal comportment toward the world is an ekstatic in/there/with structure. Although in *Being and Time* a treatment of ekstatic structure appears only in the discussion of temporality, we can generalize the notion of "*ek-stasis*" as pertaining to existence as such if we consider the 1949 *Introduction to "What Is Metaphysics?"* (P, 277–90), particularly where Heidegger articulates the meaning of "existence" in *Being and Time* (BTa, 373–75). Care is called the "ekstatic essence of Dasein," where *ek-stasis* indicates a "standing-out," but not in the sense of an "away from" the supposedly immanent "inside" of consciousness. The "out" is characterized as the openness of being itself. It may sound strange, Heidegger says, but the *stasis* is the standing in the "out" and "there" of the unconcealing presence of being. In other words, and this is important for my analysis, ekstatic structure indicates a being-in-the-there, and *not* a "projection" from an inner state of consciousness.[2] Consciousness is not the origin of the presence of beings; we are *already* ekstatically standing-in being before we distinguish "consciousness" and "things."

Accordingly, Da-sein is ekstatically *there* in its world, disclosing its meaning and significance in prereflective involvement. A basic indication of the ekstatic there is the structure of *Zuhandenheit*, as illustrated in tool use (BTa, Section 16)—indeed, only in prereflective *using* (BTa, 98), not in thinking about use. As the famous hammer example shows, in using a hammer I am not casting out mental beliefs from inside out to the practice or trying to match up objective properties and subjective intentions; rather, I am immersed in the practice, I am "there," fully "in" the activity, animated by concern (*Besorgen*) for my project and guided by a tacit, holistic circumspection (*Umsicht*) of the situational milieu. According to Heidegger, it is in breakdowns of the situation (e.g., when a tool breaks or malfunctions) that the meaning of the situation becomes reflectively evident, and where experience can be split into "objective" (*vorhanden*) properties (the hammer is too small) and "subjective" intentions (I cannot finish the job). Such delineations, however, are derived from a more original practical sphere that is neither strictly objective (being concernful use) nor subjective (being ekstatic).

Dasein's being is not only environmental in the above sense, but it also involves being-with other Daseins. But being-toward-others is ontologically different from relations with things in the world (BTa, 162). Other Daseins are not person-things but likewise concernful being-in-the-world (BTa, 156). The implication is that other Daseins are likewise needful, that they experience the radical finitude and possibility that mark existence. Where Dasein's involvement with things *zuhanden* is characterized as *Besorgen*, *Mitsein* involvement is characterized as *Fürsorge* (BTa, 157).[3] *Fürsorge* is said to be *essential* to *Mitsein*: "as *Mitsein*, Dasein 'is' essentially for the sake of Others" (BT, 160). This does not mean that Dasein always cares about others, but it does suggest something originary, because Heidegger calls indifference a "deficient" mode of *Fürsorge*, distinguished from "positive" modes (BTa, 158). Positive modes are marked by two extremes: a standing in for people's care (which can be a kind of paternalistic domination), and a releasing of people to and for their authentic care (BTa, 158). It is important to note that Heidegger indicates that there are mixed forms in between these two positive extremes, but that articulating them would lead him away from his purposes.[4]

In any case, *Fürsorge* is completely different from *vorhanden* and *zuhanden* relations, which suggests an ethically relevant contrast with objectification and instrumentality. Despite this contrast, what I want to suggest and work with later is an analogical treatment of *Mitsein* compared to other modes of ekstatic being-in-the-world. I will ask if empathy can be considered an ekstatic mode of *Mitsein* that is implicated in *Fürsorge* and can clarify the derivative nature of indifference as a deficient mode of *Fürsorge* in a way analogous to the derivative nature of the *vorhanden* out of ekstatic involvement.[5] I want to see if empathic concern can show itself as ekstatically *there* in Dasein's social world. I am encouraged in this by the fact that Heidegger initiates a discussion of empathy (*Einfühlung*) right at the end of his treatment of *Mitsein* and *Fürsorge*. More on this later.

Being-in and *Befindlichkeit*

In Section 28 of *Being and Time*, Heidegger offers a focused treatment of being-in as the existential constitution of the "there." He also associates being-in, and indeed being-in-the-world, generally, with the notion of dwelling (BTa, 80).[6] With the ekstatic connotations of existence, we can then call being-in an ekstatic dwelling. If we notice the confluence of the "in" and the "there" and draw on the specific identification of being-with and being-in (BTa, 155: "Being-in is *Being-with* Others"), we can summarize Dasein's existence as an ekstatic dwelling with a coordinated in/there/with structure. It is the existential sense of immersion and involvement that distinguishes "dwelling in" from objective, spatial conceptions of "in."

A fundamental mode of being-in that discloses the "there" is found in Heidegger's coinage of *Befindlichkeit* and its manifestations in mood (*Stimmung*).[7] Mood can be called an affective attunement (drawing on connotations of *stimmen*), a precognitive disclosure of various ways in which the world *matters* to Dasein (BTa, 176), interests Dasein.[8] Heidegger insists that moods should not be understood as "subjective" or "inner" states, which is why "feeling" and "affect" can be misleading (BTa, 178).[9] Even our language shows something here: we "have" feelings but are "in" moods (and we "find ourselves" in them). In any case, a mood is not an interior condition, because it is ekstatic in *disclosing* how the world matters, a kind of atmospheric background that precedes and makes possible any particular endeavor's various pursuits and findings.[10] A mood, then, is what I would call "ambient attunement." And it is important to note that, for Heidegger, mood can be collective and public, not simply an individual locus of experience (BTa, 178). Indeed, mood is something that constitutes being-with-one-another (FCM, 67).[11] There can even be a fundamental cultural mood (*Grundstimmung*) that marks an era or a time.[12] At any rate, mood is a pervasive and an ever-present orientation that marks any comportment toward the world.[13]

Why is the question of mood important for moral philosophy? It helps identify an ekstatic, disclosive, existential mode of dwelling, and its in/there/with structure allows us to talk of being-ethical-in-the-world in a way comparable to Heidegger's ontological analysis. Mood can open up questions of motivation that have been the province of moral psychology and speak to the limits of cognition in explaining or affecting moral action. A Heideggerian orientation, however, avoids the trap of subjectivism that usually haunts a promotion of affects and prompts the rationalized alternative of an "impartial" subject, whose reflective disinterest can appear problematical in the existential milieu of moral situations. We also can bypass the way in which rationalistic theories so often trade on beliefs as "causes" of action, which seems phenomenologically suspect. We can talk of moods and affects as disclosive of "moral import," prior to the isolation of beliefs and various appeals to rational inferences and implications.[14] We can then better understand why a reference to reasons, principles, or rules often does not *matter* to people, and why moral change often arises from a shift in affective ambiance—whether from an attempt to tap into moods or from a gradual evolution of a social atmosphere.[15] I repeat, mood cannot be sufficient for an ethics, but it may be necessary, or "essential," in Heidegger's verb-sense of *Wesen*, as a coming to presence of moral import. Rules and principles may still be important for ethics, but the question is whether moral *philosophy* can reduce ethics to rule formation or rule following.

Empathy

In accordance with the preceding discussion, I want to focus on empathy as a moral mood, as an originary, disclosive ethical attunement, and on how Heidegger's ekstatic in/there/with structure can be located in the phenomenon of empathy. I will begin with characterizations of empathy drawn largely from the field of social psychology, but such notions will eventually be refined with the help of Heidegger.[16]

Empathy has been defined as a feeling-with-another, as a vicarious sharing of an affect, which is most clearly shown when one is not directly undergoing the Other's feeling or circumstance. Empathic affect is disclosive of something outside oneself, and so is to be distinguished from more immanent, self-regarding affects. Empathy is not a "matching" with someone else's feelings but rather "an affective response more appropriate to another's situation than to one's own."[17] An empathic relation is not a "union" of self and Other (contra Rousseau and Schopenhauer); it requires a distinction between self and Other in order to be experienced *as* related to the feeling of an Other and as one's own experience of this relation (what Heidegger calls "mineness"). Empathic relations also can have an intersubjective reciprocity.[18] The emergence of empathy seems to be contextual and situational,[19] by no means constant, not universally exhibited (with variations both between and within individuals), and although strictly speaking not "active" (instigated by the will), or not entirely "passive" either. Empathy should not be seen as affective only, because it can have cognitive dimensions as well (empathic understanding), and it connects with processes such as memory, symbolic association, imagination, and role taking. Mature empathy, then, should be understood as multidimensional, as a blend of affective, cognitive, and participatory elements (see E, generally). Nevertheless, the affective element seems to be developmentally primal and appears to make the other elements possible (ED, ch. 10 and p. 63). We will concentrate on the affective dimension, although the remarks above show that empathy can be richly disclosive and can function in different ways in ethical considerations.[20]

Empathy and compassion often are used interchangeably, but empathy should be seen as the wider term and as that which makes compassion possible. Compassion is an empathic awareness of another's suffering, prompting an interest in alleviating that suffering (or at least dwelling with another's woe).[21] Empathy can include the sharing of positive feelings (e.g., one can share the joy of someone's freedom or success), and so it has a wider application than compassion. But since suffering and injury are clearly prominent in moral concerns, it is no surprise that compassion is highlighted as a crucial form of empathy.

Finally, empathy and compassion seem to be positively associated with prosocial behavior, though the association is certainly not a necessary one. Developmentally and otherwise, empathy seems to correlate with altruistic action, the formation and use of moral principles, and the operation of moral judgment (E, ch. 7; ED, ch. 4). We might conclude, then, that empathy is an existential precondition for a moral life.[22] The ethical significance of empathy would have to be associated with action in some way or to some degree in order to distinguish ethical sentiment from mere sentimentalism, or a kind of aestheticized empathy that simply dwells with the feeling and is satisfied with that, perhaps as an avoidance of the costs and encumbrances of an emotional involvement.[23]

Historically speaking, the term *empathy* originated as an English translation of the German term *Einfühlung*, which had been used in nineteenth-century German aesthetics to explain how one experiences an aesthetic object. Empathy was subsequently taken up in early twentieth-century experimental psychology in reference to how one experiences the affects of others. In any case, *Einfühlung* had generally been understood as a process of "feeling oneself into" another object or person (i.e., as a "projection" from "inside" oneself out "into" the Other). Such made sense in terms of the prevailing notion of selves as individually constituted and self-contained, so that awareness of another's affect would have to involve the projecting of one's own experiential states "into" the Other, which would then double back as a perceived experience *of* the Other's condition.[24]

I would like to spotlight the "*ein*" in *Einfühlung* in order to link up with Heidegger's conception of being-in, which would be different from a projective "into" that Heidegger himself saw as problematical. In other words, I want to interpret empathy in terms of Heidegger's ekstatic in/there/with structure, where empathy is an attunement *disclosing* the weal and woe of others, *there* in the world, *with* us, and *in* us in that it *matters*. Heideggerian ekstatics can contribute to moral philosophy by helping us overcome self-Other bifurcations that have created classic problems associated with empathy. For example: (1) Empathy as a surprising anomaly (How can we experience the misfortune of someone else if we are not directly undergoing it?); (2) Empathy as a mysterious process that needs an explanation (If understood as a projection, how does such a "transfer" from inside oneself into the Other occur?); (3) Skepticism about empathy (How can one "truly" apprehend the experience of another that is directly inaccessible to one's own consciousness?); (4) Cynicism about empathy (Given the priority of individual consciousness and self-awareness, should we not say that empathy is really only the projection of one's own interests and a surreptitious strategy for enhancing those interests?). If empathy is understood as ekstatic attunement, much in this catalogue of problems can be dissolved.

Heidegger on *Einfühlung*

At the end of Section 26 of *Being and Time*, after the discussion of *Fürsorge*, Heidegger offers some remarks about *Einfühlung*.[25] He begins by saying that disclosure of the Other arises primarily out of being-with the Other (BTa, 161). He then mentions the theoretical problem of the psychical life of others (*fremden Seelenlebens*) and the proposal of *Einfühlung* as the original way in which being toward others is made possible. But he finds the term *Einfühlung* regrettable (BTa, 162) and critiques the theory as phenomenologically inadequate, because of its sense of empathy as a "bridge" between a solitary subject that feels itself "into" the Other who is initially closed off (the psychological category of *Projektion* is mentioned here).[26] But with such self-Other divisions, disclosure of the Other will always remain a puzzle. In *History of the Concept of Time,* Heidegger had rejected the "problem" of empathy (how can one apprehend the experience of others by "feeling oneself into" them?) as a pseudo-problem, one as absurd as the problem of the reality of the external world (cf. the treatment of this latter question in BTa, Section 43). In general terms, the projective model of empathy is rejected, because Dasein's world is always already a co-world as being-with-and-toward-others, which is called an "autonomous, irreducible relationship of being" (BTa, 162); indeed, Dasein is *essentially* an *einander Verstehen,* an understanding of one another (HCT, 242). Empathy does not constitute being-with but itself is made possible by being-with (BTa, 162). For this reason, empathy is not a primordial existential phenomenon, any more than "knowing" is (BTa, 163).

It is important to clarify Heidegger's critique here. It is not the phenomenon of shared feeling that is rejected but rather the theoretical model that presumes isolated selves that somehow must venture "out" to each other. In fact, the implication is that disclosure of the Other is an original element of Dasein's being. Heidegger does not pursue an examination of *Einfühlung* along the lines of his phenomenological analysis of being-in-the-world, but he opens a door that I am trying to enter in this chapter (particularly by reading "*ein*" ekstatically rather then projectively). He admits that *Miteinandersein* and *Einfühlung* still need "phenomenal clarification," that the "ontological existential originality" of *Miteinandersein* is not obvious or self-evident, that it still needs to be pursued as an *ontological* problem (HCT, 243). He even mentions the possibility of a "special hermeneutic of empathy," which will have to show how genuine understanding of the Other gets suppressed, obstructed, and misled—for example, in the direction of an inconsiderate reckoning with others "without seriously 'counting on them' or even wanting to 'have anything to do' with them." A "proper" understanding of the Other will have to presuppose this hermeneutic (BTa, 163).

There are some remarks in *Fundamental Concepts of Metaphysics* that are helpful for my analysis. Although, again, Heidegger rejects the theoretical term *empathy* and its polarized problematic (FCM, 203), he claims that there *is* a phenomenon in which people can "share one and the same comportment *with one another,*" an "immediate experience" of a *Mitgang,* a going-along-with (FCM, 205). Although there are questions concerning the extent of this capacity, nevertheless, such a phenomenon shows that human beings can have an essential "transpositional" relation with others (ibid.). Heidegger then tries to experiment with a language that can avoid the theoretical traps of "empathy." His venture in fact resonates with the kind of interpretation I am attempting to bring to the phenomenon of empathy. Consider his remarks about "self-transposition" (*Sichversetzen*) as a "going along with" (*Mitgang*):

> In general the question at issue concerns the possibility of man's transposing himself into another being that he himself is not. In this connection self-transposition does not mean the factical transference of the existing human being into the interior of another being. Nor does it mean the factical substitution of

oneself for another being so as to take its place. On the contrary, the other being is precisely supposed to remain *what* it is and *how* it is. Transposing oneself into this being means going along with what it is and how it is. Such going-along-with means directly learning how it is with this being, discovering what it is like to be this being *with* which we are going along *in this way*. (FCM, 202)

Heidegger complains that usually such self-transposition is described as merely cognitive and hypothetical, as opposed to an existential inhabiting of the Other's sphere. Such an account, however, misses the direct experience of *my* being with the Other.

> This moment does not consist in our simply forgetting ourselves as it were and trying our utmost to act as if we were the other being. On the contrary, it consists precisely in we ourselves being precisely ourselves, and only in this way first bringing about the possibility of ourselves being able to go along with the other being while remaining *other* with respect to it. There can be no going-along-with if the one who wishes and is meant to go along with the other relinquishes himself in advance. "Transposing oneself into p. p. p." means neither an actual transference nor a mere thought-experiment that supposes such transference has been achieved. (FCM, 202–03)

I want to work with these suggestions to explore a richer phenomenology of empathy.

I have already sketched the possibility of empathy as an ekstatic being-in-there-with-the-Other, of empathic concern as a fundamental element of Dasein's social world, of indifference as a derivative and deficient mode of being-with (analogous to the *zuhanden-vorhanden* dynamic). Consider a face-to-face encounter with someone undergoing pain or misfortune. I assume that there can be moments of spontaneous, direct, affective responses, wherein we are immersed in/there/with the other person: we might wince, or tears might well up, or sadness might come—all in direct response to what is seen/sensed/felt in and from the person's words, tones, gestures, facial expressions, and body language. Analogous to the phenomenology of tool use that undermines the model of cognitive steps—of forming beliefs, drawing inferences, transferring to manual maneuvers and out to the tool—empathic concern shows moments when we are simply affectively in/there/with the person, without a sense of conjuring up feelings or beliefs "inside" and then "transferring" them to the other person, or processing perceptual data as "misfortune" and then triggering an affect and then casting it out to the other—all of this in an inferential procedure of external reception, internal processing, and projective transmission. No, the shared affect just *happens*.[27]

Of course, we might sooner or later become reflective or even self-conscious about an empathic experience and split it up into zones of "self" and "Other" in various modes and for various reasons.[28] But I think we can recognize genuinely ekstatic moments when we are not reflective or self-conscious (or strategizing or faking or merely edifying), but simply *there*. Speaking for myself, these moments are not very frequent, but when they happen I take them as "authentic," and in a sense satisfying as a clearly worthy, enhanced, and exemplary mode of human interaction and response, in other words, as fully *appropriate*.[29] I would like to think that such moments are possible for others regarding me as well. The point is that we have here an intimation of a fitting engagement, a deep sense of involvement that feels right. As Heidegger puts it, "do we not experience a new sense of elation in our Dasein each time we accomplish such going-along-with in some essential relation with human beings?" (FCM, 206).

As was mentioned earlier, empathy can exhibit intersubjective reciprocity, that is, not just a one-to-one "withness" but a productive co-presencing, where both sides *alter* each other. This is why the projective "from-into" model fails; not only is my empathic concern directly disclosive, but something happens *to* me as well; it says something about *me* as much as my relation to an Other. I feel a kind of exalted openness, that I *am* with someone, that is, *not* taken "out of myself" to some other region; rather, it is an enlargement of *me* at one of my best moments.

Conversely, I take deviations from these moments to be deficient in a sense, and noticeable *as* deviations. I am more likely in moments of indifference to ask myself why I do not care, whereas in moments of empathic concern, I am not likely to ask myself why I care. I suggest, then, that we take empathic moments to be primal, and that indifference (or worse) is *noticed* as "negative." Here we have an analogy to Heidegger's analysis of *Zuhandenheit*, where a *breakdown* in tool function is noticed as a disruption, which accordingly *illuminates* the meaning of the more primal mode of involvement. If we notice disengagement as a deviation (recall Heidegger's description of indifference as a deficient mode of *Fürsorge*), we might have phenomenological evidence for the primacy of empathic concern. Empathy could then serve as an existential "exemplar," as a kind of "measure" for a significant range of ethical matters.[30]

Empathy and Social Psychology

I would like to highlight some findings in social psychology, especially in the area of child development, which I believe can reinforce Heideggerian phenomenology and suggest developmental roots of an ekstatic in/there/with structure. Moreover, Heideggerian phenomenology can help us interpret these findings in a philosophically deepened way and challenge certain subjectivistic assumptions and prejudices that prevail in the social sciences.[31] In any case, this discussion can effectively address questions such as the following: How is it that we come to care about others? How does caring get blocked? How might caring be nourished?[32]

Face-to-face play between parent and infant (at two to three months) entails the sharing of emotion and develops an affective attunement that may be the precursor of later empathic responses (ED, 127). At ten to twelve months, babies begin to sense the emotional meaning of facial expressions; this begins their social development, which soon exhibits a capacity to respond vicariously to emotional expressions and behaviors (ED, 129).[33] Empathic experience seems to emerge in stages and in a way that makes an assumption of mere "conditioning" problematical (ED, 51): in the first year, prior to self-other differentiation, infants experience empathic distress, in which the distress of the Other is one's own (and which would seem to be a developmental base that makes later empathic forms possible).[34] In the second year, with self-Other differentiation, children can respond empathetically to the distress of others that they recognize is not their own. At two to three years, a child learns more clearly that the feelings of others are their own, and this actually enhances responsiveness to their cues. With the learning of language, empathy can relate to more complex emotions and can be aroused by the mere recounting of an absent person's misfortune.[35] It appears that a primal empathic response may be biologically coded, and yet a child's environment can influence whether or not he or she flourishes or withers.[36]

What is particularly interesting in child development is the role of motor mimicry, which is essential to an extensive range of learning experiences, and which can be considered a primal form of empathy.[37] Motor mimicry is a mode of transpositional embodiment, in which, for example, we spontaneously wince at other people's pain, smile at their delight, recoil at their peril, ape their movements, and so on. Such behavior has been generally perceived as a puzzle by psychologists (ED, 322–23): why is it done, especially when we ourselves are not undergoing the movements? It seems, though, that the role of motor mimicry in early childhood provides answers, and a Heideggerian ekstatics greatly contributes to an understanding of such behaviors. Mimetic response, especially in a child's early face-to-face engagements, would seem to be a fundamentally ekstatic phenomenon. In spontaneous mimicry, we can presume that the "outside" comes first in a way and is productive of the child's "inside." Indeed, psychologists speculate that an infant comes to learn about the self primarily through the emotional responses of others, a process that then can be looped back to allow vicarious learning about the experiences of others (ED, 136). It is important to note here that empathy should not be understood as unidirectional from either side of self and Other; it is developmentally bipolar, *inter*personal rather than *intra*personal; it is not simply an "out to" or an "in to" or even a mere "with," but a reciprocal copresencing that prefigures a significant range of intersubjective processes.[38]

In general terms, research suggests that a projective model of empathy presuming a self-centered trajectory "into" an Other is reductionistically flawed (ED, 138). The phenomenon of empathy in early child development would seem to bear out Heideggerian claims about the ekstatic nature of experience and the derivative nature of various divisions between self and Other, the internal and the external. The subsequent Heideggerian philosophical move would be that ekstatic structure remains operative in mature experience as well. Although reflective distance and various partitions of experience are necessary elements of human experience, Heidegger is at pains to point out how a reduction to such elements distorts our thinking and how philosophy must acknowledge and attempt to articulate an originary, prereflective, ekstatic dimension in Dasein's being. The point of this chapter is that ethics in particular can benefit from such a philosophical revision.

To conclude this section, research findings also speak to familiar questions of "nature" and "nurture." The development of empathic concern seems to be a confluence of innate predispositions and environmental influences (ED, ch. 7; E, ch. 4). The latter highlights the importance of upbringing and education in matters of ethics. Mimetic processes are crucial for the development of numerous capacities, particularly language, but also a moral sense. Heidegger's ekstatic configuration of being-in-the-world helps show how and why this happens, and it cues insights concerning how something like empathy can be nurtured, reinforced, or, as Heidegger says, facilitated in particular cases (FCM, 205).[39] But in addition to the importance of environment, research suggests that empathy is in some sense "natural," not in the sense of being invariant, universal, or essential, but in the sense of being intrinsic, that is, *not* conventional, arbitrary, artificial, or culturally constructed. Empathy, then, would be part of human nature in the sense of not being mere social conditioning or even a surreptitious strategy for advancing self-interest. In other words, it is natural for human beings to care about each other and feel for each other. It should be added, in sum, that being-in-the-world shows nature and nurture not as opposites along the lines of binaries such as intrinsic and extrinsic, invariant and variable, but rather as intersecting co-constituents of human development.[40] One significant consequence for ethics in all of this can be found in recent experiments that seem to validate empathic and altruistic behavior as a genuine part of human experience, contrary to egoistic suppositions that such behavior is either infeasible or ultimately based in self-interest (E, ch. 7).[41]

Empathy As Ethical Attunement

Earlier in this chapter I established the connection between the attunement of mood and ekstatic dwelling. The word "dwelling" (*Wohnen*) became a preoccupation in Heidegger's later thinking. This word in all of its resonances gave Heidegger an alternative to traditional subject-object ontologies, because it captured in one stroke both human and extra-human features (existential meaningfulness and an environing habitat). In "Letter on Humanism" Heidegger considers the Greek word *êthos* in its sense of abode or dwelling place, and he suggests that his ontological investigations might then be called an "original ethics"(BW, 235). What I am suggesting here is that we need not restrict ourselves to Heidegger's lofty "ontological ethics"; we can extend the notion of dwelling to familiar ethical concerns, particularly with regard to empathy. I am suggesting that empathy can be understood as a primal mode of dwelling or attunement with the social world, as a capacity for ekstatic being in/ there/with others with respect to existential weal and woe.

If ethics in its "evaluative" aspect always has to engage certain preferences regarding better and worse ways of living, empathy can be understood as a preconceptual, preregulatory, but nonetheless exemplary "measure" for the possibility of genuine ethical regard, particularly in terms of valuing beneficence over maleficence. As ekstatic attunement, such a measure arises neither from sheer self-regard nor from a reflective construction of principles bypassing existential comportment— in other words, empathy exhibits *self*-involvement-with-*others*. Here we can bring in Heidegger's notion of *Jemeinigkeit* and go a long way toward deflecting misconceptions of this complex term. The affective immediacy of empathy shows a being-toward-others-that-is-mine, (i.e., *my* being-toward-others). Empathy presupposes a differentiation of self and Other, rather than sheer union. But as *my* felt concern for others, mineness displays an existential "mattering," in that the fate of others matters to me. And I would surely prefer that others also be absorbed in their mineness regarding my fate, in other words, that their concern for me be heartfelt rather than an instrumental calculation, or a mere mechanical obedience to rules, or an impersonation of social expectations. So mineness in this context is anything but egoistic self-regard.[42]

Empathy, of course, exhibits various degrees of feeling and concern, which suggests another form of measuring, all the way toward so-called cognitive modes such as empathic understanding. We should not hold to a strict separation between affective and cognitive empathy. As Heidegger says, every form of understanding and knowing has its mood or attunement. Even a strict conception of moral principle would seem to require that one have an *interest* in the principle, that one care about its importance and about living up to it. Ethics as lived demands that moral "beliefs" be *animated* in the sense of being charged with existential import. The various degrees of empathy can be taken as a primal source of such import. Indeed, developmental studies suggest that empathic affect passes through various stages and continues to be implicated in supposedly more abstract moral considerations.[43]

Here in the sphere of ethics we engage the familiar distinction between the modern and postmodern conceptions of selfhood, between the unencumbered, disinterested self of detached reason and the situated self of world involvement. For all of the supposed advantages of rational universality in cognitive ethical theories, what remains problematical for such theories are fundamental questions about moral constitution and moral motivation—that is, how does one come to see a situation *as* a moral situation, and why should one *be* moral or come to see morality as an important part of one's life? Empathy can address such questions as a primal mode of ethical *interest*, as involvement in the existential weal and woe of others. Such involvement can be understood in terms of Heidegger's early concept of care and the later notion of "nearness," which is meant to contrast with the "distance" of objectified modes of being exemplified in modern technology. Cognitive moral theories consider rational disinterest a great advantage in guaranteeing universality and in preventing ethics from collapsing into the chaos of emotional forces. But we have seen that a turn to affect may in fact be a turn to the very origins of an ethical sense. Moreover, promoting disinterest should give some pause, because some of the most heinous human behaviors can be traced not to hatred but to a radical emotional detachment, a distancing from the fate of others that objectifies them to the point of permitting brutal treatment in the name of duty, order, efficiency, and so on.[44]

Empathy, then, is not simply a feeling, it is a mode of *disclosure* that generates ethical import; in its atmosphere of affective nearness, there arises the existential "draw" of the Other that can be called the prereflective condition for the possibility of, and openness to, important ethical forces such as responsibility, obligation, conscience, and guilt. The ekstatic structure of empathy also helps defend against the gambits of moral skepticism, nihilism, and relativism, which in one way or another are governed by subjectivistic assumptions and the fact-value binary. A Heideggerian analysis allows ethics to show itself as a *world* phenomenon.

Empathy and Authenticity

The preceding discussion also helps open up the question of authenticity (*Eigentlichkeit*) in a way that subverts the common belief that Heidegger meant this notion to represent radical individuation and a divorce from the social world. In general terms, Dasein's authenticity indicates an openness to radical finitude shown in being-toward-death. Dasein's authentic "self" is something that is *not* "a being" but rather a "transcendence" that is sheer "possibility" and ultimately the "impossibility" of death. Inauthenticity simply reflects the various ways in which Dasein covers up this radical finitude in its "fallen" immersion in positive states of being or familiar modes of understanding. Authenticity, then, is an embrace of finitude.

It is important to note, however, that authenticity and being-toward-death involve certain double movements, and in typical Heideggerian fashion, these movements involve a positive disclosure of meaning by a negative experience. First of all, the negativity of death discloses the existential meaning of the world as care. We care about the world *because* it is finite: the possibilities of loss, for example, show how and why things matter to us. The negativity of death therefore generates the "throw" that opens up a world of meaning.[45] Another double movement is that being-toward-death allows the possibility of discovering one's own distinctive mode of care. The disruption of death can shake off one's dependence on the distortions, superficialities, and dispersions of everyday common understanding, the familiarity of which has supplied a refuge from radical finitude. Now Dasein has the possibility of coming to its "own" (*eigen*) understanding of its existence, appropriate to itself, no longer dominated by the commonplace.

Despite this clear sense of individuation, interpreting authenticity as a sheer break with the social world is a mistake. Dasein is always situated. Being-toward-death does individuate, since one's own death is nonrelational (BTa, 293), but such individuation should be understood as a temporary interruption of world involvement that prepares a disclosive renovation, and not as a radical break with the world (BTa, 308). Dasein's transcendence surpasses all beings (MFL, 192), and yet it surpasses *itself as well* (MFL, 190). That is why in choosing itself authentically, Dasein really chooses not isolation but being with other Daseins and other beings in the world (ibid.).[46]

Several texts clearly suggest some ethical implications in the context of authenticity. Heidegger states emphatically that Dasein's for-the-sake-of is nothing like a radical egoism—that would be "madness" and "outrageous nonsense." It is rather the condition for the possibility for Dasein "to be able to be with others, for them, and through them" (MFL, 186). The individuation of being-toward-death is still connected with *Mitsein*; it opens up the potentiality for being of *others* too (BTa, 309). There remains a fundamental relation between authenticity, resolution, and being-with-others (BP, 287–88). A later work (GA 39, 72–73) suggests an ethical sense of nearness and connectedness that recapitulates the disclosive double movement of death and care. The existential "nearness of death" can be the basis of an "original community" (*ürsprungliche Gemeinschaft*); its negativity can be the source of an unqualified belonging together (*unbedingten Zueinandergehörens*). In short, our common finitude can draw us toward each other. Finally, there is a remarkable passage at the very end of *Vom Wesen des Grundes* that organizes and coordinates the double movements of death, care, authenticity, and *Mitsein*:

> And so man, as existing transcendence abounding in and surpassing toward possibilities, is a being (*Wesen*) of distance. Only through primordial distance, which he forms toward all beings in his transcendence, does there arise in him a true nearness to things. And only the capacity to hear in the distance develops for Dasein as self the awakening to the response (*Antwort*) of Mitdasein; for only in Mitdasein can Dasein sacrifice its egotism (*Ichheit*) in order to win itself as an authentic self.[47]

In view of this strong social component in authenticity, I would like to suggest the possibility of an analogous ethical authenticity with respect to the phenomenon of empathy. The movement of being-toward-death to authentic care is a general ontological configuration that Heidegger provides as an interpretive path for the thinking of being. We have noticed certain ethical registers in authenticity and are free to explore possible parallels in the "ontical" sphere of ethics, especially since Heidegger hinted that the ontological structures of conscience and guilt, though not as such indicative of a moral meaning, nevertheless can provide an existential basis for morality.[48]

Empathy (especially in developmental terms) seems to imply a primal ekstatic "nearness" along the lines of Heidegger's ontological analysis. And empathy in the form of compassion seems analogous to the double movement of authenticity, in the sense of being an openness to the finitude of suffering that discloses its meaningfulness and our responses to it. Recalling two basic aspects of inauthenticity—(1) an immersion in presence as a refuge from radical finitude and (2) a superficial leveling that conceals the depth of individuated appropriation—empathy could be understood as ethically authentic, as a dwelling-presence-in-the-midst-of-finitude that discloses the meaning, depth, and appropriate particularity of a given existential situation. Moreover, in view of the first form of inauthenticity above, could we call indifference inauthentic, as a refuge from the negativity of suffering to protect the self from the burden of perceiving the pains of life? And regarding the second form, could we call an ethics restricted to moral rules and principles, inauthentic in a way, as a "flattening" of the ethical sphere into generalizations that conceal existential comportment and its specificity?[49]

The Limits of Empathy

It is important to reiterate that empathy and its implications cannot be sufficient for an ethics. I have tried to establish that it is a crucial element in ethics, that it can be exemplary, and that it may be a primal or an originary ethical phenomenon (especially in a developmental sense). Nevertheless, empathy must be seen as a limited ethical phenomenon, and Heidegger's ontology can help articulate this limit.

For Heidegger, the radical finitude of being, the ontological correlation of presence and absence, undermines the model of constant presence that has dominated Western thought. The truth of being as unconcealment indicates that beings emerge out of concealment, and that every revealing is implicated in modes of concealing. Consequently, every form of being is limited and balanced by otherness and thus is always *ambiguous* regarding its "nature." The same must be said for ethical concerns, and a turn to Aristotle can provide some guidance on this point. Aristotle connects *phronêsis*, or practical wisdom, with *aretê*, or virtue (*Nicomachean Ethics* 1107a1–2), and virtue shows itself as a capacity to find a balance between extreme possibilities (e.g., moderation as a balance between overindulgence and denial of pleasure).[50] Heidegger, in his early writings, gave much attention to Aristotelian *phronêsis*, but primarily for ontological rather than ethical considerations.[51] In his *Sophist* course, he associates *phronêsis* with conscience and authenticity (S, 39).[52] In a later course on Parmenides, *phronêsis* is conceived of in ontological terms as a balance between concealment and unconcealment.[53]

Taking a lead from Aristotle, Heidegger's ontological phronetics of presence and absence can be shown to operate in ethical thinking and practice, as a balancing act that is indigenous to ethical finitude. For example, phronetics can negotiate a balance between self-regard and other-regarding empathic concern. The debate between egoism and altruism can be diagnosed as a struggle between "purist" theories modeled on constant presence that cannot abide otherness or ambiguity. Ethical life not only can involve the coexistence of self-interest and altruism, it also can involve an ambiguous blend of self-regarding and other-regarding attitudes and behaviors.[54]

One also could perform a phronetic analysis of the "virtue" of empathic concern as a balancing between the following extremes: (1) indifference or objectification, a general alienation from the fate of others; and (2) empathic overload, which can lead to extreme personal distress (which can prompt indifference), an overprotection or overtaking of the Other, or a revulsion against suffering.[55] Such extremes can correspond to Heidegger's distinction between the deficient mode of *Fürsorge* and its problematic, positive mode of standing in for another's care. We also can locate within this dynamic the importance of Heidegger's other positive mode of *Fürsorge*, which releases people to their authentic care.[56] We should remember as well that there are modes of *Fürsorge* between the positive extremes of overtaking and release.

Finally, there also can be a balance between the extremes of empathy for no one and empathy for everyone. The former is sociopathic, while the latter is unrealistic, if not impossible. A certain empathic partiality is probably inevitable because of the following factors: the contextuality of empathic experiences, the seemingly natural partiality toward intimates as contrasted with strangers, and the risks of emotional overload. But if empathy can remain exemplary, this can open up the importance and role of moral principles ("feed the hungry") as "proxies" for the limits of direct empathic concern. In addition, a tending toward the abstract quality of principles can actually help manage the intensity of empathic affects that can be psychically overpowering (ED, 73). The importance of empathy, then, does not supplant the role of principles in ethics, nor is it immune to certain problems that lead us to see the significance of a certain "distancing" in social life.[57] It is important to remember that Heidegger's ekstatic configuration of being-in-the-world does not discount or disparage objectification or reflective distance but simply the *reduction* of ontology to these modes of disclosure. I am not recommending the elevation of ekstatic empathy to some kind of ethical "ground" or moral absolute.[58] My proposal is simply that empathy is developmentally originary, that empathic affect, rather than reason, uncovers ethical import and predisposes one to a range of moral conceptions, and that the ekstatic structure of empathy helps surmount certain problems that have bedeviled traditional moral philosophy.

Notes

1. It also is important to establish that, in my discussion, ethics as "moral philosophy" is not a search for demonstrative certainty or rational "justification" in moral matters. It is a reflective, contextual, dialogical, performative enterprise concerning questions of how human beings ought to live with each other, an addressive enterprise that simply offers itself for response and that always presumes finitude.

For an extended discussion of my approach to ethics in light of Heidegger's thought, see my *Ethics and Finitude: Heideggerian Contributions to Moral Philosophy* (Lanham, Md.: Rowman & Littlefield, 2000). The present chapter is a revised version of chapter 6 of my book. I will not engage here the various problems associated with Heidegger and ethics, (e.g., why he did not write an ethics, or whether his thought might even be antithetical to ethics). Suffice it to say that I think his existential analysis allows for a rich articulation of ethical themes, regardless of his own misgivings or even shortcomings in such matters.

2. As Heidegger says in the context of language, Dasein is not first "inside" and then expressed "outside." Being-in-the-world is *already* "outside" (BTa, 205). When Heidegger offers a critical discussion of "projection," he refers to *Projektion*; his own notion of *Entwurf* is far from an inside-out structure, in fact, it is associated with the "throw" of *Geworfenheit* (P, 284).

3. I prefer to leave *Fürsorge* untranslated to capture the senses of caring for and caring about that can be missed in the standard translation "solicitude." In German, *liebesvolle Fürsorge* means loving care; *soziale Fürsorge* means social welfare, social service.

4. It is frustrating that Heidegger seems to find the time to discuss examples of tool use in some detail, but human relations seem to be a distraction.

5. I stress the limits of the analogy, however, because as Heidegger says, indifference is still a mode of *Fürsorge*, and so is nothing *vorhanden* (BTa, 158). Still, Heidegger himself draws an analogy between *Fürsorge* and the circumspection of *Zuhandenheit* (BT, 159).

6. See also Heidegger's "Letter on Humanism" (BW, 260), when he writes "dwelling is the essence of being-in-the-world."

7. I want to leave *Befindlichkeit* untranslated. "State of mind" has been recognized as inadequate; "disposition" is better, but it too suggests a psychic state that misses the *world*-disclosive and ekstatic senses that Heidegger aims for in the connotation of "how one finds oneself."

8. Some examples of mood disclosure would be the world experienced as frightening, exciting, boring, intriguing, comforting, taxing, mysterious, and so on. Even science, then, can have its disclosive moods, in terms of how science matters and cultivates an altered (detached) interest in things (see BT, 177).

9. In FCM (64–66), Heidegger does not summarily reject the association of mood with the notion of "feeling," only that such a category is freighted with subjectivity and therefore limited and not decisive in thinking through the nature and structure of mood. For Heidegger, though, an affect is certainly not "objective," it is not just "in us" but is disclosive of the world in some way.

10. Moods are "the 'presupposition' for, and 'medium' of, thinking and act-ing"(FCM, 68). We might distinguish between mood and feeling in the sense that a feeling is more localized than the atmospheric quality of a mood.

11. Here Heidegger talks about how a mood can be "infectious," how a certain bearing in a person can have a direct effect on the atmosphere of a social gathering.

12. See FCM, sections 16–18; GA 39, 140–41; GA 45, 197.

13. What tempts us to think that the attunement of mood simply comes and goes and is not always constitutive of experience is focusing only on intense extremes such as joy or grief, thereby missing more subtle forms such as vague contentment, slight apprehension, and so on. There is never an absence of mood but only changes of mood (FCM, 68).

14. Arne J. Vetlesen argues that emotion supplies the "constitution" of a moral object, as an affective discovery of the import of the weal and woe of others. See *Perception, Empathy, and Judgment: An Inquiry into the Preconditions of Moral Performance* (University Park: Pennsylvania State University Press, 1994), ch. 4. See also Justin Oakley, *Morality and the Emotions* (New York: Routledge, 1992).

15. In any case, Heidegger helps us see that mood shifts are not something that can be "controlled" or "directed," but they can be "awakened" (FCM, 59ff).

16. See Mark H. Davis, *Empathy: A Social Psychological Approach* (Boulder: West-view Press, 1996). Hereafter cited as E, followed by the page number. Also see *Empathy and Its Development*, edited by Nancy Eisenberg and Janet Strayer (Cambridge, Mass.: Cambridge University Press, 1987). Hereafter cited as ED, followed by the chapter number and page number.

17. Martin Hoffman, "Affect and Moral Development," in *New Directions for Child Development*, edited by D. Cicchetti and P. Hesse (San Francisco: Jossey-Bass, 1982), p. 95.

18. For example, empathic exchanges in a love relation help show the bipolar, reciprocal element well. Such emotional transactions amount to a co-constitution of selves; each person is *altered* by the relationship, which is different, then, from a mere "sharing" of feeling. I would suggest that all empathic relations have a certain degree of reciprocity in them. It should be pointed out in this regard that Heidegger does not discuss to any significant extent the *inter*subjective elements of Mitsein, some-thing treated extensively by Gadamer and Habermas. Heidegger does, however, call *Fürsorge* a "co-disclosure" (BTa, 344).

19. Empathy is contextual not simply as variegated but as situational, stemming from one's understanding of another's specific life circumstances.

20. The primacy of affective empathy can be seen as ethically significant,

because a cruel or sadistic person can be said to possess a kind of cognitive empathy. See Bernard Williams, *Ethics and the Limits of Philosophy* (Cambridge, Mass.: Harvard University Press, 1985), p. 91.

21. Empathy, however, also must be distinguished from "personal distress," which is an *aversive* experience of another's suffering that prompts various modes of flight to alleviate one's own distress (ED, 7). It also should be pointed out that neither empathy nor compassion need be associated with love, a dissociation that can have a great significance for ethics if something like universal love is seen as unlikely or impossible.

22. Vetlesen maintains that empathy is the human access to, and disclosure of, the moral domain, the import of the weal and woe of others (*Perception, Empathy, and Judgment*, 204-18).

23. For an insightful analysis of sentimentalism in this vein, see Roger Scruton, *The Aesthetics of Music* (Oxford: Clarendon Press, 1997), Ch. 15.

24. I am not arguing that such a projective and reflective model of empathy has no sense or application, only that it is not primal.

25. Heidegger also had treated this topic in *History of the Concept of Time: Prolegomena,* translated by Theodore Kisiel (Bloomington: Indiana University Press, 1985). Hereafter cited as HCT, followed by the page number.

26. Heidegger may have had Husserl specifically in mind here, since Husserl understood *Einfühlung* as the self feeling itself into the Other, with the self as the original reference point. See Rudolph A. Makkreel, "How Is Empathy Related to Understanding," in *Issues in Husserl's Ideas,* vol. II, edited by Thomas Nenon and Lester Embree (Boston: Kluwer Academic Publishing, 1996), pp. 199-212. See also the study by one of Husserl's students, Edith Stein, *Zum Problem der Einfühlung* (Halle: Buchdruckerei des Waisenhauses, 1917).

27. Empathy, then, is a direct disclosure of a co-presencing that is more than merely subjunctive or hypothetical (how I would feel if I were in another's situation). Moreover, empathic disclosure need have nothing to do with the question of "accurate" perceptions of others, something which again is generated by projective presuppositions and reflective divisions of self and Other. In the midst of an empathic experience, we do not take it as an exercise in accurate perception (only an epistemologist would see it that way). There simply emerges an affective co-presencing of another's fate. If I felt sadness in the presence of another person's misfortune, and someone were to ask me—"Do you think you genuinely felt as he did?" or "Do you think you correctly perceived the contents of his consciousness?"—I would blink in bewilderment. Cognitive categories of sameness and difference are not thematized in empathic moments, although they do exhibit a vague and an ambiguous intersection of togetherness and apartness.

28. Heidegger indicates that it is no accident that a polarization of self and Other has been conceived (FCM, 203), because part of being-with is an experience of being "apart" or merely "alongside," which can prompt a notion of a gap that needs bridging (FCM, 206).

29. Here I might borrow from Heidegger's sense of *Ereignis* and call these moments an appropriation of self and Other, their "belonging together."

30. See Werner Marx, *Is There a Measure on Earth? Foundations for a Nonmetaphysical Ethics*, translated by Thomas Nenon and Reginald Lilly (Chicago: University of Chicago Press, 1978).

31. Some might claim that bringing in a social science perspective can only subvert a Heideggerian analysis, but with care I think we can make headway. Besides, Heidegger did not reject scientific findings, only their philosophical primacy and flawed assumptions. In *Being and Time,* he suggests positive prospects for ethnology and psychological research, but first a phenomenologically adequate conception of "world" is needed before appropriate scientific findings can be considered (BTa, 76–77). Note also Heidegger's discussion of biological research in his examination of life forms and organisms (FCM, ch. 4).

32. Certainly this analysis can connect with feminist discussions of a "care ethic." Two classic works are Carol Gilligan, *In a Different Voice: Psychological Theory and Women's Development* (Cambridge, Mass.: Harvard University Press, 1982), and Nel Noddings, *Caring: A Feminine Approach to Ethics and Education* (Berkeley: University of California Press, 1984). I would hope that a Heideggerian treatment could work against any undo restriction of this issue to gender differentiation.

33. Some cases: a nine-month-old becomes overwhelmed at the distress of other infants; a fourteen-month-old sees another infant crying, begins to cry, and looks to her mother; a fifteen-month-old is arguing with another child, who begins to cry, and the first child leaves to fetch a teddy bear to bring to the crying child (ED, 119).

34. It is interesting to note that empathic distress in the case of crying seems to be specific to the sound of infant crying; when researchers produce a computer-simulated sound of comparable intensity, empathic response does not occur (ED, 149).

35. Children in later years can begin to empathically generalize about groups or grasp larger life situations and their meanings. In maturity, a broadened understanding of life and its complexities can modify empathy in various ways (ED, 52).

36. In addition to prosocial attitudes, empathy seems to be implicated in an entire range of social behaviors and attitudes (e.g., self-awareness, communication skills, and social understanding) (ED, 148–49). Such findings would lend support to Heidegger's claim that the affective dimension of *Befindlichkeit* and *Stimmung* has priority in Dasein's being-in-the-world.

37. In fact, *Einfühlung,* in its earliest usage, referred to motor mimicry (ED, 317–18).

38. Empathic responses that infants receive from others are both self-forming *for* the infant and precursors for the child's empathic responses *to* others in later development. The point is that the self from early on has *relational* needs in addition to mere biological needs based in "drives" of pleasure and pain. An inattention to relational needs is a significant flaw in most developmental theories, especially Freudian theories. See Vetlesen, *Perception, Empathy, and Judgment,* pp. 252–71.

39. Many factors seem to enhance the development of empathic concern: a secure, nurturing, affectionate environment (which diminishes excessive self-concern), modeling and identification, inductive socialization (e.g., the Golden Rule), and opportunities for, and reinforcement of, helping behaviors (ED, 150–57).

40. The history of this question can be traced back to Aristotle. In the *Nicomachean Ethics* (1134b18–35), he discusses a distinction between nature (*physis*) as invariant (universally valid) and convention (*nomos*) as variable and relative. But he suggests that there is a sense of *physis* that is changeable, that *physis* may be unchangeable for the gods, but in our world the natural can admit of change (indeed, in the *Physics* change and *physis* are identified). After Hegel and in light of evolution theory, one can say clearly that change, variation, and even disparity are not inimical to "nature." And Heidegger declares in *What Is a Thing?,* translated by W. B. Barton Jr. and Vera Deutschs (Chicago: Henry Regnery, 1967) that what is "natural" is always historical (p. 39). We should note the sense of emergence in the Greek *physis,* derived from the verb *phy,* to grow, arise, or bring forth. Aristotle connects *physis* with the self-moving (*Physics* II.1), and Heidegger wants to stress the implicit phenomenological sense of self-showing in *physis* (see "On the Being and Conception of *Physis* in Aristotle's *Physics* B,1" in GA 9, 239–301). There is a link here with Heidegger's peculiar conception of "essence," which should be understood as the verb-sense of *Wesen,* as a coming-to-presence. In this regard, calling empathy natural is not to say that it is universal, invariant, or essential in a metaphysical sense, but that it simply shows itself spontaneously in human experience, that it is in some sense intrinsic to human beings, though dependent on environmental influences for its flourishing (analogous to the natural propensity for language, which is nevertheless not automatic or self-generating). We could call empathy a natural human capacity or potential, in the same way that Aristotle called virtue a natural potential fulfilled by habit (*Nicomachean Ethics* 1103a24–26). So although empathy is not artificial or conditioned, its development is neither automatic nor necessary; it needs nurturing. Accordingly, empathy *can* be absent or concealed or lost. This gives some relief from citations of exceptions (e.g., the occurrence of radical selfishness in extreme conditions) meant to invalidate the naturalness of empathy, as though invariance or permanence were necessary conditions for the natural. The category of potentiality

provides a more balanced account. For another angle on "nature," see the discussions of the evolutionary advantages of empathy in ED, ch. 3 and E, ch. 2.

41. See also C. Daniel Bateson, "Experimental Tests for the Existence of Altruism," *Proceedings of the Biennial Meetings of the Philosophy of Science Association* 2 (1993):69–80.

42. Dasein's for-the-sake-of-itself "does not assert ontically that the factual purpose of the factical Dasein is to care exclusively and primarily for itself and to use others as instruments (*Werkzeug*) toward this end" (BP, 296). Indeed, Dasein's selfhood as a *world* phenomenon is "the ontological presupposition for the selflessness in which every Dasein comports itself toward the other in the existent I-thou relationships" (BP, 298).

43. In infants, empathic distress prepares the possibility of prosocial sympathetic distress, and empathy makes possible empathic anger at perpetrators of another's hurt, something exhibited in children as early as eighteen months old (ED, 54). The emergence of guilt feelings being the cause of another's hurt can be understood as a blend of empathetic distress, sympathetic distress, and self-directed empathic anger (ED, 55). Finally, empathic injustice arises when a child feels aversion to someone suffering undeserved misfortune or mistreatment, and such can be seen as a bridge between empathic concern and a more generalized sense of moral principle (ED, 57). Empathy and guilt function as motives for moral action and for affirming certain principles ("care for the needy") that then can function as premises in moral judgments in various social or political milieus (ED, 60). From a developmental standpoint, empathic affects emerge prior to cognizance of moral principles, and the affects seem to predispose people toward, and help activate, moral principles. Empathy allows a moral principle to be a "hot cognition" (ED, 72); indeed, moral principles can become charged enough to themselves elicit empathic responses in moral situations (ED, 73). For a discussion of the role of emotion in moral judgment and moral life, especially in contrast to Kantian and Habermasian postconventional ethics that stress cognitive validity, see Vetlesen, *Perception, Empathy, and Judgment*, ch. 6. It should be added that for Kant, respect for the moral law is a kind of feeling, but nonetheless one that is generated by reason.

44. Among the most significant examples are behaviors in the Nazi regime. See Vetlesen's discussion in *Perception, Empathy, and Judgment*, chs. 2, 4, 5.

45. MFL, 182. The transcendence of Dasein's being-toward-death opens up an abyss (*Abgrund*), which each Dasein is for itself. But this is not something apart from the world. Dasein is "held out into the nothing," but not as an empty nothingness. The nothing is a *power* that "constantly thrusts us back into being," that lets beings be as beings (FCM, 299). The nothing is not a *nihil negativum* but a *nihil originarium* (MFL, 210).

46. Again, Dasein's being is beyond all beings but not as absolute nothingness. In transcendence is found a capacity for "binding commitment," where Dasein "first can and even must hold itself to beings" (MFL, 196–97).

47. *Vom Wesen des Grundes* (Frankfurt am Main: Vittorio Klosterman, 1955).

48. Dasein's essential being-guilty is called "the existential condition for the possibility of the 'morally' good and for the 'morally' evil—that is, for morality in general and for the possible forms which this may take factically" (BTa, 332).

49. As a transition to the last section of my chapter, it should be pointed out that although the authenticity of empathy is meant to suggest a kind of exemplary ethical measure, this does not rule out inauthentic ethical modes, especially regarding principles. Heidegger's authentic-inauthentic distinction is not itself a "moral" construction implying that one should reject the inauthentic. The distinction displays, rather, a multidimensional, "layered" dynamic, that is, movements between radical finitude and presence, between wonder and familiarity, between originary depth and the customary, between individuation and the common. Authenticity is a "modification" of the inauthentic (BTa, 312), not its opposite. Even the climactic "moment of vision" (*Augenblick*) in authentic being-toward-death is just that, *momentary*; the *return* to inauthenticity is a positive part of Dasein's structure (FCM, 295–96).

50. I prefer the notion of "balance" to the Aristotelian conception of a "mean," because the latter is too freighted with exactitude for Aristotle's flexible and variegated analysis of how virtue unfolds in life.

51. For a rich discussion, see Theodore Kisiel, *The Genesis of Heidegger's Being and Time* (Berkeley: University of California Press, 1993), pp. 227–308. One interesting note is that in the Introduction to a proposed book on Aristotle, Heidegger translates *phronêsis* as *fürsorgende Umsicht*, which has clear social implications.

52. See Sections 18–24, which offer a detailed discussion of *phronêsis*.

53. *Parmenides*, translated by André Schuwer and Richard Rojcewicz (Bloomington: Indiana University Press, 1992), pp. 118–23.

54. If I experience pleasure in helping others or some vexation in a sacrifice I might make, such bearings would be problematical only for polarized conceptions of ethical regard.

55. The latter, of course, was Nietzsche's target in his critique of pity.

56. Here we notice a link to the Kantian principle of respect that allows people their freedom. See *Basic Problems of Phenomenology*, Section 13, where Heidegger analyzes Kant's notion of respect as a double-directed striving that exhibits a simultaneous attraction and repulsion. For extended discussions of the prospects for ethics in

light of Heidegger's response to Kant, see two works by Frank Shalow: *Imagination and Existence: Heidegger's Retrieval of the Kantian Ethic* (Lanham, Md.: University Press of America, 1986) and *The Renewal of the Heidegger-Kant Dialogue: Action, Thought, and Responsibility* (Albany: State University of New York Press, 1992).

57. It is well known that people who work in highly charged environments such as emergency rooms have to develop certain strategies of distancing to ward off emotional overload.

58. Werner Marx, in *Towards a Phenomenological Ethics: Ethics and the Life-World*, translated by Stefaan Heyvaert (Albany: State University of New York Press, 1992), suggests an ethical basis in compassion born out of mortality, which certainly accords with my analysis. But he also talks about a person developing a compassion for all humanity, an "all-pervading force that is alive in his overall relation to world, fellow-man, and community" (p. 140). This is way overblown, I think, and it needs to be subjected to a Nietzschean suspicion. Nevertheless, a limited empathic circle can be widened somewhat, because often it is simply absence or distance that creates indifference. Strategies of exposure often can instigate an empathic nearness that spawns an otherwise dormant ethical motivation. One of the virtues of Heidegger's conception of correlative presence and absence with respect to the self is that we are never fully present to each other, or even to ourselves, and this works against closure in all of its forms, especially in oneself. It makes possible a cultivation of openness that can have ethical implications, that is, a disposition of expansiveness, an openness to "more," to novelty and otherness, which can be productive of relatedness without collapsing into conditions of "unity" that betray their own modes of closure. The repudiation of full presence also implies a kind of humility in ethics, in that one does not possess a clear and transparent sense of being perfectly right.

Part V

Heidegger and the
Contemporary Ethos

17

Nihilism and Its Discontents

Thomas Sheehan

Although they mature in his later years, Heidegger's reflections on nihilism lie at the heart of his thought and inform his relation to practical philosophy throughout his career, from his early discussion of tool use in *Sein und Zeit*, through his engagement with Nazism in the 1930s, and up to his postwar discussions of technology. This chapter offers a reading of Heidegger on nihilism and technology that differs markedly from much of the literature on the subject. I conceive of it as a philosophical propaedeutic to understanding not only Heidegger's political error of 1933 but also the continuing danger of such mistakes today.[1]

I. Overcoming Nihilism?

Do we live in the age of fulfilled nihilism? If so, can we overcome such nihilism?

These two questions inform the extraordinary open letter that Martin Heidegger published in 1955 in a *Festschrift* celebrating Ernst Jünger's sixtieth birthday.[2] Heidegger's letter was written in response to an essay that Jünger had contributed six years earlier, in 1949, to a *Festschrift* on Heidegger's own sixtieth birthday, so there was a certain reciprocity in the exchange: a favor returned, a public gesture of respect mirroring an earlier one.

But Heidegger's letter was more than a cordial gesture toward an old friend. It was above all a philosophical engagement with the person who had inspired Heidegger in the late 1920s with his essay "*Totale Mobilmachung*" and with his book *Der Arbeiter*, published in 1932, the year before Hitler took power. These works had opened doors for Heidegger onto such themes as nihilism, technology, and *Gestell*, and since Jünger had raised some of these issues in his 1949 essay, Heidegger took the occasion to address them and, in the process, to reevaluate his intellectual relationship to Jünger.

To return to our two questions: at first glance it seems that, *ex professo*, Heideggerians would agree that we do live in the age of fulfilled nihilism—manifest in the dominance of technology—and that it is both desirable and possible that such techno-nihilism be overcome. According to this view, the long "history of being" has culmi-nated in the triumph of τέχνη over φύσις, the hegemony of the man-made over the natural. In the process, "being" seems to disappear, to count for nothing, to amount to *nihil*, a "negative nothing" (GA 9, 415.5;P, 313.35), hence, the age of complete ni-hilism. It is not that all forms of being (*das Sein des Seienden*) have disappeared (that is impossible, since as long as there are human beings, there will be being, and even ni-hilism is a formation of being). But the most fundamental kind—φύσις/nature, which underlies all other modes of being—seems to have been obliterated by those who stamp everything with their own Gestalt, turn all entities into reproductions of human will, and thus reduce the being of entities to the state of having-been-produced. In this reading, techno-nihilism means the effective death of nature. In place of φύσις—being that rises up of its own accord—nowadays the being of entities is virtually an artifact: it become entities' unlimited intelligibility and availability for production. Entities *are* whatever human beings would make of them.

Heideggerians who hold this position argue that we no longer live in a natural world that is moved from within by φύσις but in an artificial world frenetically pro-pelled from without by τέχνη into whatever human beings want it to be. The world is too much with us—in fact, it *is* us, the theater of our mirrored selves: "Think you're escaping and run into yourself."[3] The universe of modernity is a hermetically sealed world that reflects modern human subjectivity as much as the cosmos of Augustine and Aquinas reflected divine subjectivity. For those medieval philosophers, each en-tity had its being to the degree that it stood before God's mind and was held in exis-tence by his divine vision: "We see these the things you made because they exist; however, they exist only because you see them" [*Confessions* XII, 38 (52)]. Each entity was stamped into existence by God and had being to the degree that it was a reflec-tion of his own divine ideas, the *rationes aeternae*. But today, due to the power of tech-nology, this hermetically sealed world is no longer divine but human. It is referred back to ourselves, and we seem to meet nothing but ourselves *qua* producers extrap-olated into our products (GA 9, 407.12–13;P, 307.34–35). Thus the correlative of techno-nihilism is "humanism," the belief that human being is fulfilled in abetting the limitless availability of everything that is.

Based on this account, it seems that we do live in the age of fulfilled nihilism, in which the power of being is reduced to the power of human labor under Vico's rubric, *verum et factum convertuntur*.[4] Therefore, the task of Heidegger's philosophy would be to "annihilate nihilism," to overcome it by drastically limiting the power and reach of technology and making room again for nature. It seems we should turn our backs on industrialization, techno-science, the exploitation of the earth, and first of all on the rationality that drives them. We should strive to preserve ourselves from the ravages of city life and return to nature, the way Heidegger himself did by taking refuge in his simple hut in the Black Forest. Is that not the case Heidegger is arguing? Is this not why he threw his weight behind the Nazis in the 1930s? And even if his political choice was wrong, was not at least his philosophical motive commendable?

Let us see if that is so. The essay Jünger published in Heidegger's honor had been entitled "*Über die Linie*," roughly, "Across the Line." There Jünger had discussed how, with the end of World War II, Western humanity seemed to be crossing a line from nihilism into a new age when *das Sein selbst*, being-itself, was beginning once again to "turn toward" human beings and put an end to their homelessness. Jünger called this hoped-for future event *die Zuwendung des Seins*, the turning of being toward human beings, and in that phrase we might think we hear an echo of Heidegger's own language and thought. But not so. When he responded to Jünger's essay in 1955, Heidegger subtly (and sometimes not so subtly) rewrote Jünger's essay and reinscribed it, much transformed, into Heidegger's own quite different understanding of nihilism and the possibility of "overcoming" it.

Fifteen years earlier, during his 1940 seminar on the *Physics*, Heidegger had shown how Aristotle, in taking up the doctrine of the fifth-century Eleatic Sophist, Antiphon, had radically reinterpreted that doctrine by quietly incorporating it as *Unwesen* into his own vision of *Wesen* (GA 9, 294.1–7;P, 224.27–32). Something similar can be said of Heidegger's open letter of 1955, in which Jünger's earlier essay is quietly appropriated as an understandable but finally inadequate "shadow" of the essential issue. Heidegger takes almost all of the major topics that Jünger had expounded and inverts them, corrects them, or takes them beyond themselves. He transforms Jünger's *Überwindung* into a *Verwindung*; his "topography" into a "topology"; his "line" into a "zone." Above all, he shows Jünger's central thesis about a future *Zuwendung des Seins* to be an illusion: we should await no such future moment when being would "turn toward" human beings—because, he says, being is always already a *Zuwendung zum Menschenwesen*.

Heidegger's transformation of Jünger begins at the very top of the piece. Jünger had called his essay *Über die Linie*, and Heidegger gives his open letter the same title, except that he adds a set of quotation marks around the noun and thereby changes the meaning: *Über "die Linie.*" The preposition *über* can mean both "over"/"across" (Latin, *trans*) and "concerning" (Latin, *de*). Jünger had used it in the first sense, "Crossing the Line" (from nihilism to being), whereas Heidegger's quotation marks transform the title from *trans lineam* to *de linea*—*Über "die Linie,*" that is, "What about this 'line'?" This alteration effects an important shift of horizon and allows Heidegger to propose a different kind of question. The purpose of his open letter, he writes, is to take everything Jünger has to say and elevate it to the level of "a higher ambiguity that lets us experience to how the overcoming of nihilism requires that we take the turn into the essence of nihilism, at which point the desire to overcome becomes no longer tenable" (GA 9, 424.10–14;P, 320.34–37). Jünger's hope of overcoming nihilism is here cut short. Heidegger is making no predictions that techno-nihilism will ever be overcome. What counts for him, rather, is a new awareness and acceptance of *essential* nihilism. The only kind of "overcoming" that interests him is, he says, that whereby "the *essence* of the nothing, in its former kinship with 'being,' can arrive and be accommodated among us mortals" (GA 9, 410.4-6;P, 310.1-3, emphasis added).

In the 1930s, Heidegger (not unlike Jünger) had hoped that National Socialism would provide solutions to the problem of planetary nihilism, and he implied that his own philosophy might have served as the ideological superstructure of such changes. By the 1950s, however, it would appear that he was convinced that a more profound understanding of the *essence* of nihilism invalidated such naïve hopes for a remedy. Heidegger's point hangs on the distinction between

1. the essence of nihilism—the essential *nihil* that is the necessary condition for any understanding of the being of entities to take place; and

2. the historical and cultural phenomenon called "nihilism"—here, techno-nihilism—which Heidegger claims is the result of overlooking or forgetting that essential *nihil*.

Heidegger's focus on the essence of nihilism is the reason he changed the title of his open letter one last time, not simply by inserting quotation marks into Jünger's title but by directly declaring what he thought was at stake in nihilism. When he published his text as a separate pamphlet in 1956, Heidegger entitled it *Zur Seinsfrage*, as if to say the question of nihilism must be brought back to the question of being. But, for Heidegger, "being" denotes something very different from the traditional meaning of the word. In his Preface to the pamphlet, he writes: "The new title is meant to indicate that this reflection on the essence of nihilism stems from a clarification of being as ~~Being~~" (GA 9, 385.5-7;P, 291.7-9). The cross-out indicates that this ~~Being~~ is nothing entitative: it most emphatically does not refer to the being of entities (their whatness, thatness, and howness), which is the traditional topic of metaphysics. Rather, this ~~Being~~ refers to *what makes possible* the being of entities and one's relation to it. Insofar as it is nothing entitative, Heidegger crosses it out (~~Being~~), or calls it "the nothing," the essential *nihil*. ~~Being~~ is just one more name for Heidegger's central topic. ~~Being~~ = *Welt* = *Da* = *Ereignis* = *Lichtung* = the essential *nihil* = *die Sache selbst*. Thus the sentence above, from Heidegger's Preface to *Zur Seinsfrage*, sets our task:

1. to clarify ~~Being~~, that which makes possible all forms of the being of entities;

2. to clarify "essential nihilism" (the essential *nihil*); and

3. to decide whether techno-nihilism can be overcome.

In what follows I focus on Heidegger rather than Jünger, not simply because Heidegger is philosophically more interesting but also because Jünger himself eventually conceded Heidegger's points.[5] Moreover, I also propose to read the Heidegger of *Zur Seinsfrage* as he demanded (rightly or wrongly) to be read, namely, as *homo philosophicus* rather than as *homo politicus*, that is, as a thinker about Being rather than as the conservative German nationalist who inserted himself dramatically and disastrously into politics more than two decades before he published this essay. It is not that I think we should refrain from reading Heidegger politically—far from it. But regardless of whether one believes Heidegger's postwar *apologia* for his political engagement, regardless of whether one thinks he was amazingly naïve in how he understood German politics in the 1930s and world politics right up until his death, Heidegger did in fact insist to the bitter end that his reasons for supporting National Socialism had to do with his hope of overcoming nihilism and tempering the effects of technology. He claimed that we could understand his political "error" (as he called it) only if we first understood what he thought about nihilism and technology. Taking Heidegger at his word, one might argue (as I emphatically do not) that in his laudable efforts to overcome techno-nihilism he may have picked the wrong party, but at least he intended the right goal and therefore that even as we criticize him for the former, we should join him in pursuing the latter.

However that may be, I propose to investigate nihilism and technology on Heidegger's own terms and to bracket for now the political implications of his philosophy. My focus is on how he transformed Jünger's hope for an *Überwindung* of nihilism into his own vision of a *Verwindung*, a "freeing" of oneself from such nihilism by seeing its rootedness in a deeper, and an unsurpassable "essential nihilism" which is, in fact, the human condition (GA 9, 425.15;P, 321.28).

To repeat, are we in the age of fulfilled nihilism? And if so, can we overcome it? There may well be other, more direct and fruitful ways of broaching these two questions, but for now let us follow Socrates' suggestion that questions of "how to?" follow from questions of "what is?" (*Meno* 70a, 86c, 100b). Let us test Heidegger's thesis that reflecting on the essence of nihilism by reflecting on what makes possible the understanding of being will help us decide whether or not techno-nihilism can be overcome.

II. Horizon and Method

First, a remark on the horizon within which Heidegger's reflections in *Zur Seinsfrage* move. As we would expect from this thinker of "one thing only," whatever Heidegger has to say about nihilism is bound up with what he has to say about Being. Thus we must "reduce" the question of nihilism to the question of Being.

Being, we have said, is not the being of entities but what makes that possible. More accurately (since the being of entities never shows up except in correlation to human understanding), Being is what makes possible the *conjunction* of understanding and the being of things. Thus insofar as it makes possible the presence of things to human understanding, ~~Being~~ is ἐπέκεινα τῆς οὐσίας, beyond or other than being.[6]

We also said that "~~Being~~" is only one term among many for Heidegger's central topic. In other texts he calls this topic "being-itself" or "being-as-such" (in contrast to the being of entities). In his later years he preferred to call it *Lichtung* and *Ereignis*. All of these terms are about the "open" (*das Offene*), which is Heidegger's principal name for "the thing itself." "The open" also is the proper translation of "the *Da*" of *Dasein*, the prior and necessary condition for understanding the being of whatever-is. Heidegger's central question is focused exclusively on this "open" and how it gets opened up.

If there is a shade of difference between *Ereignis* and *Lichtung*, it is that *Ereignis* is the process, and *Lichtung* is the result. *Ereignis* is the opening up of the open, and *Lichtung* is the open that gets opened up. Taken together, this opening-of-the-open is what must already be the case if we are to perceive that anything *is* at all, *is this or that*, and is in *this or that way*—the thatness, whatness, and howness (= the being) of things.

Ereignis/Lichtung is not some supervenient power ("Big Being") that works upon *Dasein* from without. Rather, *Ereignis/Lichtung* names the Ur-fact that human beings are thrown out of immediacy and into discursiveness, so that worlds of possible significance are engendered and sustained. That is:

1. The finitude or relative lack-in-being that defines our essence

2. is responsible for the non-self-coincidence and thus the temporality of our being

3. and opens a space of finite presence within our being—*Da* or *Lichtung*, the realm of the "as" (i.e., of dif-ference and possible relations),

4. thanks to which entities can be taken *as* this or that and thus be understood in their current mode of being.

Under techno-nihilism, on the other hand, this Ur-fact gets overlooked and seems to disappear or "turn away." In taking things *as* this or that, and thus encountering them in their being, people might think they are meeting—presuppositionlessly—nothing but their own man-made purposes and intelligibilities, their Gestalt as "worker" locked into correlativity with "the total work-character" of everything that is (GA 9, 389.28, 402.5–5;P, 294.30, 304.2–3). On this account the crux of historical-cultural nihilism is the correlativity—in fact, the direct proportionality—between the self-assertion of the technological self as worker-dominating-the-world and the "withdrawal of ~~Being~~," (i.e., the apparent disappearance of the open as the source of all understanding of being).

But is this really so? Granted the correlativity of worker and product (i.e., of productive subjectivity and its realms of objectivity), why must the intensification of this correlativity stand in inverse proportion to awareness of the open? Why must there be a zero-sum game between the growing power of the worker and the awareness of *Ereignis/Lichtung*? These are the questions we shall examine in what follows.

If the horizon of Heidegger's discourse on nihilism is the "question of ~~Being~~," his usual μέθοδος for approaching nihilism is by *Seinsgeschichte*, the history of the ways that the open, along with the forms of being it makes possible, has been "given" from archaic Greece up to the epoch of planetary technology. Since that road is long and winding, I propose to follow not Heidegger's historical μέθοδος but a more analytical ἀτραπός, a "shortcut" that gets to the heart of the matter by raising the question of τέχνη and technology.

The shortcut consists of investigating τέχνη in light of the question of ~~Being~~ (the inquiry into the open), which means investigating it in conjunction with the notion of φύσις. Here I shall use Heidegger's reflections on Aristotle's *Physics* as a guide to understanding the alleged hegemony of the "Gestalt of the worker" in the present age (GA 9, 239–301;P, 183–230). The first step (Section III) will be to get clear on the three presuppositions that Heidegger thinks inform the text of *Physics*, B, 1. Those presuppositions, in turn, will lead us to the Greek vision of being and time as Heidegger understands that (Sections IV and V), and therefore to the fulfillment of that Greek vision in the finite infinity of the availability of things in the current epoch (Section VI). All of this will allow us to decide whether or not techno-nihilism can be overcome (Section VII).

III. Three Presuppositions: φύσις, κίνησις, φαίνεσθαι

The first presupposition that governs Aristotle's text on φύσις (*Physics* B, 1) is what I call a thoroughgoing naturalism—but in the Greek rather than the modern sense of the word. This "Greek naturalism" entails that absolutely everything that is, insofar as it is, is in an essential sense a natural entity. It has its being from and because of φύσις and therefore is moved καθ' αὐτό, of and by itself. Before φύσις designates a determined region of entities (growing things as contrasted to artifacts), it refers to the whole of reality and names the in-itself-ness of every entity.[7]

But this characterization is still too formal. It begins to take on specificity and content only when we note a second presupposition that is intimately bound up with the first. Accompanying this thoroughgoing naturalism, and in fact defining it, is an equally thoroughgoing "kineticism." For Aristotle, as for the archaic Greeks, φύσις is the ἀρχὴ κινήσεως, the principle of intrinsic movement, its origin and ongoing ordering force, which I shall call "self-movement" (κίνησις καθ' αὐτό). To say that absolutely everything that is, insofar as it is, is a φύσει ὄν (an entity of-and-by-φύσις) is to assert: (1) that every entity as such is intrinsically in movement (*Physics*, A, 2, 185 a 12), where this "self-movement" means movement *into appearance* (see below); and (2) that every entity, to the degree that it is a φύσει ὄν, has within itself the origin and directing of its own movement.

It is true, of course, that from the very first sentence of *Physics* B, 1 (192 b 8–11) Aristotle divides all entities into "those that are of-and-by φύσις" and "those that are of-and-by other causes." That is, he divides entities into (1) those that have been moved into their current shape and appearance from *within* themselves and (2) those that have been moved into their current form from *without*. These latter are ποιούμενα, or artifacts, things produced through the know-how of an artisan, the τέχνη of a τεχνίτης. Entities are divided, therefore, into φυσικά and ποιούμενα, according to whether they are intrinsically or extrinsically moved into their current appearance.

But even the artifact is made of a natural substrate. Thus even when we understand some entities as artifacts, we also co-understand them as artifacts made *of* some natural stuff and to that degree as self-moved entities, φύσει ὄντα. We evidence that co-understanding when, for example, we look at an old, beautifully crafted table and say, "Now *that* is wood!"—by which we mean something like, "This artifact shows us what wood really is and can be used for." Or for a nonlinguistic example, there is Antiphon's experiment: bury that same table in your backyard, wait a long time until it rots and germinates, and then check what comes up. The seedling will be the start not of a table but of wood.[8]

As Heidegger reads Aristotle, the self-movement of natural entities is not movement in any of the usual senses: locomotion, qualitative, or quantitative motion, or even coming-into-existence. Rather, the entity's self-movement is its *self-presentation*, its appearing-at-all and its appearing-as-this-or-that.[9] Here we encounter yet a third presupposition that underlies *Physics* B, 1, one that ties φύσις and κίνησις into what may be called, at least provisionally, Greek "phenomenology." Everything that is, to the degree that it is at all (and thus is natural and self-moving), is a process of *coming into appearance*, becoming accessible, engageable, intelligible. This is what the Greeks called φαίνεσθαι, the process of becoming a φαινόμενον.

As a unity, these three presuppositions—φύσις, κίνησις, and φαίνεσθαι, the natural movement of self-presentation—are the structure of what Heidegger calls the intrinsic disclosedness of entities, their ἀλήθεια. In Heidegger's view, there are three levels of disclosure, ranging backward from the most derivative to the most fundamental. (The natural-kinetic-phenomenological presuppositions we have been discussing operate primarily on the *second* level of disclosedness.)

ἀλήθεια₃   truth in the usual sense of the correspondence or *adaequatio* of propositions and states of affairs

ἀλήθεια₂   truth as the intrinsic disclosedness or intelligibility of an entity, according to Aristotle's dictum, "The degree of εἶναι a thing has is the degree of ἀλήθεια it has," which finds a weak echo in the medieval *verum et esse convertuntur*[10]

ἀλήθεια₁   truth in the fundamental sense of the "opened-up open" (the *Da* or *Lichtung*) that allows for all significance and thus for both the disclosedness of entities (ἀλήθεια₂) and the correctness of statements (ἀλήθεια₃)

Heidegger argues that for ancient Greek thinkers, and especially for the pre-Socratics, the words φύσις and ἀλήθεια did not name the being or οὐσία of entities, their stable and constant presence to human engagement. That would be the case with Plato and Aristotle, the philosophers of οὐσία par excellence. But if οὐσία in Plato and Aristotle is about the *presence* of entities to human engagement, φύσις and ἀλήθεια in the pre-Socratics hint at a prior *absence* (the open), which, compared to the presence of entities, is a unique kind of *nihil*. That is why, in Heidegger's eyes, the archaic Greek thinkers rank a cut above the philosophers of οὐσία: they at least are aware of and name the *source* of οὐσία, even though they operate mostly on the level of ἀλήθεια₂, without thematizing ἀλήθεια₁. Hence the need for the explicit retrieval and thematic articulation of ἀλήθεια₁ (*die Sache selbst*, τὸ πρᾶγμα αὐτό,[11] which Heidegger believed his thought provided.

All of this is commonplace in the Heideggerian literature today, as is the groundedness of the three levels of disclosure in temporality. *Sein und Zeit* argues that temporality makes possible all disclosure. The relation of temporality (*Zeitlichkeit*) to ἀλήθεια₂, and ἀλήθεια₃ is one of grounding to grounded, whereas, at the fundamental level of ἀλήθεια₁ temporality is the very structure of the open.

But Heidegger speaks not simply of *Zeitlichkeit* but also of the *Zeitigung* of *Zeitlichkeit*, one of his earliest names for *Ereignis*, the opening of the open. Unfortunately, the English translations of *Sein und Zeit* miss this crucial connection. The Macquarrie-Robinson edition misleadingly renders *Zeitigung* as "temporalizing" (BTa, 278.17), and Professor Stambaugh's version (BTb, 217.13 *et passim*) carries over this non-starter as "temporalization."

1. *Zeitigung* (literally "maturation" or "blossoming": γένεσις) would be more accurately translated as the "generation" or "coming-to-be" of *Zeitlichkeit*. Heidegger made the point in 1963: "*Zeitigung as Sich-zeitigen* means self-unfolding, emerging, and thus appearing. The Latin *natura* comes from *nasci*, 'to be born.' The Greek φύσις comes from φύειν and means 'emerging' in the sense of coming out of concealment into the unconcealed."[12]

2. But the temporality thus generated—the dif-ference, or *distentio*, within the essence of human being—constitutes the very openness of the open.[13]

3. Thus *Zeitigung* (the generation of temporality) = *Ereignis* (the opening up of the open). The resultant ἀλήθεια₁ is what makes possible both the self-presentation of entities in correlation with human powers of engagement (ἀλήθεια₂) and the correct correspondence of propositions with states of affairs (ἀλήθεια₃).

In other words, *Zeitigung* as the generation of *Zeitlichkeit* makes possible φαίνεσθαι, the appearing of a φαινόμενον in correlation with the human powers of perception and action. Hence, what we have been calling the "phenomenological" presupposition of Greek thought (ἀλήθεια₂) rests on a more fundamental "aletheiological" presupposition (ἀλήθεια₁).

We may now take the next step. Heidegger finds the three presuppositions that underlie *Physics* B, 1—naturalism, kineticism, and phenomenology—packed into the single phrase that, for him, captures both the essence of Greek ontology and the origin of techno-nihilism. Plato and Aristotle, he says, understood reality in terms of οὐσία, *beständiges Anwesen*.[14] It is these two words, *Anwesen* and *beständig*, that we must carefully unpack if we are to get to the heart of Heidegger's interpretation of nihilism.

In the usual interpretation, *das beständige Anwesen* is an entity's "stable and constant presence," where "presence" always means "presence-unto-possible-human-engagement" and, hence, "intelligibility" in the broad sense. As far as it goes, this translation is correct. But the English here misses the richness of the Greek phrase that underlies it: ἡ ἀΐδιη οὐσία. More important, the translation misses the interplay of being and time that is at work in the Greek phrase. In the next two sections, we shall consider the "Greek" relation of being and time, first by treating the being-aspect under the rubric of *Anwesen*/οὐσία (Section IV) and then the time-aspect under the rubric of *beständig*/ἀεί (Section V).

IV. Anwesen/οὐσία

Anwesen translates οὐσία and thus refers to the "self-presentation," whereby entities become intelligible to human beings. Heidegger makes this clear in his 1955 letter when he argues against Jünger's hope for a future "turning" (*Zuwendung*) of being toward human beings, as if this happened only occasionally. Heidegger makes it clear that being is *nothing but* turnedness-to-human-beings. "Presumably this turn to [human beings], even if it is still veiled, is the very thing we confusedly and vaguely call 'being'" (GA 9, 407.3–5;P, 307.26–28). Indeed, "Presence ('being') as presence is always and in each case presence unto the human essence" (GA 9, 408.22–23;P, 308.35–36). Thus, "We always say *too little* about 'being-itself' when, in saying 'being,' we omit its presence *unto* the human *essence* and thereby fail to see that this [human] essence itself co-constitutes 'being'" (GA 9, 407.22–25;P, 308.3–6).

We must take these assertions as straightforwardly as Heidegger puts them. Being occurs only in and with the essence of human beings, but being is the presence of entities as this or that. Therefore, all forms of the being-of-entities are forms of the presence of entities *to* and *for* human beings.

This presence-to-human-being is not something added on to entities; rather, to be an entity is to be always within the range of possible human engagement. For the

Greeks this is the source of the "wonder" that initiates philosophy: entities *can be engaged*, they are ontologically κατ' ἄνθρωπον, "ad hominem." This is what Heidegger means by saying that the essence of a phenomenon is "to come into unconcealment," "to be disclosed," "to stand forth in the open," and other such ways of discussing ὄν ὡς ἀληθές. Entities are intrinsically open to what the Greeks called νοῦς/νοεῖν, and therefore are νοητά (intelligible), always already correlative to a possible human νόησις.The theme recurs frequently in Heidegger's thought in the 1950s. In the spring of 1951, for instance, he told the students: "If the Greeks understand the presence [of entities] as εἶδος, and if εἶδος is thought of as an essential trait of φυσις, then this entails that presence is a relatedness to human beings."[15]

And just as this ad-hominem status is essential to entities, so likewise openness to entities—the ability of human νοεῖν to engage and know them—is essential to human being. It is this correlativity and reciprocity that Heidegger finds named in Parmenides' Fragment 5, in the τό αάτό (the "gathered-together-ness") of νοεῖν and εἶναι, a phrase echoed in Aristotle as the "sameness" that gathers together ἐπιστήμη and πρᾶγμα in actual knowledge.[16]

Recognizing the correlativity of ὄν ᾗ ὄν with human praxis, production, and thinking (what Husserl calls the "phenomenological reduction") is the first step toward asking what brings about that correlativity at all (the "transcendental reduction"). This is the question to which we now turn. How is the correlativity constituted?

The process whereby entities become humanly engageable—*Anwesung*—does not happen in entities themselves apart from human beings, nor is it superveniently ordained from beyond the human world. Rather, it occurs only with human beings and in the midst of their world. The opening of the open is precisely what brings about the "gathering-together" of εἶναι and νοεῖν. This is what Heidegger called "the wonder of all wonders,"[17] not transcendental consciousness, as in Husserl, but *Ereignis*, the intrinsic opening of the human essence so that entities can be seen *as* this or that and as engageable by a reciprocally disposed νοεῖν. By this intrinsic opening (*Zeitigung/Ereignis*, which happens only with human beings), entities are usable and knowable in praxis, discourse, and thought. *Ereignis* is what makes entities *innerweltlich*, or "innerworldly."

At the "innocent" dawn of Greek–Western history, this correlativity between human beings and the being of entities is the basis for what is altogether too loosely called Greek "humanism." Such humanism (if we may apply this much later term to archaic and classical Greece) is not first of all a celebration of the beauties of the human or a Promethean self-assertion, whereby humans take themselves as the measure of all things. Yes, such self-assertion is a possible element of Greek humanism, maybe an inevitable consequence of it, and arguably even one of its positive achievements—but not its basis.

Prior to such self-assertion there rules the fact that entities, insofar as they are, are open to human νοεῖν, are intrinsically accessible, engageable and (to take Heidegger's term *innerweltlich* in its broad and proper sense) ultimately "humanizable."

The grounds for Greek humanism are ontological, not anthropological, and they lie in the a priori correlativity that governs the openness of human beings and the "humanizability" of entities. And if Heidegger has any criticism of this Greek humanism, it is simply that it did not adequately thematize the *source* of this correlativity, the prior Ur-fact of the opening/*Ereignis*.

The human being is νοητικός (Latin: *intelligens*) in the sense of being-in-the-world and able to have access to something only mediately (i.e., *as* something). And entities are νοητά (Latin: *intelligibilia*) in the sense of falling within-world (i.e., within the province of νοῦς) and only thus able to be engaged *as* something. On the one hand, inasmuch as the open makes possible the presence of things to human beings, things themselves are "turned toward" possible human engagement. On the other hand, inasmuch as the human essence *is* the open and also "co-constitutes being,"[18] humans have access to everything that is insofar as it is. These two potentialities—the unlimited ability to know, and the unlimited ability to be known—are a priori correlative, and their correlativity is finally grounded in the Ur-fact of human finitude.

At the other end of Greek–Western history, where things are no longer so "innocent" (in this regard, Heidegger speaks of "an extraordinary danger"[19]), we see the historical outcome of this Greek humanism in the virtual inevitability of the current age of technology, rooted in that same τὸ αὐτό. Insofar as the essence of entities entails their presence to human engagement, it also entails that they are disposed to be picked up and used, to be reshaped as ποιούμενα—and endlessly so. The unlimited accessibility of the real lies at the core of the Greek-Western vision of being, which from the pre-Socratics up through Heidegger has affirmed the infinity of the intelligibility and transformability of τὸ ὄν, an infinity that is correlative to the infinite reach of νοῦς. Nor does this affirmation of infinite intelligibility necessarily depend on an entity (God) in which everything is already fully known.[20] A bad infinity will do.

Can we really include Heidegger in this vision? Yes, certainly. For if ἀλήθεια always entails the ad-hominem status and intrinsic accessibility of entities, the λήθη-dimension of ἀλήθεια most emphatically does not indicate a point where such accessibility supposedly runs out. Rather, to put it formally, the λήθη names the unsurpassable fact of such accessibility, or to put it materially, the λήθη names the lack-in-being or finitude that opens up the open. This finitude, by generating the openness wherein entities can appear *as* this or that, makes possible an infinity of significance. There is no end to the human reach into entities, even if this infinite reach is finally rooted in an unexplainable finitude. The λήθη entails the endless availability of the real, but "without [an ultimate] why."

Thus we would be doing "being" no favors if we just let entities "be" in the sense of leaving them pristine and untouched, perhaps even unknown. The proper way to let entities *be* is to let them *be present*, that is, to let them be endlessly engageable. And we do that by endlessly *engaging* them, both scientifically and practically, and, yes, by letting them be submitted to the domination of the worker in the inevitable humanization of nature and naturalization of the human. If one follows Heidegger's thinking consistently (not to mention the facts), there is no escape from this humanization/naturalization, no nostalgia for a time "before" humanity allegedly crossed the line into "too much" τέχνη, and no hope for a new age when the balance might shift back in favor of nature. Or better, if there *is* such nostalgia and hope, it has nothing to do with Heidegger's philosophy. At its worst, it is a matter of bad faith, an index of inauthenticity and flight, a refusal to accept the historical fate of Greek–Western existence that is captured in Parmenides' word τὸ αὐτό.

In Heidegger's view, the current age of technology follows from the fact that the being of entities has always been experienced as *Anwesen*, their "presence-unto" human being, all the way from archaic Greek φύσις through classical Greek οὐσία, right down to Jünger's notion of production (GA 9, 400.20-22;P, 302.35-36). Hence, planetary technology is not only inevitable but also unsurpassable—for it is empowered by the ontological *nihil* (the open), which cannot be overcome at all.

V. Beständig/ἀεί

The adjective *beständig*—the other word in Heidegger's key phrase "*das beständige Anwesen*"—points to the question of time. *Beständig* is usually translated as either "stable" or "constant," neither of which, as we shall see, is adequate. What does the adjective *beständig* add to *Anwesen* as "presence-unto"? Is it only a chance addition to the noun, or does it contain the whole secret of the turn into essential nihilism?

Heidegger explains *beständig* by reflecting on the meaning of the Greek adverb ἀει, "eternally," and the adjective ἀΐδιος, "eternal, everlasting." This procedure appears logical enough, for do not stability and constancy necessarily point toward eternity? This has been the mainstream understanding in Western metaphysics. Compare St. Augustine's "*Id enim vere est, quod incommutabiliter manet*" ["What truly is, is what remains unchanging"],[21] and Thomas Aquinas' "*Esse autem est aliquid fixum et quietum in ente*" ["Being is something unmoving and at rest in an entity"].[22] But it does not work that way for Heidegger.

Heidegger's explanation of ἀει and *beständig* comes in his commentary on *Physics* B, 1 at the point[23] where Aristotle establishes the priority of μορφή over ὕλη by rejecting what Heidegger calls the "materialism" of the Sophist Antiphon, a materialism that, interestingly enough, was intimately bound up with Antiphon's radical repudiation of τέχνη. In anticipation, we may say: Antiphon saw the constancy of presence as the hallmark of the "really real" and thus as the touchstone for discerning what is truly φύσις. In this way, Antiphon does offer an escape from τέχνη. He suggests that, yes, insofar as we are human, we must unfortunately live with τέχνη; however, insofar as we are philosophers, we must be ever in retreat from τέχνη toward φύσις. And is that not Heidegger's program as well?

In his fragmentary work ᾽Αλήθεια,[24] Antiphon puts forth the thesis that what most deserves the name φύσις is the primary and least shaped elemental matter—

τὸ ἀρρύθμιστον πρῶτον: earth, water, air, and fire—rather than (1) anything, such as iron or wood or flesh, that derives from, or is a reshaping of, those primary elements, and (2) a fortiori anything, such as an artifact, that is even further reshaped from those secondary reshapings. It would be hard to find a more absolute rejection of technology.

The reason Antiphon gives for claiming that only the most basic elements of matter are φύσις is that they are ἀΐδια: they do not change of and by themselves (οὐ γὰρ εἶναι μεταβολὴν αὐτοῖς ἐξ αὐτῶν).[25] From Antiphon's use of the word, which Aristotle apparently accepts, it would seem that ἀΐδιος must mean "eternal" or "everlasting." The most constant and stable would be the unchanging and eternal—ultimately, the divine. And even though Antiphon and Aristotle radically disagree on the *content* of that ultimate entity—"materialistic" in Antiphon's view, "idealistic" in Aristotle's—they would nonetheless agree on its *form*: eternal presence. Antiphon's retreat from human τέχνη in the direction of a chthonic φύσις is a negative mirroring of Aristotle's sublation of human τέχνη in the direction of an Olympian φύσις.

But Heidegger confounds those simple certainties. In showing how that is so, I will not go into the way that Aristotle incorporates Antiphon, as *Unwesen*, into his own interpretation of φύσις (at *Physics* B, 1, 193 a 21–31). (Briefly, we recall that Aristotle "wrests" from Antiphon's ἀρρύθμιστον πρῶτον his own very different notion of πρώτη ὕλη, so-called "prime matter.") Rather, I will present only the gist of Heidegger's reinterpretation of the meaning of ἀεί in that same passage.

Heidegger begins by noting the astonishing ambivalence of the words ἀεί and ἀΐδιος. At one end of the spectrum, these two words can mean "forever," with all of the connotations of eternity and necessity that the word bears: "that which is *always* the case." But at the other end of the spectrum, these words can refer simply to "whatever happens to be the case at a given time," as in Herodotus' ὁ αἰεί βασιλεύων, "the currently ruling king,"[26] or Aeschylus' ὁ ἀεί κρατῶν, "whoever is ruler" (*Prometheus Bound*, 937f., a phrase that David Grene masterfully renders as "whatever king is king today").[27]

The same ambivalence is found in the English word "ever" that we use in translating ἀεί and ἀΐδιος. On the one hand, "ever" can mean "always" and "eternally," with overtones of necessity (like the Latin *ne-cesse*, "not yielding or withdrawing," from *ne* + *cedo*). On the other hand, the word can refer to any specific and nonperduring occasion: "Did you ever see so-in-so?" This latter meaning continues in the suffix of words such as "whoever," "whenever," and the adverb "however," where it has the sense of "any at all, from among infinite possibilities" (as in the aforementioned phrase from Herodotus), a meaning certainly quite removed from any notion of eternity or necessity.

Ἀΐδιος and "ever" can, of course, have the sense of "perpetual" or "eternal." Plato, for example, speaks of ἡ ἀΐδη οὐσία, "eternal being," and Aristotle discusses ἀΐδιος βασιλεία, "perpetual monarchy."[28] However, the words ἀΐδιος and "ever" do not necessarily refer to time and, above all, need not indicate eternity or endless duration. Heidegger overturns the presumptive meaning of ἀΐδιος when interpreting *das beständige Anwesen* not primarily as constant presence or stable and abiding self-identity but as "*autonomously initiated*" self-presentation. He writes:

> The word ἀεί conveys the notion of "staying for a while," specifically in the sense of "being present." Something is ἀΐδιον if it is present *of and by itself without further assistance*—and for *this* reason, perhaps constantly present. . . . The decisive factor is that whatever properly is, is present *of and by itself* and therefore is encountered as what in each case is *already* there in front of you— ὑποκείμενον πρῶτον. (GA 9, 269.13-16, .30-33;P, 206.2-5, .17-20)

In this remarkable passage, we watch the meaning of *beständiges Anwesen* shift from (1) the temporally perduring ("something constantly present") to (2) the *autonomously and intrinsically present* ("present of and by itself without further assistance"), so that the entity is (3) always *priorly present* ("already there in front of you"). But this "intrinsic, prior presence" is (4) an "intrinsic, prior presence *unto*" human engagement. It is the same as what we saw in investigating *Anwesen*/οὐσία: the "ad-hominem" status of entities, ὄν ὡς ἀληθές. The factor of "alreadiness" in an entity's being "ever-already present and intelligible" indicates not some chronologically prior intelligibility (e.g., "it was intelligible even before human beings came on the scene"), but rather (5) the entity's *intrinsic* intelligibility, the a priori status of its availability for human engagement: *Das beständige Anwesen* = ἀλήθεια₂.

Again, we ask where this apriority resides. In the text above, Heidegger argues that the autonomy and apriority (ἀϊδιότης, or *Beständigkeit*) of an entity's accessibility lie neither in the primacy of entities over human knowing, as in traditional, objectivist metaphysics, nor in the primacy of human knowing over entities, as in modern, subjectivist philosophy. The apriority that interests Heidegger is the correlation of νοεῖν and εἶαι over either of the two correlata. The correlation is grounded in the open, and the open is grounded in human finitude. If there is any necessity, constancy, and stability that "temporally" determines the intelligible presence of entities, it is nothing but the always-alreadiness of the open.

Therefore, the supposed constancy of presence-unto, the ἀεί -factor that serves as the touchstone of οὐσία in the Greek version of "being and time," in no way undoes the ad-hominem status of that presence. In fact, it reconfirms it with the weightiest of inevitabilities. We might have thought that in the φύσις-centered cosmos of Antiphon and Aristotle, the most real instance of reality would be what is most removed from human beings, the unchanging and eternal, in the form of either Antiphon's pretechnological "elemental" (τὸ ἀρρύθμιστον πρῶτον) or Aristotle's meta-technological divine (ὁ θεός). But Heidegger argues that the ruling issue in the analogical structure of being-present is not eternity but the apriority of the correlation between thinking and being—which, at the other end of Greek–Western history, entails the virtual inevitability of the age of technology.

If I have spent so much time on Antiphon's response to the problem of technology, it is because his "solution" is both consonant with, and in fact prototypical of, the Right Heideggerian response to nihilism. The term "Right Heideggerian" goes back to the late 1970s, when it came to be applied to those who argued (1) that being is exhausted in presence, (2) that even the λήθη is an as-yet-hidden presence that might someday emerge from concealment in the "new dawn" of a secular parousia, and (3) that this as-yet-hidden presence could arguably be already present to itself in a transparent *Bei-sich-sein*, not unlike the God whom Thomas Aquinas allegedly experienced in a mystical ecstacy shortly before his death at Fossanova.[29]

In the intervening years, Right Heideggerians have assimilated some of the discourse about the lethic character of and accordingly shifted a bit to the left—while unfortunately continuing to metaphysicize that λήθη into an ultimately unintelligible "X." Having learned something from poststructuralism, and in the process having allegedly disabused themselves of the mythology of a hypostasized λήθη, they end up rewriting that λήθη as an untotalizable (but historically empty) asymmetry bound up with a dehistoricized and an aleatory occurrence of postethical obligation.[30] This limp gesture may be a necessary—but is certainly an insufficient—half-step toward salvaging whatever potential remains in Heidegger's discourse: necessary insofar as it tries to take social obligation seriously, insufficient insofar as it has no demonstrable resources for confronting history, either for understanding it in theory or engaging it in practice. It remains only another and much thinner form of "German ideology."

In the final analysis, the Right Heideggerians have no resources for confronting the question of techno-nihilism. They are just a step away from Antiphon, whose response to τέχνη was to search for something untouched by human beings, a φύσις with as little overlay of τέχνη as possible. Antiphon's strategy was to deny intrinsic reality to ποιούμενα, to retreat from them in the direction of φύσει ὄντα as he searched for a world where being was defined not by history and human action but by unchanging stability. But in Heidegger's telling, Antiphon's strategy is self-contradictory.

First, the supposed eternity or unmovedness of Antiphon's underlying elemental stuff denies the very reality of the φύσις that Antiphon was trying to preserve. Φύσις means the movement of self-presentation, whereas Antiphon's elemental stuff does not move at all, least of all in the direction of engagement by human beings. For Antiphon, any shaping of φύσις into a ποιούμενον is a violation; and to follow this logic to its ultimate conclusions would mean abandoning history, becoming the mad ecologist who has to leave the earth in order to preserve it.

Second, the supposed eternal unmovedness of Antiphon's φύσις also is the guarantee of its pseudo-mysteriousness, its ultimate unknowability. Insofar as φύσις, in Antiphon's scheme of things, does not move at all and keeps entirely to itself, it resists all appearance and escapes behind any attempt to shape it into εἶδος. For Antiphon, the most real is the most unknowable, an "existent" prime matter without form, a "something" without appearance. It is unknowable and thus in effect a nothing. Indeed, Antiphon's φύσις is the forerunner of the Right Heideggerians' λήθη: a something that is really nothing—or better, a nothing that has to be something insofar as it performs such mysterious acts as hiding and revealing itself, withdrawing and dispensing epochs of "being" or inspiring an impotent "obligationism-without-why."

VI. Fulfilled Nihilism: θεολογία

We have considered both terms in the key phrase that, for Heidegger, captures the Greek notion of "being and time," and from either side of *das beständige Anwesen* the conclusion imposes itself: the humanization of the world is inevitable. If *Anwesen* points to the endless engageability of entities, *Beständigkeit* (once freed from its presumed reference to constancy and eternity) reinforces that endlessness by revealing its a priori status. The confluence of these two topics has raised the question of the *source* of this a priori accessibility and offered a hint of what it means to "turn into the essence" of nihilism. We may now take the last step in our ἀτραπός, by tracing the aforementioned three presuppositions back to their natural end, the theological.

We have argued that the classical Greek versions of naturalism, kineticism, and phenomenology entail one another in an intricate perichoresis. According to the first presupposition, everything that is—from the Unmoved Mover, if there is one, down to prime matter if *per impossibile* one could speak of it as existing—is, to one degree or another, φύσις. But this presupposition entails the other two: everything in the world is kinetically self-presentative (ἀληθές), or it is not at all. The degree of that self-presentation is measured by the entity's degree of φύσις, that is, its degree of movement, and specifically its degree of return unto itself.[31] All φύσις, including God, is a ὁδὸς . . . εἰς φύσιν (*Physics* B, 1, 193 b 12), a direct or an indirect, a perfect or an imperfect, *reditio in seipsum*. An imperfect natural entity makes an incomplete return to itself, and a perfect natural entity (if there is one) makes a complete return to itself. This thoroughgoing kineticism of Greek thought is not contradicted by, but rather fulfilled in, the notion of the divine as perfectly at rest in itself (cf. ἐνέργεια ἀκινησίας: Aristotle, *Nicomachean Ethics*, VII, 14, 1154 b 27), insofar as "rest" is understood as the in-gatheredness of motion into its τέλος, and hence is not the opposite of motion but its highest instance.

Perfectly self-coincident in his return to himself, God is the perfection of φύσις/κίνησις/φαίνεσθαι, and as such sets the pattern that is imitated by all lower entities. Thus an entity of incomplete self-return is imperfectly self-presentative and only imperfectly able to know itself. The perfectly natural entity, on the other hand, is one that would be entirely self-present (to itself) and self-presentative (to others), precisely because of its complete return to itself. We may imagine this unity not as a circle as much as a point or dot: pure self-coincidence without remainder. The already achieved self-coincidence of such an entity is what makes it the most intelligible, τὸ μάλιστα ἐπιστητόν (*Metaphysics* A, 1, 982 a 31).

This analogical circumcession of nature, movement, and disclosure informs the exalted vision of human wisdom that is celebrated in the Prooemium to *Metaphysics*, where Aristotle prefaces that vision with a complex *videtur quod non* (nos. 1–7 below), followed by a weighty admonition (no. 7). In what follows, I paraphrase and summarize Aristotle's hypothetical objection (*Metaphysics* A, 1, 982 a 1 to 983 a 1).

1. If it is the case that "σοφία is knowledge of first principles and causes" (983 a 1–3),

2. and if "God is thought by everyone to be one of the causes and a first principle" (983 a 8–9)

3. so that σοφία must necessarily entail knowledge of God (θεολογική),[32]

4. it seems to follow that the transcendent *object* of such knowledge would require an equally transcendent *subject*—in other words, that "God alone would have this privilege" of knowing God (982 b 30–31).

5. Moreover, poets tell us that "the divine is by nature jealous" (982 b 32),

6. and if God is jealous of anything, He would be jealous of His privilege of being the only theologian, the only one to know God himself.

7. Therefore, it seems that human beings would do well to seek only the knowledge that befits their nature, not only because anything else would be unfitting (982 b 31-32), but also because, given God's jealousy, all who excelled in theological knowledge would be δυστυχεῖς, very unlucky indeed (983 a 1).

Thus the hypothetical objection. But Aristotle easily refutes it. Not only is God not jealous ("poets tell many a lie," as he reminds us at 983 a 4–5), but there are more important reasons, relating to φύσις, that should lead us to dismiss the objection. Precisely *when* human beings follow the knowledge that befits their nature, they find themselves on a path that leads toward the divine. In Aristotle's cosmos, where reality is diffused analogically and without rupture, wherever there is human being, there is a natural desire (cf. φύσει at 980 a 22 and 27) to see, know, and imitate God and thus, analogously, to *be* God. Can this desire be fulfilled? While Aristotle does not answer the question unambiguously, he does imply a human participation in the self-knowledge of God, as indeed he must, given the analogical nature of φύσις. He claims that σοφία (ἐπιστήμη θεολογική) is a knowledge that "either God alone can have, or God *above all others*" (983 a 9–10).

Aristotle's claim is momentous. He opened *Metaphysics* with the assertion, "All people by nature desire to know" (980 a 21), and by the second chapter of the Prooemium, we learn that the object of that unlimited desire is God. Human beings can, to some degree, know God the way God knows Himself, because in fact they participate in the same reality as the Divine. But this means that, whether or not the project is ever actually fulfilled, Aristotle has opened up to human beings the *possibility* of the total knowledge (and along with that, the total control) of everything that is. Aristotle's theology is the first technology, and modern technology is only the last theology. The "death of God" begins with the first sentence of the *Metaphysics*, and after that, historical-cultural nihilism will be only a mopping-up exercise. Whether God exists or not, whether God is the object of faith, reason, denial, or indifference, henceforth in post–Aristotelian Western thought, θεός, the highest instance of φύσις, will be a symbol for the goal and scope of technology: the humanization of nature and the naturalization of man. "God" will be the symbol *par excellence* for "*der 'unendlich ferne Mensch.'*"

God as the "infinitely distant human being": with those words, the nihilism born in the theological technology of Aristotle's *Metaphysics* comes to its fullness. The phrase, published posthumously in 1954, had been jotted down sometime between 1934 and 1937 by Edmund Husserl. It is found in an extraordinary passage in his text on the crisis of Western science. There, in reflecting on the modern relation between God, mathematics, and philosophy, and on the grounding of the infinite knownness of the real in God, Husserl had characterized what Heidegger, at about the same time, was beginning to call the fulfilled condition of nihilism.

From its Greek beginnings, Husserl writes, philosophy has pursued the ideal of the complete rationality of the real, ideally expressible in a universal science. However, the fulfillment of that ideal became possible only with the discovery of modern mathematics. "Is not nature in itself thoroughly mathematical?" he asks. "Must it not also be thought of as a coherent mathematical system?"[33] The answer is yes, because in some way the complete mathematical rationality of the world, as a created universe, is grounded in God's achieved comprehension of everything:

> One says to oneself: Compared to the absolute knowledge we ascribe to God the creator, our knowledge in pure mathematics has only one lack, namely, that while it is always absolutely self-evident, it does require a systematic process in order to bring to realization in cognition, i.e., as explicit mathematical knowledge, all the shapes that "exist" in spatiotemporal form. . . . Therefore, when conceived of as ideally complete, the universal science corresponding to the new idea [of rational, scientific philosophy] is nothing but—*omniscience*.[34]

And accompanying this progress in knowledge is a progress in technical mastery:

> Along with our growing and always more perfect cognitive power over the universe, we also achieve an ever more perfect mastery over our practical environment, a mastery that expands in unending progression. . . . Thus we truly are the image and likeness of God. Just as mathematics speaks of infinitely distant

points, straight lines, etc., so analogously one can say metaphorically that God is the "*infinitely distant human being.*"[35]

It would be difficult to find a clearer vision of the "theologian" as mathematicizing technician—or, in this case, as philosopher—marching shoulder to shoulder with Jünger's "worker" into the infinitely distant goal of the God-man. This vision had already begun to come into focus at least a century earlier. David Strauss understood himself to be merely drawing the inevitable conclusion from Hegel when he wrote at the end of *Das Leben Jesu*:

> When we say that God is *Geist* and that humankind is *Geist* as well, it follows that the two are not *per se* distinct. . . . When we ascribe reality to the idea of the unity of divine and human natures, does it mean this unity had to come about only once, in a single individual, and never before or after? [. . . .] Would not the idea of the unity of the divine and human natures be real in a far higher sense [than in traditional Christology] if I conceived *the whole of humankind* as its realization rather than just one individual man?[36]

And Feuerbach, in the first thesis of his *Grundsätze der Philosophie der Zukunft*, reduced the whole of metaphysics (and not merely, as he thought, the program of modernity) to an epigram that might serve as an epitaph: "The task of the modern era [indeed, of all Greek–Western history] was the realization and humanization of God—the transformation and dissolution of theology into anthropology."[37] It is this theological-technological project, which some call "nihilism," that comes to expression in the formula: "fulfilled naturalism is humanism; fulfilled humanism is naturalism."[38]

VII. Some Conclusions

Heidegger's discussion of nihilism moves between two foci: techno-nihilism and the essential *nihil*. The latter refers to the intrinsic "withdrawnness" or "hiddenness" of the finitude that opens the open (φύσις κρύπτεσθαι φιλεῖ). This hiddenness is largely responsible for the widespread overlooking or "forgetting" of the open, which Heidegger identifies with historical-cultural nihilism. And allegedly the forgottenness of the opening is what aids and abets the spread of technology.

But important questions remain. If the open were not overlooked but recovered and embraced in recollective resolve, would that mark the end (or at least the beginning of the end) of the technological domination of the world by what Jünger calls "the worker"? Does Heidegger's thought entail a mandate to right the balance and restore nature to the place of honor it once held before the triumph of modern technology? What conclusions can we draw from Heidegger's reflections on nihilism?

1. The hiddenness intrinsic to the opening of the open is *what allows for* the endless accessibility of entities. Without the withdrawal intrinsic to *Ereignis*, entities would not be disclosed, and humans beings would not be human. But *with* this withdrawal, entities are endlessly available to human engagement and manipulation. The technological domination of the globe is the *gift* of the finite open. Far from having a philosophically negative valence, *die Technik* is the positive outcome of *Ereignis*.

2. In Heidegger's thought, "essential nihilism" in and of itself has nothing to do with a given ratio between φύσις and τέχνη, nature and technology. 'Αλήθεια as self-presentation is the intrinsic intelligibility of entities, not their exhibition of "natural" εἴδη. Essential nihilism is a matter of the hiddenness intrinsic to the open, and historical-cultural nihilism is a matter of overlooking that hiddenness. But neither essential nihilism nor historical-cultural nihilism has any necessary relation to the domination of nature by technology, nor does limiting the scope of technology and restoring the powers of nature have any necessary relation to overcoming the oblivion of the open. One can be a historical-cultural nihilist in φύσις-rich and τέχνη-poor ancient Greece as much as in today's φύσις-poor and τέχνη-rich North America—Antiphon is proof enough of that.

3. Historical-cultural nihilism is not proportionate to the degree of human control over entities; it is not a zero-sum game in which the advances of humanization entail oblivion of the open. One can promote and affirm a world that is, in principle, completely knowable and controllable by human beings, and still remain resolutely true to the open. And one can embrace mystical worldviews (as the dying Aquinas allegedly did) which, to the degree that they are oblivious of the open, are formally no different from the materialist worldviews of Antiphon or Stalin.

4. The self-coincident and all-knowing God, who lies far beyond the open, remains untouched by essential nihilism. But for human beings, who cannot escape the open, the essential *nihil* marks a certain death of God. *Moritur* νόησις νοήσεως, *incipit* κένωσις κενώσεως, the groundless self-emptying that makes possible the endless knowledge and manipulation of the world. The Heideggerian discourse on the gradual triumph of technology should change its lugubrious tones and become an Ambrosian *Exultet* to the *felix culpa* of a historical unfolding that at last opens our eyes to the *nihil* that is both the essence of being-itself and the fate of human beings.

5. The Ur-fact of *Ereignis* entails that everything is comprehensible, except the comprehensibility of everything. This formula might seem to raise the specter of closure and totalization, but it asserts the exact opposite. This view refuses to locate the open "behind" τέχνη, whether behind artifacts in some pristine φύσις, as Antiphon argues, or behind "the worker" in some transrational and transethical *Dasein*, as Right Heideggerians would have it. The point, rather, is to salvage the λήθη (the opening of the open) from all efforts to locate it, either over the edge of this world, where human νοεῖν supposedly runs out of steam, or in "its own proper dwelling place" (ἀεὶ..ἐν τῇ οἰκείᾳ ἕδρᾳ),[39] in an eternal Beyond whence it might intersect and interrupt history, or in an empty, aleatory obligationism. The task is to reinscribe the λήθη where it belongs: at the heart of human being, where it makes possible the endless, untotalizable project of the historical engagement with and humanization of the world. This "economizing" of the λήθη confirms the finitude both of humankind and of all forms of being, precisely by generating an infinity of possibilities for the reshaping of the world. It shows that the mystery of *Ereignis* inhabits and empowers planetary technology. Therefore, we live into the mystery of *Ereignis* not by being less nihilistic but more.

6. Just as the locus of the mystery shifts to the horizontal and historical, so too our engagement with nihilism must shift from the "what" to the "how," from discourse about the essence of nihilism to decisions about how best to carry out the task of the endless humanization of the world. This was clearly not Heidegger's move, but it should be our own.

From his early course on the phenomenology of religion (1920–1921) up through his last writings, Heidegger remained ever focused on the essence of "eschatology." I do not mean the so-called "eschatology of being,"[40] according to which *Ereignis*, long overlooked, has allegedly dispensed to us, in these latter days, the most extreme possibility of being. Rather, I draw on the original sense found in Heidegger's 1920–1921 course, where the eschaton, no longer a mythical supernatural event at the end of time, is understood as radical finitude, the always arriving but ever unfathomable enabling power by which humans are drawn into realms of significance, and in the face of which they live in utter uncertainty. The words "eschatology" and "eschatological" have to do with living into and out of the finitude of the open, the ultimate, unsurpassable *Urfactum*. Eschatology means *Geschichtlichkeit*. But when it came to the question of "What is to be done?" the best Heidegger could offer was a redoubling of his eschatological vision. To his assertion that human being is pulled into the mystery of the open (ἦθος ἀνθρώπῳ δαίμων) he adds a purely formal, empty protreptic to *Gelassenheit*, that is, to letting oneself be pulled into that mystery: γένοι᾽ οἷος ἐσσί μαθών. *"Werde wesentlich!"* ["Become what you already are"].[41]

This move is hardly sufficient to the claims made on us by thinking and acting, not only in terms of political responsibilities but first of all in terms of philosophical ones. Indeed, on its *own* terms, Heidegger's reflections on the essence of nihilism demand the dismantling of the ahistorical, utopian obligationism to which Right Heideggerians abandon the eschatological. The task, rather, is to reinscribe the eschatological within the concrete order of power—economic, social, political, and ideological (including the philosophical)—where alone the future of "nihilism" (should we choose to use this unfortunate word) will be decided. Such a reinscription does not require in the first instance the elaboration of new political philosophies or schemata of moral obligation. Those either will or will not come in their own good time. The first step, rather, is to recognize that whereas the essence of nihilism can be worked out in the realm of thought, the actual course of the humanization of nature and naturalization of the human is decided not in classrooms or philosophy conferences and not in libraries or texts. Rather, it is being decided in the hills and the streets and in the boardrooms and the *maquilas*. Anything philosophy has to say must come as a reflection on that.

To return to Heidegger's demand that he be read as a *homo philosophicus* rather than as a *homo politicus*: the present reflections suggest that what Heidegger has to say about the essence of nihilism—important though it might be—cannot realistically serve as a philosophical platform for grounding political options. One would no more want to take Heidegger's reflections on the essence of nihilism as the basis for political decisions than one would want to take the apocalyptic discourses attributed to Jesus of Nazareth as a blueprint for running a revolution. You may not like technology and its products, the possibilities it opens up at the expense of the ones it closes off. You may not like the current constellation of the management of technology or the distribution of its effects. But Heidegger's philosophy—for whatever light it may shed on the question of essential nihilism—will not help one bit with changing the real powers that drive τέχνη today. Taken strictly, Heidegger's discourse does not even encourage you to work to change the direction of history. To motivate and to enact such a change require other strategies and other tactics, and they do not come from Heidegger.

This chapter has sought to be one thing only: a philosophical propaideutic to understanding Heidegger's political "error" of 1933—and the continuing possibility of such errors today. If we bracket for now the other and more interesting reasons that Heidegger had for joining the National Socialist German Workers Party, if we focus only on the philosophical justifications that he gave *ex eventu* for his choice, it seems that he joined the Nazis because he thought that they could help overcome nihilism. If we remain at the superstructural level of philosophical discourse, we conclude that his error was not that he picked the wrong party for overcoming nihilism but that he thought nihilism, could be overcome at all.

Notes

1. Citations in these notes frequently refer to texts by page and line. The line count does not include the "header" or any empty lines on the page but does count the lines of section titles. Further documentation for the theses of this text can be found in the author's "Nihilism: Heidegger/Jünger/Aristotle," in *Phenomenology: Japanese and American Perspectives*, edited by Burt C. Hopkins (Dordrecht: Kluwer Academic Publishers, 1998), pp. 273–316.

2. Martin Heidegger, "Zur Seinsfrage," in GA 9, 385–462;P, 291–322.

3. James Joyce, *Ulysses* (New York: The Modern Library, new edition, 1961), p. 377.

4. Giambattista Vico, *On the Most Ancient Wisdom of the Italians Unearthed from the Origins of the Latin Language*, translated by L. M. Palmer (Ithaca, N.Y., and London: Cornell University Press, 1988), pp. 45–46.

5. See *Martin Heidegger*, edited by Michel Haar (Paris: Cahiers de l'Herne, 1983), p. 149.

6. See Plato, *Republic*, VII, 509d.

7. GA 5, 324.4-9;EGT, 15.21–25.

8. See *Physics* B, 1, 193 a 12–15, and Hermann Diels, *Die Fragmente der Vorsokratiker*, 2d. ed. (Berlin: Weidmannsche Buchhandlung, 1907), p. 594.29–31.

9. In the latter case, μορφή/εἶδος: GA 9, 277.32/212.18.

10. *Metaphysics*, 1, 993 b 30–31; compare Thomas Aquinas, *Summa Theologiae* I-II 3, 7 c.: "*Eadem est dispositio rerum in esse sicut in veritate.*"

11. Plato's Seventh Letter, 341c.

12. Martin Heidegger, *Zollikoner Seminare: Protokolle—Gespräche—Briefe*, edited by Medard Boss (Frankfurt am Main: Vittorio Klostermann, 1987), p. 203.7–11.

13. GA 2, 539.15-17;SZ, 408.7-8;BTa, 460.20–21.

14. See GA 9, 266.24;P, 204.5.

15. *Übungen im Lesen*, winter semester (1950–51), April 18, 1951.

16. Diels, *Die Fragmente der Vorsokratiker*, p. 117.7; Aristotle, *De Anima*, III, 5, 430 a 20, and III, 7, 431 a 1.

17. GA 9, 307.23–24;P. 234.17–18.

18. GA 9, p. 407.24-25;P, 308.6.

19. GA 9, p. 389.14-15;P, 294.18-19.

20. See Aristotle, *Metaphysics* 12, 9, 1075 a 4-5.

21. *Confessions*, VII, 11 (17), *Patrologia Latina*, XXXII, p. 743.

22. *Summa Contra Gentiles*, I, 20, quarta obiectio (24), in *Opera Omnia* (New York: Musurgia, 1948-1949), V, 17A.

23. Section X of Heidegger's commentary: GA 9, 336ff;P, 203ff.

24. Diels, *Die Fragmente der Vorsokratiker*, pp. 591-97.

25. *Physics* B, 1, 193 a 26-27.

26. *Historiae*, 3rd. ed., edited by Charles Hude (Oxford: Clarendon, 1927, reprinted 1954), II.98 (vol. I) and IX.116 (vol. II).

27. *Prometheus Bound*, translated by David Grene, in *The Complete Greek Tragedies*, edited by David Grene and Richmond Lattimore (Chicago: University of Chicago Press, 1959), vol. I, p. 345.

28. *Timaeus* 37e, and *Politics* V, 1, 1301 b 27, respectively.

29. The Right Heideggerian position finds its classical expression in John D. Caputo, *Heidegger and Aquinas: An Essay on Overcoming Metaphysics* (New York: Fordham University Press, 1985). Compare Thomas Sheehan, "A Way Out of Metaphysics," *Research in Phenomenology* 15 (1985): 229-34.

30. See John D. Caputo, *Against Ethics* (Bloomington and Indianapolis: Indiana University Press, 1993).

31. See Sheehan, "Nihilism: Heidegger/Jünger/Aristotle," pp. 291.5-292.4.

32. See *Metaphysics*, E 1, 1026 a 19 and K 3, 1064 b 3.

33. Edmund Husserl, *Die Krisis der europäischen Wissenschaften und die transzendentale Phänomenologie, Ergänzungsband. Texte aus dem Nachlass 1934-1937*, edited by Reinhold N. Smid (Dordrecht: Kluwer, 1993), p. 67; *The Crisis of European Sciences and Transcendental Philosophy*, translated by David Carr (Evanston: Northwestern University Press, 1970), p. 67. Hereafter cited as *Krisis*, followed by the German and English pagination and line numbers.

34. *Krisis*, p. 55.33-35/55.8-13; *Krisis*, p. 66.21-23/65.18-19.

35. Ibid., p. 67.15-32/66.6-9, 16-19.

36. David Friedrich Strauss, *Das Leben Jesu kritisch bearbeitet* (Tübingen: C. F. Osiander, Erster Band, 1835; Zweiter Band, 1836). Here, II, §146, p. 729.20-22; II, §147, p. 734.15-18, and p. 734.24-29, my translation. The English translation by

George Eliot (Mary Ann Evans) is taken from the significantly changed fourth edition (1839) of the work *The Life of Jesus Critically Examined*, 3 vols. (London: Chapman Brothers, 1846; reissued: Philadelphia: Fortress Press, 1972).

37. Ludwig Feuerbach, *Gesammelte Schriften*, edited by Werner Schuffenhauer (Berlin: Akademie-Verlag, 1970), vol. IX, p. 265.

38. Karl Marx and Friedrich Engels, *Werke* (Berlin: Dietz, 1968ff); Ergänzungsband, Erster Teil), 1968, p. 536 (manuscript 3); in MEGA, I/2, 263.

39. Plotinus, *Enneads*, IV.8.6.

40. GA 5, 327.17–18;EGT, 18.15.

41. Pindar, *Pythian Odes*, II, 72; Martin Heidegger, *Zur Bestimmung der Philosophie* (Frankfurt am Main: Vittorio Klostermann, 1999), p. 534.

18

Is There an Ethics for the "Atomic Age"?

PIERRE JACERME

> We stand at once within the realm of that which hides itself from us, and hides itself just in approaching us.
>
> —Heidegger, *Discourse on Thinking*

The "atomic age" began for humanity (and there is only one) in Hiroshima, on August 6, 1945, at 8:15 A.M. But for what "humanity," that is the question. Is humanity the same before and after the explosion of the bomb? Does the term *ethics* mean the same thing before and after "Hiroshima"? Aristotle wrote that "its name *ethikê* is one that is formed by a slight variation from the word *ethos* (habit)," and "moral virtue comes about as a result of habit."[1] But with Hiroshima do we not see the appearance of the *strangest* and most *uncanny*? Can this uncanny be thought of in a *positive* way? And what impact [*empreinte*] does it have on that ethical character, especially since we know that "Hiroshima" is the realization of the possibility—that can be repeated just for the purpose of domination—of the destruction of humanity and its world, *on the basis of the very procedures of rational calculus?* Either reason proves to be in contradiction with the possibility of any ethics, or on the contrary, ethical care in its sway opens reason to the uncanny nature of its being, a nature that is concealed by the language of calculation.

> Here something turns in on itself. Here something coils in on itself but does not close itself for it uncoils itself at the same time. (PR, 14)

Of course, Heidegger had already spoken, through Hölderlin and Nietzsche, of the growing "danger," of the threatening "chaos," and more directly, of the "grasp" of "objectification" that extends a "fleeting cloud," a "shadow" over a "concealed land."[2] But after "Hiroshima," the tone changes, as early as "The Letter on Humanism," addressed to Jean Beaufret in December 1946. In an important passage, Heidegger responds to a question from Beaufret on "the relation of an ontology with a possible ethics. " He brings together three points: "the obvious perplexity of man," soaring "to immeasurable heights," the necessity of devoting the greatest care to fostering an "ethical bond," and the distress of "technological man," who can only act in obedience to the demands of technology. He does so on the basis of an interpretation of what had just happened in "world history" at Hiroshima, as though that event could make man sense the urgency for another thought.

> Can thinking refuse to think being after the latter has lain hidden so long in oblivion but at the same time *has made itself known in the present moment of world history by the uprooting of all beings [durch die Erschütterung alles Seienden]?* (BW, 232)

That same year, at the beginning of the "Anaximander Fragment," Heidegger asks: "Do we stand in the very twilight of the most monstrous transformation our planet has ever undergone?" (EGT, 17).

With Hiroshima, something other, heretofore latent, emerges in the light of day; something that Kenzaburo Oe named in 1965 "an incomparably larger abominable reality still hidden in the darkness."[3] It is the innermost depths of this "thing" that Heidegger attempted to think after 1945—always more radically and deliberately—by increasing his interventions, including courses, lectures, "dialogues," colloquia, seminars, interviews, and various publications. This increased number of interventions is all the more remarkable since, after *Being and Time*, he exhibited the tendency to *withhold* his texts. It is as though this "thinking of Being," confronted by the most extreme "distress," manifested itself in a more exoteric practice, a more distinct engagement in "being-in common," and as though, at the very moment when a calculating thinking finds itself in a dead end, it was necessary to show man—who had gone astray—the possibility of another path by sketching some preparatory steps. I would like in this chapter to retrace those steps, through a questioning on the being of man and on originary ethics.

After these texts from 1946, there was in 1949—in the Bremen lectures on technology (*The Thing, The Ge-Stell, The Danger, The Turning*)—an attempt to configure an *ethos* of man equal to the "danger" that "concerns" [*regarde*] his being. In 1954, there was a thoughtful meditation (presented as a "Dialogue" between a Japanese person and an inquirer) which, unable to rely on an all too compromised representational thinking, tried to bring out the *resonance* of reason, rather than its reasoning, from the forgotten heart of its language. In 1956, in Heidegger's last public course, *The Principle of Reason*, there was a long and thorough development on the meaning of the atomic age. At the same time, on October 30, 1955, in a celebration in his hometown for his countryman, composer Conradin Kreutzer, Heidegger delivered a lecture ten years after "Hiroshima" that he published in 1959 under the title *Gelassenheit.* Professor Kojima Takehiko would indeed write to him on July 5, 1963, that the text "almost appeared to us, Professor, as a wish on your part to address yourself to us Japanese.[4] Moreover, following a demonstration on April 8, 1958, against atomic armament of the Bundeswehr, a movement was formed "against atomic death," and Heidegger joined the group.

Can human beings still be *touched* when the distress is precisely the "absence of distress"? If that which remains hidden in the present is the only thing that can truly touch us, then perhaps an evocation of what was not felt at that time could *prepare* us to be touched and in that way initiate a new sensitivity.

On August 6, 1945, at Hiroshima, a "great many signs," to use Parmenides' expression, appeared. It is important to bring these signs into view to gain a *vision that speaks* (in the sense of the Chinese proverb, cited by Heidegger in his *Heraclitus* seminar with Fink): "Once pointed out is better than a hundred times told"[5] concerning what happened that day to the inhabitants of the city, transforming them into shadows or cinders, turning them inside out, staggering them and rendering them silent. The only reference left for the survivors was their crazed bodies. This is indeed a fragile reference, when the earth collapses, and when the tremendous white light of a sun—all of a sudden, so close, as if it could be touched—produces blindness: "I'm blind . . . I could no longer see anything. . . . With the fingers of my left hand I touched my face lightly; my eyebrows, my cheeks, and my mouth, my forehead, my cheeks, my mouth, felt like a mixture of bean curd and gelatin. My face was swollen, like a big sponge; it was as if I had no nose" (HN, 177).

> Their faces were wholly burned, their eye sockets were hollow, the fluid from their melted eyes had run down their cheeks. . . .[6] The human is reduced to the vegetal, the mineral. The shadow of man spreads on the concrete:
>
> . . . the flash of the bomb . . . had, in some places, left prints of the shadows that had been cast by its light.
>
> . . . a painter on a ladder was monumentalized in a kind of bas-relief on the stone façade of a bank building on which he was at work, in the act of dipping his brush into his paint can.
>
> A man and his cart on the bridge near the Museum of Science and Industry, almost under the center of the explosion, were cast down in an embossed shadow which made it clear that the man was about to whip his horse. (H, 95–96)

These anecdotes seem emblematic: confronted with the horrible, it is as though the monstrous fire still had to be like an artistic fire, and as though man still succeeded, due to the gathering produced by the gesture, in maintaining his superiority over animals at the very moment when he was reduced to the barest life. It is this last point that Bataille noted when he reported on John Hersey's text, which reconstituted the fate of several survivors during the twelve days after the explosion, then during the following months: "The individual in the streets of Hiroshima, dazzled by an immense flash—which had the intensity of the sun and was followed by no detonation—learned nothing from the colossal explosion. He submitted to it *like an animal*, not even knowing its gigantic scope."[7] Human solidarity is broken: "But it is in isolation and in complete ignorance of what was suddenly upon them, that the revelation—the meager, shattering, unending revelation—began for each of them" (GB, 500).

Hence, the cry of the poet Tôge Sankichi, which is engraved on a stone in the Peace Park:

> Give me back myself
> Give back the human race. (HN, 24)

As Bataille notes, it is this *isolation* that above all reduces man to animal; Hersey's fragmented montage intensifies this. To reduce the reporting to a succession of multiple views offered by the memory of the witnesses results in these recollections being "reduced to the dimensions of *animal* experience" [. . .] "since in them the immediate experience of the catastrophe is isolated" (GB, 501). Bataille emphasizes this point in relation to M. Tanimoto, a Methodist pastor in Hiroshima, who survived due to the protection of a huge rock. "M. Tanimoto's representation, on the other hand, has only *sensory* value, since what there is of *intelligence* in it is mistaken. Error is the human aspect in the description, while what stands out in it as true is what the memory of an animal would have retained" (GB, 502). It will be necessary to better understand this transfer of the "true" to the level of the "animal," and this paradox of a "view of the *animal*, walled-in, deprived, by an error, of a passage into the future, deprived of an event whose essence is to alter the destiny of man" (ibid.). Even the concern for humanity that Tanimoto professes, as it were, becomes like an instinct—for the human slips through his fingers when, on the bank of the Ota River, he tries to save the wounded from the rising tide.

> He reached down and took a woman by the hands, but her skin slipped off in huge, glove-like pieces. He was so sickened by this that he had to sit down for a moment. . . . *He had to keep consciously repeating to himself, "These are human beings."* (Hersey, cited in GB, 505, emphasis in original)

The human is but a litany, a leitmotif that unfolds mechanically in order to avoid sinking. Hence, the stupor and the silence of all. "*Almost all had their heads bowed, looked straight ahead, were silent, and showed no expression whatever*" (Hersey, cited in GB, 505, emphasis in original). Progressively, the tide covers the wounded.

> Countless people were struggling to get to the stream under the bridge. I could not distinguish men from women. Their faces were swollen and gray; their hair

stood on end. Then, raising both hands skyward and making soundless groans, they all began jumping into the river, as though competing with one another. (HN, 176)

Indeed, "Hiroshima" is, as Kenzaburo Oe says twice in his book, "the most difficult matter to handle," a matter that is encountered "at a basic level" (HN, 180). But what is this basic level? Are we free to decide to speak, as he wishes, of "the nature and extent of *human* misery, not just the destructive capacity, of an atomic bombing" (ibid.)? Can we avoid the grip of technology that is such that it still determines us, even when we denounce it? And what does "the nature and extent of human misery" mean when man is seen as an animal? To describe "Hiroshima" from the perspective of the wounds, symptoms, medical research, to speak of illness or healing, as Oe does at the beginning of his book—"in the hope that, as one with only a peripheral place in the world, I can find decent and humanistic ways to contribute to the healing and reconciliation of all peoples"—is to remain a prisoner of technology precisely when one attempts to move away from it (HN, 11). In fact, as a physician from Hiroshima actually explained to him in a letter (a physician who actually belonged to the group of the *Hibakusha,* or people who have suffered the bomb), "Hiroshima" must first be the object of a silent reappropriation that happens in and through silence, a silence that Heidegger calls, in "A Dialogue on Language" and also in *Gelassenheit,* the "*peaceful calm of silence*": "People in Hiroshima prefer to remain silent until they face death. They want to have their own life and death" (letter from Matsusaka Yosihitaka to Kenzaburo Oe [HN, 19]).

What are we to make of the *silence* proper to Hiroshima? What are we to make of the blurring of the distinction between man and animal? The "most difficult matter to handle" of Hiroshima itself delineates an ethics, as Oe must recognize progressively as he travels through Hiroshima. Such an ethics not only does not coincide with its initial "humanistic" project but calls for an "overcoming" of *humanism* that is still difficult to formulate. With respect to a woman who was deprived of her stillborn monstrous child and who had said: "If only I could see my baby I would have courage," Oe, struck by the usage of the word "courage," engages in this thoughtful discussion.

> If a mother wants to see her dead deformed child so as to regain her own courage, she is attempting to live at the minimum limit under which a human being can remain human. This may be interpreted as a valiant expression of humanism *beyond* popular humanism—a new humanism sprouting from the misery of Hiroshima." (HN, 83)

What does the necessity ("*we have* to understand these words") of such a "beyond" indicate? It indicates that it is at the level of language itself that we should situate ourselves. Now, a bit further in his book, Oe notes that in *French* literature, three words (the essential words of the ethics born from "Hiroshima") carry tremendous weight but are *neglected in Japanese: dignity, humiliation, and shame.* He writes: "The sentence, 'That boy is full of dignity,' for example, does not flow naturally in Japanese syntax. It sounds like a sentence translated from a foreign language" (HN, 104). The ethics that delineates itself from the "most difficult matter to handle" of Hiroshima cuts into the Japanese language. The linguistic discomfort felt by the writer is the sign of a deeper malaise, of a metaphysical nature. There is a need for a "place at the margins," as Oe says, a need for the "excess" of "the man of *sovereign sensibility*" who "subordinates" reason, as Bataille says: "Indeed, the man of sovereign sensibility is not unrelated to the birth of the atomic bomb: his excessive nature corresponds to that of the science, which is to say of reason" (GB, 508-09).

But instead of "responding" in an excessive way to excess and declare, "it is better to live up to Hiroshima" (GB, 511)—while at the same time prophesying that "the world, trapped in a corner, is doomed to abrupt metamorphosis" (GB, 513)—should we not, rather, in order to *be* "up to Hiroshima," instead of subordinating reason, restore its *provenance* and follow the indication given to Oe by the "feeling of language"? For us, such an indication is priceless: "Hiroshima" generates a new ethical concern, which obliterates traditional humanism and its all too centered *discourse.* *More* dignity, *more* humiliation, *more* shame, in and of itself. The Japanese cannot say that easily; there arises for it the experience of foreignness. Whence comes the measure of this "*more*"? How can we encounter it?

It is not an accident if the critique of humanism—of man as a master of beings— a critique already present at the end of the 1942 essay *Plato's Doctrine of Truth*, assumes a considerable importance in the December 1946 letter to Jean Beaufret, when Heidegger interpreted "this moment of world history" as "the uprooting of all beings," and therefore as the possibility of giving attention once again to Being and its withdrawal.

Indeed, over what would man still reign if everything is able to collapse, a collapse that is actually due to the work of reason that has served to ensure its domination? The essential problem is no longer a problem of mastery. An ethics can no longer be an ethics of the subject in the sense of the "thinking" subject who represents its own representation to itself in order to ensure its certainty and found upon it a system of obligations and responsibility. Ethics can no longer be based on *representational* thinking, and dialectical thought as well is on the side of power. The question rather becomes: After Hiroshima and the atomic "disassociation," on what basis can we find the measure of an ethical "bond," given that ethics can no longer have a normative aim with respect to any domain of being, nor have a "categorical" (in the sense of Kant's "categorical" imperative) aim transcending the totality of beings?

What is a measure which is no longer a measure for entities but which on the contrary arises from the "uprooting" of entities—that is, a *call*, a "sending on our way," coming from "Being itself" (i.e., from Being in its proper truth), which gives itself in a lighting flash? The stakes of a thought that thinks the truth of being as the "primordial element of man, as one who ek-sists" would be for Heidegger "original ethics."[8] Any ethical "bond" whatsoever implies that one give a positive meaning to man; now, what Hiroshima makes patently clear—since the totality of beings is uprooted and *will remain so*—is that this will only be possible on the basis of the truth *of being*, and on the condition of renewing the thought of man by thinking him as a *relation to that truth*—and not as the lord of the earth or of the cosmos. Therefore, only a *decision* of thought, one that will let the truth *of being* be said *without any concern for entities*, will permit one to give thought to the *humanity* of man. "To think the truth of Being at the same time means to think the humanity of *homo humanus*. What counts is *humanitas* in the service of the truth of Being, but without humanism in the metaphysical sense" (BW, 235).

As Heidegger explains: "Are we really on the right track toward the essence of man as long as we set him off as one living creature among others in contrast to plants, beasts, and God? [. . .] But we must be clear on this point, that when we do this we abandon man to the essential realm of *animalitas* even if we do not equate him with beasts but attribute a specific difference to him" (BW, 203). The critique of this type of humanism, which culminates in the negation of humanity, should allow access to something other—by avoiding the tendency to reduce man to animals—something that happened at Hiroshima and perhaps remains in reserve, hidden in the *silence* of the survivors. It is this silence that we should attempt to understand better at this point. At Hiroshima, the importance of the withdrawal of being became manifest, and the *silence* indicates to us the *ethical experience* undergone by those who have *sojourned* in such withdrawal when it manifested itself. At that time, Being emerged from its oblivion and thus at the same time manifested this oblivion as such. How can we speak of the "uprooting of all beings," the occurrence of the *nothing* (that "other of beings")—as in the case of the experience of "anxiety"—and with this occurrence, speak of the approach of the "non-appearance" of being itself and of the abyssal correspondence between being and reason ("the groundless"), except by *silence?*

Hiroshima allows us to undergo this complex experience, but on the condition of not understanding it as a mere devastation leading to a new form of mastery. In another way, negatively, by threatening to uproot everything, the atomic age confirms the current primacy of beings. We have been given the chance to perceive the extreme form of the withdrawal of Being through this flash, which also gives us the extreme modality of a givenness of presence, that is, a coming to the fore of entities so that our only possible action is to constantly reinforce our domination over them—if need be by fragmenting them, by atomizing them. The paradoxical effect is that it is the call of Being that makes itself heard.

Hence, Heidegger's anger and sarcasm when he sees his contemporaries neglect this crucial event in favor of superficial activities: "Defiant man is utterly at a loss simply to say what *is*" (EGT, 57). And close to anger, there is a passionate hope, akin to despair. "Perhaps the world's time is now becoming the completely destitute time. But also perhaps not, not yet, not even yet, despite the immeasurable need, despite all the suffering, despite nameless sorrow, despite the growing and spreading peacelessness, despite the mounting confusion."[9] This is why we need to understand that what is essential can only come from Being itself and not from the management of entities, or the entity man, even when he lives with "atomic fear": "Long is the time because even terror, taken by itself as a ground for turning, is powerless as long as there is no turn with mortal men. But there is a turn with mortals when these find the way to their own being [*Wesen*]" (PLT, 93, trans. slightly modified). How can we dwell in our "proper being"? On the basis of the instancy in the "truth of Being." The atomic bomb is nothing but another sign—neglected, as in the case of the others—of what has existed from the beginning, namely, the lack of concern for Being itself in favor of the will to control everything: "What is deadly is not the much-discussed atomic bomb as this particular death-dealing machine. What has long since been threatening man with death, and indeed with the death of his own nature, is the unconditional character of mere willing in the sense of purposeful self-assertion in everything" (PLT, 116). Hence, the atomic bomb can have the inverse effect of blinding man about being and concealing the fact that "the terrifying has already taken place": "Man . . . stares at what the explosion of the atom bomb could bring with it. He does not see that the atom bomb and its explosion are the mere final emission of what has long since taken place, has already happened," namely, "the *way* in which everything presences [. . .] despite all conquest of distances the nearness of things remains absent."[10] What is "terrifying" is that there is no concern whatsoever for *presence* as such, which remains in the withdrawal: "Science's knowledge, which is compelling within its own sphere, the sphere of objects, already had annihilated things as things long before the atom bomb exploded [. . .] the thing as a thing remains nil" (PLT, 170). This annihilation deprives all that is of its life. "Atomic physics [. . .] observes nature (*phusis*) insofar as nature exhibits itself as inanimate."[11] Here appears the first demand of the "originary ethic": to see what *is*, "Instead of shying away from this demand, by taking refuge in powerless determinations of goals which are limited to safeguarding humanity."[12] "Demand," because even if he concerns himself with entities alone, man is still able to hear (although not always aware of it) a call of *Being* that speaks to him through language. Rockets, atomic bombs, reactors, those things that are, are "what they are in the name of their name"; "hurry" acts insofar as it *speaks* to man and to that extent "has" its being: "If that call to such hurry had not challenged him and put him at bay, if the word framing that order and challenge had not spoken: then there would be no sputnik."[13] In the word the withdrawal of being speaks, and according to this modality we are given various dispensations of presence on the basis of which entities will be present to us in various ways (as *phenomena*, as *objects* , or as *standing reserve*, etc.). Therefore—and this is another demand of "original ethics"—man is always in a relation to a call, and always called to a destiny of *unveiling*. In 1955–56, in *The Principle of Reason,* Heidegger noted that "the characterization of an epoch as the atomic age probably touches on what is" (PR, 29). This *nomination* will help us determine the *fundamental mood* on the basis of which we would be able to feel and then characterize the modality of givenness of presence that determines our being. According to Heidegger, this mood is "uncanniness" hidden under "an apparently harmless naming." This *uncanniness* lies in the fact that, "Humanity defines an epoch of its historical-spiritual existence by the capacity for, and the availability of, a natural energy" (ibid.). Now, "there would be no atomic age without atomic science," and no microphysics without reassembling the manifold of elementary particles into a new unity, that is, without obeying the call of the principle that reason be given (ibid.). On that basis we reach an *ethical* characterization in the sense of that which concerns the *sojourn* or *dwelling* of *existent* man: "As the global epoch of humanity, the atomic age is distinguished by the fact that the power of the mighty Principle, of *the principium reddendae rationis,* displays itself (if not completely unleashed) in a strange manner in the normative domain of human existence" (PR, 30). Why strange [*unheimlich*]? Because "the demand to render reasons threatens everything of the humans' being-at-home [*alles Heimische*] [. . .] it robs them of the roots of their subsistence [. . .] the more decisively humans try to harness the "mega-energies" [. . .] the more impoverished becomes the human faculty for building and dwelling in the realm of what is essential" (PR, 30–31). In what form is presence given to us when we feel this uprooting? In fact, not only have not there not been "things" for us for a long time now, but "we already move in a world where there are no more ob-jects" (PR, 33). That point is important in order to determine correctly *that which is,* that is, "what approaches us from what has-been and, as this, is what approaches" (PR, 80).

> The very presence of nature in the thematic region of nuclear physics remains unthinkable as long as we still represent it as objectivity and not as "orderability" (*Bestellbarkeit*), which means that the entity is present in a sense of "proposed to . . . ordered to . . . (*bestellt*) while being at the same time summoned, provoked . . . (*Gestellt*).[14]

The consequence of this, as Heidegger explains in a carefully worded letter to Kojima Takehiko on September 2, 1963, is that "through modern technology the energy hidden in nature is unleashed, unleashed is transformed, what is transformed is amplified, what is amplified is set forth, and what is set forth is organized" (*Philosophie,* 14). The modality of the withdrawal of being that governs this deployment resonates as a call to place everything under a regulation that is itself guaranteed by what Heidegger names *Die Macht des Stellens* [*The power of summation*]; we also could render that expression as follows: the force of the summon. "Everywhere reigns the provocative, calculative, and justifying summon (*Stellen*)" (ibid.). It follows, then, that "everything that can be and is" only *gives itself* as a "stable calculable ground *(Bestand)*" and is only experienced from the perspective of securing that ground. Such a power, be-cause it is not human, always "calls" for more security, more summons, more guar-antees—we also should add, in remembrance of the survivors of Hiroshima, more dignity, more humiliation, more shame—and rules over technology, science, industry, economy, *and the rest*, without anything—coming from man—being able to oppose it: "the ineluctable and irresistible character of this summoning force leads to the unfolding of its domination over the entire planet" (ibid., 15).

It is therefore this force that provides the *measure*. It modifies man "under the growing threat of losing his humanity": "Man can no longer be who he was previ-ously before the summoning force took over" (ibid., 15). The *danger* is that man would not reach "his proper being" and would be expropriated from it:

> In what way is man exposed to the summoning force? Man is himself sum-moned without knowing it. That is to say that man is challenged to enframe [*Bestellen*] the world to which he belongs as a thoroughly calculable ground and securing himself at the same time in view of the project of this enframing. In this way man remains prisoner of the will to enframe through the calculable and its achievement. Surrendered to the summoning force, man conceals that path that leads to his proper Dasein from *himself*. (*Philosophie*, 16)

Such is for the humanity of man "the most dangerous" threat. But, on the other hand, if we look at the summoning force not as an "object" but as an open "en-counter," then through this experience of *Ereignis* we are able to understand how much being needs man: "Its summoning force requires that this call be addressed to man" (*Philosophie*, 17).

For our part, that is, in an uprooting uncanniness, we experienced something similar to what the contemporaries of Heraclitus underwent—even more radically—when, near an oven in an ordinary, familiar place, he revealed the presence of the Gods to them (BW, 231), except that we live at the time of the vanished God, and we can no longer "discern the default of God as a default" (PLT, 91). This means that we have the possibility of discovering our belonging to being itself.

> The challenging addressed to man for the enframing (that is to say, for the de-ployment (*Erschliessung*) of the world as a technological world), a challenging ruling in the force of the summon, betrays the belonging of man to Being it-self. It constitutes that which is most proper to his humanity. Indeed, it is only on the basis (*Grund*) of a belonging to being that man can apprehend being. It is only in relation to being that what we call reason (*Vernunft*) can be said. (*Philosophie*, 18)

Thus the heart of originary ethics is this identity between *being* and *reason*, which attests that the proper of man does not belong to him and that, therefore, his vocation is not to master it, and that it is not reason's sole function to ground beings or to secure being in order to ensure its stability and development (Being = reason = the groundless). Hence, the importance of an "open encounter" with the "summoning force," which paradoxically includes within it and shelters a "tracing of what is proper to man and only to him" (*Philosophie*, 17). Consequently, "that which is proper to man lies in the fact that he does not belong to himself" (ibid., 20). It is in this sense that man entails uprooting and the uncanny. "We do not need atomic bombs at all [to uproot us]—the uprooting of man is already here. All our relationships have become merely technical ones."[15] To the extent that technology *requires* man to *be* in this relation, man is in that sense an "instrument" of being. And of this he knows nothing, (TB, 72). When people these days seek "an ethics" for everything (cloning, the Internet, a method of feeding chickens, refereeing soccer games, etc.), this means that they want to cover up the lack of law with a "morality." They want *regulations* that would have the (unquestionable) status of principles, and above all would be such that they "de-responsibilize" the subject. A subject, being, as it were, short-circuited, hidden behind this wall of "principles," in fact, would let the process of enframing take place, that is, this "summoning power" that *commands* any acts whatsoever (on the basis of *its* power). "Modern man" is subjected to "imperatives" that are only the constraints of reality; he is the "slave to the forgetting of being." This passage is from the Thor Seminar (September 11, 1969). Twenty-three years earlier, meeting Jean Beaufret for the first time in September 1946, Heidegger spoke to him about "man of the earth in his most extreme distress," that is, he adds, "as I sometimes say, in the *forgetting of Being.*"[16]

And in December 1946 the same idea is expressed in the sentence just cited where we find the allusion to Hiroshima: "Can thinking refuse to think being after the latter has lain hidden so long in oblivion but at the same time *has made itself known in the present moment of world history by the uprooting of all beings [durch die Erschütterung alles Seienden]*" (BW, 232). Publicly, it is in the "Letter on Humanism" that Heidegger recognized that *Being and Time* was thought in light of the experience of the "forgetting of Being." The forgetting of Being is a subjective genitive, in the sense that Being "withdraws while it discloses itself in entities," but it also is our own forgetting in the sense that we have forgotten the forgetting, that is, the *lêthê* of Being, the form of its withdrawal that gives us our destiny of being, as Beaufret used to say, the "men of entities." When entities disintegrate (or threaten to disintegrate), is it not the "non-appearance" of Being that appears? This forgetting appears to us positively as desired by Being and that can but provoke us, for once, to think Being "without regard for entities." The truth of Being can once again enlighten us even *more radically*, because going "beyond the Greeks," we can speak positively of what the Greeks thought in a privative way, when they spoke of *alêtheia* (where the *a* is privative). The unconcealment of Being can enlighten us as clearing and not as *alêtheia* (in the sense that the withdrawal is not thought at its core, because it is considered negatively).

No doubt it is always a withdrawal of Being that frees the presence of entities, but we moderns can think of the *withdrawal itself* as the *withdrawal for the opening* (even if it is the "dim light" of "objects" or the "standing reserve"). But the Greeks did not give thought to the withdrawal itself positively (forgetting Heraclitus' fragment 123 too quickly: "Nature loves to hide"), because, as early as Parmenides, they had *defined* and *determined alêtheia* in terms of *constant presence* and had prioritized the moment of openness so far as to "forget" the withdrawal—and this is the beginning of metaphysics.

It is for this fundamental reason that Jean Beaufret, in April 1964, when translating the *End of Philosophy and the Task of Thinking*, suggested that the reference to *alêtheia* in fragment 1, line 29, of Parmenides' poem be translated as "open-without-withdrawal" [*ouvert-sans-retrait*]; this would show the difference that Heidegger makes between *die Lichtung*, that is, the clearing of the open, which does entail withdrawal, and *Unverborgenheit*, which does convey the open and its clearing but in such a way that the open entails no more withdrawal.[17] Only weak thinking could attack Jean Beaufret's translation by saying that it is false, alleging that for the Greeks, there was the "withdrawal"!

Heidegger and Beaufret have clearly neither thought nor said that the Greeks did not have the idea of "withdrawal," but what they do claim is that the Greeks have quickly "covered over what they had uncovered" (Nietzsche), and that they did not concentrate or focus their thinking on the withdrawal but, on the contrary, on the constancy of presence that would engender the onto-theo-logical idea of being.

Taken in a nonmetaphysical sense, Being is nothing but that *movement of approaching by withdrawing*, and it is this movement *insofar as it draws us toward it* that Heidegger's "fundamental ontology" attempts to question and reconstitute. This no longer has anything to do with "ontology" in the metaphysical sense.[18] This is why Heidegger, at a certain moment in his path of thinking, would cross through Being to indicate the site of the "movement" in question: "the sign of this crossing through cannot, however, be the merely negative sign of a crossing out. It points, rather, toward the four regions of the fourfold and their being gathered in the locale of this crossing through."[19] The twofold movement of *coming into presence* and *withdrawal*, which is Being, unfolds as the "fourfold" (*Geviert*: the earth, the sky, the divine, the mortals), the way in which *difference* ("being as such") rules. And the world according to which the *Geviert* opens an era is the "thing itself" to be thought, coming into being, staring at us, *regarding* us (both in the sense of that which fulfills the view and that which becomes the noema of our concern)—"truth of being" leading us to our selfhood: *Ereignis*.

Ever since the "Letter on Humanism," although I used term *Sein*, I had *Ereignis* in mind (Heidegger, in the Thor Seminar); in 1981, Beaufret said, "It is an aberration to name difference itself with the metaphysical name of Being." (DH, 124)

If Greek philosophy as a whole is the forgetting of Heraclitus' fragment in which Being is referred to as *phusis*, we must dare say that the Greeks philosophized on the basis of the "open-without-withdrawal" and did not reflect sufficiently on the withdrawal itself, dazzled as they were by the "overabundance of presence" that culminated in "present" beings (then perceived as "beautiful," or "completely unveiled" and "appearing fully"), while the *presence* itself of beings remains "non-apparent" within them. All that took place for the Greeks on the basis of an indifference to the withdrawal, even though it was the very origin of the phenomenon—an origin that is known and sometimes even recognized, but denied nonetheless, so powerful was the nocturnal power of the concealment, the force of the *lêthê*, which placed all values on the side of the uprooted truth, as though it were necessary to separate oneself from that source, a source too difficult to master.

> When the understanding of Being settles on Being as *Anwesenheit*, that is to say, as *Unverborgenheit* [it is this term that Jean Beaufret renders as "open-without-withdrawal"] then it is the essential moment of *Lêthê* in *alêtheia* which itself remains in the *lêthê*. (DH, 124)

What took place for the Greeks through a kind of denial of *Lêthê* can only take place violently, brutally, for us, "men of entities," on the basis of the disappearance, not of an "overabundance of presence" but of the "overpowering of entities," and in such a way that in a fleeting flash the withdrawal suddenly touches and regards us: it regards and concerns us, and we must both respect and shelter the *nothing* that arises beyond all devastation, when at Hiroshima the "uprooting of all beings" occurs. This *nothing* concerns us *insofar as it has not been thought through by Western metaphysical thought*. It reaches us as "unthought." How can we escape this fire, that which in thought has still not been thought? We must rather leap through it, as "through a flame" (PR, 60). "Hiroshima" thus appears not as an event of the past but as a *precursory* event in the sense in which *Time and Being* speaks of a thought that looks ahead by stepping back.

If everything seems to take place between Heraclitus' "lightning" or "thunderbolt, which "pilots all things" (fragment 64), and Hiroshima's lightning, and if the bomb seems to have already exploded long ago in the pre-Socratic sky, it is then actually "in reverse" that everything takes place and is illuminated. "Hiroshima" compels us to reinterpret Heraclitus (see the 1966 seminar). Because the "withdrawal" as such has not been thought through, *logos* gained priority over *êthos* and covered it so much that, as Heidegger noted in his courses on Heraclitus (GA 55, 215), man is defined as "a living being for whom *logos* is proper" and not "a living being for whom *êthos* is the most proper." In fact, *logos* is a *comportment* of man and thus already belongs to *êthos*. Logic is a kind of ethics, but due to the insistence on present beings, logic has superceded ethics, leading to the triumph of cybernetics. *Logos*, as a *judicative statement*, has superceded *speech*. Conforming to this orientation, ethics itself in Western thought has been *determined* on the basis of the understanding of being as *constant presence (habit)*. As Schopenhauer explains when he cites Aristotle, it is *the constancy of the habit* that has served to designate the *constancy of character* expressed in *morals*.[20]

In Homer already, *êthos* designated a place habitually frequented, a familiar place, for example, the stallions go where they know the cavalry stands. Bringing out ethics from "forgetting" thus requires us to construct the *êthos* on the basis of the nonhabitual, and this is where the thought of an "originary ethics" encounters "the uncanniness" of the "atomic age," whose effects Hiroshima intensifies in a place that is to be thought as a fourfold. How could the *nonhabitual or the uncanny* be a dwelling *place*? On the basis of what *withdrawal* and what *approach* of being can we inhabit a new way of being instead of acquiring a habit? In order for logic to find the ethical dimension again, a dimension *from which it springs*, one would need to try to *unfold language*—that resonance that is ours, corresponding to the movement that is being—before it becomes a *judicial statement* therefore, to unfold language from the *distance* of its "proximity" (see Heraclitus, fragment 122). Perhaps it is only in this way that a "rootedness" could be granted to "uprooting."

At the end of March 1954, Professor Tomio Tezuka paid a visit to Heidegger in Freiburg and had a conversation with him. "He then asked me, 'In Japanese there is presumably a word for language, so called:' "What is the original meaning of this word?" I replied, "The word you are asking about is: *kotoba*. . . . I suppose that the koto is connected to with *koto* [meaning matter] of *kotogara* [meaning event or affair (*Sache*)]. The *ba* is a sound transformation of 'ha' and has connotations of 'many' or 'dense,' as with leaves (ha) on a tree. If this is right, then the *koto* of 'language' and the *koto* of 'matter' are two sides of the same coin: things happen and become language (*kotoba)*. The words '*kotoba*' may have its roots in ideas of this kind. This explanation seemed to fit well with Heidegger's ideas."[21]

A bit later, in a "Dialogue on Language between a Japanese and an Inquirer," this exchange was as follows:

I: Then as the name for language what does *Kotoba* say?

J: Language, heard through this word, is: the petals that stem from *Koto*.[22]

This flower of speech is there like a homage to Shuzo Kuki, a student of Heidegger's at Marburg and a dear friend, who "died too young" (in 1941). Kuki, the first, explored the proper Japanese *êthos* on the basis of the uncanny of Western *ethos* (which Heidegger had explored in his "hermeneutics") in his 1930 essay *Iki No Koso* [*The Structure of Iki*]. His grave welcomes us at the threshold of Heidegger's text, which effects an inverse movement with the aim of encountering the *uncanny* proper to Japan. "*I*: I am happy to have photographs of Kuki's grave and of the grove in which it lies" (OWL, 1).

Kuki's grave is a homage as well, through him, to all those who died "too young," who in Hiroshima suffered the most "uncanny" suffering, thus inciting speech to another saying, *leading ethics, as ethics, to ethics*, "rooting" it in "the atomic age."

Notes

This chapter was translated by François Raffoul and David Pettigrew.

1. Richard McKeon, *Introduction to Aristotle* (New York: Random House 1947), p. 331.

2. Martin Heidegger, "The Age of the World Picture," in QCT, 153.

3. Kenzaburo Oe, *Hiroshima Notes*, translated by David L. Swain and Toshi Yonezawa (New York: Marion Boyars, 1995), p. 181. (Hereafter cited as HN).

4. M. Heidegger–Kojima Takehiko: Une correspondance, in *Philosophie*, vol. 43 (Paris: Minuit, 1994), p. 5. (Hereafter cited as *Philosophie*, followed by the page number.)

5. Martin Heidegger and Eugen Fink, *Heraclitus Seminar* 1966/67, translated by Charles Siebert (University: University of Alabama Press, 1979), p. 17.

6. John Hersey, *Hiroshima* (London: Penguin Books, 1946), p. 68. (Hereafter cited as H.)

7. Georges Bataille, "Concerning the Accounts Given by the Residents of Hiroshima," in *American Imago* 48:4 (1991): 500 (emphasis added). (Hereafter cited as GB.)

8. Martin Heidegger, "Letter on Humanism," in BW, 231.

9. Martin Heidegger, "What Are Poets For?" in PLT, 93.

10. Martin Heidegger, "The Thing," in PLT, 166.

11. Martin Heidegger, "Science and Reflection," in QCT, 171.

12. Heidegger, *Langue de tradition et langue technique* (Paris: Lebeer Hossman, 1999), p. 31.

13. "The Nature of Language," in OWL, 62.

14. *L'affaire de la pensée* (Toulouse: TER, 1965), 20 (and note p. 43).

15. "Only a God Can Save Us": in *Heidegger: The Man and the Thinker*, edited by Thomas Sheehan (Chicago: Precedent Publishing, 1981), p. 56. (5/31/1976 interview published just after Heidegger's death)

16. "The Basic Question of Being As Such," *Heidegger Studies*, vol. 2, 4 (1986):5.

17. On this crucial problem, see Jean Beaufret, *Dialogue avec Heidegger*, vol. 4 (Paris: Minuit, 1985), p. 78. (Hereafter cited as DH.)

18. On this issue, see Pascal David's illuminating article, "L'ontologie n'est pas fondamentale," in *Philosophie*, vol. 62 (Paris: Minuit, 1999).

19. Martin Heidegger, "On the Question of Being," in P, 310-11.

20. See Arthur Schopenhauer, *The World As Will and Representation*, translated by E.F.J. Payne (New York: Dover, 1969), §55.

21. "Tomio Tezuka, 'An Hour With Heidegger,'" translated by Graham Parkes, in *Heidegger's Hidden Sources* (London: Routledge, 1996), p. 60.

22. Martin Heidegger, "A Dialogue on Language between a Japanese and an Inquirer," in OWL, 47.

19

Praxis and *Gelassenheit*
The "Practice" of the Limit

ANDREW MITCHELL

According to Heidegger, the thought of practice—the thought of all that has unfolded from the Greek delineation of πράξις—reaches its culmination at the end of metaphysics in Nietzsche. For Nietzsche, a practical activity lies at the foundation of all living beings (the organization and schematization of a surrounding chaos), and without this act, there is no life. Heidegger's confrontation with this Nietzschean end position (as well as with the corresponding ascendancy of the *animal rationale* therein) determined his thought of practice in the years to come. In the 1939 lecture course *Nietzsche's Doctrine of the Will to Power As Knowledge* (GA 47), Heidegger showed that Nietzschean practice is the imposition of a *limit* upon chaos, and that this limit is always overstepped in the constant expansion of the will to power. Six years later, in the 1945 conversation entitled "'Αγχιβασίη" (GA 77), Heidegger returns to the thought of practice as an act of limitation, though now, for Heidegger, that limit is neither imposed from without nor always to be overstepped. Rather, it is a limit that arrives from the things themselves, in what Heidegger here for the first time calls "releasement" (*Gelassenheit*). Releasement expresses Heidegger's mature understanding of practice, and it is only arrived at by going through Nietzsche.

The Praxis of the Will to Power in Stabilizing Chaos

Heidegger's confrontation (*Auseinandersetzung*) with Nietzsche is at its most strenuous in the 1939 lecture course *Nietzsche's Doctrine of the Will to Power As Knowledge* (GA 47). Here Heidegger presses the thought of the first Nietzsche course (*The Will to Power As Art* [GA 43]) even further, with results decisive for his final understanding of Nietzsche,[1] particularly in regard to life. It is no exaggeration to say that the thought of life, the ground of both art and knowledge for Nietzsche, is ultimately what is at stake in the Heidegger–Nietzsche confrontation. Life likewise provides the context for Heidegger's considerations of practice in *The Will to Power As Knowledge*. Here Heidegger doggedly pursues Nietzsche's thought of truth as a necessity of life past its easily misunderstood biological couchings, past its unwitting restatement of truth as correctness, and into the heart of its claim to necessity, into the Nietzschean concept of chaos.

The analysis begins with a note from the spring of 1888, first published in *The Will to Power*: "Not 'to know' [*erkennen*] but to schematize—to impose upon chaos as much regularity and form as our practical need requires."[2] Nietzsche seeks a more fitting name for what commonly passes as knowing, the process of a subject becoming familiar with the world. Knowing is nothing theoretical for Nietzsche, but instead is something practical, a comportment he calls a "schematizing." Schematizing, in turn, entails the imposition of regularity and form upon chaos. "Knowing" and "schematizing," "practice" itself and the "need" requiring it, all rest upon the abyss of chaos. A requisite for Heidegger's course, then, is a long look into the abyss.

Chaos surrounds us, presses in, forces itself upon us—"washes over us," Heidegger says (GA 47, 152;Niii, 78). This is the world as Nietzsche understands it—"The total character of the world, however, is in all eternity chaos"[3]—an unstable world of force and becoming. This swirling confusion is not simply somewhere "outside" of us; on the contrary, we too are rife with chaos—"I say unto you: you still have chaos in yourselves"[4]—a chaotic multiplicity of sensations is harbored "inside" each of us. Could one then say that, like the embattled Freudian ego caught between an external reality and an inner unconscious, that this "we," too, is poised at the interface of chaos external and internal? No, for the chaos "tunnels through us"[5] as well: "It is what is nearest. It is so near that it does not even stand 'next' to us as what is over against us, but we ourselves, as bodily beings [*als leibliche Wesen*], are it" (GA 47, 152;N iii, 79). Chaos outside us, chaos inside us, chaos inside and outside of chaos itself, this thickened chaos is all.

To say that we are this chaos as bodily beings is to say nothing less than that we are this chaos as long as we live, for "Life lives in that it bodies."[6] Nietzsche's understanding of the body cannot be cut out from its place in the midst of chaos and enshrined as a predecessor of so much of the thought of the twentieth century, without a certain violence being done to that body, without a severance of its necessarily effusive chaos-character. Life is that embodiment which opens out onto chaos, inseparably joined to a surrounding world of will to power. In addressing this conception of embodiment, Heidegger takes up the phenomenological *Körper/Leib* distinction. Nietzsche's body is not the *Körper*, a material-body occupying a mathematical space with a certain weight; "the living-being [*das Lebendige*] 'has' no mere body [*Körper*] in the aforementioned sense" (GA 47, 159). To be sure, even "having" is the wrong way to understand the living being's bodiliness. Rather, "the living-being *is* bodily [*leiblich*]," where bodily names its way to be. This body (*Leib*) neither encapsulates the living-being, nor encumbers it. Distinct from the discrete body of the *Körper*, the living body, the *Leib*, "is transmission and passage at the same time,"[7] an opening onto Chaos.

But the translation may mislead one here. "Transmission and passage" translates "*Durchlaß und Durchgang*," and without a doubt the most common meaning of *Durchgang* is "passage." However, a literal rendering is not only more to the point but more fruitful as well. The body (*Leib*) is both a letting-through (*Durchlaß*) and a going-through (*Durchgang*) at the same time, and this in regard to chaos; the body both lets Chaos through *and is itself that which goes through* (i.e., Chaos). Insofar as it is chaos, the body goes through and lets itself through . . . itself. This is the structure of the "thickened" Chaos, mentioned above. The body is our belonging to the world, streamed through with chaos: "Through this body flows a stream of bodily life."[8] And we too as bodily beings are only a different formation of this chaos streaming through: "That Chaos of our region of sensibility which we know as the region of the body is only *one section* of the great chaos that the 'world' itself is" (GA 47, 153;Niii, 80). Like a cookie cut out of dough, there is no essential difference between us and the world: "*This world is the will to power—and nothing besides!* And you yourselves are also this will to power—and nothing besides!" (WTP, §1067;KSA XI, 611).

Yet, life is not simply rampant dissolution and wild destruction; it also is stability and repose. More, life is being. Heidegger does not miss a note of Nietzsche's from the mid-1880s: "Being—we have no idea of it apart from the idea of 'living'—How can anything dead 'be'?"[9] Living can provide a model for being, only because the living-being must establish itself within chaos. Where life is, there being will be. Life requires a fixing, forming, and mastering of chaos if it is to endure. The body itself is such a formation, a "structure of dominance"[10] or mastery (*Herrschaftsgebilde*), a modulation of the chaos surrounding it: "Our body bodies as a wave in the stream of chaos" (GA 47, 156;Niii, 82, tr. mod.). Thus while chaos rips life forth into its stream, life also must take a stand. Heidegger thinks this coincidence of streaming chaos and stabilized life by the word "urge" (*Drang*). As far as life is this "chaotic bodying and throng of excessive self-urging [*umdrängte Sichüberdrängen*]," life must coevally "withstand the urge and the excessive urge [*Drang und Überdrang*]" (GA 47, 162;Niii, 85). The logic of the urge is peculiar, however, and as an essential component of life it warrants a moment's attention.

Heidegger points out that the urge cannot be an urge that drives [*drängt*] the living being to its destruction or annihilation (it is not a death drive, for instance), since in this case the urge "would simply have driven itself away [*sich selbst verdrängte*] and would never be able *to be* an urge" (GA 47, 162;Niii, 85). This persistence of the urge is precisely what is so urgent about it. The urge of Chaos urelentingly urges life toward dissolution, without ever delivering life from the urgency of that urge. Life has always already opposed the urge to dissolution simply by being alive. For life to feel the urge of chaos it is necessary that life already have established itself; the urge requires such an established life if its urgency is to be felt at all. Heidegger writes that within the essence of the urge, there lies an urge "to *not* succumb to the onslaught, but to withstand it, even if only in order to be able *to be* wholly urgeable and excessively *self*-urging [*sich überdrängend*]." The resistance necessary for the urgency of the urge is itself something urged and urgent. The urge is in its essence an antagonism of urges. The urge, *life*, is inescapable.

In this, the structure of the will to power as interpreted by Heidegger is recognizable, a doubled movement of establishing and overcoming.[11] The similarity between the logic of the urge and the will to power is made clear in the recapitulation that opens the next sitting of Heidegger's course. Life must in a certain way establish itself, he says, "In a certain way, i.e.: through a stabilization of the urge, this urge must not be laid to rest [*stillgelegt*], but rather must only be so fixed [*festgelegt*] that in it and through it there persists precisely something fixed [*Festes*] that can be urged beyond and overcome [*überdrängt und überwunden*]" (GA 47, 168). The fixating of the urge is necessary so that life may continue to overcome itself. It supplies a hurdle for life to leap over in its excessive self-urging. In his first lecture course on Nietzsche, Heidegger identifies this peculiar urging with the will: "It [the will] is not only a feeling of something urging [*etwas Drängendem*], but is itself something urging [*etwas Drängendes*]" (GA 43, 61;Ni, 52). The insatiability of the will keeps open "our very state of being," which Heidegger reciprocally terms "an urging [*Drängen*]" (GA 43, 61;Ni, 52). This state of being is only open, however, because it must continually go beyond itself in order to be itself; it is an openness for the continued appropriation of the world (chaos). But since no essential difference can obtain between the self and the world while both are of the same chaos, the world is simply a hitherto unformed and yet to be appropriated aboriginal self. The will is thus open for the incessant appropriation of . . . itself. Willing must seize the self outside of itself in order to be itself. "Willing always brings the self to itself; it thereby finds itself out beyond itself. It maintains itself within the urging [*Drängen*] away from one thing toward something else" (GA 43, 61;Ni, 52). The body opens onto chaos, where it is willfully urged beyond itself. Such is life for Nietzsche, life as will to power.

With this, the importance of practice for Nietzsche comes into view—it is a necessity of life. Life must stop up the flow of chaos if it is to live, especially since, as we have seen, life is precisely the overcoming of such temporary stoppages of flow. This stopping up and fixing is what leads Nietzsche to replace "knowing" with "schematizing": "Not 'to know' but to schematize—to impose upon chaos as much regularity and form as our practical need requires" (WTP, §515;KSA 13, 333). Schematizing forms chaos, lends it *Gestalten*, schemata, and this is a practical act, an act that is ultimately the work of reason ["reason is in its essence 'practical reason,' as Kant saw" (GA 47, 166;Niii, 88)]. The thought of reason as just such a practical strategy of life is commonplace in Nietzsche. Reason stands in the service of life, and in this regard it is no different from the hide, claws, or teeth of an animal, all of which are likewise furnished for the furtherance of life: "Just as certain sea animals, for example, the jellyfish, develop and extend their tentacles for grasping and catching, the animal 'man' uses reason and its grasping instrument, the principle of contradiction, in order to find his way around in his environment, in that way securing his own subsistence [*den eigenen Bestand zu sichern*]."[12] But there is a difference, perhaps, between the use of reason and the flailing of a psuedopod, for the object which reason fixes (*das Feste*) is the particular being (*das Seiende*). Looking out into chaos, reason apprehends (*vernimmt*) "the particular being *as* particular being,"[13] and fixes it: "Something fixed, however, is called [. . .] a particular being" (GA 47, 176;Niii, 92, tr. mod.). The practice of life is the constitution of a world of beings.

Consequently, schematizing is the most practical of practices—a practice more "practical" than either eating or drinking—the practice of world formation. Heidegger calls this original schematizing a "praxis," one that "belongs to the essence of life."[14] The traditional view of praxis as a "deed" or an "activity" by which goals are realized and intentions carried out misses the necessity of praxis for life.[15] Heidegger claims that, thought originally, praxis first means neither "deed" nor "activity" but rather the sheer "performance of life" (*Lebensvollzug*), the "liveliness" of the living being (i.e., nothing other than the stabilization of chaos).

Now Heidegger describes this stabilization in terms of a limitation; the living being looks out upon chaos with an eye toward "a fixing and thus a limiting [*Eingrenzendes*]"[16] of the confusion it encounters. The delimited world is never free from this surrounding chaos but is exposed to it in essence. Consequently, the limit of the world (the boundary between beings and chaos) takes the form of a horizon (τό ὁρίζον): "To the essence of the living in its liveliness, to stabilization in the manner of a requirement for schema, there belongs a horizon" (GA 47, 163-64;Niii, 86, tr. mod.). But a horizon cannot be understood to be impenetrable and set in place. It is instead a flexible boundary, expandable and restrictable. And life requires it so; the reason that establishes the world of beings is a "projective perception" (*entwerfendes Vernehmen*) that must first gaze out into the chaos in order to fix it (GA 47,166;Niii, 88). The horizon, then, must in some sense be translucent, and Heidegger does not fail to reiterate its permissive qualities: along with "translucent" (*durchscheinend*), it also is pervious (*durchlässig*), somehow traversed or measured through (*durchmessen*) and, in "a broader sense of 'seeing' and 'looking,'" something likewise "seen through" (*durchblickt*).[17] Because of this permissiveness of the horizon, the living being is exposed "to what is not-fixed, what becomes and can become, to the possible" (GA 47, 165;Niii, 87). The horizon makes possible a further appropriation and stabilization of chaos (i.e., growth). Life thrives on chaos and sets itself a limit so that it may be exposed to chaos. The necessity of schematization is nothing other than a necessity for a still more unfixed chaos.

The horizon drawn by reason "sets limits and stabilizes," and for this reason it is what "first lets chaos appear *as* chaos" (GA 47,166;Niii, 88). If the horizon did not establish a limit to the chaos, chaos could not appear *as* chaos, for there would be nothing other than chaos. To appear *as* chaos, chaos also must be able to appear as something else. Chaos appears *as* chaos to something other than that chaos. Chaos cannot appear *as* chaos to chaos itself when there is nothing other than chaos. For chaos to appear *as* chaos there must be a living being, a fold or formation within the sea of chaos (a "wave," Heidegger says). For chaos to appear *as* chaos, there also must be chaos *as* life. Now if the horizon were not translucent, chaos could not *appear* at all. The translucency of the horizon exposes the living being to chaos. When Heidegger claims that "praxis and chaos belong essentially together,"[18] he can only do so because the limit is translucent, because at their limit chaos and praxis touch. This belonging together brings a mutuality or reciprocality to praxis and chaos. Praxis needs chaos for its work of life, while chaos needs praxis to appear as chaos.

Nevertheless, the thought of belonging together demands a stronger claim. Chaos appears as chaos to a living being mortally dependent upon the stabilization of chaos. But this is as much to say that chaos can only appear as chaos to a will that seeks to stabilize it. The belonging together of praxis and chaos means that chaos cannot be other than for praxis, that praxis cannot be without this chaos which is for it. This is of drastic importance in Heidegger's understanding of Nietzsche. Because life itself is only a formation of chaos, that is, nothing other than chaos, nothing in the "world" is inherently other to life. Life is a wave upon the sea of chaos in a world where land is nowhere in sight. Consequently, nothing necessarily resists the appropriations and schemings of life. As such, there is no sense of chaos apart from life. Chaos is only the yet-to-be-formed material of life. This is the reasoning behind one of the most "violent" moments of interpretation in the *Nietzsche* courses, Heidegger's claim that chaos for Nietzsche is a hidden order: "Nor does Nietzsche mean by chaos what is tangled as such in its confusion, the unordered, arising from the removal of all order; rather, chaos is what urges [*Drängende*], flows, and moves, whose order is *concealed*, whose law we do not immediately know [*kennen*]."[19] The order of chaos is its stabilization; the concealedness of that order is that stabilization as yet-to-be. Heidegger's claim that chaos bears a hidden order arises from his consideration of the belonging together of chaos and praxis. The belonging together of chaos and praxis means that chaos exists as yet-to-be-ordered. But this yet-to-be-ordered affects chaos in essence. Chaos *is* life to be (possibility). Because there is no essential difference between bodily life and the surrounding chaos, because there is nothing sacred to the will and nowhere to hide from life's appropriations, chaos exists as orderable in essence, as the always already to-be-ordered.[20]

Praxis is the practice of setting limits to life. But the limit that praxis sets is always only to be transgressed—it must be, for life is nothing more than this transgression. Life is born of such overstepping and first begins from the limit. Heidegger expresses this in a thought recurrent throughout his work, that a limit is not an ending but a beginning: "The liveliness of a living being does not cease at this *limiting* scope [eingrenzenden *Umkreis*] but continually takes its start from it."[21] Life begins at the limit—this is the fruit of Heidegger's Nietzsche confrontation.

Letting the Limit Be

Despite his criticisms of Nietzsche, Heidegger does not abandon the thought of a fundamental act of delimitation at the essence of existence. Rather, he strips the thought of everything emblematic of Nietzsche and takes it up as his own. Gone is the idea of the living being which must always overstep its bounds. Gone too is the world of one body with this being. Both of these only served to further install the dominance of the technological "subject," by Heidegger's account. Gone finally is the term *praxis*. This practical act of life in its liveliness gives way to what Heidegger terms *Gelassenheit* ("releasement"). This new practical act of delimitation is neither an action (releasement lies "outside of the distinction between activity and passivity"[22]) nor anything practical (releasement is "neither theoretical nor practical" but is said to "occur before this distinction"[23]. Heidegger's thought of releasement emerges from his engagement with Nietzsche and is most fully presented some five years after *Nietzsche's Doctrine of the Will to Power As Knowledge* in "Αγλιβασίη" (1944–1945), a conversation between a scientist, a scholar, and a sage.[24] The discussion of releasement is first arrived at only after a consideration of horizon.

The horizon, again first considered visually as "an open field of vision [*Gesichtskreise*],"[25] is regarded as essential to human existence as such: "The human is a horizonal being [*ein horizontales Wesen*]" (GA 77, 83). The horizon plays a constitutive role in the experience of such a being, and this relationship is found throughout the history of philosophy. Heidegger points to the Greek/Aristotelian understanding of τέχνη and the Kantian notion of the transcendental as paradigmatic here, but the charge is easily extrapolated to Nietzsche's understanding of praxis, as depicted in the 1939 lecture course. At issue in the thought of the horizon is a movement that would overstep the givens of experience and, in leaping over them, first render them susceptible to experience.

For the Greeks (read Aristotle), τέχνη denotes a bringing to presence, not primarily of an individual product but of an appearance (*Aussehen*) of the thing's essence.[26] This essential appearance, the εἶδος ἐν τῇ ψυχῇ, must be sighted beforehand, prior to any particular thing's coming to be.[27] The arena for the coming into view of these appearances is the field of vision (*Gesichtskreise*) (i.e., the horizon), and this includes the psyche. By τέχνη, "a field of visible appearances [*Umkreis des sichtbaren Aussehen*] of the things, the field of vision, is held open" (GA 77, 86). Consequently, τέχνη cannot be restricted to craft production in any narrow sense but stands for a way of letting things appear. Following Aristotle, τέχνη is a happening of truth (ἀληθεύειν).[28] Even in the simple viewing of a tree, the scholar says, we always see more than the tree; we look "over and out away from what we see" into treehood and thereby "first see the individual tree by means of this looking out beyond" (GA 77, 86). The sage cautions that we do not produce these essential appearances ourselves but rather receive or "welcome" (*empfängt*) them to the psyche. "Treehood, indeed the entire field of vision . . . is not our work. The horizon goes out over us and our abilities. Insofar as we look into the horizon, we see and step out beyond ourselves" (GA 77, 87).

The situation is similar with Kant, where such overstepping is regarded as "transcendental." Here one steps over the particular objects of experience and into their conditions ("I term *transcendental* all knowledge which is occupied not so much with objects as with the mode of our knowledge of objects insofar as this mode of knowl-edge is to be possible *a priori*" [CPR, A 11-12/B 25]). The transcendental "contains a view into the appearance of the objective [*die Aussicht in das Aussehen des Gegen-ständlichen*]. . . . This view, as field of vision, encompasses the perceptual representa-tion of individual objects. It is the horizon of these objects and of the perception directed upon them" (GA 77, 98). As with Greek τέχνη, this horizon is arrived at by stepping over the particular things seen. Heidegger calls this transcendental condi-tioning of experience a representing (*Vor-Stellen*), and its function is similar to the Nietzschean "projective perception" of reason. It is a representing that "going out over the individual objects, delivers to perception a view into the possible appearance of objects [*eine Aussicht in das mögliche Aussehen von Gegenständen zu-stellt*]. This rep-resenting that delivers [a view into the possible appearance of objects] forms the hori-zon for all representation" (GA 77, 98). The horizon of objectivity conditions the objects of experience within it by providing for their representation by thought.[29] In doing so, representing goes beyond the objects of experience, so again the horizon is only encountered through an overstepping of particular beings.

The conversation partners in "᾽Αγχιβασίη" mention Nietzsche only in passing as falling within this metaphysical tradition of horizonal-representational thought—"Nietzsche, too, though with a difference befitting him, thinks the same in his doc-trine of the perspectival constitution of the will to power" (GA 77, 97-98)—yet the analysis in *The Will to Power As Knowledge* leaves no doubt as to the appropriateness of their claim.[30] The "perspectival" constitution of the will to power mentioned in the conversation is connected in the lecture course to the permissiveness of the hori-zon. Heidegger had claimed of the horizon that it was "somehow always measured through and, in a broader sense of 'seeing' and 'looking,' 'looked through [*durch-blicken*]'" (GA 47, 165;Niii, 87, tr. mod.). This widened sense of "looking through" must be understood in connection with what we would call our point of view or, in more Nietzschean terms, our perspective: "Praxis as performance of life maintains it-self within such [acts of] looking through—'perspectives'" (GA 47, 165;Niii, 87, tr. mod.). The praxis of life, as an expression of the will to power, requires such per-spectives, and Nietzsche says as much in *The Will to Power*. "Every strengthening and increase of power opens up new perspectives and means believing in new horizons—this idea permeates my writings" (WTP, §616;KSA XII, 114). Heidegger strictly dis-tinguishes between horizon and perspective; for him, perspective names the projective act of stepping out into chaos with an eye toward establishing a horizon. Perspective and horizon thus belong together: "The perspective is a route of looking through [*Durchblicksbahn*], cleared in advance, in which a horizon is formed. *The character of looking through and looking ahead, together with the formation of a horizon, belongs to the essence of life*" (GA 47, 165;Niii, 87, tr. mod.). One's perspective, then, is the work of one's practical reason ("projective perception"), and it is equipped with all of the categories that Nietzsche views as essential for the living being's ordering of experience (identity, cause, effect, event, subject, object, etc.). This projective ordering constitutive of experience is what Nietzsche calls that "necessary perspectivism by virtue of which every center of force—and, not only man—construes all the rest of the world from its own viewpoint" (WTP, §636;KSA XIII, 373). Nietzsche's perspectivism—Heidegger goes so far as to label it a "Platonism, albeit transposed to modern thinking"[31]—places him firmly within the tradition of horizonal-representational thought.

Each of these positions thinks of the horizon of experience as first opened up by a movement of overstepping. This one movement, known by so many different names throughout the history of philosophy, Heidegger calls a willing.[32] Willing encounters the horizon of experience by stepping over the given. The horizon, however, remains determined by the "steps" that lead up to it: "Horizon and transcendence are thus experienced starting from the objects and our representing, and are determined only in relation to the objects and our representing" (GA 77, 111;DT, 64, tr. mod.). The horizon is not only a horizon of the will but a horizon of representation as well. Heidegger sees in representing the willful activity of jumping past what is given in order to make of it a possible object of experience; what is *represented* in this manner becomes an *object* of representation. As a result, the thought of thinking as representational is inextricably bound up with the will; representing is a striving and a willing.[33] The representational horizon—and this means the limit of representation—is an effect of the will. One could thus make the provocative claim that Aristotle, Kant, and Nietzsche are all representational thinkers.

To step over something, however, there must be room for movement, an openness that in some sense precedes the overstepping and makes it possible. Precisely, this open expanse remains unthought within representational thinking. The metaphysical tradition of willful/representational thought—exemplified here by Aristotle, Kant, and Nietzsche—sees the will to lie at the base of experience. Now Heidegger could partly agree with this, provided that the will is understood as the ecstaticity of Dasein, and experience is thought of as an event in the open or clearing, in which case, ecstatic Dasein could be held to open a clearing. What Heidegger cannot abide is the determination of this open taking its start in things. The representational tradition objectifies the open by thinking of it from the overstepping of things. In its objectified form, the open appears as horizon: "The horizonal [*Das Horizonthafte*], then, is but the side facing us of an openness which surrounds us; an openness which is filled with views of the appearances of what to our re-presenting are objects" (GA 77,112;DT, 64, tr. mod.). The openness that comes to meet us clothed as horizon is called in the conversation *Gegend* ("region"), but as this still thinks the region in its relation to us, a new name is found for the openness itself, *Gegnet* ("that-which-regions").

The failure of representational thinking to think that-which-regions, that is, openness, as anything other than a horizon for the representation of objects bars any further inquiry into the openness itself, into its regioning, and this is to say, at the same time, that it bars any inquiry into Being itself. Friedrich-Wilhelm von Herrmann stresses the central role of regioning in Heidegger's thought: "From regioning [Geg-nen] as the self-opening of the open, Heidegger thinks the essence of truth, of Being, of time, of space, and of the world. From this regioning, the particular being receives its unconcealment or openness, its constitutive Being, its temporality, its spatiality, and its belonging to a world."[34] To think this would require a thinking that did not represent, a thinking that would not be determined by a willing.[35] Within the conver-sation "'Αγχιβασίη," the sage repeatedly claims that he wants non-willing, a think-ing that does not represent. He does not wish to flee out beyond the objects but to abide alongside them in the breadth of things. Heidegger names this thinking a wait-ing.[36] Waiting is "in essence releasement"[37]–it is the "practice" of releasement.

Waiting (Warten) is a way of being in the world, a comportment that "has no ob-ject" and must therefore be distinguished from expectation (Erwarten), the latter counting on something that has not arrived (GA 77, 115;DT, 68.). In fact, if waiting could be said to wait upon something at all, then what waiting would wait upon would be something that had already arrived, even if only in the mode of not yet ar-riving. Waiting would wait for what is not-yet, but without expecting it. That is, wait-ing does not search for anything beyond the not-yet that is already here. But because the not-yet is already here, there is no reason to wait for it. The not-yet names no pres-ence and thus no object for a waiting. If we take the words of the sage literally, he says nothing less than this. In discussing how the overstepping of particular beings deter-mines the objectified appearance of the horizon, the sage emphasizes that "what lets the horizon be what it is, is entirely not yet [noch gar nicht] experienced" (GA 77, 112;DT, 64). This statement hints that the Gegnet is experienced in the horizon as not-yet. The scholar, too, makes a similar claim shortly thereafter: "We are appropri-ated to that-which-regions; but we do not yet experience it as that-which-regions [wir erfahren sie aber noch nicht als die Gegnet]" (GA 77, 124). We are not yet within that-which-regions.

But here we must not be misled; the scientist in the conversation voices a possi-ble misunderstanding: "That sounds as if before then we had been outside that-which-regions" (GA 77, 121;DT, 72). The sage answers both yes and no: "That we are, and yet we are not." Even though we must be admitted into the region, this does not mean that we are outside of it: "We are not and never could be outside that-which-regions." We are always in the Gegnet, even when all we see of it is the horizon, "the side of that-which-regions turned toward our re-presenting" (GA 77, 121;DT, 73). From another point of view, however, we are outside of the region in that we have not yet released ourselves for it by waiting. Both views are correct. The question of our being left outside or admitted into that-which-regions is a meaningful one, but only on the condition that the human has already been admitted into this undecided situa-tion. The sage can claim that "waiting lets itself into the open itself,"[38] but this is still dependent upon a prior acceptance into the open on the part of the open itself. With-out this, there can be no waiting.[39] For this reason, the scientist is wrong to say that waiting, as a being let loose (Los-Gelassensein) from the transcendental relation to the horizon, is "the first moment of releasement [*Gelassenheit*]" (GA 77, 121;DT, 73, tr. mod.). Waiting cannot simply wait its way into the open without further ado. The first moment of releasement is the regioning of that-which-regions. Waiting, however, fulfills releasement. Releasement is thus a letting oneself into something for which one has already been pre-admitted: "We belong in that upon which we wait."[40] As noted by von Herrmann, Heidegger's thinking of releasement here structurally reflects the thinking of *Ereignis*, "The thinking of releasement belongs to the thinking of *Ereignis* and shows the same traits as the latter."[41]

For the human, who belongs to that-which-regions *by essence*, to not be released into that-which-regions is nevertheless to still bear a relation to that-which-regions. The yes/no answer of the sage to the question of our being outside of that-which-regions points to this peculiarity of the human essence. The scholar, too, recognizes this ambivalence; when the question turns to whether we actually are appropriated to the region, he responds, "Thus we are and we are not," a situation described by the scientist as "again this restless back and forth between yes and no" (GA 77, 123). This ambiguous position between yes and no is not something to flee from but rather is itself the human essence that allows admittance into the open. Suspended between yes and no, our "residence [*Aufenthalt*] in this between is waiting"[42]; a residence that is elsewhere described as a dwelling (*wohnen*): "dwelling, after all, already means: the residence of the human on earth."[43]

To dwell within this in-between (in this "dimension"[44]) is to practice releasement, the Heideggerian counter to the praxis of Nietzsche. Waiting in residence between yes and no, the mortals (for this is who we have been speaking of all along) refrain from deciding the fate of things according to their own human, willful needs. Neither do they leap out beyond the things to view them against a horizon. Because waiting does not willfully determine things through a horizon, things no longer have the character of objects (*Gegenstände*) of representation (*Vor-stellen*). It would be wrong to say that they lose their object character, since "they never first attain it" (GA 77, 125). The sage carries this point to its conclusion: "Not only do they no longer stand over against us [*stehen . . . uns . . . entgegen*], rather they no longer stand at all" (GA 77, 114;DT, 67, tr. mod.). In place of this standing—and the connection of *stehen* with *stellen*, and thus with *Gestell*, should not be overlooked—things rest (*ruhen*).[45]

The practice of dwelling is the letting be of this resting. In regard to the thing, to let a thing rest means "to wait upon its thing-essence [*Dingwesen*]," instead of "ambushing it as an object with physical explanations" (GA 77, 133). A few years later, Heidegger will call this ambushing a "challenging-forth" (*Herausfordern*)[46] and see in it the demand that nature reveal itself to us as "purely present,"[47] without remainder. To wait upon a thing's thing-essence, then, is precisely not to challenge it forth, not to decide in advance how it is to be revealed (i.e., as fully so, in accordance with our will and greed), and not to demand that it be purely present. Rather, to wait upon a thing's thing-essence is to let the thing rest *in its essence*, and that means *to not be purely present.* The essence of a thing is a space of concealment, a hiding place from revelation.[48] When things are allowed to essentially show themselves (when a thing *west*), they preserve this hiddenness and self-concealment, and only then can they be said to be whole (*Heil*). The way of being in the world that lets things be what they essentially are is dwelling.

In the lecture "Building Dwelling Thinking" from 1951, Heidegger identifies the "fundamental trait" of dwelling in what he calls a "sparing" (*Schonen*). "The authentic sparing is something *positive* and occurs when, in advance, we leave something in its essence, when we properly shelter it back [*zurückbergen*] in its essence [. . .] *The fundamental trait of dwelling is this sparing*" (VA, 143;PLT, 149, tr. mod.). In dwelling (as sparing), we shelter (*bergen*) what is concealed (*verborgen*) and allow it to remain concealed. Strangely enough, Heidegger uses the exact same term to describe the occurring of that-which-regions in "'Αγχιβασίη." "Regioning is a gathering and sheltering-back [*Zurückbergen*] to a broad resting in an abiding [*zum weiten Beruhen in der Weile*]" (GA 77, 114;DT, 66, tr. mod.). Dwelling is a waiting that admits itself into the regioning of that-which-regions. The sage says that in waiting, "we leave open what we wait upon,"[49] and this can only mean that we leave it *concealed in essence.*

In dwelling, then, things show themselves according to their own measure and not as "purely present." The hiddenness of their essence shines in their presencing. Dwelling brings a limit to willful human encroachment. We are brought back to our place of spending awhile in the breadth of things (our mortal participation in the fourfold). But this becoming mortal on our part (an exposure to *our* limit, death) likewise brings the limit to the things we spare; there is a limit to their revealing. The thing challenged forth—a piece of the standing-reserve (*Bestand*)—is purely present and thus *in excess* of itself. The letting things rest that is practiced in dwelling returns these things to their proper measure, limits their unconcealment, and lets them abide as things. Dwelling attends to this limit between concealment and unconcealment and shelters it. From their limit, the mortals are exposed to this limit of things. Thus the limit does not mark the end of something, but rather "the limit is that from which *the essence* of something *begins* [sein Wesen beginnt]" (VA, 149;PLT, 154, tr. mod.). To wait is to cease overstepping things and to come to dwell near them. This is the meaning of ἀγχιβασίη, a word from Heraclitus, "letting-oneself-into-nearness."[50]

Conclusion

Heidegger's confrontation with Nietzsche in the 1930s made clear to him the extent to which Nietzsche was the culmination of a metaphysical "practical" tradition already in effect with Aristotle and running through Kant, a tradition Heidegger found to be dominated by transcendence, overstepping, and overcoming. In other words, it is a tradition dominated by the will. Nevertheless, we cannot simply have done with Nietzsche, with the entire philosophical tradition, it cannot be so simply overcome—"to cease [*abzulassen*] overcoming,"[51] Heidegger will later name our task. Overcoming is not open to us as human, for we dwell in the between. The scientist is doubly wrong to call waiting (dwelling) a "restless [*ruhelose*] back and forth between yes and no" (GA 77, 123). First, because dwelling is a letting things rest and nothing restless[52] (the scientist himself comes to see this: "Thus there is no restless hanging, rather a calm resting [*ruhige Beruhen*]" [GA 77, 123]). Second, because there is no yes and no. Immediately after convincing the scientist that waiting is a resting, the group agrees that, consequently, hanging is an inappropriate description of it. It is the sage once again who brings the thought to its conclusion: "Just as little do the supposedly fixed pins of yes and no exist, between which we are supposedly hung" (GA 77, 124). In dwelling, things are preserved in their essence, and nothing is purely present; this is a motif that Heidegger considers again and again. It appeared above in the analysis of waiting, where it was said that waiting waits for the not-yet that is already here. We can never be totally removed from that-which-regions. We are always already within it, even if only as not-yet admitted. Alternately, we can never be over and done with gaining admittance to that-which-regions—"the inclination to such out-goings [*Hinausgehen*; i.e., overstepping] does exist, moreover, it is indeed firmly rooted in the human" (GA 77, 95). Rather than free us from responsibility, this situation only heightens it. We can never escape the in-between, undecided and always to be decided.

For this reason, there is still something positive to be found in the nightmarish world of will to power as painted by Nietzsche, a trace of something otherwise. This is the thought of the limit that Heidegger later develops in his thinking of *Gelassenheit*. But this limit, might it not also be a trace, a tracing of another limit, between belonging and non-belonging, the (un)world of will to power and the fourfold?

Notes

1. The analysis of justice, for example, with which the course ends (NI, 632–48;Niii, 137–49), has been given too little attention. "Justice" is one of Nietzsche's five "basic words," according to Heidegger (in "Nietzsche's Metaphysics," NII, 314–29;Niii, 235–46), and provides a second pivot point—after the "new sensibility" of the first course—on which to consider any "twisting free" of metaphysics by Nietzsche.

2. *The Will to Power*, edited by Walter Kaufmann and translated by Walter Kaufmann and R. J. Hollingdale (New York: Vintage Books, 1968), §515. (Hereafter cited as WTP followed by the English pagination.); *Sämtliche Werke. Kritische Studienausgabe.* 15 vols. 2d. ed., edited by Giorgio Colli and Mazzino Montinari

(Berlin: Walter de Gruyter, 1988); KSA, vol. 13, pp. 333–34. (Hereafter cited as KSA, followed by the German pagination. All KSA references are indebted to the indexical work of Scott Simmons, published in the inaugural issue of *New Nietzsche Studies*.)

3. Nietzsche, *The Gay Science*, translated by Walter Kaufmann (New York: Vintage Books, 1974), §109; KSA III, 468.

4. *Thus Spoke Zarathustra: The Portable Nietzsche*, edited and translated by Walter Kaufmann (New York: Viking Press, 1954), Prologue §5; KSA IV, 19.

5. GA 47, 152; Niii, 78.

6. GA 47, 152; Niii, 79, trans. mod. D. F. Krell translates *leibt* as "bodies forth," which seems unnecessary and may perhaps add an unwarranted allusion to something ecstatic in the term. The question of ecstasis here is not to be lightly passed over, especially if the "world" of the body is shown to be a unilateral one, an *un-world* lacking the difference constitutive of world, as I, in fact, take it to be.

7. GA 47, 153; Niii, 79.

8. GA 47, 153. The published *Nietzsche* volume omits the word "bodily" from the phrase "a stream of bodily life"—certainly due to its *redundancy*; cf. NI, 565; Niii, 79.

9. WTP, §582; KSA XII, 153. The quotation also is central to Heidegger's interpretation of Nietzsche's "alleged" biologism; cf. GA 47, 58–60. Also see WTP, §581; KSA XII, 369, "'Being' as universalization of the concept 'life' (breathing), 'having a soul,' 'willing, effecting,' 'becoming.'"

10. GA 47, 154; Niii, 80.

11. One of many statements to this effect, from "Nietzsche's Metaphysics": "In order that the will to power as overpowering be able to advance a stage, that stage must not only be reached but also established and secured. . . . Power can only empower itself to an overpowering by commanding *both* enhancement *and* preservation" (NII, 267–68; Niii, 196–97).

12. GA 47, 195; Niii, 103, trans. mod. I have changed the translation of *Bestand* from "permanence" to "subsistence." The securing of a horizonal region of life is anything but permanent, as Heidegger is at pains to exhibit throughout his course. Rather, life itself as will to power must secure itself only in order to overcome itself. This is at the heart of Heidegger's interpretation of the will to power.

13. GA 47, 181; Niii, 96, trans. mod.

14. GA 47, 162; Niii, 85. Heidegger goes so far as to equate the living being with praxis in the published *Nietzsche* lectures: "The living being *as* praxis . . . is first

installed in chaos as chaos" (NI, 575; Niii, 88, emphasis added). This is a pointed change from the earlier manuscript, which reads, "The living being according to its praxis . . . is first installed in chaos as chaos" (GA 47, 166).

15. Heidegger had, of course, dealt with πρᾶξις in that most traditional of sources, Aristotle, some twelve years prior in his lecture course on Plato's *Sophist* (GA 19; see, e.g., §6c and the whole discussion of φρόνησις and σοφία, esp. §16). For an overview of Heidegger's indebtedness to the Aristotelian notion of πρᾶξις (and the *Nicomachean Ethics* in general), see F. Volpi, "*Being and Time:* A 'Translation' of the *Nicomachean Ethics?*" in *Reading Heidegger from the Start: Essays in His Earliest Thought,* edited by T. Kisiel and J. Van Buren (Albany: State University of New York Press, 1994), for whom πρᾶξις plays a dominant role in Heidegger's conceptualization of Dasein. In Heidegger's readings of Aristotle in the early 1920s, according to Volpi, "*theoria* is no longer viewed as the highest vocation that is to be preferred for human being. Rather, in the context of Heidegger's ontologizing, *praxis* in each of its comportments is elevated to serve as the basic determination of the way of being belonging to human being, that is, as its ontological structure" (p. 202).

16. GA 47, 163; Niii, 86, trans. mod. "*Das Schemabedürfnis ist bereits Ausblick auf Festmachendes und damit Eingrenzendes.*"

17. GA 47, 165; Niii, 87. See also GA 47, 170: "The horizon is not that of 'the eyes,' but rather that of the thinking of beings as such."

18. GA 47, 166; Niii, 88.

19. GA 47, 153; Niii, 80; trans. mod. See also Heidegger's opening review from the course's next meeting; chaos itself " in its essence is no mere confusion, but rather, concealed and not unfolded in its law and structure, the becoming of life as a whole" (GA 47, 160).

20. Michel Haar takes Heidegger to here betray a predilection for a "primacy of forms," a primacy that goes against Nietzsche's "deeper intention" (Haar, "Heidegger and the Nietzschean 'Physiology of Art,'" in *Exceedingly Nietzsche: Aspects of Contemporary Nietzsche Interpretation,* edited by David Farrell Krell and David Wood (New York: Routledge, 1988) p. 27). So Haar construes Nietzschean chaos as "the wealth of forms hidden and waiting to be discovered." In this view, chaos is a superficial strata that serves to veil (and never to compromise) the underlying order and regularity of this supposed storehouse of forms. Heidegger would consequently conceive of "an order in and of itself of forms latent in chaos," a "reservoir of forms" (p. 27), leading Haar to ask, "Isn't Heidegger closer to the Aristotelian notion of form immanent in nature than to the Nietzschean notion of nature of chaos?" (p. 16). Now this simply is not the case. The hidden order of chaos, as shown above, is by no means a field of predetermined possibilities awaiting their

actualization (here to be equated with a coming out of hiding). Rather, what Heidegger sees in Nietzsche is the absence of anything truly beyond the grasp of the rational/practical living being. From this point of view, the chaos of chaos is not chaotic enough. It is, in Haar's own words, "the bottom, the base, or the primary material of the Will to Power" (see "Life and Natural Totality in Nietzsche," translated by Michael Gendre, *Journal of Nietzsche Studies* 3 (spring 1992): 83). Life must exceed itself in order to be alive. There must be ever-more chaos for life to ever increasingly master. The "hidden order of chaos" does not refer to an order somewhere beneath a mere appearance of the chaotic but is rather a determination of that chaos itself. Chaos is determined *as* chaos solely by the possibility of such ordering for life. It is the precondition for the ordering activity of the will to power. Chaos is simply the name for that which is liable to the ordering, that is, delimiting, praxis of the will to power. Despite whatever "puritanism" Haar may find in Heidegger (p. 23), Heidegger's criticism of Nietzsche on this point is ultimately that Nietzsche is not radical enough. The antagonism of life and chaos is certainly of interest to Heidegger, but in the case of Nietzsche, both parties in the contest are isogenous. It is this absence of difference—a difference constitutive of world for Heidegger—that Heidegger criticizes in Nietzsche. It is Nietzsche who is closest to the monist that Haar would like to see in Heidegger, while Heidegger himself, for all of his alleged fixation on Being, is the advocate of difference.

21. GA 47, 164; Niii, 86, trans. mod. Heidegger expresses this thought of beginning from a limit in connection πέρας in 1951's "Building Dwelling Thinking" ("The limit [*Die Grenze*] is not that at which something stops, but rather, as the Greeks recognized, the limit is that from which something *begins its presencing,* [Wesen]," *Vorträge und Aufsätze* 7th ed. (Stuttgart: Verlag Günther Neske, 1994), p. 149; PLT, 154, trans. mod. [*Vorträge und Aufsätze,* hereafter cited as VA, followed by the page number], and in the 1956 *Zusatz* to "The Origin of the Work of Art" ("The limit in the Greek sense does not block off; rather, being itself brought forth, it first brings to appearance what is present [*das Anwesende erst zum Scheinen*]," GA 5, 71;PLT, 83, trans. mod.). In "The Question Concerning Technology" (1953) the thought is expressed in a discussion of τέλος ("Circumscribing [*Das Umgrenzende*] gives bounds to the thing. With these bounds the thing does not stop; rather from out of them it begins to be what, after production, it will be" (VA, 13; QCT, 8). More citations could be added. The GA 47 citation is perhaps Heidegger's first formulation of this important thought.

22. GA 77, 109; DT, 61, trans. mod.

23. GA 9, 358; P, 272: "*Es ereignet sich vor dieser Unterscheidung.*" This quotation from "The Letter on Humanism" occurs within a discussion not of releasement but of thinking. The "Letter," however, is written in the year following "'Αγχιβασίη," wherein Heidegger repeatedly stresses the essential relationship between thinking

and releasement (see, for one example among many, "Thinking is releasement to that-which-regions because its essence lies in the regioning of releasement" [GA 77, 123; DT, 74, trans. mod.]).

24. In fact, the conversation begins by acknowledging its indebtedness to an earlier conversation on the topic of knowing (*Erkennen*; GA 77, 3). The conversation "'Αγχιβασίη: *Ein Gespräch sebstdritt auf einem Feldweg zwischen einem Forscher, einem Gelehrten und einem Weisen*" (1944/1945) in *Feldweg-Gespräche* (GA 77, 1-159) is the source from which was drawn the published "Conversation on a Country Path about Thinking" (in the 1959 volume *Gelassenheit*, 27-71; DT, 58-90, and GA 13, 37-74). The published version, however, is less than a fourth of the size of the source text and differs from it in some important respects: (1) The name of "sage" (*der Weise*) is changed to "teacher" (*Lehrer*) in the published version. This brings the sage by name to a closer connection with the scholar (*Gelehrter*). The scholar is well versed in the history of philosophy and makes that history available to the conversation. The tight relation between *Lehrer* and *Gelehrter* in the published version of the conversation would seem to underscore the necessity of an appropriation of the historical before any possible "overcoming" of it (which is to say again that the history of philosophy must be *verwindet* and not simply *überwindet*). At one point in the conversation, the sage considers the meaning of his name, claiming that a sage (*ein Weiser*) is not someone who knows (*den Wissenden*) but someone who is able to point (*weisen*) to the way (*die Weise*) the human is to follow the hints that come to him or her (GA 77, 84-85). Historical references (*historische Hinweise*) often have helped the conversation along (GA 77, 97), for such references as the scholar provides throughout the conversation oftentimes are those hints (*die Winke*) that the sage will follow. (2) There is a more precise usage of the term "*nötig*" in the published version, which would seem to reflect the continuing evolution of "*Not*" and "*Notwendigkeit*" as philosophical matters for Heidegger's thought (cf. G, 29; GA 77, 105; G, 32; GA 77, 107; G, 32; GA 77, 108). (3) For *Gelassenheit*, Heidegger eliminates the tight connection he had forged between thing and world in the "'Αγχιβασίη" conversation. To this end, the word "*Welt*" is systematically replaced by "*Gegnet*" in the crucial closing pages of the conversation (cf. G, 65-68; GA 77, 149-51), and a long excursus on the thing is removed (GA 77, 126-38), exemplifying that the thing in these pages is a jug, and much of this discussion had come to light in the 1950 essay "The Thing" (VA, 157-79; PLT, 165-86). A comparison between the two conversations consequently helps to better understand the trajectory of Heidegger's thought between 1944 and 1959.

25. GA 77, 83.

26. "Nevertheless τέχνη does not first of all mean the bringing forth of an individual thing but rather the producing and delivering of the sight [*Anblicks*] and the appearance [*Aussehens*] of a thing; according to this appearance, the thing is each time produced into presence as appearing as such and such. Τέχνη is the

letting be seen and bringing-into-view of what a thing is according to its essence" (GA 77, 13).

27. Aristotle, *Metaphysics* VII, vii, 1032b22, Τὸ δὴ ποιοῦνώ, ἐὰν μὲν ἀπὸ τέχνης, τὸ εἶδος ἐστι τῇ ψυχῇ ("The thing which produces . . . is the form in the soul, if the process is artificial"); also see 1032b3, 'Απὸ τέχνης δὲ γίγνεται ὅσων τὸ εἶδος ἐν τῇ ψυχῇ ("Things are generated artificially whose form is contained in the soul"). Insofar as the *eidos* in the soul of the artisan is a cause of the product, part of the artisan's craft is a receptivity to such forms. It is the form in the soul that is brought forth in τέχνη. The form is "something brought to view, which we have received, I do not know from where or how" (GA 77, 87).

28. Cf. Aristotle, *Nicomachean Ethics*, VI, ii, 1139a18.

29. Heidegger had said as much in the 1929 *Kantbuch*: "Knowledge of beings is only possible on the grounds of a prior knowledge, free of experience, of the constitution of the Being of beings. [. . .] For its own possibility, therefore, the finite knowledge of beings requires a knowing which does not take things in stride [*nicht-hinnehmendes*] (and which is apparently nonfinite), such as a 'creative' intuiting" (GA 3, 38; KPM, 26–27). The famed treatment of the transcendental imagination that follows lends further support to the claims of the conversation.

30. One could productively consult the section of *The Will to Power As Knowledge*, entitled "The Poetizing Essence of Reason" (§15), for an equally appropriate casting of Nietzsche within this tradition.

31. GA 47, 181; Niii, 97.

32. Heidegger's notion of will, it should be noted, is sufficiently broad to stand synonymous with a host of concepts from throughout the history of philosophy: "By the word 'will,' in fact, I do not mean a faculty of the soul, but rather—in accordance with the unanimous, though scarcely thought out doctrine of Western thinkers—that which grounds the essence of the soul, of spirit, of reason, of love, of life" (GA 77, 78).

33. A full elaboration on this point would require an examination of Leibniz, above all, and his distinction between *perceptio* and *appetitus*: "In the way in which I define perception and appetite, all monads must necessarily be endowed with them. I hold *perception* to be the representation of plurality in the simple, and *appetite* to be the striving from one perception to another" ("Letter to Louis Bourguet," December 1714, in *Philosophical Papers and Letters*, edited by Leroy E. Loemker (Dordrecht: Kluwer Academic Publishers, 1976), pp. 662–63, hereafter cited as PPL. Cf. "The Monadology," in PPL, §§14–15, 644). For Leibniz, the appetitions of the monad are "its tendencies from one perception to another—which are the principles of change" (see "The Principles of Nature and of Grace, Based on Reason" in PPL, §2, p. 636). It

is Heidegger's task to think the belonging-together of perception and appetite as a key moment in the history of will and representation.

34. Friedrich-Wilhelm von Herrmann, *Wege ins Ereignis: Zu Heideggers. "Beiträgen zur Philosophie"* (Frankfurt am Main: Vittorio Klostermann, 1994), p. 381. Hereafter cited as WE.

35. This is a point of disagreement between von Herrmann and Emil Kettering. For Kettering, "Heidegger attempts to overcome [*verwinden*] every form of thinking as willing" (Emil Kettering, NÄHE: *Das Denken Martin Heideggers* [Pfullingen: Verlag Günther Neske, 1987], p. 251, hereafter cited as DMH), and for this reason we are only admitted into that–which-regions, "In that we stop all willing and representing and, waiting, admit ourselves into the open of that-which-regions" (DMH, p. 257). Von Herrmann's position is the more reasonable: "The essential determination of thinking and of the human as releasement does not somehow set out to deliver a repudiation of the will as a whole. Much more does it solely concern a thinking of the essence of the human and of his thinking which does not take its start from the will and subjectivity as in the modern tradition" (WE, p. 376). Given the importance that Heidegger attaches to appropriative recovery (*Verwinden*) in opposition to simple overcoming (*Überwinden*; cf. GA 77, 110–11; DT, 63), it would be strange for Heidegger to suddenly advocate a complete abandonment of the will. To be sure, he is quite clear that there is not only a "definite relation" ("*bestimmten Verhältnis*," GA 77, 106; DT, 59, where "*Verhältnis*" points to a relation of essence, cf. GA 77, 120; DT, 72) between willing negation and not willing at all, but something itself that calls for thought in this relationship. In the words of the scholar, "Not only do I see this relation, I confess that ever since I have tried to reflect [*nachzudenken*] on what moves our conversation, it has appealed to me, if not wholly called to me [*Ich bin von ihm . . . angesprochen, wenn nicht gar angerufen*]" (GA 77, 107; DT, 59, trans. mod.). It is von Herrmann's position that informs the understanding of non-willing (*Nicht-wollen*) in the following.

36. Cf. GA 77, 122; DT, 74, trans. mod. "In releasement, then, thinking changes from such a representing into the waiting upon that-which-regions."

37. GA 77, 123; cf. G, 51–52; DT, 75.

38. GA 77, 116; DT, 68, trans. mod.

39. Von Herrmann: "Every essential move from the reign of the region must be given beforehand to thinking so that thinking may let itself into it. That which has been given beforehand, the pre-gift [*Vorgabe*], occurs from out of the region itself, in the manner of a self-opening and self-showing" (WE, 382).

40. GA 77,122; DT, 74, trans. mod. The complexities of this thought are concisely captured by von Herrmann in the statement, "What is to be thought, the open

of being itself, *admits* thinking into itself, so that thinking can respectively *admit itself* into the self-opening open" (p. 383).

41. WE, 384.

42. GA 77, 123; DT, 75, trans. mod.

43. From "Poetically Man Dwells" (1951), VA, 186; PLT, 217, trans. mod.

44. See VA, 189; PLT, 220; trans. mod. "This between is measured out for the dwelling of man. We now term the alloted traversal, through which the between of heaven and earth is open, the dimension."

45. The term *Ruhe* is a term of art for Heidegger around this time and as such requires some comment. In "The Origin of the Work of Art," the work of art *rests* in the unity of Earth and World. "This is the unity we seek when we ponder the self-subsistence of the work and try to express in words this closed, unitary repose of self-support [*Ruhe des Aufsichberuhens*]" (GA 5, 34; PLT, 48). Heidegger cautions against taking *Ruhe* here to be any absence of movement. "It is at any rate not an opposite that excludes motion from itself, but rather includes it. . . . Where rest includes motion, there can exist a repose which is an inner concentration of motion, hence, a highest state of agitation, assuming that the mode of motion requires such a rest" (GA 5, 34–35; PLT, 48). This is the way that the work of art rests, a rest that also is a struggle (*Streit*) of truth's occurring: "The actual reality of the work [*Die Wirklichkeit des Werkes*] is defined by that which is at work in the work, by the happening of truth. This happening we think of as the fighting of the conflict [*Bestreitung des Streites*] between world and earth. In the concentrated agitation of this fighting, rest occurs [*west die Ruhe*]. The self-repose [*Insichruhen*] of the work is grounded here" (GA 5, 45; PLT, 57–58; trans. mod.). Rest, then, is a tense repose, and it arises in two contexts within the "'Αγχιβασίη" conversation: (1) *Ruhe* holds together those "opposites" that belong together. When Heidegger differentiates the same (*das Selbe*) from the identical (*das Gleiche*), he does so by recourse to *Ruhe*; the same is that in which seeming opposites belong together, "Only the different can be the same; yes, in the most different there rests the purest same; I would almost yet like to proclaim the reverse: in the pure same there rests the different" (GA 77, 88–89). (2) *Ruhe* is not the absence of motion. When the scientist claims *Ruhe* to be the negative of both movement and work, pronouncing work to be "the life-element for the modern human" (GA 77, 69; cf. VA, 68; EP, 85, trans. mod.: "the human as *animal rationale*, i.e., now as the working being"), he is led to see that "Every doing, then, is necessarily once again a movement, and thus the renunciation of rest" (GA 77, 69). But the scholar completes the thought. Rest itself is no mere not-doing, and the essence of the human is not merely work. The human must "also reside [*aufhalten*] somewhere in the *Ruhe*" (GA 77, 70). The *Ruhe* is the residence between yes and no, the tensed opening of truth.

46. In 1949's Bremen Lecture, *"Das Ge-Stell"* (GA 79, 27).

47. Cf. GA 79, 25: "Indeed, this objective representation, which seems to first let us encounter the presencing [*das Anwesende*], is in its essence already an attack upon that which approaches us [*das uns Angehende*]. In the appearance of the purely present [*der reinen Gegenwart*], which proffers the ob-jective [*das Gegenständige*], the objective [*das Objecktive*], there is concealed the greed of representing calculation."

48. In a thorough presentation of the fluctuating history of the term *Wesen* in Heidegger's thought, Alfons Grieder notes this sense of "hiding" as well, though he limits it to the work of the 1930s (particularly to the essay "On the Essence of Truth," where one can indeed read, "We want to show that the essence of truth is not the empty 'generality' of an 'abstract' universality but rather that which, self-concealing [*sich verbergende*], is unique in the unremitting history of the disclosure of the 'meaning' of what we call Being" [GA 9, 200; P, 153]). Grieder finds at least two senses in which essence may be said to hide, first in the forgetfuless of Being (since, as Heidegger says, "in the concept of 'essence,' philosophy thinks being" [GA 9, 200; P, 153]), and second in that Heidegger holds "that all disclosure of Essence, Being, and beings as beings is necessarily tied to closure" (p. 190). It is this second sense of hiding that I seek to show operative in Heidegger's thinking of essence during the 1940s.

49. GA 77, 116; DT, 68, trans. mod.

50. GA 77, 155; DT, 89.

51. ZS, 25; TB, 24, trans. mod.

52. It is worth noting the antagonism of a world of restful dwelling and the conception of a world of chaos. According to Heidegger, this antagonism is a somewhat late development. Heidegger explains that in Hesiod (cf. *Theogony* 116) χάος originally means something like an opened "yawning" and "points in the direction of a measureless, supportless, and groundless gaping opening" (GA 47, 149; Niii, n. 77, trans. mod.). Later, however, the word comes to be indissociably linked to movement. "In its later significance, chaos also always means some kind of 'motion'" (GA 77, 150; Niii, 77). A world of chaos would thus appear incompatible with a thought of rest. In a footnote to the manuscript, Heidegger quickly sketches some comments as to why the basic experience named by chaos did not come to master the handed-down meaning but was rather overtaken by motion: "Collapse of ἀλήθεια: the open of unconcealment, of the arising presence and remaining [*des aufgehenden Anwesens und Bleibens*]—and the open of the gaping, of the arising of what remains out [*des Aufgehens des Ausbleibenden*], of the self-withdrawing and thus of the empty, stand in a veiled essential connection" (GA 47, 150, n. 1). Heidegger connects χάος to ἀλήθεια elsewhere too. In a note dated May 1937, Heidegger writes of the question concerning the essence of truth as a question entirely removed from any type of epistemology or logic. This question receives its true significance, he claims, when it

becomes a questioning back into "the first beginning," where it "first makes visible ἀλήθεια and with this φύσις–χάος–τέχνη–οὐσία–νοῦς in their concealed essence and thereby points to the concealment of Da-sein in philosophy before now, allowing an intimation of the reason [Grund] for this" (GA 43, 285). Along similar lines, David Farrell Krell provocatively links χάος to another ancient word elsewhere employed by Heidegger, χώρα (cf. Nii, 91–92 n.; the word is found at GA 40, 70–71; IM, 53–54).

20

Psychoanalytic Praxis and the Truth of Pain

WILLIAM J. RICHARDSON

The truth of pain is pain itself.

—Anonymous

T his chapter was written as a contribution to a *Festschrift* in honor of Patrick Heelan, Ph.D., on his seventy-fifth birthday. He and the writer had been colleagues and friends since their first meeting in graduate school. Heelan has continued to explore the contributions of phenomenology to the philosophy of science. The writer [of this chapter], originally concerned with the question of Being and its truth in Heidegger, had broadened his interest to include the philosophical foundations of psychoanalysis. There the question of truth remained central, however. In fact, even Heidegger's conception of truth as *alêtheia* returned serendipitously to center stage. To salute the occasion, it seemed appropriate for the writer to reflect briefly on the relation between science and truth as this issue is posed now in the work of French psychoanalyst Jacques Lacan, the so-called "French Freud." He spoke at different times and in different ways about both subjects, but he thematized the two together in a well-known essay, "Science and Truth."[1] It is hardly a major landmark in his thought, but it can serve here as a convenient point of reference for this brief, unavoidably incomplete, reflection.

Science

Lacan's interest in science was a function of his effort to clarify in what way psychoanalysis can be considered a science. Clearly Freud wanted to qualify it as such, for this was the only way, he thought, to give his discovery of the unconscious intellectual respectability in the scientifico-cultural world of his time. The classical

hypothetico-experimental methodology of nineteenth-century science held for
Freud an abiding fascination, and his ambition, initially at least, was to develop a
theory of psychoanalysis that could approximate an analogous certitude. But the
classic methodology rested on an epistemology that was positivistic in nature,
where objects of research were essentially accessible through sense perception, and
any contribution of the subject to the knowability of the object could be, in principle, disallowed by the rigor of procedure. For Lacan, however, the scientific paradigm of choice was not nineteenth-century physics but twentieth-century
linguistics. Here the role of the subject, especially when the method is applied to
psychoanalysis, is inseparable from the research procedure itself, and the scientific
character of the process must be conceived of differently. That difference was
marked by the methodology of structuralism, to which Lacan was introduced by
the work of Lévi-Strauss. Where natural science for Freud was "grounded" in a positivist (physically measurable, cause-effect) epistemology, the structuralist method
was "grounded" for Lacan in the sheer formalism of the process:

> This is the problem of the grounding that must assure our discipline its place
> among the sciences: a problem of formalization. . . .
>   Linguistics can serve us as a guide here, since that is the role it plays in the
> vanguard of contemporary anthropology. . . .
>   And the reduction of every language to the group of a very small number
> of these phonemic oppositions, by initiating an equally rigorous formalization
> of its highest morphemes, puts within our reach a precisely defined access to
> our own field.[2]

Lacan's espousal of this formalizing methodology as it occurs in Lévi-Strauss'
work appears in the following:

> It is clear that [Lévi-Strauss] . . . can argue for a certain recuperation occurring
> in chemistry, owing to a physics of sapid and odorous qualities, otherwise
> stated, to a correlation between perceptual values and molecular architecture
> arrived at by means of a combinatory analysis, i.e., by a mathematics of the sig-
> nifier, as has been the case in every science to date.
>   What's more, when, after having extracted the combinatory element in
> the elementary structures of kinship, [he] reports that a certain informer, to
> use the ethnologist's term, is himself fully capable of drawing the Lévi-Strauss-
> ian graph, what is he telling us if not that, here again, he extracts the subject
> from the combinatory in question—the subject who on the graph has no other
> existence than the denotation ego? (ST, 10)

It is the search for a comparable formalism that accounts for Lacan's always expand-
ing effort to schematize, logicize, mathematicize, and finally topologize his own spec-

ulative conceptualizations: "Mathematical formalization is our goal, our ideal. Why? Because it alone is matheme, i.e., it alone is capable of being integrally transmitted."[3] And all this was in the effort to make scientifically congenial, in terms, at least, of what he preferred to call *conjectural* science, the structuralist ideal that he adopted.[4]

Now this trajectory was made possible for Lacan by his conception of the subject of science, a conception that would serve likewise as a model for the subject of psychoanalysis. Both were born with the *cogito* of Descartes:

> It is unthinkable that psychoanalysis as a practice and the *Freudian* unconscious as a discovery could have taken on their roles before the birth—in the century that has been called the century of genius, i.e., the seventeenth century—of [modern] science. (ST, 6)

By this, Lacan means that the unconscious that Freud discovered has no meaning except with reference to consciousness, as described in the Cartesian *cogito*.

Lacan makes his own Alexander Koyré's (1892–1964) account of the emergence of modern science: how mathematicization of the physical universe through the work of Copernicus, Kepler, Galileo, and others found its philosophical complement in the work of Descartes. Those familiar with Heidegger's critique of technology will recognize the similarity between Heidegger's interpretation of this event and Lacan's. The difference? Heidegger sees in it the birth of the subject-object dichotomy that then spawns scientific positivism with its fateful consequence in the guise of modern technology. Lacan is interested only in the structure of the subject itself that is at issue.

It is this subject, discovered through the *cogito*, that Lacan calls the "subject of science." For him, it is as though the entire scientific enterprise—its history, its institutions, and all of the virulence of its burgeoning power—may be conceived of as the function of a single hypostasized, egoless subject: the "correlate" of science as such, taken as a whole:

> This correlate, as a moment, is the aftermath (*défilé*) of [Descartes'] rejection (*rejet*) of all knowledge [in the hyperbolic doubt], but is nevertheless claimed to establish for the subject a certain anchoring (*amarrage*) in being; I hold that this rejection of all knowledge constitutes the subject of science in its definition. (ST, 5)

Note that this subject is not the subject of limpid self-awareness that the *ego* of *sum* often is taken to be, for it includes the confounding obscurity of the *un*conscious that Freud discovered in it. Rather it is a subject, somehow anchored in "being," that remains after all "knowledge" has been rejected, like the empty field, some of what would eventually be called a *mathesis universalis*. The model for such a subject may be found in game theory, "which takes advantage of the thoroughly calculable character of a subject, strictly reduced to the formula for a matrix of signifying combinations"

(ST, 9). Such a subject is not the concrete, singular scientist who plays the game but the *position* of correlative subject that a given scientist occupies in the game.

Now this same egoless, disembodied subject, Lacan asserts, is the subject of psychoanalysis. Its depersonalized character is insisted upon to distinguish it from the subject with an identity all its own by which it can assume "responsibility," that is, become an individual "responsible" subject (ST, 11). But how can such a subject be disengaged from *cogito*? Lacan replies:

> It is not vain to restate that in the test (*l'épreuve*) of writing *I am thinking:* "*therefore I am*" with quotes around the second clause, the notion is legible that thought only grounds being by knotting iself in speech where every operation goes right to the essence of language. (ST, 13)

I take him to mean that if the subject can say with certitude that "I am," the ground of that certitude is not in the thinking of it but in the *saying* of it. Descartes himself focuses on the thinking of the subject without adverting to the saying through which the illation comes to pass:

> What about thinking? Here I make my discovery: thought exists; it alone cannot be separated from me. I am; I exist—this is certain. But for how long? For as long as I am thinking, for perhaps it could also come to pass that if I were to cease all thinking I would then utterly cease to exist.[5]

In all rigor, however, the illation from *cogito* to *sum* is valid not when thinking is taking place but when the subject *says* that it is taking place, and in that sense it implicitly affirms that it itself undeniably *exists* at that moment precisely in the saying. It is in this sense that "thought only grounds being by knotting itself in speech where every operation goes right to the essence of language" (ST, 13).

The Cartesian subject, for Lacan, then, is before all else a speaking subject, a subject of language. For that very reason it is the subject of the unconscious, for "the way opened up by Freud has no other meaning than the one I have made my own, namely, that the unconscious is language" (ST, 15). Since the beginning of his public teaching (1953), Lacan has reiterated the thesis: "the unconscious is structured like a language."[6] For the cognoscenti, then, the only thing new here is the force of Lacan's assertion: the unconscious *is* language, not simply "structured" by it.

The importance of this remark is that the subject who enters psychoanalysis is not simply the singular human individual that requests it but essentially a "divided" subject. The sense is that the subject is split between a conscious level, dominated by the "ego," which, for, Lacan, is essentially an "imaginary" function as he understands that term,[7] and an unconscious level that is subject to the laws of language operating through it and comes to expression beyond control of the conscious ego. The latter he refers to most frequently not as the "unconscious of the subject" but as the "subject of the unconscious," that is, the unconscious *as* subject, governed by the laws of language.

In explaining how the unconscious works, Lacan utilizes the distinction that Saussure stresses between signifier (speech sound) and signified (concept represented by the sound). There is this difference in usage, however: for Saussure, the signifier refers directly to a signified, but for Lacan, the signifier refers rather to another signifier. The result is that a congeries of signifiers becomes a "signifying chain" that functions like "rings of a necklace that is a ring in another necklace made of rings" (E, 153/502). And the subject? It is not to be identified with the chain of signifiers as such but rather as an effect of them, suspended from them as it were. "Conveyed (*véhiculé*) by a signifier in its relation to another signifier, the subject is to be rigorously distinguished from the biological individual as from the psychological evolution subsumable under the subject of understanding (*compréhension*)" (ST, 23). And, clearly, the signifier must be distinguished from a sign:

> Signs . . . represent something to someone. . . . The register of the signifier is instituted in that a signifier represents a subject to another signifier. That is the structure of all unconscious formations: dreams, slips of the tongue, and puns. The same structure explains the subject's originary division.[8]

This is the subject that speaks through the analysand (*sujet de l' énonciation*) as distinct from the subject of the statement made by the analysand (*sujet de l' énoncé*), which appears on the level of conscious self-awareness.[9] How the signifying chain functions according to such basic laws of language as metonymy and metaphor is too complex a story to be repeated here,[10] but it is such laws as these, taken in the ensemble, that govern the functioning of the unconscious.

For Lacan's disciples, all of this is old hat. He takes time to remind them only that in the seminar of the previous year, *Crucial Problems for Psychoanalysis* (1964–65),[11] he had stressed on the momentary (*ponctuel*), pulsating, peek-a-boo way in which the unconscious irrupts in consciousness. But what sense does it make to say that "the subject on which we operate in psychoanalysis can only be the subject of science" (ST, 7)? Surely the subject is always instantiated in a singular analysand, designated by a name and marked by all of the modalities of identification that go with it. I take Lacan to mean that the basic structure of the unconscious as delineated above prescinds from any singularizing factors and is transindividual, quasi-absolute in nature (like the subject of game theory), the way the subject of science is a position that functions independently of the concrete activity of any individual scientist. This, at any rate, is how I understand the "thoroughly calculable character of a subject [as] strictly reduced to the formula for a matrix of signifying combinations."

Once this much is said, little more is offered explicitly to clarify Lacan's conception of science. He does remark, however, that everything so far concerns the subject of science, but that nothing has been said about its object, a matter that has "remained unelucidated since the birth of science" (ST, 12). As for the "object" of psychoanalysis, Lacan has already spoken of it as *object a* what for Freud was the "lost,—that is, no longer present "object" of the subject's fundamental quest (SE, 19, 237). As "lost," this object is irretrievable; as "cause of desire" (Lacan's formula), it is unattainable. The subject itself (of science as well as of psychoanalysis), then, is marked by an irreparable lack/absence/hole that scars its structure with an ineluctable negativity. If all of this characterizes the object of psychoanalysis, surely "the object of science as such will be thereby modified" (ST, 12)—but Lacan does not take the matter any further here.

Truth

In the aerie of Lacanian theory, what has been said up to now is fairly straightforward. But what can "truth" mean for a subject of this kind? The question for Freud was much simpler than for Lacan. In his *New Introductory Lectures on Psychoanalysis*, he characterizes "scientific thinking" as follows:

> Its endeavor is to arrive at correspondence with reality—that is to say with what exists outside us and independently of us and, as experience has taught us, is decisive for the fulfillment or disappointment of our wishes. This correspondence with the real external world we call "truth." It remains the aim of scientific work even if we leave the practical value of that work out of account. (SE, 22, 170).

As for the truth of psychoanalysis, Freud would probably add nuance to the term *reality* with his distinction between "psychical" and "material" reality (SE, 4/5, 620), but his method would still be analogous to natural science, that is, to search out the causes at play in any given phenomenon under investigation. Evidence for this appears in the frequency with which he refers to his endeavor, especially in the early years, as an "aetiology"] a science (*-logos*) of causes (*aitia-*).[12] But all of this is the language of classical positivism, where truth consists of correspondence between a subject's judgment and an object judged.[13] What happens to truth in psychoanalysis when the positivist ideal is rejected out of hand?

By the time Lacan broaches the question of truth in "Science and Truth," there is a considerable backlog of his remarks on the subject that he can presume his listeners have in mind. In the early years of his teaching, he made much of the distinction between "empty" speech and "full" speech: "empty speech takes place when the subject seems to be talking in vain about someone who, even if he were his spitting image, can never become one with the assumption of his desire" (E, 45/254); "full" speech is achieved not by examination of the "here and now," nor by the examination of resistances, but by *anamnêsis*:

In psychoanalytic *anamnêsis* it is not a question of reality, but of truth, because the effect of full speech is to reorder past contingencies by conferring on them the sense of necessities to come, such as they are constituted by the little freedom through which the subject makes them present. . . . It is certainly this assumption of his history by the subject, insofar as it is constituted by the speech addressed to the other, that constitutes the ground of the new method that Freud called psychoanalysis. (E, 48/256-57).

The truth of the subject comes about then through the speaking that constitutes the psychoanalytic process. It is not based on any kind of correspondence; it is essentially revelatory in nature and takes place when meaning (*sens*) is discovered in a historicizing process. It has no other foundation than the efficacy of the language that utters it and prescinds completely from the "reality" that characterizes the world of its conscious activity. Founded thus in language itself, truth has an inexhaustible resilience: "Even if [language] communicates nothing, the discourse represents the existence of communication; even if it denies the evidence, it affirms that speech constitutes truth; even if it is intended to deceive, the discourse speculates on faith in testimony" (E, 43/251-52).

There is another element in Lacan's backlog: the negativized nature of truth. As early as 1955, in "The Freudian Thing," a paper commemorating in Vienna the centenary of Freud's birth, Lacan delivered a grotesque prosopopeia in the name of truth to the evident consternation of his audience. "Men, listen, I am giving you the secret. I, Truth, will speak." His point is that there is no such thing as total truth—especially in psychoanalysis—and truth arrives at best as damaged goods. Eventually he will claim that no truth can ever be whole (SXX, 92/85). Here, however, he underlines not simply the manifestation but the inevitable *distortion* of truth as it comes to expression:

> For you I am the enigma of her who vanishes as soon as she appears. . . . The discourse of error, its articulation in acts, could bear witness to the truth against evidence itself. . . . For the most innocent intention is disconcerted at being unable to conceal the fact that one's unsuccessful acts are the most successful, and that one's failure fulfills one's most secret wish. . . . I wander about in what you regard as being the least true in essence: in the dream, in the way the most far-fetched conceit, the most grotesque nonsense of the joke defies sense, in chance, not in its law, but in its contingence, and I never do more to change the face of the world than when I give it the profile of Cleopatra's nose. (E, 121-22/408-10)

Truth, then, carries the scars of negativity. In other words, "Error is the habitual incarnation of truth. . . . Error is the usual manifestation of the truth itself—so that the paths of truth are in essence the paths of error."[14] Clearly, any complete account of truth also must consider for the error and distortion (i.e., non-truth) that infiltrate it. Given this much of the backlog recalled, this chapter warrants three further comments.

Truth and Language

The shock effect of the prosopopea (delivered some ten years previously) Lacan recalls in "Science and Truth" with restrained but obvious relish. "Why doesn't he say the truth about the truth?" someone is alleged to have asked. His response:

> Everything that can be said of the truth, of the only truth . . . [comes to this:] there is no such thing as meta-language, . . . no language being able to say the truth about truth, since the truth is grounded in the fact that it speaks, and that it has no other means with which to do so. (ST, 16)

Evidently truth and language are intertwined for Lacan, and since there is no meta-language, there is likewise no "meta"-truth (truth about truth). But why? This goes back to a fundamental principle of Lacan's entire conceptualization: "There is no Other of the Other." By this he means that the Other is the locus of the signifier, language as such, the ultimate resource of the whole signifying system. Within this system, "any statement of authority has no other guarantee than its very enunciation." Inasmuch as the Other thus understood is an "ultimate resource," there is nothing beyond it or outside of it (i.e., no *meta*-language) to serve as its foundation.[15] It is in this sense that "there is no Other of the Other" (E, 310–11/813).

Truth and Unconscious Knowing (Savoir)

It is important to note that the term *savoir*, usually signifies theoretical knowing of an abstract nature or very practical knowing of a concrete nature, that is, know-how (*savoir-faire*). Thus *savoir* in the context of science will refer to that knowledge which is the result of scientific research. In the context of psychoanalysis, however, *savoir* for Lacan refers rather to the *savoir-faire* of the unconscious or, more precisely, to the "network of signifiers which concretely determine, in a structure of repetition, the relation of a subject to the real."[16] He takes pains to make clear that the division of the subject (between unconscious and conscious levels) is one between the *savoir* of the unconscious and truth. He suggests a topological model for this relationship, namely, the Möbius strip, to indicate that "the division where these two terms join together is not to be derived from a difference of origin" (ST, 5). Subsequently he suggests another metaphor: the relation between unconscious *savoir* and truth is like an inscription that "does not etch into the same side of the parchment when it comes from the printing-plate of truth and when it comes from that of [unconscious] *savoir*" (ST, 13).

Clearly there is a profound compatibility between unconscious *savoir* and truth, but how to explain it? *Prima facie*, one might surmise, given what is available in the present context, that since language and truth are thought together, it may be the articulation in speech that transforms *savoir* into truth by liberating it from repression. But that would be too easy, for there is a profound ambiguity in Lacan's use of *savoir* here: is the *savoir* in question science (hence, conscious) or psychoanalysis (hence, unconscious)? And if the latter, does the denotation of "truth" remain univocal in each case?

Leupin takes the *savoir* here to be science and interprets "truth" accordingly. He cites Lacan's own criteria for evaluating the success of any scientific enterprise:

> The only thing important for the scientist is that the phenomenon be communicable in some language (condition of the *mental order*), capable of being registered under some form (condition of the *experimental order*), and that he might be able to insert it in the chain of symbolic identifications where his science unifies the diversity of its own object (condition of the *rational order*). (E, 79)

But is the net result truth? Not at all:

> Truth in its specific value remains foreign to the order of science: science can be honored for its alliances with truth; it can propose to itself as object the phenomenon and its value; [but] it can in no way identify (*identifie*) it for [science's] own purposes. (E, 79)

Truth and [the *savoir* of] science, then, are heterogeneous, irreducibly different, though not "incompatible" with each other).[17] But how is "truth " here conceived in its differentiation from science? Leupin makes it clear that "truth" designates first of all the fruit of the conjectural sciences, that is, the "social" ("human") sciences of the tradition; its application may be extended to areas that may be described as "affective," "aesthetic," "analytical," and to the whole world of what is loosely called "the arts" (LHS, 5). To explain the relationship between the *savoir* of science (which he summarizes with the word "exactitude") and the truth of "conjecture" in the sense just described, he expands Lacan's reference to the Möbius strip (LHS, 9).[18]

If we take a normal strip of paper and, after marking one side "truth" and the other side "exactitude," imagine a homunculus on one side trying to get to the other, there is no way he can do so without leaving the one side in order to gain the other by some kind of magical leap onto a surface that is essentially external to the one from which he starts. Moreover, the strip will necessarily be a limited one and capable of orientation in one direction or another. But if we make the same piece of paper into a Möbius strip by half-twisting it and joining the ends

> our homunculus' situation has completely changed. While he still believes he is walking toward a horizon (that his progress has a direction), he is in fact circling

the strip (a Möbius strip is not orientable [in one direction alone]). Moreover, although he still believes that [exactitude] and [truth] are opposed, in fact they are now inscribed on the same side of the strip, since a Möbius strip has only one surface and one side. In other words, the opposition between the two sides is no longer external; it is internal to the structure. The subject of science is at the same time in and out of both truth and exactitude. (LHS, 9–10)

This is an admirable piece of exposition, and its clarity makes it appealing. Two difficulties remain, however:

1. The *savoir* in question here is science, and clearly on the level of con-sciousness. Can the analysis be simply transposed to psychoanalysis where the *savoir* is the unconscious, where universality, predictability, and the insertion of the phenomenon "in the chain of symbolic identi-fications by which this science unifies the diversity of its own object (which is the condition of the *rational order*)" are hardly the order of the day? In any case, the *savoir* at stake for Lacan is clearly the unconscious, for he begins the present lecture by recalling that he had terminated the seminar of the previous year by formulating the "experienced divi-sion of the subject as a divison between knowledge and truth" (ST, 5). The correlation between *un*conscious *savoir* and truth still remains to be explained.

   Would the analogy of the Möbius strip be equally pertinent in the latter case? An important distinction may be made, it seems, be-tween the *savoir* of the fundamental structure and the *savoir* of the psychoanalytic experience.[19] In the first case, one might postulate a compatible reciprocity between *savoir* and truth, according to which each may reflect the repression of the other. But in the psychoana-lytic experience, there comes a moment when *savoir* and truth are *one*—that time when the subject discovers at last the uniquely singu-lar structure of who she *is* and can say "Thou art that." This, I take it, would be the moment of truth, when "the real journey begins" (E, 7/100).[20]

2. Is the scientific attitude operative here, taking exactitude as its goal instead of truth, congruous with what contemporary scientists actu-ally do when engaged in research? Exactitude (and all that it implies) is certainly necessary for re*search*, but it is not, I submit, what the sci-entist searches *for*. Exactitude characterizes a methodology, nothing more. It is a means, not an end, to determine the way things *are* in the physical world around us, however provisional the discernment must be. What motivates the scientist is surely not exactitude for its own

sake but what lies beyond the horizon of the known, daring him to venture beyond it. Any conception of truth worthy of science must account for this vocation to endless discovery.

Truth and Cause

Most curious is Lacan's proposal to consider truth as cause. One can think in these terms for Freud, perhaps, since, positivist that he was, he could well say that the discovery of the patient's truth (e.g., in "Little Hans" or the "Rat Man") "caused" a relief of symptoms. One might even use this language for the early Lacan, insofar as the achievement of "full" speech would, in principle, cause the liberation of a patient, at least partially, from her neurosis. But what does it mean here?

> The medium which will serve us at this point is one I brought up earlier. It is the cause: not the cause as logical category, but as causing the whole effect. Will you psychoanalysts refuse to take on the question of the truth as cause when your very careers are built upon it? (ST, 17)[21]

What, in fact, is Lacan trying to say? He argues by comparison with other disciplines where truth allegedly also functions as cause: magic, religion, and science. He manages this by introducing Aristotle's language about the four causes, though Aristotle himself might be startled by this claim to paternity. Be that as it may, for Lacan—in magic, truth functions as efficient cause; in religion, as final cause; in science, as formal cause; and in psychoanalysis, as material cause. None of this is self-evident; still less is it satisfactorily argued. For example, what can it mean to say that truth as cause in psychoanalysis comes under the guise of material cause, because of "the form of impact (*incidence*) of the signifier" that Lacan ascribes to it (ST, 22)? How can psychoanalysis, with its "impact of the signifier," which derives from the primordiality of the symbolic, be a *material* cause for science as a formal cause, when science itself, along with whatever "causal" power it has, is grounded in the same symbolic system? In any case, how could the two ever be considered separate and independent? And if we take truth as a formal cause (science) and truth as a material cause (psychoanalysis), what is the effect of this reciprocal causality? Is it truth as such, causing itself to be true? What, then, *makes* it true? What is truth itself? Lacan's thought goes begging here, I am afraid (see ST, 23).

How does one evaluate "Science and Truth" as a contribution to the evolution of Lacan's thought at this period of its development? Anything thorough would have to address the heart of he matter: the identification (here) of the subject of psychoanalysis and the subject of science. But that would make for a long day at the office. More tractable is to comment on Lacan's conception of truth, but even here logistic restrictions make it impossible to do more than sketch the bare essentials of a critique. I shall confine my remarks to three: (1) concerning the fundamental nature of truth; (2) concerning the relation between truth and language; and (3) concerning one fundamental difficulty that must be addressed.

1. Lacan's conception of truth, to the extent that it leaves the achievements of the *savoir* of science beyond its ken, I find deeply flawed. Scientific method, whatever its rigor, is not an end in itself but the means of discovering the way things *are* in the physical world of human experience. The first ingredient of a viable conception of truth must be the discovering of what is the case. More radically, Lacan cites with approval but without elaboration the gnome of a contemporary philosopher, whom he leaves nameless: "The truth of pain is pain itself" (ST, 18).[22] I take this to mean that the truth of pain is not in a judgment about it but in the simple fact that it is what it is and "makes itself seen," that is, "evident" as such.[23] My claim is that e-vidence in its most radical sense of making (letting itself be seen) is the fundamental nature of truth from which all other versions of it derive. Any version of truth (e.g., concordance, coherence) is secondary to the originary manifestation of what is, in fact, the case. I submit that this is the most plausible way to explain the truth revealed by the structuralist method of Lévi-Strauss that Lacan cites with approval, the "correlation between perceptual values and molecular architecture arrived at by means of combinatory analysis, i.e., by the mathematics of the signifier" (ST, 10). The e-vidence (truth) is in the sheer manifestation of the correlation as an index of the way things *are*.

Obviously the notion of originary truth as e-vidence/dis-covery/dis-closure/self-manifestation recalls Heidegger's thematizing of the Greek word for truth, *a-lêtheia*: a combination of *-lêthê* (what lies hidden in concealment) and *a-*, the alpha prefix indicating privation. Taken together, they identify truth as non-concealment, or re-velation. Of course Lacan was fully aware of Heidegger's conception of truth and apparently was quite comfortable with it in 1953 when describing the psychoanalytic process: "In psychoanalytic anamnesis it is not a question of reality, but of truth, because the effect of full speech is to reorder past contingencies by conferring on them the sense of necessities to come, such as they are constituted by the little freedom through which the subject makes them present" (E, 48/256). Apparently he lost interest in the conception as he turned more and more toward the formalism of Lévi-Strauss to develop the "scientific" character of psychoanalysis.

What Heidegger adds to the conception of truth as e-vidence (discovery) is a frequent reflection on the negative component of truth, *-lêthê*. The negativity in question is not simply an absence of manifestation but includes a dynamic quality that Heidegger articulates especially in the essay "On the Essence of Truth." There, after showing that truth as correspondence is made possible by a prior openness (what I have been calling "e-vidence," etc.) between knower and known prior to, and enabling, the judgment of correspondence, he asserts that no account of the essence of truth is complete without a parallel analysis of a corresponding "non-truth," since no re-velation in a finite world can be total, that is, "whole" (*pas toute*). This non-essence of truth takes two forms: mystery (*Geheimnis*), the concealment of what still remains unrevealed, and errancy (*Irre*), a compounding in forgetfulness of this double concealment:

> Errancy is the essential counteressence to the originary essence of truth. Errancy opens itself up as the open region for every counterplay to essential truth. Errancy is the open site for and ground of *error*. Error is not merely an isolated mistake but the kingdom (the dominion) of the history of those entanglements in which all kinds of erring get interwoven.

In conformity with its openness and its relatedness to beings as a whole, every mode of comportment has its manner of erring. Error extends from the most ordinary wasting of time, making a mistake, and miscalculating, to going astray and venturing too far in one's essential attitudes and decisions. . . . By leading them astray, errancy dominates human beings through and through. (P, 150–51, amended)

My suggestion is that this conception of a non-essence (i.e., negativity) of truth is comprehensive enough to make room for the hypostasized Truth of the famous prospopeia as well as for the residual distortions and lies that contaminate truth. This certainly would account for the fact that no truth can be "whole" (*pas toute*). And if we go this far, may we not have a suggestive reading of the following passage?

> This lack of truth about truth, necessitating as it does all the traps that meta-language—as sham and logic—falls into, is the true place of *Urverdrängung*, i.e., of primal repression which draws towards it every other repression. (ST, 16)

To claim a correlation between *-lêthê* for Heidegger and "repression" for Lacan (here even "primary" repression) would be a daring move. But if it worked, we might go one step further and ask if there might not be a discernible similarity between -*lêthê* (Heidegger) and the real (Lacan). If so, the next question would be to ask if the event of *a-lêtheia* (privation of -*lêthê*) might not be thought as the event in which the World, through the functioning of the symbolic and the imaginary, were constituted. But none of these extensions is necessary for Lacanians to find in Heidegger's experience of *a-lêtheia* the valuable philosophic support for Lacan's experience of truth in psychoanalysis, of which he is in need.

Be that as it may, does an *a-lêtheic* conception of truth offer us a way of thinking truth as cause? As a matter of fact, Heidegger does suggest that Aristotle's four causes combine to constitute a process of revelation. To clarify the notion of *technê*, he writes:

> *Technê* is a mode of *alêtheuein*. It reveals whatever does not bring itself forth and does not yet lie here before us, whatever can look and turn out now one way and now another. Whoever builds a house . . . reveals what is to be brought forth, according to the perspectives of the four modes of occasioning. This revealing gathers together in advance the aspect and the matter of house . . . with a view to the finished thing envisioned as completed, and from this gathering determines the manner of its construction. Thus what is decisive in *technê* does not lie at all in making and manipulating nor in the using of means, but rather in the aforementioned revealing. It is as revealing, and not as manufacturing, that *technê* is a bringing forth. (QCT, 13)

Aristotle's four causes coalesce, then, in a process of revelation. If this revelatory coalescence can be conceived as "cause," what would be its "effect"? Using language as loosely as Lacan does, may we not say that the "effect" of *alêtheia* is freedom—not in any voluntaristic sense, of course, but simply as a liberation from darkness (*lêthê*)? More precisely, the effect of a successful analysis would be the experience of freedom that comes to an analysand through the discovery that "Thou art that," the moment when "the real journey begins" (E, 7/100): "The truth of pain is pain itself."

2. Lacan insists on one more point—the close correlation between truth and language: "Since the truth is grounded in the fact that it speaks, . . . [it] has no other means by which to do so" (ST, 16). For Heidegger, this correlation is based upon his interpretation of the meaning of *logos* for the early Greeks, as may be seen, for example, in the work of Heraclitus (EGT, 59–78). Although *logos*, from early on, was asso-

ciated with speech, the original sense of it for Heraclitus came from *legein*, meaning "to gather" (as one gathers wood), or "to bring together" into some kind of unity that thereby becomes manifest as what it is. Like *physis*, *logos* was, from the beginning, associated with the coming to pass of *a-lêtheia*, the unconcealment of everything that is. The task of human beings would be to collaborate with the process by letting beings be seen as what they are. Eventually, it became possible to think of this gathering process (the coming-to-pass of truth) as aboriginal Language, and the task of human beings as bringing it to expression in words. Heidegger does not argue that Heraclitus saw this clearly himself, but claims rather to be articulating what Heraclitus left unsaid yet somehow inscribed in the language he used. At any rate, the vocation of human beings as such is to bring to articulation the language of Being/Logos itself, a task for which the poets serve as models.[24] Transposed into the context of Lacanian psychoanalysis, this would mean, I suggest, that "truth is grounded in the fact that it speaks," because *a-lêtheia* comes-to-pass through the *logos* operating in the very action through which the analysand achieves full speech: "It has no other means with which to do so."

3. *But* all of this founders on the irreducible fact that "there is no Other of the Other," and Being/*A-lêtheia*/*Logos* must certainly be considered as Other than the language of psychoanalysis—or so the objection goes. I have dealt with this issue at length elsewhere and shall recall briefly only what is relevant to the present context.[25] When Lacan speaks of Being, he refers to it as some kind of substance:

> There is no metalanguage. When I say that, that means apparently no language of Being. But is there Being? . . . Being is, as they say and Non-being is not. . . . This Being can be supposed only for certain words—individual, for example, or substance. (SXX, 118/107–08).

But is the Being Heidegger speaks of a "substance"? No! It is neither a substance nor any other kind of thing that "is"—the classic analysis in *Being and Time* reveals it precisely as "No-thing," *Nichts*) (SZ,184–91;BTa, 228–35). In no way can it be considered a metalanguage—a language that "is" beyond language. Rather than something that "is," Being/Logos is the process by which everything that "is" is empowered to *be* what it *is* and show itself (become e-vident) *as* what it *is*. Profoundly different from whatever "is," Being functions as the Power that empowers everything that is to be present, manifesting itself as what it is and able to function as such. For a case in point, in

Seminar XX 1972–1973 Encore, Lacan distinguishes between *exis-tence* and *ex-sistence*, and Fink elucidates the difference:

> In Lacan's terminology, existence is a product of language: lan-guage brings things into existence (makes them part of human reality), things which had no *existence* prior to being ciphered, symbolized, or put into words. The real, therefore, does not exist, since it precedes language; Lacan reserves a separate word for it, . . . : it "ex-sists." It exists outside of or apart from our reality. Ob-viously, insofar as we name and talk about the Real and weave it into a theoretical discourse on language and the "time before the word," we draw it into language and thereby give a kind of exis-tence to that which, in its very concept, has only ex-sistence.[26]

But whether Lacan speaks of *existence* or *ex-sistence*, each one *is* what it *is* as different from the other in order to mean anything at all. The Power that enables them to be what they are—precisely in their differ-entiation from one another—is what Heidegger understands by Being. Without something of the sort, Lacan's entire speculation, I submit, can have no meaning at all.

To conclude: Once Lacan identifies the subject of psychoanalysis with the sub-ject of science, obscurities persist with regard to the analogy between the respective modes of *savoir* to be found in each discipline when one considers their respective re-lation to truth. Surely truth must be allowed a place in science beyond the ken of the sheer methodology of exactitude, but as to how that truth is to be conceived to be dis-coverable both in science and psychoanalysis (in however analogous a fashion) must remain for now an open question. In 1965, Lacan leaves us completely in the dark. The hypothesis ventured here is that a conception of truth as e-vidence/dis-closure— in short, as *alêtheia* for Heidegger (including the non-truth that this comports)—goes a long way toward satisfying Lacan's need for the concept. How much further can it go? For now, that remains to be seen.

Notes

1. The essay, published separately in *Écrits* (Paris: Éditions du Seuil, 1966), pp. 855–77, was the opening lecture of *Le Séminaire. Livre XIII. L'objet de la psych-analyse* (1965-1966) (unpublished). This essay has been translated into English by Bruce Fink, "Science and Truth," *News Letter of the Freudian Field* 1:4–29 (1989). (Hereafter cited as ST, followed by the English pagination.) All references in this chapter to Sigmund Freud's *Standard Edition of the Complete Psychological Works of*

Sigmund Freud, translated and edited by James Strachey (London: The Hogarth Press, 1966) are cited as SE followed by the volume number and the page number.

2. Jacques Lacan's *Écrits: A Selection*, translated by A. Sheridan (New York: W. W. Norton, 1977), pp 73/285. (Hereafter cited as E, followed by the English and French pagination).

3. Jacques Lacan, *The Seminar of Jacques Lacan: Book XX (1972–1973) On Feminine Sexuality, the Limits of Love and Knowledge*, edited by J.-A. Miller and translated by B. Fink (New York: W.W. Norton, 1998), p. 119 [*Le Séminaire, Livre XX, Encore*, 1972–73 (Paris: Editions du Seuil, 1975), p. 108]). (Hereafter cited as SXX, followed by the English and French pagination.)

S. J. Costello, in "The Real of Religion and Its Relation to Truth as Cause," *The Letter* 13:69–81 (1998), gives an overview of this trajectory, and Jonathan Scott Lee, in his text, *Jacques Lacan* (Boston: Twayne, 1990), p.190 (hereafter cited as JL, followed by the page number), summarizes Lacan's critique of classical positivism.

4. Lacan prefers to call Dilthey's *Geisteswissenschaften* "conjectural" rather than "human" or "social" sciences, because "conjectural" allows the suggestion of exact calculability (in terms, at least, of probability theory), whereas "human" and "social" leave room for an anthropocentric humanism that he repudiates. The term allows a closer approximation of "conjectural" science to "exact" science: "The opposition between exact sciences and conjectural sciences is no longer sustainable once conjecture is subject to exact calculation (using probability) and exactness is merely grounded in a formalism separating axioms from laws for grouping symbols" ("Science and Truth," p. 11). Psychoanalysis would be just such a conjectural science.

5. René Descartes, "Meditations on First Philosophy," in *Discourse on Method and Meditations on First Philosophy*, translated by D. A. Cress. (Indianapolis: Hackett, 1998), p. 65.

6. Explanations of this thesis abound: see, for example, Lee's *Jacques Lacan*; Dör's *Introduction to the Reading of Lacan: The Unconscious Structured Like a Language*, edited by J.-F. Gurewich and S. Fairfield (Northvale, N.J., and London: Jason Aronson, 1997); J. P. Muller and W. J. Richardson, *Lacan and Language: A Reader's Guide to the Ecrits* (New York: W. W. Norton, 1983), pp. 1–25.

7. The "ego" for Lacan is essentially a unified image, perceived as though reflected in a mirror embodied in some other that gathers into unity the still-disordered elements of the becoming subject. See Lacan's. *Écrits: A Selection*, pp. 1–7; 93–100. (Hereafter cited as E, followed by the page number.)

8. Jacques Lacan, *Position of the Unconscious*, translated by B. Fink, in *Reading Seminar XI: Lacan's Four Fundamental Concepts of Psychoanalysis*, edited by R. Feldstein,

B. Fink, and M. Jaanus (Albany: State University of New York Press, 1995); p. 269. See also Lacan, *Écrits*, p. 840.

9. Leupin notes in his *Lacan and the Human Sciences*, edited by A. Leupin (Lincoln: University of Nebraska Press, 1991), p. 204 (hereafter cited as LHS, followed by the page number), that when Lacan rewrites Descartes' *cogito* as *I think*, "*therefore I am*," as cited above, he intends to underline the division between the (speaking) "subject of the enunciation" and the (spoken) "subject of the enunciated."

10. R. Grigg,"Metaphor and Metonymy," *Newsletter of the Freudian Field* 3 (1989):59-79.

11. J. Lacan, *Le Séminaire de Jacques Lacan. Livre XII. Problèmes Cruciaux Pour la Psychanalyse* (1965, unpublished).

12. See for example, "On the Grounds for Detaching a Particular Syndrome under the Description Anxiety Neurosis. Incidence and Aetiology of Anxiety Neurosis" (SE, 3); "Obsessions and Phobias: Their Psychical Mechanism and Their Aetiology" (SE, 3); "Heredity and the Aetiology of the Neuroses" (SE, 3); "Further Remarks on the Neuropsychoses of Defence: The Specific Aetiology of Hysteria" (SE, 3); "The Aetiology of Hysteria" (SE, 3); "Sexuality in the Aetiology of the Neuroses" (SE, 3); "My Views on the Part Played by Sexuality in the Aetiology of the Neuroses" (SE, 7); "Introductory Lectures on Psychoanalysis: General Theory of the Neuroses." "Some Thoughts on Elements and Regression—Aetiology" (SE, 15-16); and so on.

13. For a succinct analysis of the nature of truth both as correspondence and coherence, and each as distinct from meaning, see M. Cavell, *The Psychoanalytic Mind: From Freud to Philosophy* (Cambridge, Mass.: Harvard University Press, 1993), pp. 17-18.

14. Jacques Lacan, *The Seminar of Jacques Lacan: Book I: Freud's Papers on Technique: 1953-54*, edited by J.-A. Miller, translated by J. Forrester (New York: W. W. Norton, 1988), pp. 263 and 269.

15. *Metalanguage*, in formal semantics, [is] a language used to describe another language (the object language). The object language may be either a natural or a formal language. The goal of a formal semantic theory is to provide an axiomatic or an otherwise systematic theory of meaning for the object language. See the *Cambridge Dictionary of Philosophy*, edited by R. Audi (New York and Cambridge: Cambridge University Press, 1995), p. 486.

16. R. Chemema and B. Vandermersch, eds., *Dictionnaire de la Psychanalyse* (Paris: Larousse, 1998), p. 377.

17. Jacques Lacan Radiophonie, *Scilicet* 2/3:5-99 (1970), pp. 92-93.

18. Note that the Möbius strip is circular, hence, the homunculus' journey (presumably in submission to the chain of signifiers) is, in principle, "end"-less. Note too that the center of the circularity is, in principle, empty, symbolic of the ineluctable hole (i.e., void) that characterizes every human subject (LHS, 11).

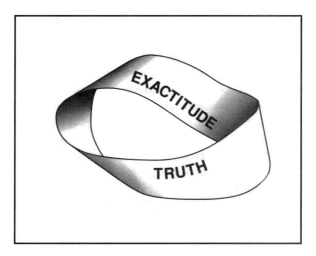

The figure "Exactitude and Truth" is reprinted from *Lacan and the Human Sciences*, edited by Alexandre Leupin, with permission of the University of Nebraska Press, ©1991, University of Nebraska Press.

19. This distinction was suggested to me by Willy Apollon, M.D., and Danièle Bergeron, M.D. Responsibility for this use of it, however, is my own.

20. Lacan will return to the problem of the relationship between *savoir* and truth in much greater detail in *Le séminaire. Livre XVII. L'envers de la psychanalyse* (Paris: Éditions du Seuil, 1969–1970). (This will be a significant development of his later thought, much too complex for discussion here. Any future development must necessarily have passed through this point.)

21. The word "cause," to begin with, is highly ambiguous, and Lacan makes much of this ambiguity. Bowie summarizes this on p. 119 of his *Lacan* (Cambridge, Mass.: Harvard University Press, 1991): "Lacan toys relentlessly with a single pun, on the word *cause*: the unconscious is the cause of truth (causes it, makes it happen), and analysis has sole responsibility for defending truth's cause (its interests, its standing): this piece of word-play is confidently executed and has the support of etymology: the Latin *causa* had both senses and also, for that matter, gave birth to the thing (*chose*) so elaborately played upon in "The Freudian Thing." But does the pun portray or disguise its own incoherence? The two senses of *cause* can scarcely have equivalent and co-active roles in the *causerie!* of psychoanalysis."

22. Who the philosopher was is a matter of conjecture. Fink suggests that is was Merleau-Ponty. (See Fink, "Science and Truth," p. 28.) But Dany Nobus, in a private communication, notes that Merleau-Ponty died in 1961, five years earlier, and could hardly be referred to as "a philosopher [recently] awarded full academic honors."

23. *The Oxford Dictionary of English Etymology* notes "evident" from the Latin *e-videre* as having originally the sense of the middle voice as "making itself seen." At the risk of annoying the reader, I shall hereafter hyphenate the word "e-vidence" to emphasize the middle-voice sense in which I am using it.

24. It should be noted that Lacan personally translated this article into French (EGT, 59–79).

25. William Richardson, "Psychoanalysis and the Being-question," in *Interpreting Lacan,* edited by J. H. Smith and W. Kerrigan (New Haven: Yale University, 1983); William Richardson, "Heidegger Among the Doctors," *Reading Heidegger, Commemorations* (Chicago: University of Chicago Press, 1990); and William Richardson, "*La vérité dans la psychanalyse, Lacan avec les Philosophes,* edited by R. Major (Paris: Albin Michel, 1991).

26. Fink, "Science and Psychoanalysis," p. 25.

Contributors

Miguel de Beistegui teaches philosophy at the University of Warwick. His books include *Heidegger and the Political* and *Philosophy and Tragedy*, co-edited with Simon Sparks. He has published numerous articles on Hegel and contemporary phenomenology.

Peg Birmingham is chair of the Philosophy Department at DePaul University in Chicago. She is the co-editor of *Dissensus Communis: Between Ethics and Politics* and the author of articles on Heidegger, Arendt, Foucault, Derrida, and Irigaray. She is presently completing a manuscript on Hannah Arendt, entitled, *The Predicament of Common Responsibility: Hannah Arendt and the Right to Have Rights*.

Walter Brogan is professor of philosophy at Villanova University. He is the co-translator of Martin Heidegger's *Aristotle's Metaphysics Theta 1–3: On the Essence and Actuality of Force* and the co-editor of *American Continental Philosophy: A Reader*. He has written many articles on the intersection of contemporary continental philosophy and Greek philosophy and is the current co-director of the Society for Phenomenology and Existential Philosophy and a member of the founding board of the Ancient Philosophy Society.

Françoise Dastur is professor of philosophy at the Université de Nice Sophia-Antipolis. She is the author of several books, including *Death: An Essay on Finitude*, *Hölderlin Le Retournement natal*, *Comment Vivre Avec la mort?*, *Heidegger and the Question of Time*, and *Telling Time: Sketch of a Phenomenological Chronology*. In 1993 she founded *L'Ecole Française de Daseinsanalyse*, of which she is president.

Jean Greisch is professor of philosophy at the Institut Catholique de Paris. He has written numerous books, including *Ontologie et Temporalité: Esquisse d'une interprétation intégrale de Sein und Zeit*, *L'arbre de vie et l'arbre du savoir: Le chemin phénoménologique de l'herméneutique heideggérienne (1919–1923)*, *Le cogito herméneutique: l'herméneutique philosophique et l'héritage cartésien*, and *La Parole Heureuse: Martin Heidegger entre les choses et les mots*.

Lawrence J. Hatab is professor of philosophy at Old Dominion University. He is the author of *Nietzsche and Eternal Recurrence, Myth and Philosophy: A Contest of Truths, A Nietzschean Defense of Democracy: An Experiment in Postmodern Politics,* and *Ethics and Finitude: Heidegger's Contributions to Moral Philosophy.*

Pierre Jacerme was for many years *Khâgne* professor of philosophy at the prestigious Lycée Henri IV in Paris, where he trained generations of future professors of philosophy. He has published numerous articles, most notably "*A propos de la traduction française d'Etre et temps,*" in *Heidegger Studies,* vol. 34 (1987–1988).

Theodore Kisiel is presidential research professor of philosophy at Northern Illinois University. He is the author of the *Genesis of Heidegger's Being and Time,* the co-editor of *Reading Heidegger from the Start,* the translator of Martin Heidegger's *History of the Concept of Time: Prolegomena,* and the author of numerous articles on hermeneutic phenomenology and continental philosophy of science.

Andrew Mitchell teaches philosophy at California State University at Stanislaus. He is currently completing his Ph.D. at the State University of New York at Stony Brook, entitled "The Fourfold and Technology: Heidegger's Thinking of Limit." He is presently translating Heidegger's *Vier Seminare* (with François Raffoul).

Jean-Luc Nancy teaches philosophy at l'Université Marc Bloch de Strasbourg. His principal books published in recent years include *Being Singular Plural, L'intrus, La pensée dérobée, L' "il y a" du rapport sexuel,* and *La création du monde ou la mondialisation* (forthcoming).

François Raffoul teaches philosophy at Louisiana State University. He is the author of *Heidegger and the Subject* and the editor and translator of numerous volumes. He is currently preparing a manuscript on the origins of responsibility.

William J. Richardson, professor of philosophy at Boston College, is the celebrated author of *Heidegger: Through Phenomenology to Thought* (preface by Martin Heidegger) and the co-author, with John Muller, of *Lacan and Language: A Reader's Guide to the Ecrits* and *The Purloined Poe: Lacan, Derrida, and Psychoanalytic Reading.* He has written widely in the fields of philosophy and psychoanalysis and at present is preparing a study on the ethics of psychoanalysis. He maintains a private practice in psychoanalysis in Newton, Massachusetts.

Jacob Rogozinski teaches philosophy at the University of Paris VIII. He was program director of the *Collège International de Philosophie* from 1986 to 1992. His books include *Kanten, esquisses kantiennes,* and *Le don de la loi.* He also has published numerous articles on Kant and Heidegger.

John Sallis is Edwin Erle Sparks professor of philosophy at Pennsylvania State University. He is the author of a dozen books, including *Force of Imagination: The Sense of the Elemental, Chorology: On Beginning in Plato's "Timaeus," Shades—Of Painting at the Limit, Double Truth, Stone,* and *Echoes—After Heidegger.*

Frank Schalow is the author of *The Renewal of the Heidegger-Kant Dialogue: Action, Thought, and Responsibility, Heidegger and the Quest for the Sacred, Language and Deed, Imagination and Existence,* and co-author of *Traces of Understanding.* He served as Secretary-Convenor of the North American Heidegger Conference and is currently a member of the Editorial Advisory Board of *Heidegger Studies.* Frank Schalow is an Assistant Professor at the University of New Orleans.

Dennis Schmidt is professor of philosophy at Villanova University. He is the author of *The Ubiquity of the Finite* and *On Germans and Other Greeks: Tragedy and Ethical Life.* He has translated Ernst Bloch's *Natural Law and Human Dignity.*

Charles E. Scott is Edwin Erle Sparks professor of philosophy at Pennsylvania State University. His recent books include *The Question of Ethics, Advantages and Disadvantages of Ethics and Politics, The Time of Memory,* and *A Companion to Heidegger's Contributions to Philosophy* (co-editor).

Thomas Sheehan is professor of religious studies at Stanford University and professor emeritus of philosophy at Loyola University in Chicago. He has published widely on Heidegger and most recently has co-edited, with Richard Palmer, volume 5 of Edmund Husserl's Collected Works, *Psychological and Transcendental Phenomenology and the Confrontation with Heidegger.*

Jacques Taminiaux is Adelmann professor of philosophy at Boston College and the former director of the Center for Phenomenological Studies at the University of Louvain-la-Neuve. His books include *Heidegger and the Project of Fundamental Ontology, Poetics, Speculation, and Judgment,* and *The Thracian Maid and the Professional Thinker: Arendt and Heidegger.*

David Wood is professor of philosophy at Vanderbilt University and honorary professor of philosophy at the University of Warwick, England. He has edited some ten books on continental philosophy and is the author of *Philosophy at the Limit* and *The Deconstruction of Time.* He is currently completing three books: *Thinking after Heidegger, Time and Time Again,* and *Things at the Edge of the World.* He also is researching a book on philosophy and trees.

Index